THEORY AND INTERPRETATION

OF NARRATIVE SERIES

SURPRISED BY SHAME

Dostoevsky's Liars and Narrative Exposure

Deborah A. Martinsen

The Ohio State University Press
Columbus

Copyright © 2003 by The Ohio State University Press
All rights reserved.
Library of Congress Cataloging-in-Publication Data
Martinsen, Deborah A.
    Surprised by shame : Dostoevsky's liars and narrative exposure / Deborah A. Martinsen.
        p. cm. — (The theory and interpretation of narrative series)
    Includes bibliographical references and index.
    ISBN 0-8142-0921-1 (alk. paper) — ISBN 0-8142-9008-6 (CD-ROM)
    1. Dostoyevsky, Fyodor, 1821-1881—Criticism and interpretation. 2. Shame in literature. 3. Truthfulness and falsehood in literature. 4. Deception in literature. 5. Narration (Rhetoric) I. Title. II. Series.

PG3328.Z7 S526 2003
891.73'3—dc21
                    2002153881

Other identifiers: ISBN-13: 978-0-8142-5903-0 (paper)

Cover design by Dan O'Dair
Type set in Adobe Garamond Pro

*For my parents,
Marge and Harry Martinsen,
with thanks and love*

contents

	ACKNOWLEDGMENTS	ix
	INTRODUCTORY NOTE	xiii
1	Surprised by Shame	1
2	Something about Lying	18
3	Shame's Legacy: Fathers and Children	52
4	General Ivolgin: Narratives of Shame and Identity	62
5	Confessional Moments	92
6	Stepan Trofimovich Verkhovensky: Leaving the Narrator Behind	103
7	Divided Selves	135
8	Lukian Lebedev: Narrative and Exposure	147
9	Metaliterary Identity	170
10	Captain Lebiadkin: Pretender Politics and Poetics	184
11	Father and Son: Legacy of Shame	207
	CONCLUSION	217
	NOTES	225
	BIBLIOGRAPHY	257
	INDEX	267

acknowledgments

The fullest praise and sincerest thanks only begin to express my great gratitude to the family, friends, and colleagues who have supported me and my writing. First, I thank Bob Belknap, who inspired me to investigate Dostoevsky's epideictic liars. Mentor and muse, Bob encouraged me to embrace ambiguity and paradox as I analyzed some of Dostoevsky's funniest prose. As he has discussed, read, and commented on my endless revisions, Bob has also been a fun and unflagging fellow traveler. Next, I thank Robin Feuer Miller for blazing the path I followed through Dostoevsky's complex narratives and for providing me personal and academic support. Her bright presence and insightful remarks on myriad conference papers lifted my spirits and helped me find the way in dark moments. To Ganna Bograd I give special thanks for an amazing walking tour of Pavlovsk; for incredible map tours of Petersburg and Staraia Russa; and for generously sharing her knowledge, insight, detective stories, and enthusiasm for Dostoevsky.

Thanks to the institutions and individuals who provided opportunities to develop my work: to the Harriman Institute for including this book in their series and for awarding me Pepsico grants to attend Dostoevsky conferences in Staraia Russa; to the Columbia Slavic Department for inviting me to teach the graduate Dostoevsky seminar; to the National Endowment for the Humanities for the chance to attend two summer seminars that marked this project's beginning and its turning point; and to the University Seminars at Columbia University for their help in publication. Special thanks to Peter Rabinowitz, who recognized the book's theoretical sea change and who inspired me, with great editorial insight and humor, to write some of its hardest prose. Thanks to members of the University Seminar on Slavic History and Culture for sharing ideas and references. Thanks to Saul Morson, Jim Phelan, and their seminars' members for sharing their ideas on Russian counter-traditions and on rhetorical theories of narrative. Thanks to Heather Lee Miller, Eugene O'Connor, and Jennifer Shoffey Carr at The Ohio State University Press for guiding me through the publication process. Thanks also to my colleagues in the Petersburg and Staraia Russa Dostoevsky House-Museums, especially to Natasha Ashimbaeva, Natasha Chernova, Boris Tikhomirov, and Vera Bogdanova, for inviting me, publishing me, and sharing their Fedor Mikhailovich with me.

Endless thanks to all who have read during the last ten years one or more manuscript drafts. Your collective wisdom has significantly improved this work. I offer special thanks to Roger Anderson for encouraging deeper analysis; Ellen Chances for organic criticism; Kathy Eden for a kind, close reading; Caryl Emerson for erudite encouragement and charitable hyperbole; Nicole Fermon for deepening the social analysis; Carol Flath for identifying the missing links; the late George Gibian for love of Ivolgin; Robert Maguire for supporting my early theorizing; Olga Meerson for linguistic perspicacity; Ron Meyer for editorial grace and generous expertise; Tetsuo Mochizuki for keen affirmation; Irina Reyfman for thoughtful reading and metaliterary references; and Nancy Workman, my general counsel, for wise questions and comments.

For helping me understand pretender politics and for sustaining me with humor, I thank Her Serene Fullness Marcia Morris. For collegial friendship and helpful correspondence, I thank Marina Balina, Ksana Blank, Svetlana Grenier, Becky and Joe Hogan, Hilde Hoogenboom, Malcolm Jones, Tanya Kasatkina, Gina Kovarsky, Richard Kuhns, Amy Mandelker, Cathy Nepomnyashchy, Donna Orwin, Ludmila Saraskina, Ellen Scaruffi, Carol Ueland, and Vladimir Zakharov. Thanks to Eileen Gillooly for understanding the demands of Logos. Extra thanks to Janine DeNovais for being my heavenly twin at the office while I met publication deadlines at home. For teaching my son how to be a kitty while I was writing or teaching, many thanks to Natasha Shnurov. Special thanks to my guardian angel Virginia Phelan for deep listening and belief in this book.

Finally, no thanks are adequate for my husband, Randall Butler, musician, philosopher, and poet, my academic, emotional, and financial supporter as well as my most exacting editor. Thanks for clarifying my thoughts, for fine-tuning my terms, and for so often finding the right word. Thanks to both Randy and our son Rory for enduring my Dostoevskian monomania in all its many forms (special thanks to Rory for "Dstevsky" and other word fun). Warmest thanks to my wonderful mother-in-law, Wanda Butler, whose generous care of my menfolk has allowed me to attend Dostoevsky conferences all over the world. I conclude by offering boundless thanks to my parents, Marge and Harry Martinsen, for the many ways they have shaped me—and this project—through their role modeling, generosity, and love.

While others have inspired and guided me, including those I have forgotten to thank, I bear sole responsibility for this book's shortcomings. May Fedor Mikhailovich forgive me.

introductory note

Ever the explorer of the heart's deep core, Dostoevsky has created work that has been mined by psychologists, philosophers, social scientists, theologians, and literary critics for over a century and a half. In choosing his liars as subjects, I have plunged most deeply into the fields of narrative and shame studies. Following Dostoevsky, who identifies shame at one's identity as a fundamental source of lying, and using the narrative insights of Slavists and narratologists alike, I came to realize that Dostoevsky uses the dynamics of shame as a narrative strategy, collapsing the intersubjective distance between characters and readers by having us witness scenes of shame. This is the starting point of my study. For psychologists and other shame researchers, I provide a discussion of varieties of shame and shamelessness that can be seen as a series of Dostoevskian case studies. For literary critics and other students of narrative, I explain how Dostoevsky takes shame from the realm of character analysis and plot motive and embeds it into the narrative dynamic of three great novels—*The Idiot*, *Demons*, and *The Brothers Karamazov*. For Dostoevsky scholars and the general reader, I group characters who are not customarily studied together, thereby recontextualizing Dostoevskian thematics in a way that yields new insights about the author's narrative goals. For all readers, I show how Dostoevsky uses lying (*vran'yo*) as an indicator of subconscious processes that motivate characters, thereby illuminating his sense of what drives much social discourse not only in nineteenth-century Russia, but also in the world at large.

The main title of this book, *Surprised by Shame*, explains in shorthand Dostoevsky's enterprise. Dostoevsky transforms universal shame dynamics—which hinge on unexpectedness, contagiousness, and paradoxicality—into narrative dynamics. By positioning readers as witnesses to exposed shame, Dostoevsky makes us experience our post-lapsarian heritage, thereby dramatizing his social, political, and metaphysical message of human interconnection. By creating and exposing his liars, whose narcissistic stories manifest their shame, Dostoevsky reveals fiction's function not only to expose but possibly also to save readers as he affords us ethical awareness and thus the impetus to change.

So why was Dostoevsky interested in shame? Shame lies on the boundary between self and other and is thus intimately linked to the question of identity. Its boundary status also explains shame's great importance for forming and policing personal and social identity and thus its importance for psychological and social studies. But to see shame is to feel shame, and so early psychologists avoided its study. The last decades of the twentieth century, however, have witnessed an interest in all varieties of affect. Shame is back.

Shame researchers come from many fields. Four shame study pioneers illustrate this variety: Gerhart Piers, an anthropologist; Milton Singer, a psychoanalyst; Helen Merrill Lynd, a sociologist; and Helen Block Lewis, a psychoanalyst. Lewis's clinical experience led her to study shame. Troubled by some of her patients' recidivism, Lewis determined that while they had worked through guilt issues in their analysis, shame issues remained unresolved. Her account of shame's role as a motive force, along with her insights into the shamefulness of shame itself, inspired many psychoanalysts and psychologists to investigate shame issues further. She and other shame theorists have helped psychoanalysis move away from drive theory by complicating and broadening the picture, allowing for a greater range of motives than the classic sex and death drives.[1] They are not alone in this work; theorists who do not directly discuss shame issues have also introduced a broader range of emotions into analysis. Heinz Kohut is an example. Although Kohut does not use the word "shame" often, he clearly views it as an essential element of narcissistic personality disorders. Andrew Morrison, whose work I cite, has an essentially Kohutian approach and views shame as the central affect in narcissistic rage. Finally, most shame researchers have developed some variant of Kohut's call for empathic healing of narcissistic injury as part of the return from shame.

Another landmark figure for shame studies is Silvan Tomkins, the founder of contemporary affect theory. Tomkins identifies nine innate biological affects as the moving forces of human behavior: the positive affects—interest-excitement and enjoyment-joy; the negative affects—fear-terror, distress-anguish, anger-rage, shame-humiliation, dissmell and disgust; and the neutral affect of surprise-startle. (The hyphenation indicates a range of intensity from mild to extreme.) Tomkins explains complex psychodynamics as the result of conflicts caused when shame, one of the negative affects, binds with other affects and drives.[2]

Shame studies have much to offer literary studies. Narratologists will find Tomkins's script theory particularly interesting. Tomkins and some of the psychotherapists influenced by him, such as Gershen Kaufman and Donald Nathanson, examine the way that individuals manage painful affect by constructing scripts out of scenes and images stored by their memory. As Adamson and Clark point out in the introduction to their edited volume, shame theory's examination of the affective sources and consequences of social injustice can illuminate current discussions of race, class, and gender. They also show how Lacanian concepts such as *désir* or his discussion of the scopic drive and the complex interplay of the eye and the gaze can be understood better when discussed in terms of affect.[3]

Philosophers have also contributed importantly to shame studies. My favorite is David Velleman, who sees shame as anxiety about exclusion from the social realm where individuals act as self-presenting agents. He introduces the ideas of free will and privacy into his discussion of shame, arguing that an agent's capacity to resist desires (i.e., to exercise his free will) enables him to choose which desires his behavior will express. Thus, when an agent shows something private, he fails to manage his self-image, which becomes an occasion for shame. This differs from standard analyses of shame, which focus on negative self-assessment or the thought of being an object of an observer's regard, or both.[4] Sartre most clearly states the idea that shame involves a reflected assessment of the self.[5] The necessary corrective for his negative view of intersubjective awareness, however, can be found in the work of philosophers such as Vladimir Solovev, who sees the positive functions of shame as protection of privacy and indication of moral awareness,[6] and Emmanuel Levinas, whose focus on the ethics of the face offers valuable insights for shame studies.[7]

Dostoevsky's work on shame has much to offer researchers in many fields. Part of his appeal may derive from the way that nineteenth-century Russian experience models trends in the twentieth century generally. A patriarchy, Russia marginalized, disempowered, or ostracized large segments of its population, men and women alike. The humiliated rage experienced by a wide range of Russians often turned inward, as seen in the soaring suicide rate, but when it turned outward, as seen in political terrorism, it rocked the entire country. From his earliest to his most mature work, Dostoevsky provides countless case studies of shame—shame turned inward, as in the case of the underground man, or shame directed outward, as in the case of Peter Verkhovensky. He portrays the shame of poverty, of social class, of terminal illness, of deformity, of mediocrity; the shame of fallen women, superfluous men, political intriguers, liars, criminals, gamblers, eccentrics, and misfits; and the hidden shame of respectable people. Dostoevsky also reveals the personal and social dynamics behind shame's many faces: shame at self and shame as a failure of self-presentation. In short, Dostoevsky documents shame's part in the universal search for personal, social, national, and metaphysical identity.

This book examines a class of Dostoevskian characters, his liars, who are at the center of Dostoevsky's shame dynamics. As his liars lie and are exposed as liars, Dostoevsky surprises them and readers with shame, engages readers with paradox, and delights us with metaliterary play. The stories his liars tell to conceal the shame of their actual identity reveal their desire to be other. Dostoevsky portrays their identity crises in painful, mimetic detail. He places these identity crises in thematic and social contexts that reveal their political and metaphysical implications. Finally, he celebrates the similarities between lying and fiction with metaliterary play that affords aesthetic pleasure to his readers. And he does all this by constantly exposing shame's paradox—its ability to both isolate and relate. For shame makes us self-conscious of how we differ from others at the same time that it makes us feel our common postlapsarian heritage. Dostoevsky's power as a writer derives, in part, from his playing on the boundary between self and other—the edge of shame's paradox. Dostoevsky willingly embraces and portrays paradox, exposes readers to shame, and risks losing us to save us.

The structure of this book requires some explanation. It begins and ends with Fedor Karamazov; it also juxtaposes Fedor Karamazov with each of Dostoevsky's major liars. Instead of moving from novel to novel chronologically, my chapters move from shamed liars (General Ivolgin and Stepan Verkhovensky) to shameless liars (Lukian Lebedev and Captain Lebiadkin). Before each chapter devoted to these characters is a minichapter that juxtaposes one of Fedor Karamazov's outrageous stories or statements with one of theirs. I have woven these discussions of Fedor Karamazov throughout my book because he is a shameless liar who defends against his shame with an aggressive shamelessness that marks him as Dostoevsky's greatest violator of social norms and decorum. He is linked to recurrent Dostoevskian thematics. And he is the site of his creator's greatest metaliterary play. It is no accident that he is Fedor Dostoevsky's namesake. As I show, Dostoevsky inscribes his awareness of the difference between lying and fiction in all of his liars' shocking stories and statements, thereby relieving some reader discomfort at their scandalousness by providing comic relief. By juxtaposing each liar with Fedor Karamazov, I reveal his roots in earlier liars, show the continuity of certain Dostoevskian thematics, and demonstrate how Dostoevsky inscribes serious messages in his liars' buffoonish performances.

Chapter 1 locates Fedor Karamazov at the center of Dostoevsky's exposition of shame. Chapter 2 examines Dostoevsky's discussion of lying as a response to shame at one's identity and desire to be other but also as the rhetoric of shame, a rhetoric that reveals as much as it conceals. Starting with chapter 3, I then offer four pairs of chapters that consist of one minichapter, juxtaposing Fedor Karamazov with General Ivolgin, Stepan Verkhovensky, Lukian Lebedev, and Captain Lebiadkin, followed by a larger chapter devoted to each of these characters. In the minichapters, I respectively examine how General Ivolgin and Fedor Karamazov present themselves as sons rather than fathers; how Stepan Verkhovensky and Fedor Karamazov use confession as a rhetorical strategy of self-presentation; how Lebedev and Fedor represent themselves as divided selves; and how Lebiadkin and Fedor share a delight in wordplay, which contributes to their deaths. These juxtapositions culminate in chapter 11 with Ivan Karamazov's devil and the Karamazov patriarch. Here Dostoevsky returns to the rhetoric of confession—Ivan's devil tells the story of a confession that recapitulates one of Fedor Karamazov's stories—with a difference that identifies Ivan's devil with Ivan's father as liars and Ivan as a writer. Throughout the book I show how Dostoevsky uses his mimetic, thematic, and metaliterary savvy to show readers how to escape shame's legacy.

Readers can follow this exposition of how Dostoevsky uses shame as a narrative strategy by reading cover to cover. I also recommend a beginning-to-end reading for those who want to look at Dostoevsky's many liars as case studies in shame. On the other hand, readers can glimpse Fedor Karamazov's developmental history by reading the minichapters. Or readers can choose those chapters pertaining to the novel of their interest—*The Idiot, Demons,* or *The Brothers Karamazov.* To all I recommend the first two chapters, which first show how Dostoevsky turns shame into a narrative strategy and then explain why.

chapter one

Surprised by Shame

To see shame is to feel shame. Dostoevsky exploits this property of shame and uses it as a narrative strategy. Shame collapses the intersubjective boundaries between characters and thus accounts for the emotional intensity of Dostoevsky's scandal scenes. Shame also collapses the intersubjective boundaries between characters and readers and thus accounts for readers' emotional involvement in the text. In mobilizing shame as a narrative strategy, Dostoevsky adds shame's affective and cognitive synergy to the recursive relations among author, readers, and text. The activity of writing exposes characters to readers' views; the activity of reading positions readers as witnesses. Portrayed shame overflows textual bounds. Just as shame disrupts individuals' unexamined sense of self and their sense of the world, so portrayed shame disrupts readers' sense of personal inviolability and their narrative expectations. By positioning readers as witnesses to exposed shame, Dostoevsky catches us off-guard and entangles us in an archaic, anxiety-fraught experience that accounts for those who recoil, never to return. Nonetheless, as I will show, by aggressively implicating readers in the painful experience of exposure and self-consciousness, Dostoevsky uses shame as an instrument of social conscience that gives us as readers the opportunity to know ourselves not as self-sufficient subjects but as members of a social and metaphysical community.

Dostoevsky aptly titles Book Two of *The Brothers Karamazov* "An Inappropriate Gathering" (*Neumestnoe sobranie*), thereby preparing his readers for the scandal that ensues. The words in the Russian title, in fact, pinpoint two major components of Dostoevskian scandals: *sobranie*—a gathering, meeting, assembly, literally "a bringing together," that is *neumestnoe*—inappropriate, untimely, unfitting, literally "not in place." Like much else in a Dostoevskian text, the book's title suggests multiple meanings: the time is not right, the place is not right, the meeting is not right. And, as is so often the case in a Dostoevskian text, all of these meanings obtain. Having read Book One, "The History of One Little Family," readers know that the unprecedented gathering of a histrionic father and three unlikely sons—a former army officer, an intellectual journalist, and a novice monk—at a time when father and eldest son are openly feuding, in a sacred place, for a secular purpose, in the company of mixed onlookers, is a set-up for scandal.

Scandals proliferate in Dostoevsky's work. But why? Scandals move personal crises into the public realm. Personal crises express social and political tensions. By shaking individuals up, crises provide them with an opportunity to move beyond the quotidien and focus on the spiritual.[1] Personal crises exposed to public view awaken voyeuristic fascination. By exposing readers to characters' crises, Dostoevsky implicates us in their lives and thus entangles us in their ethical and metaphysical dilemmas.

This book will argue that shame precipitates scandals, that for Dostoevsky scandal is the exposing of shame, and that Dostoevsky uses exposed shame as a narrative strategy to implicate readers in the ethical action of his texts. Indeed, Dostoevsky could have written the entry for "scandal" in the dictionary of the nineteenth-century Russian lexicographer Vladimir Dal'. Whereas the *Old English Dictionary* does not once use the word "shame" in its definitions of scandal, Dal's first three entries are words denoting shame: *sram, styd, pozor*. In addition to their figurative meaning of "shame," both *sram* and *styd* signify the sexual organs, with *sram* having the stronger physical connotations.[2] The noun *pozor* denotes "a spectacle" and thus incorporates the visual dimension into its meanings of "shame" and "disgrace." Dostoevsky also activates the Greek root *scandalon*, which denotes a trap or moral stumbling block. As I will show, Dostoevsky uses shame's unexpectedness, contagiousness, and paradoxicality to ensnare his readers. Shame's unexpectedness in particular allows Dostoevsky to unleash the affective and cognitive synergy of three properties of the shame experience: disruption, disorientation, and self-consciousness. No wonder the word "suddenly" (*vdrug*) abounds in his work. Dostoevsky surprises readers with shame.

In Book Two, Chapter Two of *The Brothers Karamazov*, a chapter titled "The Old Buffoon" (*Staryi shut*), Fedor Pavlovich Karamazov aggressively shames his cousin-in-law Petr Aleksandrovich Miusov. He begins by mimicking Miusov's bow to Zosima, a parodic gesture that calls attention to an action that is already "out of place." As the narrator notes, Miusov had fully intended to ask for Zosima's blessing, perhaps even kiss his hand, but discomfited by the monks' deep ceremonial bows, with fingers touching the ground, Miusov instead makes a deep civilian bow, hands at his side. Feeling out of place,

Miusov acts out of place. Fedor's parody accentuates Miusov's gesture, highlighting its inappropriateness. Miusov avenges himself by insulting Fedor Pavlovich. Thus begins the cycle of aggressive clowning and antagonistic response, shame and counter-shame, exposure and counter-exposure, that characterizes their interaction. In this scene, as elsewhere in Dostoevsky's work, scandal and shame go hand in hand. The agonistic in-laws vie to expose each other before those assembled, heightening onlookers' sense of impending disaster. The narrator heightens readers' expectation of scandal by reporting onlookers' responses. For example, as he watched his father's apish bow, "Blood flooded Alesha's cheeks; he became ashamed (*emu stalo stydno*). His evil forebodings were coming to pass" (14:36;39).[3] By reporting this and other shame responses, the narrator dramatizes shame's contagiousness.

In response to Miusov's second round of shaming, Fedor Karamazov appeals to the elder Zosima:

> In those seconds when I see that my joke isn't going over, my cheeks, reverend father, begin to stick to my lower gums; it feels almost like a cramp; I've had it since my young days, when I was a sponger on the gentry and made my living by sponging. I'm a natural-born buffoon, I am, reverend father, just like a holy fool; I won't deny that there's maybe an unclean spirit living in me, too, not a very high caliber one, by the way, otherwise he would have chosen grander quarters, only not you, Petr Aleksandrovich, your quarters are none too grand either. But to make up for it, I believe, I believe in God. It's only lately that I've begun to have doubts, but to make up for it I'm sitting and waiting to hear lofty words. I am, reverend father, like the philosopher Diderot. Do you know, most holy father, how Diderot the philosopher came to see Metropolitan Platon in the time of the empress Catherine? He walks in and says right off: "There is no God." To which the great hierarch raises his finger and answers: "The fool hath said in his heart, There is no God." Right then and there our man fell at his feet: "I believe," he cries, "I will accept baptism!" And so they baptized him at once. Princess Dashkova was his godmother, and Potemkin his godfather. . . . (14:38–39;41)

As this passage makes clear, shame has been Fedor Karamazov's companion from an early age. He describes how shame affects him physically, like a cramp. He demonstrates how shame has affected his self-image: he calls himself "a natural-born buffoon" and confesses to having an unclean spirit—a sign of dirty, thus shameful, contents. Then he tells a plagiarized story that marks him as a *vrun*, an exhibitionist liar. He thus engages in a form of rhetoric that his creator, Fedor Dostoevsky, has identified as the rhetoric of shame.

In an 1873 *Diary of a Writer* article titled "Something about Lying" (*Nechto o vran'e*), Dostoevsky's narrative persona identifies shame as a critical motive for lying (*vran'yo*). He hyperbolically argues that all Russians lie because they sense a discrepancy between their actual and ideal selves: "The second thing at which our general Russian lying hints is that we are all ashamed of ourselves. In fact, every one of us carries in him an almost innate shame at himself and at his own identity; the moment Russians are with others, they all try as quickly as possible, no matter what, to appear surely different from what they are in reality. Everyone hastens to assume a completely different identity" (21:119). Dostoevsky's *Diary* writer cannily associates shame with exposure, identity, and pain. Twentieth-century shame experts have corroborated his observations, defining shame as a painful affect originating in exposure (seeing, being seen, or both) that prompts (1) self-consciousness, consciousness of others, or both; (2) negative self-assessment; and (3) feelings of weakness, defectiveness, dirtiness, estrangement, or any combination thereof.[4] Positioned on the boundary between self and others, shame derives and reinforces its particular power from a fundamental duality of human experience: self in relation to self, self in relation to others. The pain of shame is caused by a sense of being exposed that arouses a person's feelings of inferiority, inadequacy, or defectiveness vis-à-vis self or others. The source of shame can be internal or external, imagined or real. Furthermore, shame can be experienced privately or publicly.

In the chapter "The Old Buffoon," Dostoevsky demonstrates how shame propels the action as Fedor Karamazov and Miusov compete to expose one another. In making Fedor Karamazov a liar, however, Dostoevsky also parades his own poetics and trains his readers by showing how lying conceals shame yet signals its concealment. Fedor Karamazov's Diderot story, for example, is a conversion tale featuring shame as the instrument of change. Fedor Karamazov tells this story as an artful ruse, ensnaring his audience with their own inappropriate laughter, thereby shaming them. Fedor Dostoevsky exploits the old buffoon's prankishness to mask an authorial message: positively confronted, shame can lead to revelation and change. Shame normally engenders painful self-consciousness that produces a desire to cut self off from others, thereby ridding the self of the pain. But this painful self-consciousness can also produce a desire to reconnect with others and to reorient the self, thereby healing the pain. This second scenario describes the action of the Diderot story. Fedor Karamazov deliberately tells a story that pits an atheist against a believer. Fedor Dostoevsky situates this story in a novel about atheism and belief, the secular and the sacred, alienation and community, the West and Russia, the devil and God in the human soul. Both Fedors tell a story in which a European atheist challenges a Russian man of God who calls him a "fool," thereby awakening his self-awareness and moving him to convert. Dostoevsky, however, adds thematic resonance and metaliterary play to the story. In Dostoevsky's world, atheists have isolated themselves from human community: having denied God, they deny the ties that bind—the image of God within all humans. In his story, the atheist moves from intellectual isolation to spiritual community.

Dostoevsky also uses this storytelling scene as a metaliterary opportunity, that is, as an occasion to reveal his own poetics. For example, the words that reputedly affect Diderot so dramatically are not Metropolitan Platon's own words, but a repeated quotation from the first lines of Psalms 14 and 53. Fedor Dostoevsky thus has Fedor Karamazov tell a story (about Diderot) that refers to another story (about the fool who says in his heart that there is no God), both of which have subjects who question God's existence. Fedor Karamazov tells the story; Fedor Dostoevsky frames it. Fedor Karamazov identifies with Diderot; Fedor Dostoevsky uses his character's identification with Diderot, whom Platon identifies with the unbelieving fool (*bezumets*) of the Psalms as a triple *mise en abyme* to situate the old buffoon's comic crisis of identity and belief in a literary, historical, and metaphysical continuum that moves backward from the nineteenth to the eighteenth century to the time of the prophets—a time of direct struggle with God the Father. Under the mimetic cover of Fedor Karamazov's clowning, Fedor Dostoevsky thus reveals his authorial hand. He creates a liar who tells a story about atheism and belief that reflects his novel's thematics.

Dostoevsky also fashions a narrator who maintains a critical, though not hostile, distance from Fedor Karamazov so that both author and narrator can tell a far richer story than the old buffoon. Here, as elsewhere, Fedor Dostoevsky does not share his characters' narrative limitations. For instance, Fedor Karamazov's story is based on a historical event—Diderot's meeting with Metropolitan Platon. Fedor Dostoevsky exploits the literary resonance in the historical name "Platon"/Plato to tell a story that recapitulates the dramatic action of a Platonic dialogue in which an uninitiated seeker of knowledge moves from ignorance to *aporia*, a position of perplexity that can lead to enlightenment. Although Platonic *aporia* is not identical with Dostoevskian shame, in both experiences the person becomes conscious of a lack, a critical awareness that for both Plato and Dostoevsky can inspire change. Dostoevsky thus inscribes clues to his own poetics in his character's story, thereby enhancing his authorial audience's aesthetic pleasure.

Furthermore, by making Fedor Karamazov a storyteller who can manipulate audience response, Dostoevsky demonstrates his own talent. The two Fedors tell stories for different reasons, however, thus illustrating a major difference between lying and fiction. For Dostoevsky, fiction places mimetic truth in the service of poetic truth. Exhibitionist lying, on the other hand, ignores truth and uses hyperbole and plagiarism as protective covers. The liar's narcissism impedes his narrative efficacy. Fedor Karamazov can manipulate his audience, but he cannot get what he really wants, because he fashions and then flaunts a provocative self-image. Blinded by his narcissistic injury, he cannot engage in sincere dialogue. The Diderot story locates Fedor Karamazov at the center of shame's paradox, caught between his conflicting desires to alienate and to join his fellow men. Telling the story enacts his dilemma. By violating the spirit of the place, he challenges every auditor in the cell. Yet his specific challenges to Zosima and Miusov dramatize his inner conflict. He challenges Zosima, a spiritual father, to read his heart and convert him. He challenges Miusov, his worldly cousin-in-law, to defend the decorum violated by the story's provocative content. As he anticipates, Zosima pierces his heart with wisdom, and Miusov creates a scene that compounds the scandal. Faced with the choice of accepting Zosima's offer or responding to Miusov's counter-provocation, Fedor Pavlovich remains on the familiar side of shame's paradox. His narcissistically motivated desire to avenge himself proves greater than his desire to be one with God's community. The inertial force of habit wins.[5]

Miusov accuses Fedor of lying, thereby sharing the shame he feels at being witness to Fedor's buffoonery. The aggressiveness of his accusation adds to the scandal and reveals Dostoevsky's authorial hand.

> "Fedor Pavlovich, this is unbearable! You know yourself that you are lying and that that stupid story isn't true. Why are you clowning?" Miusov said in a trembling voice, completely unable to restrain himself.
>
> "All my life I've had a feeling that it wasn't true!" Fedor Pavlovich exclaimed with enthusiasm. "I, gentlemen, will tell you the whole truth. Great Elder! forgive me, that last part, about Diderot's baptism, I invented myself just now, this very minute while I was telling it to you. It never even entered my head before. I made it up for its piquancy. That's why I'm clowning, Petr Aleksandrovich, to be more endearing. Though sometimes I don't know myself why I do it. As for Diderot, I heard this 'the fool hath said' maybe twenty times from local landowners when I was still young and lived with them; by the way, I also heard it, Petr Aleksandrovich, from your aunt, Mavra Fominishna. All of them are still convinced that the godless [*bezbozhnik*] Diderot went to Metropolitan Platon to argue about God. . . ." (14:39;42)

This interaction dramatizes a long-standing social tension and thus reflects the characters' mimetic functions. Though both ostensibly members of the same class—the landowning gentry—Miusov and Fedor Karamazov travel in very different social circles. Miusov is a hereditary landowner, a liberal westernized member of the intelligentsia, who lives on the income from his estate and spends large periods of time in Europe. Fedor Pavlovich hails from an impoverished landowning family, starts his career as a sponger, and acquires capital by his first marriage to Miusov's cousin. After her death, he goes south, increases his capital, returns to her property, and invests in land and taverns. Miusov is ashamed of their family connection. Fedor Pavlovich gets his revenge for Miusov's social snobbery by stressing their family tie and shaming him socially. Miusov's loss of control in this passage demonstrates the depth of his concern for decorum, a concern that makes him emblematic of many aristocrats.[6] His interaction with Fedor Pavlovich thus mimetically reflects an actual historical situation and metapoetically evokes the comic tradition in which clowns unmask their social superiors. By exposing Fedor Pavlovich as a liar, Miusov attempts to shame him, thus placing distance between them. Fedor Pavlovich, however, deftly collapses the distance by claiming Miusov's aunt as a source for his story. The two thus work from opposite ends of shame's paradox: Miusov uses shame to separate himself from his unwanted relative; Fedor Pavlovich uses shame to recall their connections. However scandalously, Fedor Pavlovich thus acts as the bearer of Dostoevsky's authorial message about human interrelatedness.

Fedor Pavlovich's contradictory response to Miusov raises questions of intention and poetics. He claims that he lies intentionally ("to be more endearing") and without reason ("though sometimes I don't know myself why I do it"). He admits to plagiarizing the story but confesses to fabricating a new ending.[7] In claiming that he lies to ingratiate himself with his audience, Fedor Pavlovich echoes Dostoevsky's journalistic observation that Russians lie for hospitality's sake, sacrificing themselves to their listeners to produce an aesthetic impression and provide pleasure (21:117). Fedor Pavlovich's conscious clowning does not aim to please, however, but to provoke. He plagiarizes and hyperbolizes aggressively, not hospitably. He plays the clown and humiliates himself, but he also exposes his audience both to the pain of witnessing and to the pain of exposure.

Although Fedor Pavlovich claims that he does not know why he lies, Zosima provides an answer: "And most importantly, don't be so ashamed of yourself, for that is the cause of everything" (14:40;43). Fedor exclaims that with these words, Zosima

> . . . seems to have pierced me right through and read me from inside. Indeed, it seems to me that when I enter a room I'm baser than everyone and that everyone takes me for a buffoon, so "Why not, indeed, play the buffoon, I'm not afraid of your opinions because you are all, to a man, baser than me!"

> That's why I play the buffoon, I'm a buffoon out of shame, Great Elder, out of shame. From touchiness alone I riot. If only I were sure, when I entered, that everyone would take me at once for the nicest and smartest of men,—Lord! what a good man I'd be! (14:41;43–44)

This interchange elucidates the scene's shame dynamic. As Schneider observes, "Shame arises when something doesn't fit."[8] Fedor Karamazov declares that he feels out of place when he is with others because he believes that they hold him in contempt. He responds to this social shame with a buffoonish verbal aggression that he acknowledges to be a defense. His hyperbolic rhetoric must be seen, and read, as a clown's weapon.

Miusov characterizes Fedor Pavlovich as a "Pierrot," a character associated with *commedia dell'arte*. Like Pierrot, Fedor Pavlovich is a performer who subverts hierarchies. He admits to recycling the Diderot story, a time-honored tradition, yet he claims credit for improvising the baptism. He thus follows the generic conventions of *commedia dell'arte*, which "unscrupulously stole from other theaters, taking up the latest hit, turning it inside out and offering it back as parody."[9] By exaggerating the encounter's outcome, Fedor Karamazov provides a parodic conversion story. The story's source, Snegirov's biography of Metropolitan Platon, portrays Diderot as a deliberate blasphemer who plans to confuse and mock Platon with his atheistic announcement. Unfazed, Platon notes that Diderot's atheism is not original but is anticipated by David's psalms. Shamed by this response, Diderot respectfully embraces Platon. This mild story certainly differs from Fedor's. The move from embracing Platon to embracing Christianity may be Fedor's own hyperbole, or it may have been part of the story by the time he heard it. Either way, Diderot's conversion illustrates the point in Dostoevsky's article on lying that all stories are exaggerated in the telling. In both scenarios, Fedor Pavlovich is just one in a series of narrators. Finally, whether Diderot's conversion belongs to Fedor Pavlovich or his sources, the atheist's flamboyant conversion suits the authorial thematics of Dostoevsky's Johannine epigraph of the seed (John 12:24). Fedor Karamazov thus exemplifies and enacts the part of Pierrot: he conveys an authorial message by playing the role of the clown who steals a story and parodies it by exaggerating and improvising.

Fedor Karamazov's improvisation of Diderot's conversion also bears an authorial imprint. Old Fedor may have chosen Dashkova and Potemkin as godparents for their historical verisimilitude as well as for Potemkin's scandal value. As two of the best-known figures of the time, Dashkova and Potemkin were cultural clichés, mimetically apt choices for a plagiarist. Fedor Dostoevsky's choice of these two as godparents, however, resonates richly with the novel's thematics. Dashkova was involved in the conspiracy that placed

Catherine on the throne. Dostoevsky thus has Diderot blessed by at least one person who had revolted against the God-ordained emperor (Peter III), replacing him with a secularly oriented empress (Catherine II)—an apt association for a novel about parricide/regicide/deicide as well as the conflict between atheism and faith. Furthermore, Princess Dashkova, in addition to being a famous salon hostess who knew Diderot personally, was also Catherine the Great's literary rival, appropriate for a novel full of rivalries. Potemkin was the creator of "Potemkin villages," those masks for the reality behind Catherine's ideal for the Russian empire, a form of architectural lying.[10] This synthetic detail thus accentuates Dostoevsky's metaliterary play as it calls attention to Fedor Karamazov's lying.[11] Catherine's most well-known lover, Potemkin, links lying and sensuality, making him a worthy parallel for Fedor Pavlovich himself. In fact, commenting on Diderot's baptism, Fedor Pavlovich associates his verbal ingenuity with "piquancy," a word that connects his rhetoric both to Ivan's newspaper articles, which are "piquantly" composed (14:15;16),[12] and to his own sensuality,[13] which finds expression in his view that Lizaveta Smerdiashchaia "could be regarded as a woman, even very much so, and that there was even some piquancy in it of a special sort, and so on and so forth" (14:91;98). Dostoevsky thus deliberately links verbal ingenuity and sensuality, an association further underscored by allusions to Diderot, whose first commercial literary work, *Les bijoux indiscrets*, centers on the world of courtesans. The association with Ivan's writing also links father and son in a significant way that Dostoevsky reveals late in his novel and that I will discuss in chapter 11.

In fashioning Diderot's baptism as an unholy trio united in a holy rite, Dostoevsky exposes the conflict between Fedor Karamazov's metaphysical longing for community and his materialistic longing for power. He also reveals Fedor Pavlovich's unconscious desire for spiritual guidance and a way to rejoin the community he provokes to reject him. In short, Dostoevsky shows that while Fedor's story may serve to conceal his shame, it also functions as a sign of the cover-up. Dostoevsky thus supplies readers with a trail that moves from the story's overt to its latent content.

Dostoevsky first encrypts Fedor Karamazov's desire for acceptance into his Diderot story. Then he exposes the shame dynamics that lead Fedor to conceal it. Anticipating rejection, Fedor aggressively provokes it. His verbal aggression acts out a defensive hostility. By attacking his audience with stories, Fedor Karamazov not only moves from passive to active; he also reveals part of what he intends to hide. By having Zosima identify shame as the source of Fedor Karamazov's lying, Dostoevsky provides readers with the key to the old buffoon's stories. By showing readers how to identify Fedor's desire for acceptance, Dostoevsky creates a common ground between the sensuous old buffoon and his authorial audience. Distracted by the scene's scandal and metaliterary play, readers may overlook this area of commonality. Yet Dostoevsky announces it at the novel's outset. At the end of Book One, Chapter One, which focuses on Fedor Pavlovich, the narrator declares: "In most cases, people, even wicked ones, are far more naive and simple-hearted than we generally assume. And so are we ourselves" (14:10;9). The shocking last sentence (*Da i my sami tozhe*) warns readers that Dostoevsky is going to breach the distance between characters, even wicked ones, and readers. Indeed, Dostoevsky reprises this idea polyphonically at the novel's end as the townspeople discuss the defense lawyer's speech at Dmitry's trial. One person calls the speech "serious," another "true." A third then pipes up: "Us, too, he summed us up, too . . . at the start of the speech, remember, that we're all the same as Fedor Pavlovich?" A fourth voice agrees, "At the end, too" (15:151;723).[14] The seven hundred pages that separate these passages bespeak an authorial message. Fedor Karamazov may be gone, but Fedor Dostoevsky has not forgotten him.

Dostoevsky scandalizes readers by suggesting that we are all the same as Fedor Karamazov. The idea disrupts our unquestioning sense of self; it disorients us; it makes us self-conscious. This, I argue, is Dostoevsky's goal: to surprise readers with shame, to expose shame as the post-lapsarian heritage we share with Fedor Pavlovich, with all of Dostoevsky's characters, with all human beings. Shameless exhibitionism aggressively transgresses and collapses the intersubjective boundaries between characters, but also among characters, readers, and text. In behaving like a buffoon, Fedor Karamazov aggressively arouses shame in those positioned as witnesses. In writing this and other scandal scenes, Fedor Dostoevsky aggressively confronts his readers with shame. He also provides us with opposing models of response. In "An Inappropriate Gathering," Dostoevsky opposes the responses of Miusov, who perpetuates the cycle of shame, to those of Zosima, who empathically reflects Fedor Pavlovich back to himself, giving him the opportunity to confront his shame and return to community. What Zosima does for Fedor Karamazov, Dostoevsky does for his authorial audience. He provides us with the opportunity to confront our shame—the shame we experience as we witness another's shame. In having Zosima plunge beneath the surface to reveal to Fedor Karamazov that his shameless behavior springs from his shame, Dostoevsky shows us how we, like Miusov, perpetuate shame cycles. Fedor Dostoevsky thus gives us the opportunity to confront our shame and to know ourselves—not as self-sufficient subjects but as members of a social and metaphysical community. The idea that we are all the same as Fedor Karamazov also gives new meaning to the word "brothers" in the novel's title. In this unconventional way, Dostoevsky dramatizes his social, political, and metaphysical message of human relatedness.[15]

In fashioning scenes of shame, Dostoevsky engages an archaic experience that evokes anxiety. Even when Dostoevsky portrays shame as content and as motive (thus as plot mover), he arouses reader discomfort. When Dostoevsky uses shame as a narrative strategy, he takes the greater risk of losing some readers.[16] In return, he gains access to those who remain. On the mimetic as well as synthetic levels, Dostoevsky exploits shame's affective and cognitive synergy, heightening readers' self-consciousness and thus engaging us emotionally as well as intellectually. He seduces readers by arousing our voyeuristic instincts. He taps shame's paradoxical capacity to isolate and relate. He employs shame's comic potential to create intimacy as well as to entertain.[17] He also uses and demonstrates shame's potential to link the ethical with the aesthetic.

Shame is experienced intersubjectively, making it a rich ground for exploring ethical interactions. Shame is also experienced contextually, thereby lending itself to aesthetic evaluation, for shame is experienced when people or things are exposed, which literally means that they are out of place. Both the English verb "to expose" and its Russian equivalents, *oblichat'*, *razoblachat'*, *raskryvat'*, indicate the placing out, disrobing, depriving of shelter, laying open, placing in an unsheltered or unprotected position of something or of someone (the Russian verb *oblichat'* contains the root *lik*, or "face," which stresses the human). This spatial aspect of exposure locates shamed persons aesthetically—in a dissonant or disharmonious relationship with their surroundings. This strong linking of the aesthetic with the ethical derives from a long tradition in Russia, where even language reinforces it. The Russian word for icon, *obraz*, also means "image," while the Russian word for the ugly, disgraceful, disfigured, and scandalous is *bezobrazie*, or "without image."[18] At the personal, social, and metaphysical levels, individuals can relate respectfully and thus preserve this deep sense of aesthetic/ethical propriety, or they can violate boundaries, breaking down aesthetic/ethical structures.

Dostoevsky's liars are excellent vehicles for studying shame and narrative because they are shamed, shameless, or both. In fact, in diagnosing shame at one's identity or the desire to be other than who one is as a central motive for lying, Dostoevsky identifies lying as the rhetoric of shame. Furthermore, Dostoevsky's liars not only fall into social cracks, making them out of place or misfits; they also *feel* out of place. Consequently, liars flirt with or violate social norms. Finally, lying and fictionalizing share much common ground, making liars apt agents for Dostoevsky's metaliterary play. While Dostoevsky's liars try to fit themselves into society by citing literature, Dostoevsky assimilates himself into the Western canon.

My inquiries into shame and lying overlap notably. I examine the content of lying as shame content made manifest. This illuminates each liar's particular shame issues but also opens up a whole range of questions about shame, rhetoric, misrepresentation, and narrative. Liars are self-fashioners, whose self-representing disclosures function simultaneously as unconscious self-exposures. Dostoevsky thus plays with narrative's paradoxical ability to reveal and conceal. The authorially supplied surplus vision of Dostoevsky's texts reveals a gap between the narrative abilities of character-narrators and author, a gap that reveals how character-narrators' narcissism (a symptom of their shame) blinds them, but not their author (or his audience), to the larger thematic and metaliterary depths of their stories. Dostoevsky's personalized (semi-embodied or embodied) heterodiegetic narrators also expose his homodiegetic character-narrators; the author, in turn, may expose his narrator as an exposer.[19] To write about lying allows Dostoevsky to write about fictionalizing. To expose readers to shame allows Dostoevsky to collapse the intersubjective boundaries between characters and readers.

For Dostoevsky, reading is a redemptive tool that stimulates ethical changes. His prose fiction "translates the interactive problems of ethics into literary forms."[20] While Dostoevsky does this in a variety of ways throughout his literary career, in his novels after *Crime and Punishment* he develops a narrative strategy that involves his readers' immersing themselves in the experience of shame. In *Crime and Punishment*, Dostoevsky's third-person narrator enters Raskolnikov's fevered brain, thus generating reader sympathy for his antihero. Yet he retains the requisite omniscience for violently agitating readers' moral sensitivity. Dostoevsky thereby evokes a dual response, making readers complicit with Raskolnikov, yet arousing our ethical qualms. By gradually revealing the psychology behind a shame-driven crime, Dostoevsky implicates readers in the text's ethical action. But the exposure of shame does not fuel the action as it will in his later texts. After *Crime and Punishment*, Dostoevsky turns shame dynamics into narrative dynamics by exploiting shame's unexpectedness, contagiousness, and paradoxicality. Shame is unpredictable and thus has no standard script. Shame is contagious and thus provokes painful responses from witnesses to shame (characters and readers alike) and from the shamed (characters). Shame is also cognitive, partially because the shamed and the witnesses to shame engage in the cognitive processes of heightened self-consciousness and evaluation. In his post-1866 novels, Dostoevsky exploits shame's affective and cognitive synergy on the mimetic and synthetic levels. He unleashes shame's paradoxical power both to isolate and to relate. Dostoevsky thus adds the peculiar synergy of shame dynamics to the recursive relations among author, readers, and text.

Dostoevsky explores and exploits disgrace-shame, the shame that follows exposure, but also keeps discretion-shame, the shame that helps prevent exposure, alive for characters and readers alike.[21] He does this by targeting his readers' internal divisions as well as our divided roles as members of the narrative and authorial audiences.[22] As James Phelan points out, narratives require that audiences judge characters.[23] In the narrative audience, where we participate as observers of the text's mimetic illusion and as addressees, we experience with the characters portrayed the full force of disgrace-shame. As members of the narrative audience, we respond to shame viscerally, much as the characters portrayed do. Like them, we tend to respond negatively to exposed shame. In the authorial audience, where we have a double consciousness of the text's mimetic and synthetic dimensions, we witness and experience the disgrace-shame, yet with the cognitive engagement, surplus vision, and aesthetic pleasure that provide the distance necessary to separate act from actor. Dostoevsky supplies additional help for his authorial audience by providing shame-sensitive characters who model appropriate responses for us. These characters know or intuit that shame is a source of suffering. They can thus condemn the act without losing compassion for the actor.

This schema, however, does not account for the shame overflow released in the Dostoevskian text. Shame occurs in the intersubjective space between self and others. As discretion-shame, it defines and preserves boundaries between self and others. As disgrace-shame, it violates and collapses those boundaries. Whether shame involves actual exposure or the threat of exposure, it unleashes affective energies that linger long after the self has derived some comfort from the cognitive energies that have been harnessed to contain them. In adopting this authorial strategy, Dostoevsky takes a leap of faith. The epigraph to *The Brothers Karamazov* (John 12:24) expresses Dostoevsky's larger authorial plan: his novels are like seeds. They participate in his organic metaphor for the ethical activity of reading. The lingering affect, I believe, acts as the germinating power of his texts. Given the proper soil, they cast off their cognitive shells and take root in readers' guts.

Shame is central to Dostoevsky's poetic power. He exploits shame's visual, spatial, ethical, aesthetic, epistemological, and metaphysical dimensions, especially in *The Brothers Karamazov*, a novel that repeatedly refers to the biblical myth of shame's origins, a myth that links cognition and affect. After Eve and Adam eat the fruit and their eyes are opened, they learn they are naked, and they cover themselves. Then they hide from God. This myth couples knowing and seeing as well as knowing and feeling. Eve and Adam *see* that they are naked, but they must also *feel* naked, since their first impulse is to cover themselves. In learning that they are naked, Eve and Adam become conscious of themselves; they develop objective self-awareness.[24] The myth thus demonstrates shame's intimate connection to identity. In sensing that nakedness is inappropriate to that environment, they intuit something about the world outside themselves; they develop a knowledge of standards, rules, and goals. Shame thus involves the cognition of their "real," that is, their "fallen" condition. In the Garden, Dostoevsky learns that shame heightens both cognitive and affective faculties, knowledge that he will exploit by using shame to manipulate readers' emotions while engaging our intellects. Furthermore, the myth shows that the pain of exposure lingers. Even though Eve and Adam have covered themselves, *they still feel naked*. As it turns out, their attempts at concealment (an aesthetic response to shame) show God that they have eaten from the tree. Dostoevsky perceives and plays on the similarity between such visual cover-ups and verbal cover-ups. As I will show, the stories that his liars tell to cover their shame reveal as much as they conceal.

In the myth, God also exiles Eve and Adam from the Garden of Eden so that they will not eat from the Tree of Life. The myth thus links transgression and exile, thereby enlarging its etiological scope. For once they develop objective self-awareness and awareness of the world's standards, rules, and goals, human beings lose their spontaneous, unmediated relationship to self and world. The myth of the Garden thus accounts for the divided self—humans' sense of separation from self, other, and God. Exile from Eden emphasizes metaphysical separation. The myth problematizes the issue of shame's relationship with guilt by linking transgression, shame, and separation. Since the myth also differentiates between two kinds of knowledge—knowledge of good and evil, that is, knowledge of the world's standards, rules, and goals, and knowledge of self, that is, objective self-awareness—it is tempting to correlate these with guilt and shame. Nonetheless, the myth, like all rich stories, defies such easy correlation. And so does Dostoevsky.

Shame relates broadly to human identity; guilt relates more narrowly to human action. Although affect theorists argue that guilt is a form of moral shame, all theorists agree that guilt involves a moral component. Shame arises when a person negatively evaluates his/her whole self in relation to an ideal self,[25] thereby arousing feelings of inferiority or inadequacy. Guilt arises, in contrast, when a self acts so as to transgress against personal, moral, social, or legal norms. Self and object thus meld in shame, but are differentiated in guilt. Shame and guilt can be related, but need not be so. (Dmitry Karamazov does not feel guilty for his dirty socks and underwear, for example.) While shame has no fixed script, guilt often follows the sequence—transgression, punishment, redemption.[26] In Christian scenarios, the transgressor repents and expiates the offense. No single action, however, can heal feelings of shame. Shame's negative intensity also shields it from examination and discussion. Shame triggers more shame: individuals are ashamed at feeling shame. Shame's fecundity and contagiousness explain the individual and social discomfort that engender social taboos surrounding it.[27]

The myth of the Garden shows that shame works paradoxically: it both violates individual integrity and protects it. Its positive function, discretion-shame, correlates with knowledge of good and evil; it is normative, as it defines social standards, rules, and goals.[28] It thus reflects and sustains the individual and social ordering of the world. On the other hand, its negative function, disgrace-shame, correlates with knowledge of self. Disgrace-shame is a painfully experienced disintegration of the world, reflecting a break in the self's relationship with self, others, or both. Both discretion-shame and disgrace-shame involve cognition and self-evaluation. Discretion-shame focuses on social norms and tends to foreground the preservation or repair of the appropriate[29]; disgrace-shame focuses on self and tends to foreground the experience or control of narcissistic injury. Both functions reveal how high shame stakes are: they involve nothing less than one's identity as a self-presenting agent. Because shame threatens one's qualifications to present oneself in the public sphere, shame's drama devolves through issues of inclusion and exclusion. Dostoevsky's liars all experience the disgrace-shame of exclusion. Consequently, they either struggle to prove their worth as self-presenting agents or actively share their disgrace with others, or both.

On the mimetic level, Dostoevsky makes shame an ethical drama by activating the literal meaning of the Russian words that designate persons and characters: *litso, deistvuiushchie litsa*—"face," "acting faces."[30] One need only think of expressions such as "losing face" and "saving face" to see how closely the whole person is identified with her or his face. Such expressions also highlight the recursive relationship between individual and social identity. We can lose or save face only vis-à-vis an other or others. The Russian word for modesty, propriety, or decorum, *prilichie*, literally "in the presence of face," likewise emphasizes this recursive relationship. As Leslie A. Johnson shows, Dostoevsky hinges the ethical action of *The Idiot* on interactions between faces/persons. While Dostoevsky always paid much attention to faces, in *The Idiot* he introduces the metaliterary play on the word *litso*, which he keeps active in later works. Faces mark the external boundaries between self and others. Also, as centers for verbal and visual interactions, faces become a locus for identity. Readers as witnesses judge interactions between characters by interpreting words, facial expressions, and body language, determining from these clues whether characters violate or demonstrate respect for self and others.

On the synthetic level, Dostoevsky involves readers in the ethical drama of shame by collapsing the intersubjective boundaries between characters and readers. Portrayed shame derives its peculiar affective and narrative power from three basic properties of the shame experience: disruption, disorientation, and painful self-consciousness. Shame is sudden and unpredictable; it comes upon shamed persons unawares, exposing them—to themselves, to others, or to both. Following unexpected exposure, shamed persons cannot control the autonomic responses that betray shame: pounding of heart, averting of eyes, contracting of posture, sweating, blushing. Because these involuntary responses often further expose shamed persons, they further disrupt their sense of self and relation to the world. A person possesses a coherent sense of self and the world only when his or her experience itself is coherent by virtue of predictably recurring elements (an entirely random, unpredictable flow of events cannot be intelligible). To the extent that shame introduces unexpected exposure, disrupted expectations, and the like, it renders experience, and thereby a sense of self and of the world, less coherent. Shamed persons, however inarticulately, are aware of this disruption and pained by it: they perceive, more or less clearly, that their sense of self—hence their identity—is at risk. As a corollary, shame devastates the sense of connection to others. Shame engenders painful self-consciousness that in turn produces the desire to hide, disappear, die, or otherwise rid the self of the pain (all forms of alienation), yet it can also produce the desire to rejoin the community in such a way as to heal the pain.

Just as predictably recurring events enable a person to form a coherent sense of self and the world, so narrative predictability orients readers in the fictional world. Portrayed shame, on the other hand, disrupts readers' expectations and sense of personal inviolability. Shame is always unexpected. It disorients and rouses self-consciousness in the shamed person and witnesses alike. When Dostoevsky surprises his readers with shame, readers experience a similar disruption, disorientation, and self-consciousness. We see and feel shame—which we, like Dostoevsky's liars, and most human beings, try to avoid. Dostoevsky thus reveals our complicity in the status quo. He exposes our desire to keep the covers up.

As Dostoevsky knows, the pain of exposure lingers. Even once the authorial audience has separated from its plunged-into-the-action-and-affect role as narrative audience, pain's memory remains. Moreover, visual memory frequently accompanies the affective memory. Dostoevsky includes the persisting affect and image in his redemptional plan. Like Dante in his *Divine Comedy* or like St. Augustine in his *Confessions*, Dostoevsky knows that while authors can model a salvational path for their readers, they cannot force readers to follow. St. Augustine and Dante portray character-selves who are internally divided but who eventually follow the voice of conscience rather than their physical or political instincts. Dostoevsky retains such internal divisions and projects them outward onto characters' sociopolitical and metaphysical relationships. Like his redemptively minded forebears, Dostoevsky also attempts to stir readers' desire to follow the authorially approved path by appealing to readers' internal divisions, particularly to readers' sense of shame experienced as conscience (knowledge of right action).

In moving from the portrayal of shame as subject or motive or both to the use of shame as a narrative strategy, Dostoevsky capitalizes on the parallels between the act of reading and the action of the Fall. The forbidden fruit has nutritional, aesthetic, and epistemic appeal: it is good for food, appealing to the eye, and desired as a source of knowledge.[31] When we read, we feed our souls, participate in an aesthetic experience, and learn—about both the world and ourselves. In reading Dostoevsky's late novels, we witness others' shame, thus recapitulating in our post-lapsarian world a sudden fall from innocence to knowledge. Our eyes are open and we see and feel our separation from self and others. In short, we experience the shame of exposure. We are thus given the opportunity to know ourselves, to confront our shame positively, and to return to community, which, for Dostoevsky, means a return to God.

chapter two

Something about Lying

Dostoevsky's fiction, like Shakespeare's drama or Freud's psychology, reveals secrets. In exposing that which lies hidden, all three writers hoped to effect change—first in individuals and then in society. Like the ancient Greeks before them, all three diagnosed private pains as symptoms of public ills and vice versa. Like the Greeks, Shakespeare sought to persuade his audiences of this truth through dramatic exposition, by involving them in the cathartic action of his plays. Freud did this by posing as a private/public investigator, inviting his readers to participate in his ongoing search into the human and social psyche. Dostoevsky does this largely by surprising his audiences with shame, thereby pricking our public conscience and implicating us in the ethical action of his work.[1]

While Dostoevsky's narrative strategies and thematics have earned him a place in the canon of world literature, he also holds a special place in the Russian canon. Like other Russian writers, Dostoevsky aggressively tries to mold his readers. While Karamzin aims to feminize readers, Pushkin to remasculinize them, and Lev Tolstoy to estrange and educate them, Dostoevsky aims to save them.[2] The most modern of Russia's nineteenth-century writers, Dostoevsky nonetheless embraces the unity of sociopolitical and metaphysical that characterizes the medieval worldview. Like Dante, Dostoevsky believes that to engage in right action both socially and politically means to live in right relation to God. Dostoevsky proposes to help readers return to the Garden by changing the way we look at the world. By uncovering shame, Dostoevsky implicates us in the painful experience of exposure and self-consciousness that can lead to individual and social redemption.

In time-honored fashion, Dostoevsky masks some of his most serious social criticism with comic forms. His liars, a rather uproarious and motley group, can thus be seen as trenchant social critics who expose individuals and social institutions while exposing themselves. In Dostoevsky's work, exposure works both ways. In this, Dostoevsky self-consciously follows Gogol's lead. For example, when asked which of three characters he would like to play in Gogol's *The Inspector General*—for a performance to benefit the Literary Fund—Dostoevsky chose Shpekin, the postmaster who exposes the central character Khlestakov as an impostor. Delighted, Dostoevsky declared, "It's one of the most comic roles not only in Gogol but in all of the Russian repertory, and besides, is filled with deep social significance."[3] The letter that Shpekin opens and reads aloud exposes Khlestakov as an impostor or pretender, a figure of decided sociopolitical significance in Russian history, which witnessed numerous popular uprisings led by men pretending to be the "true" tsar. The letter also serves as Khlestakov's exposé of the play's major characters and thus reflects Shpekin and his townsmen back to each other and to themselves. In choosing Shpekin's role, Dostoevsky revealed his preference for expressing social criticism through the voices of characters who unintentionally expose themselves while intentionally exposing others.

In his first novel, *Poor Folk*, Dostoevsky assumes the role of Shpekinesque postmaster, the novelist who reveals his characters' secrets.[4] An epistolary novel, *Poor Folk* portrays the correspondence of an impoverished minor clerk and a fallen woman—a relationship largely confined to letters for the sake of social decorum. This early work thus evidences a capacity Dostoevsky develops in his later works—a deep understanding of the recursive relationship between personal and social identity. In striving to define themselves, his characters land in the chasm between real and ideal, the nexus of self-fashioning. Makar Devushkin is the first of Dostoevsky's characters who attempts to bridge that chasm through the act of literary creation.[5] He tries to transcend his personal, social, and economic inadequacies, the marks of his shame, by donning the writer's mantle and creating a compensatory identity.

Poor Folk also demonstrates Dostoevsky's attention to narrative strategy and authorial concealment. Responding to the mixed, though largely positive reviews of his story, Dostoevsky wrote to his brother, Mikhail: "Our public, like every crowd, has instinct, but not book-learnedness [*obrazovannost'*]. They don't understand how it's possible to write in that style. They are used to finding the author's mug in everything, whereas I didn't show them mine. And they haven't a clue that it is Devushkin speaking and not me, and that Devushkin can't speak any other way. They find my novel drawn out, when it doesn't contain one extra word" (28.I:117–18).

As Bakhtin has argued in his book on Dostoevsky's poetics, Dostoevsky writes polyphonically, giving his characters their own words.[6] But Dostoevsky does not relinquish authorial message. As I show, he inscribes clues for interpretation into the very structure of his work. He orchestrates the words and deeds of his characters, thereby revealing gaps and creating situational rhymes that supply surplus vision. He conveys his message through contextualization. Makar Devushkin serves as one vehicle for Dostoevsky's social message; Dostoevsky's liars serve as others. Like their progenitor, Khlestakov, they are verbal self-fashioners. Like Khlestakov, they are full of shame and attempt to gain social acceptance with their verbal fabrications. Like Gogol's postmaster, Dostoevsky exposes their secrets.

Shame Dynamics

Dostoevsky's liars offer only one example of his mastery as a portrayer of shame and shame dynamics. His keen understanding of the self's fragile coverings helps explain the particularly poignant and unexpected quality of his literary work. Shame concerns identity; thus shame exposed has the power to shake us to the core of our being. Unlike guilt, which involves a sense of transgression and has as its object what we do, shame has as its object who we are and involves a sense of inferiority or inadequacy and a fear of exposure. The states of feeling ridiculous, embarrassed, chagrined, mortified, humiliated, and dishonored are all variant shame states, all of which abound in Dostoevsky's work. Dostoevsky even chooses titles that convey shame states, for example, *The Humiliated and the Injured* and "Dream of the Ridiculous Man."

Shame arouses anxiety because it touches on taboo areas.[7] There are legal taboos such as murder and incest—and there are social taboos, such as brutal truth-telling, that allow human beings to coexist relatively peacefully. Dostoevsky explores the shame and guilt surrounding all kinds of taboos. In his novel *Crime and Punishment,* for example, Dostoevsky confounds his readers by preparing us to expect Raskolnikov to live on the guilt-identity axis, while he experiences life on the shame-identity axis. We are therefore puzzled throughout the novel by Raskolnikov's thoughts and actions. We expect guilt, but he feels shame. Raskolnikov is ashamed that his superman theory was wrong, that he is not among those who can heedlessly commit atrocious crimes in humanity's name. He dwells on his sense of failure. He is not the Napoleon he wants to be. His agonized perception of his crime as ugly rather than glorious, insignificant rather than earth-shattering, reflects his sense of self.

Raskolnikov's agonizing both illustrates and illuminates shame and guilt dynamics. In his case, guilt and shame are interwoven. He is guilty of murder. While he can never restore life to his victims, he can make restitution to society by accepting his guilt and serving time in prison. The shame dynamic is more hidden. By murdering the old pawnbroker and her sister, Raskolnikov exposes himself to a humiliating self-examination. He must confront the crushing fact that he is not the hero he wants to be. While both shame and guilt lead him to commit murder, his shame intensifies afterward because he believes that his crime was a failure.[8] Not in the physical sense, for he did kill the two women, but in the figurative sense, for he also kills his dream of greatness. His crime forces him to confront himself and to recognize, however painfully, that his theorizing about crime masked his sense of powerlessness and insignificance. His ideas camouflaged the reality of his poverty and impotence. While in Siberia Raskolnikov must work through both his guilt and his shame—he must repent his crime and he must learn to accept himself. Once his dream of the trichinae reveals that his theory was a destructive cover, he can see his crime's ethical evil and repent. Shame leads him to self-examination and acceptance of responsibility for his action. Here and elsewhere in Dostoevsky's work, shame and guilt meet in the ethical realm. Raskolnikov teaches Dostoevsky's readers a few important lessons that the novelist will reiterate and that the journalist will describe. Denial exacerbates transgression. Only by recognizing, acknowledging, and accepting one's shortcomings can one return to community.[9]

Jane Austen also portrays the dynamic of self-confrontation that follows shame exposed. In *Pride and Prejudice*, Elizabeth Bennet confronts herself after receiving a letter from Mr. Darcy, whose proposal of marriage she has just vehemently rejected. The letter informs her that Darcy had indeed interfered with Mr. Bingley's courtship of her sister Jane, but it also informs her that Mr. Wickham, who flirted with her earlier, is a wastrel and gambler who had tried to seduce Mr. Darcy's sister the previous summer.

> She grew absolutely ashamed of herself. Of neither Darcy nor Wickham could she think without feeling that she had been blind, partial, prejudiced, absurd.
> "How despicably have I acted!" she cried; "I, who have prided myself on my discernment! I, who have valued myself on my abilities! who have often disdained the generous candor of my sister, and gratified my vanity in useless or blamable distrust. How humiliating is this discovery! Yet, how just a humiliation! Had I been in love, I could not have been more wretchedly blind. But vanity, not love, has been my folly. Pleased with the preference of one, and offended by the neglect of the other, on the very beginning of our acquaintance, I have courted prepossession and ignorance, and driven reason away, where either were concerned. Til this moment I never knew myself."[10]

Austen portrays a moment of shame confronted, a critical moment when Elizabeth's acknowledgment of her personal shortcoming allows her to change her relationship with significant others. By reading Darcy's letter fairly, Elizabeth is able to view her family critically, which prepares her for her separation from them.[11] She also comes to view Mr. Darcy differently, recognizing in him a potential life partner. Austen thus shows readers how a character who confronts her shame positively can integrate healthily into her community.

Like Austen, Dostoevsky treats shame as a subject. Unlike Austen, Dostoevsky uses shame as a narrative strategy. The shame dynamics in Dostoevsky's works explain much reader discomfort, for shame involves both seeing and being seen. Whenever we experience shame, we feel that there is nowhere to hide. Conversely, when we see another experience shame, we see that other as uncovered before our gaze. This reminds us of our own protective coverings. Like the shamed, we suddenly feel acutely self-aware and vulnerable to others and their gaze. Shame's contagious force overturns our complacency, our unself-conscious sense of self. Helen Block Lewis observes, "shame is an acutely painful experience for both the person who suffers it and the sympathetic observer. . . . Shame evokes a tendency for both the sufferer to hide and the observer to look away."[12]

While reading about Elizabeth Bennet's shame, readers feel safe. First of all, she confronts herself in a private setting—she has no homodiegetic (character) audience. Second, Elizabeth is in control, and so are we; we do not look away from her shame, because she does not. Third, Elizabeth is a sympathetic character with whom readers identify. The same does not obtain when reading Dostoevsky. Frequently, exposed characters are not sympathetic. Dostoevsky breaks down the intersubjective boundaries between readers and even unsavory characters by making readers witnesses to their shame. Dostoevsky thus uses shame as an instrument of social conscience that not only expands readers' moral imaginations but also makes us examine our own collusion in the status quo. By inducing social shame, Dostoevsky produces social disgust and inspires social reform. We readers are persuaded to remake ourselves according to the models he suggests.

Dostoevsky knew shame first-hand. He knew the sting of poverty, of rejection, of social awkwardness; he knew the shame of being a convict, a debtor, and a gambler; he fell from boastful glory (following his first work, *Poor Folk*) to near-oblivion (following his second work, *The Double*). He also experienced shame vicariously by reading books ranging from *The Iliad* to *Père Goriot*. Dostoevsky utilized his knowledge to become a master portrayer of shame psychology. His rival, Tolstoy, masterfully depicts moments of shame and embarrassment in social settings, focusing on the more socially acceptable defenses against shame—denial and desire to flee. Dostoevsky, on the other hand, delves into the psyche of the humiliated and the narcissistically injured, exploring the back alleys of his characters' shame experiences and documenting a full range of shame defenses—including aggressive anger.[13] While Tolstoy and

Dostoevsky both present shameful moments that engender a character's embarrassment and desire to flee, Dostoevsky's depiction of passed-on shame, that is, of shame experienced wrathfully and inflicted in turn on others, intensifies readers' discomfort and desire for flight. Characters who lash out and strike back at their offenders violate the social norms governing human interactions. The eruption of such uncontrollable energies cries out for containment. Readers long for order to be restored. By letting shame out of the box, Dostoevsky creates an almost unbearable dramatic tension.

In portraying scenes of shame, Dostoevsky exploits three properties of the shame experience: disruption, disorientation, and painful self-consciousness. In contrast with guilt experiences of transgression, repentance, and reparation that offer readers certain expectations that authors can satisfy, delay, or thwart, portrayed shame, like the shame experience itself, is always unexpected. It disorients and rouses self-consciousness in the shamed person and witnesses alike. If the author controls the shame experience, as Austen and Tolstoy do, readers feel safe. But when authors like Dostoevsky surprise their readers with shame, readers experience a similar disruption, disorientation, and self-consciousness. Reading Dostoevsky rattles yet rivets us.

Dostoevsky not only dramatizes scenes of exposure but describes the shame dynamics involved. The following two sentences, from Dostoevsky's 1873 *Diary of a Writer* article, "Something about Lying" dramatize the shame dynamics of an exposed lie. The narrator is the *Diary* writer:

> Tell me, haven't you passed on a story [*anekdot*], as though it had happened to you, to the very person who told you that story about himself? You surely forgot, when suddenly halfway through the story you remembered and guessed something about it which was clearly confirmed in your listener's suffering gaze, stubbornly directed at you (for in such cases, for some reason, one looks the other in the eye with ten-fold tenacity); remember how, despite everything and already deprived of your sense of humor, you nonetheless, with courage worthy of a great objective, continued to mutter your tale and, having finished as quickly as possible, with nervously hurried courtesies, shaking of hands and smiles, you fled in different directions, so that when suddenly in the burst of a last convulsion you were possessed for no reason whatsoever to shout down the stairs to your listener, who was already hurrying down them, a question about his auntie's health, he didn't turn around and didn't answer then about his auntie, which remained in your memory as the most tormenting of everything from all of that story [*anekdot*] that happened to you. (21:118)

The lie in this passage is plagiarized—someone else's story told as one's own. It is exposed as a plagiarism by the speaker's own memory and confirmed by the interlocutor's gaze. The speaker both sees and is seen. The shameful experience causes a deflating affect (loss of sense of humor). His interlocutor's shame as witness to the plagiarism intensifies the speaker's shame at being exposed. While guilt allows for expiation, shame is irreversible. As Helen Merrill Lynd notes, "No single, specific thing we can do can rectify or mitigate such an experience."[14] Disoriented by shame, the speaker entangles himself further, first by denial (persistence in telling the story), then by further denial (the question about the auntie's health). The speaker thereby compounds the mutual shame. His listener has the same set of responses, and Dostoevsky manages to make his reader, another listener, experience them too, under the guidance of the listener in the text.

As Lynd points out, the memory of shame is bound to minute, concrete detail.[15] In the cited passage, the *Diary* writer describes the shame experience in great detail—prolonging the reader's vicarious experience by documenting every one of the speaker's reactions. Finally, the *Diary* writer claims that it is a small detail, the listener's nonresponse to the speaker's question, that lingers most painfully in his memory. Its power derives from its symbolic function as a trigger, a detail that torments the speaker, a tangible sign of the wedge established between him and his listener. This affective detail represents a disruption of the relationship between speaker and listener: the speaker loses the sense of individual and social identity, the validation of self-worth, provided by a listener's appreciative response. Finally, this detail emblemizes the paradox of shame: a profoundly isolating experience, it intimately relates us to the universe and our place (or lack of place) in it. Shame has revelatory and implicative power, as many involuntary responses do, for it painfully points to the deep connection between the shamed and the witnesses to that shame.

Shame isolates.[16] The plagiarist above experiences a devastating sense of loss—of connection to the other. Speaker and listener can never meet again without reliving that moment of shame, unless either or both can forget or somehow make peace with it. Lynd explains: "To a person oriented more to the shame-identity axis, other persons, the They, or at least some of them, are parts of himself as he is part of them."[17] In other words, the community participates in the constructing and policing of identity. In Russian society, the nobility's tight embrace of the honor code exemplifies this dynamic.[18] Throughout most of modern Russian history, the upper classes were subordinated to the will and whimsy of the tsarist state. They thus lived with the constant threat that their lives would be painfully and shamefully disrupted. The nobility responded by opposing state policies regarding corporal punishment—a profoundly shame-filled form of discipline from which they had no guaranteed legal protections. To counter a potential form of discipline imposed from without, they imposed on themselves a code of behavior that also worked by shame: anyone who violated the honor code was subject to exclusion. The honor code enabled the nobility to forge a sense of class identity that could hide the profoundly humiliating reality of their actual situation. In doing so, however, they created a social dynamic that made them extremely vulnerable to others' opinions.

Because it involves the self's relationship to others, the shame dynamic also touches on one of the tenets of Russian Orthodoxy—the mutual interdependence of all human beings. Vladimir Solovev, the Russian religious thinker Dostoevsky knew and liked most, describes in ethical terms what shame researchers describe in psychological terms—the recursive relationship between personal and social identity. For him, shame is the innate quality that differentiates humans from beasts. A sign of our ethical identity, shame manifests itself in conscience,[19] which, in turn, leads to ethical action. As a writer, Dostoevsky provokes readers' shame, thereby piquing our consciences and moving us to act ethically, which, in turn, improves the world in which we live.

In discussing the ethical functions of shame as discretion-shame and disgrace-shame, Carl Schneider identifies their area of commonality: "The two forms of shame—being ashamed and the sense of shame—share a common element, for *at its core, shame is intimately linked to the human need to cover that which is exposed*. This common element is apparent in the Indo-European root *(s)kem-; *(s)kam-, meaning 'to cover.'"[20] The Russian scholar N. D. Arutiunova notes that the Russian word *styd* derives from the common Slavic root *stud'/styd'*, which means "that which makes something contract, freeze, stiffen, be cold." After contrasting this with the "hot" responses to shame, such as burning and blushing, she points out that there are also "cold" responses to shame, which indicate a distancing, between self and shame or between self and other.[21] In the Garden of Eden, for example, Eve and Adam eat the fruit of the Tree of Knowledge, learn they are naked, and cover themselves.

Schneider notes that for English speakers, shame is largely synonymous with being ashamed, with disgrace. We thus fail to understand the significant role that the sense of shame or discretion-shame plays as a positive, restraining influence.[22] Solovev's conception of shame (*styd*) focuses on what Schneider identifies as discretion-shame. Dostoevsky's work illustrates the dynamics of shame (*styd*) exposed, what Schneider calls disgrace-shame. While Solovev emphasizes shame's role as a deterrent and Dostoevsky examines a whole range of roles for shame, particularly shame after the fact, both recognize the positive importance of others or the Other in shame experiences. Part of the searing pain in shame experiences derives from the devastating sense of loss of connection to others.[23] Shame thus acts as a form of self-regulation. Dostoevsky shows that what holds true for actions holds true for metaphorical impulses. When one gets carried away by one's passions, either physically or verbally, one oversteps the bounds of propriety, violating social norms. One thus places oneself outside of the habitual sphere of personal interaction. To preserve one's connection with others, one adopts appropriate patterns of behavior. Though initially a set of limits is imposed from without (as with the honor code or Orthodox ethics), individuals internalize them. Social regulation becomes self-regulation. With a sensitivity to apophaticism typical of his philosophy and theology, Solovev elaborates on this aspect of the shame experience—even though shame is experienced as a negative self-valuation, the very fact that shame is experienced speaks of a positive self-valuation.[24] Only if we think ourselves capable of a better connection can we experience the pain of falling short.

Since there are times and places in all phases of human life where covering is appropriate and even imperative, shame serves yet another constructive role: "shame guards the separate, private self with its boundaries and prevents intrusion and merger. It guarantees the self's integrity. . . . More specifically, it shields the self against overexposure and intrusive curiosity."[25] This protective function of shame makes Dostoevsky's liars more paradoxical than his many other shamed figures, for example, Makar Devushkin, merely an aspiring author: to create an acceptable and perhaps even praiseworthy public persona, liars must expose themselves to public scrutiny. Their willingness to expose themselves to bridge the perceived gap between themselves and others makes them very powerful. Impelled by their need for social recognition, liars take risks that other characters do not. They also frequently exceed the accepted limits for lying in public and thus overexpose themselves. They must then protect their fragile, overexposed selves.

Dostoevsky's liars are not a homogeneous group, nor do they respond to shame uniformly. While they mostly try to protect their selves from shame in standard ways—through flight, denial, or self-concealment—they occasionally confound all witnesses by flaunting their overexposed selves. They share the shame experienced as loss of privacy by violating others' privacy. They aggressively expose themselves and others to humiliation and pain in public arenas. Characters like Fedor Karamazov do this all the time. They thus share their shame by behaving shamelessly, provoking scandal by flouting the social norms that would have them respond to shame in more socially accepted ways.

Reader Response

In portraying exposed shame, Dostoevsky relies on shame's capacity to unnerve and yet transfix readers. He positions readers as witnesses, relying on our instinctive voyeurism, our desire to see that which is normally hidden, our pleasure in breaking a taboo. If we read on, we are implicated in the text's action. He deploys shame's paradox: as witnesses to shame we experience both separation from the shamed and communion with them. He counts on shame's contagiousness to make us self-conscious. He creates an image to haunt our ethical imaginations. He also inscribes his own poetics into such scenes, thereby affording us aesthetic pleasure.

The passage about the exposed plagiarism reveals Dostoevsky's strategies. The two sentences cited address readers directly. The *Diary* writer thus asks us to remember a painful moment when we were exposed to shame. The second detailed sentence relentlessly forces us to experience this moment as we read, but also asks us to reexperience the pain from a shameful moment in our own lives. Dostoevsky thus places readers in the position of both seeing and remembering. In this case, Dostoevsky exploits the potential of second-person narration to pull the actual reader into the role of the addressee,[26] thus directly transmitting the lived experience.

Dostoevsky as journalist borrowed extensively from Dostoevsky the novelist's narrative strategies. Throughout his *Diary,* Dostoevsky the journalist speaks in the voice of his narrative persona, the *Diary* writer, who is often but not always identical to Dostoevsky the journalist/author.[27] Since the *Diary* writer's discussion of lying accords with Dostoevsky's fictional portrayal of liars, however, I attribute his views to Dostoevsky. In his article, the *Diary* writer explores the universality of lying in Russia. His direct address to readers amply illustrates his point that "anyone" has engaged in the activity of lying, "anyone" in turn being an educated Russian. Because it is seminal for my discussion of lying, I will cite the long, highly illustrative opening paragraph of Dostoevsky's "Something about Lying." (Note the build-up to the earlier-cited passage.)

> Why, in our country, does everyone lie [*lgut*], every single one of us? I'm convinced that right now people will stop me and shout: Ah, nonsense, not everyone by a long shot! You don't have a topic, so here's what you've thought up to start more effectively. I've already been reproached for lacking topics; but here's the thing, I'm really convinced just now in the universality of our lying [*lgan'ia*]. For fifty years you live with an idea, see and feel it, and suddenly it appears in such a form that it's as though you've never known it before. A short time ago, the thought occurred to me that among us in Russia, in the intelligentsia classes, there can't even be a person who doesn't lie [*nelgushchego cheloveka*]. That's just because among us even completely honest people can lie [*lgat'*]. I'm convinced that in other countries, for the most part, only scoundrels lie [*lgut*]; they lie [*lgut*] for practical gain, i.e., directly with criminal intentions. But among us even the most honorable people with the most honorable intentions can lie [*lgat'*] completely gratuitously. Among us, for the most part, people lie [*lgut*] for hospitality's sake. One wants to produce an aesthetic effect in the listener, to grant pleasure, so that people lie [*lgut*], even, as they say, sacrificing themselves to the listener. Let anyone at all

remember—hasn't it happened twenty or so times that he's added, for example, to the number of miles per hour that the horses carrying him sometime galloped, if only it was necessary to intensify the listener's joyful impression? And wasn't the listener actually so overjoyed that he immediately began to persuade you that he knew a troika, which on a bet had overtaken a train, and so forth and so forth? Well, and what about hunting dogs, or about the false teeth you were fitted for in Paris, or about how Botkin healed you here? Haven't you told such wonders about your illness that, though of course you believed yourself in mid-story (for in mid-story you always begin to believe yourself), yet, however, lying down to sleep at night and remembering with pleasure how pleasantly struck your listener had been, you suddenly stopped and involuntarily uttered: Ah, how I lied [*vral*]! However, that's a weak example, for there's nothing more pleasant than to talk about one's illness, if only one finds a listener; and once one begins to talk, it's already impossible not to lie [*lgat'*]; it even cures the patient. But, returning from abroad, haven't you talked about thousands of things which you saw with your own eyes... however, I'm going to take back that example as well: it's impossible for a Russian person returning from there not to exaggerate about abroad; otherwise there would be no reason to go there. But, for example, what about the natural sciences! Haven't you discussed the natural sciences or the bankruptcy and flight abroad of various Petersburgians or yids, knowing absolutely nothing about those ylds and not knowing a thing about the natural sciences? Tell me, haven't you passed on a story, as though it had happened to you, to the very person who had in fact told it to you about himself? You surely forgot, when suddenly, halfway through the story you remembered and guessed something about it which was clearly confirmed in your listener's suffering gaze, stubbornly directed at you (for in such cases, for some reason, one looks the other in the eye with ten-fold tenacity); remember how, despite everything and already deprived of your entire sense of humor, you nonetheless, with courage worthy of a great objective, continued to mutter your tale and, having finished as quickly as possible with nervously hurried courtesies, shaking of hands and smiles, you fled in different directions, so that when suddenly in the burst of a last convulsion you were moved to shout to your listener, who was already fleeing down the stairs, a question about his auntie's health, he didn't turn around and didn't answer then about his auntie, which remained in your memory as the most tormenting part of the story that happened to you. In a word, if anyone were to answer to all that: *no*, i.e., that he hadn't passed on any stories, hadn't touched on Botkin, hadn't lied [*lgal*] about yids, hadn't shouted down the stairs about the auntie's health and that nothing similar had ever happened with him, then I simply won't believe it. I know that the Russian liar [*lgun*] more often than not tells lies [*lzhet*] quite imperceptibly to himself, so that one might not even notice at all. This is how it happens: as soon as a person tells a lie [*solzhet*] successfully, then he likes it so much that he includes the story into the number of indubitable facts of his own life; and he acts completely conscientiously, for he believes it completely himself; indeed, it would sometimes be unnatural not to believe. (21:117–19)

This passage provides Dostoevsky's thumbnail sketch of exhibitionist lying. The *Diary* writer immediately establishes his solidarity with Russian liars by referring to Russia in the first person plural—"in our country" (*u nas*). In referring to lying as "our lying," he distinguishes Russian lying from the falsification he claims characterizes other countries. To emphasize his point about lying as a form of hospitality, the *Diary* writer switches to the third person—"Let anyone at all remember. . . ." After expanding on lying as hyperbole (horses' speed) given in the third person, he then slips into the second person plural—"the listener starts to persuade you. . . ." The *Diary* writer then insists that "you" must have told hunting dog stories, exaggerated about doctors' cures, fabricated stories about places you've seen during your travels; that "you" must have discoursed about the natural sciences or other subjects, knowing nothing whatsoever about them; that "you" must have plagiarized someone else's story and been caught out. As the *Diary* writer verifies his claims, he reverts to the impersonal mode—"In a word, if anyone. . . ." Finally, he identifies the subjects of his discourse as "Russian liars." The *Diary* writer thus ends where he began—with a hyperbolic claim about Russian lying. By employing hyperbole and therein lying, Dostoevsky not only challenges the veracity of his claims, he also exhibits his rhetorical skill.[28]

By including the description of a plagiarism exposed into his peroration of the kinds of lying, the *Diary* writer involves readers in the shame experience both as members of the narrative and authorial audiences. In the narrative audience, we experience the full affect of Dostoevsky's embedded text. In the authorial audience, we also recognize its metaliterary aspect, for the embedded text tells the story (*anekdot*) about the telling of a story (*anekdot*). Dostoevsky thus provides readers with two means of experiencing the shame: affectively and cognitively, as participants and as observers. He also supplies relief from the painful affect described. First, after implicating the narrative audience in the shame experience both by mimetically replicating such an experience and by directly asking us to remember one, the *Diary* writer shifts back to the impersonal mode, allowing the narrative audience to universalize the experience. He thus positions us to experience shame and then releases us. Second, the authorial audience experiences relief through our aesthetic appreciation of the text's metaliterary construction. Third, the text engages us cognitively in the final discovery that such experience is pan-human. Cognitive engagement and aesthetic pleasure thus alleviate, but do not eradicate, the pain of witnessing.

Finally, Dostoevsky the author challenges his authorial audience to consider the relation of this embedded text to its host paragraph. The paragraph ends with the *Diary* writer's assertion that it is natural to steal others' stories and assimilate them into one's own life story. Jefferson Singer's and Peter Salovey's research confirms the importance of stories, real or imagined, for our sense of identity: "What is most intriguing to us about the self is that identity may be as determined by events we believe happened to us as ones that did. Our illusions, fantasies, and manufactured memories are as much a part of our identity as our mental representations of objective past and present events. We are what we imagine ourselves to be, and we strive to motivate others to cooperate in this construction of the self."[29] Stolen stories resemble manufactured memories: their authenticity is not an issue. Dostoevsky condones this form of self-fashioning, but points to a catch, for he stipulates that we must succeed. Success entails discretion: we must plagiarize without being noticed or even noticing it ourselves. The embedded text reveals the danger inherent in this natural activity: the shame of exposure. If we are caught out, we experience the double edge of shame's paradox: we lose our sense of connection to the very community that the plagiarism shows we are trying to join. The pain of separation then forces us to examine ourselves and our relation to others. In Solovev's words, shame signals conscience. Exposed to the other's gaze and to our own self-scrutiny, we are compelled to examine our motives. Why would we want to plagiarize another's story? The *Diary* writer identifies the motive as shame—shame at ourselves, desire to be other. By stealing another's story we can close the felt gap between others and ourselves.

Kinds of Lying and the Truth Factor

Plagiarism is only one kind of exhibitionist lying (*vran'yo*). The *Diary* writer describes three: (1) hyperbole, (2) bullshitting, and (3) plagiarism. Hyperbole is a figure of speech that exaggerates for emphasis. This is not only a beloved device of Dostoevsky himself, but one he uses in writing his article. Bullshitting is the verbal activity of making assertions without concern for their truth value,[30] an activity the *Diary* writer strongly condemns. Plagiarism is the act of taking another's story and presenting it as one's own. These three kinds of exhibitionist lying are intimately related and can, but need not, overlap.

The *Diary* writer also specifies three functions for exhibitionist lying—entertainment, aesthetic pleasure, and mutual hospitality. He does not distinguish among liars who engage in varieties of *vran'yo*; rather, he distinguishes between exhibitionist liars and falsifiers. Falsifiers, the *Diary* writer claims, lie for "practical gain" (*lgut iz prakticheskoi vygody*). The Russian word for this kind of lying is *lozh'*, which I translate as "deliberate lie." In his work, Dostoevsky distinguishes between the two nouns *lozh'* (which carries a strong, negative, moral charge) and *vran'yo* (which is loaded with social and semiliterary meaning). Yet, in his article, as elsewhere, he uses the verb *lgat'*, which means to lie and to speak or write a lie, a falsehood, or that which opposes truth, more frequently than the verb *vrat'*, which has a broader range of meanings that not only encompasses those of *lgat'*, but also includes to talk nonsense, to bullshit; to blather, to humbug; to boast, to tell a fable as truth,[31] because in polite usage in the nineteenth century as well as today, the verb *lgat'* is preferred; *vrat'* is more familiar and is used with children.[32] Dostoevsky complicates any translator's job by using prefixes such as *na/so/pere* to denote the verb's perfective aspect as well as its hyperbolic qualities. Though ideally I should be as precise as Dostoevsky, the English language does not allow for these distinctions, so I have included the Russian verb in parentheses. I translate *vrat'/lgat'* as "to lie," "to tell lies," and, occasionally, "to fabricate." Readers will see for themselves the infelicity of trying to be completely consistent.

While Dostoevsky's exhibitionist liars occasionally accrue material benefits from their lying, they lie epideictically—to display themselves, to enhance their image in others' eyes. By specifying entertainment, aesthetic pleasure, and hospitality as lying's function, Dostoevsky emphasizes its social nature: lying occurs largely in the public sphere. Like any form of discourse, lying requires an audience. Since liars publicly engage in verbal self-fashioning to gain audience approval, the audience is cathetically charged. Dostoevsky's liars enthusiastically hyperbolize, plagiarize, and ignore the truth. By engaging in excess, stealing from others, and disregarding truth, they violate boundaries, thereby setting the stage for scenes of exposure. When liars are exposed, as they invariably are in Dostoevsky's texts, shame comes into play. Dostoevsky, as I show, counted on this.

Dostoevsky's liars are not a homogeneous group, nor do they respond uniformly to the threat or to the shame of exposure. I divide them into the shamed and the shameless based on the way they manifest or confront their shame. I examine the content of their lies, their performance as liars, and the narrative dynamics of the scandal scenes in which they are exposed or expose themselves as liars. The ways in which shame moves each liar to perform shape his performance. Liars who attempt to conceal their shame, for instance, perform differently from those who flaunt theirs. The concealers also evoke more reader sympathy. In the narrative dynamics of scandal scenes, my dual inquiries coalesce. After *Crime and Punishment*, the protagonist of which is a murderer, a character who violates moral boundaries,³³ Dostoevsky's novels abound with liars, characters who flirt with or violate social boundaries.

Liars are performers. Like fiction writers, they display their verbal talents in the public sphere, the social nexus where identity is negotiated. Their sense of self depends on their success and thus on their ability to entertain, to provide aesthetic pleasure, to create an arena of reciprocity (the liar's narcissism often complicates this arena, as we will see). As a writer of fiction, Dostoevsky well understood how amplified stories may produce an aesthetic effect that enhances the pleasure of both liar and interlocutor. As the *Diary* writer points out in his first example of hyperbole (the troika outracing the train), a listener's aesthetic enjoyment of hyperbole may inspire him to further hyperbole—one good lie outdoes another—a fact that leads to mutual satisfaction. In fact, the *Diary* writer hyperbolically claims that reciprocal lying is a norm of social interaction among all educated Russians at all social gatherings (21:119). The unspoken rule is that one lies and allows others to lie—a social contract. Mark Twain, in his essay on lying, praises mutually hospitable lying: "I think that all this courteous lying is a sweet and loving art, and should be cultivated. The highest perfection of politeness is only a beautiful edifice built, from the base to the dome, of graceful and gifted forms of charitable and unselfish lying."³⁴ The *Diary* writer holds a similar position, arguing that only the "truthful" or "literalist" "dullard" (*pravdivaia tupitsa*), the "untalented" (*bezdarnye*), and the "heartless and hemorrhoidal" (*besserdechnye i gemorroidal'nye*), that is, people without creative talent and aesthetic sensibility, do not accept lying as a social norm.³⁵

On the other hand, the *Diary* writer points to the consequences of accepting lying as a social norm—truth becomes a rarity:

> We Russians fear truth most of all, that is, we don't fear it, if you like, but constantly consider truth [*istina*] as something already too boring and prosaic for us, insufficiently poetic, too ordinary; consequently, by avoiding it constantly, we have made it in the end into one of the most unusual and rare things in our Russian world (I'm not talking about newspapers). In this way we've completely lost the axiom that truth, especially in its purest form, is more poetic than anything that exists in the world, and, moreover, that it's even more fantastic than anything that the habituated human mind can fabricate [*nalgat'*] or conceive for itself. In Russia the truth almost always has a completely fantastic nature. Indeed, people have finally made it so that everything that the human mind can fabricate or overfabricate [*nalzhet i perelzhet*] for itself is already much more understandable to them than truth, and that goes for everywhere in the world. Truth lies on the table in front of people for a hundred years, and they don't take it, but chase after invented things, all because they consider truth fantastic and utopian. (21:119)³⁶

In this passage, Dostoevsky uses the verbs *nalgat'* and *perelgat'*. While the unmarked perfective prefix for the verb *lgat'* is *so-*, the prefixes *na-* and *pere-* both indicate a kind of excess, an adding-it-on (*na-*) or an over-and-above (*pere-*) quality that emphasizes lying's constructed nature. Here, as elsewhere,[37] the *Diary* writer articulates a Platonic vision of the world in which the mimetic obfuscates the metaphysical: human constructions hide the ultimate unity of all human beings. Lying is thus associated with an ephemeral, socially constructed reality that presupposes a social contract to disregard truth. By choosing the noun *istina*, as opposed to *pravda*, to designate "truth," the *Diary* writer further invokes poetic, biblical, and metaphysical concepts of an eternal absolute. By contrast, lying is grounded in the mimetic, not the poetic, in the material, not the metaphysical, realm.

The *Diary* writer later argues that this disregard for truth induces a "mindlessness" (*legkomyslie*) that the philosopher Harry Frankfurt identifies as typical of bullshitters[38] and that Dostoevsky recorded repeatedly in his notebooks as a deeply disturbing fact of contemporary life. In fact, the *Diary* writer opens his 1876 edition with a discussion of "contemporary Khlestakovs" whom he characterizes as narcissistic, vain, and unthinking. He declares that they are capable of committing suicide out of shame and that they never entertain "Hamletian" questions about the soul's immortality. After negatively comparing their "thoughtlessness" (*bezmyslie*) with the sincere searching of the eighteenth-century atheist philosophers Diderot and Voltaire, he condemns their complacency (*spokoistvie*) and their worldliness.

Vran'yo, in general, ignores truth. Hyperbolists delight in amplification. Plagiarists tend to their public image.[39] Finally, as Frankfurt argues, bullshitters disregard truth altogether.[40] Falsifiers must know the truth to deviate consciously from it, but the bullshitter engages in a different enterprise. None of these liars worries in the least about truth.

Frankfurt's observations on the differences between falsifiers and bullshitters illuminate the differences between falsifiers and Dostoevsky's liars:

> The liar is inescapably concerned with truth-values. In order to invent a lie at all, he must think he knows what is true. And in order to invent an effective lie, he must design his falsehood under the guidance of that truth.
>
> On the other hand, a person who undertakes to bullshit his way through has much more freedom. His focus is panoramic rather than particular. He does not limit himself to inserting a certain falsehood at a specific point, and thus he is not constrained by the truths surrounding that point or intersecting it. He is prepared to fake the context as well, so far as need requires. This freedom from the constraints to which the liar must submit does not necessarily mean, of

course, that his task is easier than the task of the liar. But the mode of creativity upon which it relies is less analytical and less deliberative than that which is mobilized in lying. It is more expansive and independent, with more spacious opportunities for improvisation, color, and imaginative play. This is less a matter of craft than of art. Hence the familiar notion of the bullshit artist.[41]

In describing bullshit artists, Frankfurt might easily have been describing Dostoevsky's liars. They improvise, exaggerating for effect. They fake context as well as facts. They appropriate whatever materials are at hand to serve their exhibitionist ends. They are not deliberate deceivers, but self-promoters. Falsifiers, like Dostoevsky's Peter Verkhovensky[42] or Ivan Karamazov's Grand Inquisitor, lie for identifiable purposes. They have concrete social or political objectives. Dostoevsky's exhibitionist liars, on the other hand, are less concerned with the actual state of affairs in the outside world than with their own self-image. While they may want wealth, power, or social status, they lie not to obtain those ends but to create the illusion that they have them. Above all, they want to be accepted as qualified self-presenting agents.

Similarly, possession of knowledge counts less for them than does the appearance of knowledge. The *Diary* writer gives the example of someone discoursing on chemistry, knowing only the word "chemistry" (21:121). Improvising from sources that could be acceptable only to a thirteen-year-old schoolboy, this speaker produces an "incredible effect" on his audience and "left, respecting himself incredibly," as the *Diary* writer rather wryly observes (21:122). The *Diary* writer emphasizes that the speaker values self-presentation over content. He scorns facts in favor of delivery: he speaks "weightily and unhurriedly releasing his words"; his tone is "haughty." In short, the goal of the exhibitionist liar is social acceptance. His self-image is determined by audience response.

The *Diary* writer's example of the discourse on chemistry flags another distinction between falsifying and bullshitting, a distinction that holds equally for plagiarism. Both are forms of fakery. As Frankfurt notes:

> For the essence of bullshit is not that it is *false* but that it is *phony*. In order to appreciate this distinction, one must recognize that a fake or a phony need not be in any respect (apart from authenticity itself) inferior to the real thing. What is not genuine need not also be defective in some other way. It may be, after all, an exact copy. What is wrong with a counterfeit is not what it is like, but how it was made. This points to a similar and fundamental aspect of the essential nature of bullshit: although it is produced without concern with the truth, it need not be false. The bullshitter is faking things. But this does not mean that he necessarily gets them wrong.[43]

While the falsifier engages in a kind of factual discourse that can be adjudged veracious or mendacious, the bullshitter engages in a kind of discourse that may contain mimetic but not poetic truth, or poetic but not mimetic truth. The bullshitter fakes things, but he may accidentally get them right. As Dostoevsky's readers well know, truth often appears in the mouths of his liars, fools, and scoundrels. The utterance's source may be compromised without compromising the utterance itself.

This leads to the question of liars' motives. Unlike falsifiers, Dostoevsky's liars are not in the business of deception. As Frankfurt notes,

> Since bullshit need not be false, it differs from lies in its misrepresentational intent. The bullshitter may not deceive us, or even intend to do so, either about the facts or about what he takes the facts to be. . . . His eye is not on the facts at all, as the eyes of the honest man and of the liar are, except insofar as they may be pertinent to his interest in getting away with what he says. He does not care whether the things he says describe reality correctly. He just picks them out, or makes them up, to suit his purpose.[44]

While Frankfurt does not specify a motive for bullshitters, Dostoevsky provides one for his liars.[45] They lie because they are ashamed of themselves. They do not intend to deceive others but to create a public persona that will be accepted and admired. They lie to affirm their own self-worth and thus their social worthiness.

The Russian Context: Identity and the Divided Self

The *Diary* writer locates the question of identity at the root of lying. Identifying shame as one of lying's two primary sources, he claims that all Russians tell lies because they are ashamed of their actual selves and want to be other, a keen (and universally applicable) observation disguised as an unverifiably hyperbolic statement. He thus argues that Russians sense a discrepancy between their actual and ideal selves (21:119). In examining the intrapsychic conflict that gives rise to lying, Dostoevsky points to sociopolitical and metaphysical conflict as well. He dates the psychic split between private and public selves, and the subsequent rise of a national inferiority complex, to Peter the Great's reforms. And, in his fiction, he returns to biblical roots, seeing shame and the lying it spawns as the fruit of the fall.[46]

Dostoevsky's most conspicuous liars—General Ivolgin, Lukian Lebedev, Captain Lebiadkin, Stepan Verkhovensky, and Fedor Karamazov—are all Russian men, all in their forties and fifties, and all of equivocal social status. Although in "Something about Lying," Dostoevsky initially claims that all educated Russians tell lies, he then, with Karamzinian chivalrousness, exempts women. Throughout his article, but particularly at the end, he employs a common tactic of epideictic rhetoric—praise or blame by contrast. First, he hyperbolically defines men as a class of liars: "there is not a Russian man who doesn't lie" (*net nelgushchego russkogo mushchiny*), thereby anticipating his claim that women are paradigms of social morality. What earlier Dostoevsky praised as a virtue, male liars' desire to please others (apparent altruism), he then contrasts with women's commitment to social welfare (genuine altruism). This negative comparison also reveals the shallow narcissism of male liars' concern about their public image. While Dostoevsky contrasts men and women for publicistic purposes, he maintains the opposition in his fiction. Although neither all of Dostoevsky's male characters are liars, nor all of his female characters altruists, Dostoevsky never created a full-blown female liar.[47]

The fictional predecessor for Dostoevsky's liars is Gogol's Khlestakov, the archetypal Russian liar. As Iurii Lotman observes, Khlestakov not only lies, he is characterized by a poverty of imagination that makes him a consumer, as opposed to a generator, of romanticism,[48] by a desire to escape from himself that leads him to divide the world into his own space (worthless) and foreign space (highly prized), and by a short memory that makes him incapable of complex calculation and so contributes to the "ingenuous simplicity" that Gogol reminded his actors was so essential to Khlestakov's personality.[49] Lotman's characterization can be used as a portrait of shame. Khlestakov is ashamed of his actual identity as an insignificant bureaucrat from Petersburg; he thus tries to pass himself off as an inspector general in the provincial town where he gets stuck from lack of money. Like Khlestakov, Dostoevsky's liars disregard truth altogether and represent themselves as they would like to be seen. Like Khlestakov, they are more interested in appearing successful than in actually being so. Likewise, they want to be admired and respected, yet they are entirely unconcerned with having the virtues that would make them so. Furthermore, Khlestakov embodies other important negative aspects of lying that characterize Dostoevsky's liars: its potential for mindlessness (*legkomyslie*), boundlessness (*bezbrezhnost'*), and narcissism. Nevertheless, though Dostoevsky's liars follow the Khlestakovian model, they move progressively away from it, General Ivolgin (*The Idiot*, 1868) being the most Khlestakovian and Fedor Karamazov (*The Brothers Karamazov*, 1880) the least. General Ivolgin, for example, craves admiration and respect; Fedor Karamazov, on the other hand, settles for the power over others that derives from displaying his shame. Likewise, General Ivolgin is the most ingenuous of Dostoevsky's liars, while Fedor Karamazov is the most self- and audience-conscious of them.

Unlike Khlestakov, who is a young man in his twenties, created when

Dostoevsky was in his twenties, Dostoevsky's most striking liars are in their forties and fifties. General Ivolgin and Fedor Karamazov are both fifty-five years old; Stepan Verkhovensky is fifty-three; Captain Lebiadkin is forty; and Lebedev is pushing fifty (like Ivan Karamazov's devil). This means that Dostoevsky was their historical contemporary, but it also means that Khlestakov is their fictional contemporary, for Dostoevsky's liars are aged Khlestakovs. Aware of the parallels between lying and fiction, Dostoevsky creates this pantheon of highly entertaining liars to flaunt his metaliterary skill.

National Identity Crisis

Though Dostoevsky uses his liars as loci of metaliterary play, he also grounds them in nineteenth-century reality as emblems of the national identity crisis. Studies have shown that a vacillation between self-aggrandizement and desire to merge with an ideal characterizes shame.[50] Amplified in the context of mid-nineteenth-century Russian society, this vacillation can be seen in the conflicting pulls of Westernizer and Slavophile values—autonomy and community. In the context of Dostoevsky's worldview, it can be seen in a wavering between the two value systems embodied in the Russian intelligentsia and the people—an imported value system that emphasizes individual self-sufficiency and a native Christian value system that emphasizes human interdependence. Seen in the sociopolitical context of Dostoevsky's fiction and journalism, his liars embody the national identity crisis. Seen in metaphysical terms, this vacillation expresses the struggle between the devil and God in the human soul.

Unlike Dostoevsky's shame-ridden underground men who withdraw, his liars, driven by the desire for social recognition, propel themselves into the public sphere. Not introspectors but exhibitionists, Dostoevsky's liars occupy themselves with self-fashioning. Nineteenth-century possibilities for social mobility motivate these men and contribute to their identity crises.

Two areas of psychological study dealing with vacillations in personal identity—studies of lying and studies of shame—illuminate Dostoevsky's liars. Studies of lying show that there are two crucial periods for children as regards lying: (1) ages three or four, when children become capable of telling a deliberate lie, and (2) adolescence, when children challenge authority and the legitimacy of many social rules.[51] Throughout childhood, children also vacillate between their conflicting desires for dependence and independence regarding their families. Adolescence further exacerbates children's susceptibility to peer pressure. Lotman observes that "As a trait of historical, and not individual psychology, lying indicates infantile tendencies in a mature person, group, or generation."[52] Their adolescent-like traits—obsession with being recognized socially as an individual yet accepted as a conforming member of a group, revolt against authority, and focus on the immediate present—explain why Dostoevsky's liars are so exasperating and appealing.[53]

Dostoevsky's journalistic and fictional works prescribe some cures for the Russian divided self. On the sociopolitical level, Dostoevsky's doctrine of *pochvennichestvo* prescribes merging the attributes of the intelligentsia and the people to heal the split between them. On the individual and metaphysical levels, Dostoevsky has Zosima, a spiritual healer, diagnose shame as the disease ravaging Fedor Karamazov's psyche and soul: "And above all do not be so ashamed of yourself, for that is the cause of everything" (14:40;43). Zosima here suggests that shame of one's self may lead to sinful actions (à la Raskolnikov). Like the *Diary* writer, Zosima thus prescribes truthfulness as the cure: "And above all, above everything else—do not lie" (14:40;44).

The Ethics of Discourse

In his "Fourth Reverie of the Solitary Walker," Jean-Jacques Rousseau likewise identifies shame as a motive for lying and recommends truth as a healing agent, concluding that truth is "an homage that the good man pays to his own dignity."[54] Like Zosima, Rousseau links the concepts of truth and self-respect, arguing that the first promotes the second. In fact, Rousseau's entire "Fourth Reverie" raises many critical issues addressed in Dostoevsky's journalistic argument and his fictional portrayal of lying. Since Dostoevsky was an avid reader of Rousseau, with whom he polemicized most of his life,[55] Rousseau's "Reverie" may well have served as a catalyst for Dostoevsky's own thoughts on lying, fiction, and truth. Both Rousseau's "Fourth Reverie" and Dostoevsky's "Something about Lying" conclude by discussing the links between shame and self-respect. Like Rousseau, Dostoevsky explores varieties of lying and reveals his own preoccupation with the ethics of discourse.

Rousseau distinguishes between lying and fiction on ethical grounds. First, he defines lying as an activity that involves concealing "a truth which one ought to make known."[56] He elaborates this ethical criterion by further defining lying as "everything which by being opposed to truth offends justice in any way."[57] Fiction, on the other hand, does not entail an ethical offense: "[T]o lie without advantage or disadvantage to oneself or others is not to lie; it is not falsehood but fiction."[58] Rousseau explains: "[E]verything which although opposed to truth does not affect justice in any way is no more than a fiction."[59] For Rousseau, it is always bad to lie or misrepresent and thus lie by proxy, but, given his belief that we all live in a corrupted world, he allows fiction (a corrupt form) to serve as a vehicle for sociopolitical reeducation.[60] In this view, fiction's ethical potential depends upon authorial intention.

Dostoevsky follows Rousseau in categorizing statements according to ethical criteria. A speaker's motives distinguish falsifying from exhibitionist lying (*vran'yo*). Falsifying is motivated by "practical gain" and "criminal intentions."[61] On the other hand, Dostoevky views exhibitionist lying as "innocent" (*lgan'yo nevinnoe*), perhaps because of its "lack of advantage or disadvantage to oneself or others."[62] In Rousseau's terms, lying is closer to fiction than is falsehood.

Nonetheless, lying is not identical with fiction. As I have argued earlier, Dostoevsky locates lying in the mimetic sphere, the world of appearances. He locates good fiction, on the other hand, in the poetic and metaphysical spheres. For Dostoevsky, lying obfuscates all truth—factual, moral, and poetic. In his 1873 article, the *Diary* writer both notes the liar's "scorn for facts" (21:122) and deliberates on Russians' lack of respect for truth (21:119). Viewing truth as boring, prosaic, and ordinary provides a tremendous impetus to embellish reality—by hyperbolizing or plagiarizing—or to disregard truth altogether—by bullshitting. As Frankfurt affirms, "It is just this lack of connection to a concern with truth—this indifference to how things really are—that I regard as of the essence of bullshit."[63] We best understand Dostoevsky's liars as liars who disregard truth, rather than as liars who falsify for personal gain.

While Dostoevsky and Rousseau agree upon the power of fiction to effect personal and social change, they diverge in their views on the relationship between lying and truth-telling. Here authorial intent and target audience play critical roles. Rousseau wrote his *Reveries* in part to change public perception of his autobiographical persona, to salvage the self-image that suffered so greatly after the publication of his *Confessions*.[64] His autobiographical persona thus discusses only his own practices, which include hyperbole, but not other kinds of lying: Rousseau mentions neither plagiarizing nor bullshitting. Dostoevsky's *Diary* writer, on the other hand, writes largely in the third person as an observer of the contemporary Russian social scene. He describes a full spectrum of lying and demonstrates his solidarity with Russian liars by writing hyperbolically. Unlike Rousseau's autobiographical persona, who characterizes himself as a *solitaire*, Dostoevsky's *Diary* writer thus identifies fully with his narrative audience. After establishing this identification, he uses it to model a negative response to the practice of bullshitting, which he views as a source of harm to both self and others.

Both Rousseau and Dostoevsky make a case for lying as a form of hospitality intended to entertain an audience. Dostoevsky adds that in amusing his audience the speaker "sacrifices himself" to them, thus representing such lying as apparently virtuous. Nonetheless, both he and Rousseau conclude by condemning such seeming altruism. Rousseau concludes that "one should not debase oneself in order to amuse others"; Dostoevsky concludes that the apparent altruism of entertaining others differs from the genuine altruism of social activism.[65] By stressing liars' concern for appearances, he exposes their apparent self-sacrifice as self-aggrandizement.

Dostoevsky's position on the relationship between lying and shame also resembles Rousseau's. Rousseau confesses, "I have often lied out of shame, to avoid embarrassment in trivial affairs or affairs that concerned only me, as when in order to keep a conversation going I have been forced by the slowness of my ideas and my lack of small talk to have recourse to fiction for something to say."[66] Dostoevsky goes further, declaring that "The delicate reciprocity of lying is practically the first condition of Russian society—of all Russian meetings, parties, clubs, scientific societies, and so forth" (21:119). The *Diary* writer hyperbolically characterizes lying as social glue, the kind of discourse that facilitates social interactions (which he, unlike Rousseau and Tolstoy, does not characterize as meaningless). Though rooted in shame, lying can serve a positive social function.

That social function is jeopardized when lying (*vran'yo*) starts down the slippery slope toward lie (*lozh'*), however. In *The Brothers Karamazov*, Zosima links lying to shame and shame to identity by noting the speaker's shame sensitivity. After he points out that Fedor Karamazov's buffoonery is rooted in shame, Zosima counsels the old buffoon, "not to be so ashamed of yourself," but also to refrain from drunkenness and from verbal licentiousness. "[A]nd above all, above everything else—do not lie." Fedor Pavlovich asks whether Zosima is referring to his Diderot story. Zosima replies:

> No, not about Diderot. The important thing is not to lie to yourself. The person who lies to himself [*lgushchii*] and who listens to his own lie [*lozh*] gets to the point where he cannot distinguish the truth either in himself or around him and consequently he loses respect for himself and for others. Respecting no one, he ceases to love, and, having no love, in order to occupy and amuse himself, he gives himself up to passions and coarse pleasures and becomes a beast in his vices, and all of this comes from continuous lying [*bespreryvnoi lzhi*] to others and to himself. (14:40–41;44)

By condoning the Diderot story, Zosima distinguishes between the lying that constitutes the Russian social contract, which promotes community, and deliberate lying, which destroys community. Once a person lies to himself deliberately, he lies to others. Deliberate lying leads the liar away from self-knowledge. It undermines the mutual trust and respect necessary for the development of community. Once habituated to lying, the liar loses all sense of connection to others and thus to God.

Zosima tells Fedor Pavlovich not to lie, but, more importantly, he tells him not to be so ashamed of himself. Zosima thus points to the escape from lying: self-respect. As Zosima demonstrates in his own story later in the novel, a person must overcome his shame sensitivity to feel he is part of the human community. He thus propagates the lesson learned by Dostoevsky's ridiculous man, a fictional character from the *Diary of a Writer,* who has a dream of unity with others that frees him from his fear of seeming ridiculous.

Interestingly, both Rousseau's solitary walker and Dostoevsky's gregarious *Diary* writer conclude their reflections on lying by discussing the ethical consequences of indulging in verbal excess. Rousseau sums up, "Truth is an homage that the good man pays to his own dignity. When my lack of small talk forced me to fill the silence with harmless fiction, I acted wrongly, because one should not debase oneself in order to amuse others, and when the pleasure of writing led me to embellish reality with ornaments of my own invention, I acted even more wrongly, because to decorate truth with fables is in fact to disfigure it."[67] Rousseau thus concludes with two points that Dostoevsky will elaborate in different ways. First, following Rousseau's example, the *Diary* writer moralizes that pandemic lying obfuscates truth. Second, Dostoevsky's journalism and fiction both manifest concern for the personal and social consequences of self-debasement. In his fiction, Dostoevsky demonstrates that his shameless liars' decision to play the fool harms not only them but those around them.

In closing, Rousseau condemns even the embellishment of reality. Dostoevsky, on the other hand, clearly enjoys his liars and their stories. Furthermore, he makes their discourse serve his authorial truth. And, while Dostoevsky's *Diary* writer criticizes hyperbole, he wholeheartedly engages in it. He thus deploys a rhetorical strategy that he will later use to great advantage in his 1876–77 *Diary,* coopting the very rhetorical practices which he is denouncing.[68] In concluding, the *Diary* writer expresses shock at the gentlemen who discourse pompously yet ignorantly. He censures this display's shamelessness as a source of despair for Russia's future. The *Diary* writer attributes such shamelessness to a lack of conscience: "It [shamelessness] manifests an indifference towards the self-judgment by one's own conscience, or, what is the same thing, an extraordinary true lack of self-respect . . ." (21:124). Dostoevsky thus echoes Rousseau's conclusion that "Truth is an homage that the good man pays to his own dignity." Dostoevsky and Rousseau agree that some kinds of lying cause no short-term harm to self or others; rather, they do cause a long-term harm,[69] for a lack of self-respect can lead to shameless behavior. The *Diary* writer thus invokes the Solovevian sense of shame as conscience, a sense of moral discretion or appropriateness that restrains a person from shameful display or action. In other words, he condones hyperbolic lying, and even plagiarism, but he condemns bullshitting, as it can potentially lead others astray.

While Rousseau defines all lying that is "without advantage or disadvantage to oneself or others" as fiction, Dostoevsky's definition of *vran'yo* encompasses a broader range of discourses. Like fiction, lying expresses a powerful psychic energy. In both his journalism and his fiction, Dostoevsky describes lying as a fundamental human activity. Taking his cue from the philosophers, Dostoevsky has Razumikhin declare in *Crime and Punishment*:

> I love when people lie [*vrut*]! Lying [*Vran'yo*] is the single privilege humans have over all organisms. If you lie [*Sovresh'*]—you get to the truth! I am a human being, because I lie [*Potomu ia i chelovek, chto vru*]. Not one truth has ever been reached without first lying [*ne sovrav*] fourteen times, or maybe a hundred and fourteen, and that's honorable in its way; well, but we can't even lie [*sovrat'-to*] with our own minds! Lie [*vri*] for me, but lie [*vri*] in your own way, and I'll kiss you for it. Lying in one's own way [*Sovrat' po-svoemu*] is almost better than telling the truth in someone else's way; in the first case you're a human being, and in the second you're only a bird! (6:155)

In a statement that clearly parodies Descartes's famous dictum, one of Dostoevsky's most sympathetic characters posits lying as the quintessential human activity. In this deliberately hyperbolic view, Razumikhin argues that human beings are governed not only by reason, which allows them to think and speak, but also by a transcendent impulse. Like the *Diary* writer, Razumikhin hyperbolizes while discussing hyperbole. His rhetorical strategy, in turn, exemplifies his point: as an implicitly comparative rhetorical trope, hyperbole points beyond itself—to the reality that serves as its implicit starting point and to something transcendent, like truth, that the verbal excess attempts to express.[70] In Razumikhin's view, hyperbole thus expresses a metaphysical impulse rooted in the idea of the transcendent.[71]

While at first glance the *Diary* writer's view that lying is rooted in shame seems to contradict this account, shame's paradox reveals their common ground in the desire to be other. Like hyperbole, shame implies comparison. Thus an individual's sense of lack presupposes a standard, norm, or ideal which he or she does not live up to. Razumikhin posits a sense of metaphysical lack, a desire to reach a transcendent truth through the nontranscendent medium of language. The *Diary* writer posits a psychological or material lack, a desire to be other, to have what the ideal other has. Both accounts thus explain the metaphoric impulse, the use of hyperbolic language to close the gap between the actual and the ideal. In fiction after *Crime and Punishment*, Dostoevsky emphasizes the desire to exhibit one's self, but he does not drop metaphysical desire, which rears its head, however comically, in the discourse of his liars.

Razumikhin qualifies his statement by differentiating between kinds of lying—"lying in one's own way" and "telling the truth in someone else's way"—descriptions that point to Dostoevsky's early concern with human identity as well as his interest in the debate between romanticism and classicism over the functions of creativity and imitation. "Lying in one's own way" can be seen as a romantic concept, identified with selfhood, with an individual's creative resources, the ability to create or fashion a self, while "telling the truth in someone else's way" can be seen as a classicist concept that points to imitation. When imitation involves the mindless repetition of others' ideas or stories, a practice that Dostoevsky repeatedly condemned,[72] it can describe plagiarism. Dostoevsky reveals the pitfalls of story-stealing by playfully exposing plagiarists.

Implicating the Reader

In the following passage from *The Idiot*, General Ivolgin tells a plagiarized story that explains his social fall. Ivolgin thus tells the truth under cover. His lie serves both as the cover-up and as the sign of the cover-up. By having the fallen woman Nastasia Filippovna expose Ivolgin's story as a plagiarism, Dostoevsky trains readers to plunge below the story's surface, and accept its poetic truth while rejecting its mimetic veracity. Dostoevsky also implicates us in the action of passing on shame, thereby complicating our response to the novel's central drama—the story of Nastasia Filippovna's shame.

> "A stupid story, and in two words," the General complacently began. "Two years ago, yes! almost, just after the opening of the new —skii railroad, I (already in civilian garb), busy with incredibly important affairs concerning the resignation of my commission, bought a ticket, in first class: I went in, I sit down, I smoke. That is, I continue to smoke; I lit a cigar earlier. I am alone in the compartment. Smoking is not prohibited, but it's not permitted either; like this, it's semi-permitted, as usual; well, depending on who you are. The window is lowered. Suddenly, just before the whistle, two women with a lapdog position themselves, just opposite. They are late. One is dressed up most lavishly, in light blue; the other more modestly, in black silk with a cape collar. They are by no means ugly, look around haughtily, speak English. I'm not bothered, of course; I smoke. That is, I almost turn it over in my mind, but nonetheless, continue to smoke—since the window is open—out the window. A lapdog is lying on the light blue lady's lap. It's small, all in all the size of my fist, black, with white paws, even a rare breed. A silver collar

with a crest. I'm not bothered. I only notice that the ladies, it seems, are angry, about the cigar, of course. One stares with a lorgnette, tortoise-shell. Once again I'm not bothered: because in fact they don't say anything! If they had said something, gave warning, asked, there is, after all, a human language! But as it is they are silent . . . suddenly,—and without the slightest warning, I tell you, that is without the very slightest, so it's absolutely as if she'd gone off her rocker,—the light blue one grabs the cigar from my hand and out the window. The coach is flying, I look—like a half-wit. The woman is a savage; a savage woman, quite certainly of a savage background. And yet a portly woman, fulsome, tall, blonde, ruddy (even too much so), her eyes flash at me. Without saying a word, I, with extraordinary politeness, with the most perfect politeness, with the most refined, as they say, politeness, approach the lapdog with two fingers, take it delicately by the neck and hurl it out the window right after the cigar! It only yelped! The coach continues to fly. . . ." (8:93)

The company applauds and the General swaggers: "And I'm right, I'm right, I'm triply right! . . . because if cigars are prohibited in train cars, then dogs are all the more so." Kolia cheers his father, but Nastasia Filippovna demonstrates that he lifted the story in minute detail from a newspaper.

In his 1873 article, Dostoevsky claims that Russian lying has two basic roots: the fear that truth is prosaic, and shame at oneself and desire to be other (21:119). When the two converge, as in the case of a person's identity, the person feels his own life deficient in interest and borrows or embroiders facts of another's life (fictional or actual) and presents them as his own. In this case, General Ivolgin skirts the possible mundanity and shame of the actual story of his break with the Epanchins and fashions himself as other. Ivolgin thus appropriates another's story. His audience applauds him for actions that are, as Nastasia Filippovna reveals, those of a Frenchman written up in a Belgian newspaper.

While Ivolgin steals his story from the newspaper, he contextualizes in a telling manner. Significantly, he sets the action in a first-class train compartment, thus establishing his social status. The act of smoking, which is "semi-permitted, . . . depending on who you are," further underscores his class privilege. Yet the moment is ripe for shame: he locates it during his transition from military to civilian life, a time when he was self-conscious about his civilian dress. The women first snub him with their hostile silence then shame him brutally.

Nastasia Filippovna follows their example. She exposes his plagiarism by repeating five times that it is "exactly the same" as the newspaper story. Her brutal exposure of the General signals the novel's poetic self-consciousness, just as the *Diary* writer's account of an exposure scene that involves mutual recognition does.[73] Both scenes demonstrate shame's contagiousness by portraying witnesses' embarrassed responses. Dostoevsky highlights audience response, but he also underscores narrative awareness. For instance, the *Diary* writer claims that stealing others' stories is natural. Yet Ivolgin ultimately fails. He owes his initial success to his sympathetic listeners. But Ivolgin fatally misjudges his audience. He expects admiration, not exposure. He does not see Nastasia Filippovna as a social outcast who intends to expose his son Gania as an equally fallen creature. Instead of accepting the shame of her fall, Nastasia Filippovna lashes back at those responsible—the fathers who have betrayed instead of protecting her. Ivolgin's own narcissistic injury blinds him to hers.

Dostoevsky, on the other hand, keeps his reader focused on shame. In this scene, he piles up portrayals of passed-on shame. Ashamed of his fall in social status, General Ivolgin steals another's story. Ashamed because Generals Epanchin and Totsky plan to marry Nastasia Filippovna off to him, Gania plans to shame her. But she has the upper hand. Ashamed of her own fallen status, she shames father and son alike. Dostoevsky stockpiles shame until character-witnesses and readers are paralyzed by it. Then the doorbell rings, and Rogozhin arrives. The arrival of another out-of-place character interrrupts the exposition of shame and creates an expectation of further scandal, an expectation Dostoevsky gratifies. Dostoevsky briefly deflects attention from General Ivolgin's shame to reveal the broader picture of shame that nineteenth-century Russian society colludes in—the exclusion/containment of a fallen woman. Dostoevsky exposes the cost of social harmony. He moves from the specific nineteenth-century Russian reality to the universal human condition.

Dostoevsky's *Diary* article reveals that he understands the complexities of shame dynamics and knows how to implicate his readers in the shame experience. Furthermore, he understands the discomfort arising from witnessing another's shame (whether in life or in fiction) as well as the affective connection that obtains between vicarious and remembered experience. In the article's exposed shame scene, consciousness of shame arises from within. Furthermore, the one witness to the speaker's shame flees. This example thus portrays internally induced shame and two responses to a shame situation—denial and flight. In the novel, shame comes from without. Moreover, a whole roomful of characters witness the General's shame. The private sphere can inhibit personal exposure and embarrassment. The public sphere can encourage public exposure, the violation of social norms, and thus scandal. By portraying scandal, Dostoevsky taps into the universal unease that attends the witnessing of shame situations. We cannot witness another's exposure without feeling vulnerable ourselves. Portrayed shame overflows textual bounds.

Dostoevsky deliberately uses the parallels between shame dynamics and narrative dynamics to involve his readers. Like the speaker in the article, the General tries to deny his plagiarism, but Nastasia Filippovna aggressively blocks his attempts. Moreover, her assaultive accusation complicates readers' responses. We would normally distance ourselves from a character like Dostoevsky's alcoholic General—but Dostoevsky creates sympathy for him by exposing his shame publicly. We might normally feel that as a seduced minor Nastasia Filippovna deserves our sympathy, but her aggressive passing on of shame unsettles us. By augmenting sympathy for Ivolgin and diminishing sympathy for Nastasia Filippovna, Dostoevsky makes us complicit with the status quo.

Narrative Ethics

Throughout his career, Dostoevsky unites ethics and aesthetics. In *The Brothers Karamazov* (1881), Ivan Karamazov declares that he refuses to accept social harmony if it has to be based on the suffering of even one small child. Twelve years earlier, in *The Idiot*, Dostoevsky portrays one woman's refusal to allow social harmony based on her own suffering and humiliation. Dostoevsky exposes her shame and suffering. By evoking our discomfort and uncovering our desire to contain/marginalize her, Dostoevsky implicates us in the social injustice she experiences. We cannot pass judgment on her without examining our own motives. Dostoevsky thus places us in a very contemporary dilemma.

As a journalist, Dostoevsky uses hyperbole to make his point about hyperbole. As a novelist, Dostoevsky uses the dual nature of the shame experience—its affective and cognitive aspects—to implicate us in universal experiences. We may want to run, but Dostoevsky will not let our consciences hide. When we accept the status quo we collude in the perpetuation of social injustice.

Portraying shame allows Dostoevsky to circumvent Russia's heavy censorship and address politically charged issues like the woman question. In *The Idiot*, Dostoevsky moves the political to the personal. This, in turn, illustrates an important difference between lying and fiction. For Dostoevsky, fiction is a tool for social change. While Ivolgin tells a story to conceal the truth of his social fall, Dostoevsky tells stories that address social ills in the guise of individual cases of shame. He thus awakens the public imagination and makes us understand private pains more fully as public ills. Like Rousseau, Dostoevsky uses fiction to arouse readers' desire for positive ideals. For Dostoevsky, lying may entertain, but all good literature effects moral change.

Dostoevsky's liars and fiction writers differ in how they use their sources.

Dostoevsky draws on world literature and the Bible for their deep cultural roots and memories; he also draws on anecdotes and newspaper accounts. Dostoevsky's liars employ the same sources, but shallowly. Dostoevsky transforms his sources; his liars do not. Dostoevsky shapes his sources into instruments of truth; his liars passively palm them off as their own experience. Contrast how General Ivolgin incorporates the lapdog story into his own biography and how Dostoevsky incorporates it into his novel.[74] Ivolgin borrows the story and embellishes it. He unconsciously uses it as an analogue story, providing his audience with autobiographical information by modeling the protagonists in his purloined narrative on actual people. Dostoevsky, on the other hand, does this consciously, furnishing his authorial audience entry into his character's psyche. Ivolgin, for instance, links the resignation of his commission with the trip. Dostoevsky, on the other hand, gives Ivolgin's trip a metaphoric twist—his journey ends in exile both from the army and from first-class society. Furthermore, Dostoevsky creates this scene of lying and exposure to make explicit the terms of what I call, in chapter 8, the Russian social contract: one lies and then allows one's interlocutor to do the same.[75] By violating this contract and not permitting General Ivolgin to lie, Nastasia Filippovna points to a fundamental collusion at the base of polite society. She raises our awareness of the conventions by which we live.

Dostoevsky also uses this scene to draw his authorial audience's attention to his novel's synthetic dimension. Throughout *The Idiot*, Dostoevsky raises questions about the nature of fiction,[76] especially its contractual dimension. Authors abound in *The Idiot*. Prince Myshkin and Ivolgin tell stories; Lebedev fabricates legal speeches and anonymous letters; Keller writes a newspaper article (which Lebedev edits); Ippolit writes a lengthy suicide note; Aglaia recites and revises Pushkin's "Poor Knight" to voice her vision of Prince Myshkin as a Don Quixote figure; Aglaia and Nastasia Filippovna correspond. These authors are extremely concerned with audience response, but they are rarely sensitive to their audiences (Myshkin is the exception). Dostoevsky thus examines the ways that narcissism undermines rhetorical efficacy.[77]

Unlike fiction, lying knows no measure.[78] It lacks modesty and discretion, what might be called a healthy sense of shame. General Ivolgin, while telling Prince Myshkin about how he served as Napoleon's page boy and confidant, gets carried away: "'O Prince!' cried the General, so intoxicated by his own story that perhaps he was unable to stop short of even the most extreme indiscretions" (8:416). In crossing discretion's boundary, General Ivolgin violates the social norm permitting a measure of hyperbole. He thus makes himself vulnerable to public exposure. Myshkin understands his own no-win situation: "He also understood that the old man had been transported by the ecstasy of his success. Nonetheless, he sensed that he was one of that order of liars, who, though they lie to voluptuousness and even to self-oblivion, still, at the very height of their ecstasy, suspect all the same that they will not be believed, that they cannot be believed. In the present situation, the old man might come to himself, be endlessly shamed, suspect the Prince of limitless compassion for him, and be offended" (8:418). Discretion-shame protects the individual from overexposure.[79] Transgressing social norms places both transgressor and witnesses in limbo: when norms are violated, behavior cannot automatically follow socially prescribed rules. Shame does not follow a set script.

By making the Prince his focalizer[80] in this scene, Dostoevsky places his readers in the same position as Myshkin. We understand that Ivolgin has crossed a boundary, but, like Myshkin, we are powerless to help him. Nonetheless, Dostoevsky models a way out. Like his only relative Mme. Epanchina, Myshkin understands that while there is no easy return from shame, an empathic audience permits restoration to community. As the General flees an earlier shame-filled situation, Mme. Epanchina extends a metaphorical hand to him, saying, "[S]tay a minute; we are all sinners; when you feel that your conscience reproaches you less, come see me, we'll sit and chat about old times" (8:204). Mme. Epanchina appeals to the General's sense of disgrace-shame as well as to his sense of discretion-shame; she attributes to him the ability to confront his own shame and get beyond it. Most importantly, however, she empathically identifies with him ("we are all sinners"). She recognizes that the first step toward recovery must occur internally—the General must face his own conscience. In proposing "a chat about old times" as further cure, Mme. Epanchina acts on her understanding that the second step occurs in the social sphere. Empathic discourse can heal shame. Dostoevsky provides his authorial audience with a model of proper response, a code for social interaction.

Dostoevsky the journalist, of course, uses different kinds of rhetoric than Dostoevsky the novelist. Dostoevsky the journalist employs a kind of rhetoric that Dostoevsky's liars use: epideictic, a form of rhetoric that displays the speaker's performance.[81] In the classical world, epideictic speeches were regarded in the same light as dramatic spectacles or athletic performances. Unlike forensic rhetoric, which concentrates on interpreting the past, or deliberative rhetoric, which rationalizes action to be taken in the future, epideictic rhetoric focuses on the present. Furthermore, while forensic and deliberative rhetoric have practical aims (winning a court case, moving an audience to action), epideictic rhetoric serves, rather, to affirm values. Epideictic is the genre of praise and blame, and equally of amplification. As much at stake as the subject of praise or blame is the speaker's rhetorical skill, for the speaker must produce an aesthetic response in his audience, whereby he demonstrates the qualities that make him worthy of audience approval or even worthy to address an audience. Significantly, audience response is critical for epideictic rhetoric, which works more through intuitive comprehension or insight than cognition.[82] Dostoevsky's *Diary* writer employs epideictic rhetoric to promote a sense of *communitas* through shared values. Dostoevsky's liars, on the other hand, employ it to promote themselves.

The *Diary* writer employs epideictic rhetoric to both praise and condemn lying. Instances of praise for lying include the descriptions of polite lies that constitute all social interaction. His article also commends lying as a cure for illness (anticipating Freud). Yet he writes most about the bullshitters. By elaborating on their practice of speaking on subjects about which they know nothing, Dostoevsky reveals lying's negative face.

In his fiction, Dostoevsky portrays lying's positive and negative aspects. On the positive side, the profoundly appealing Razumikhin from *Crime and Punishment* (1865) praises lying (discussed earlier). In *Raw Youth* (1875), Dostoevsky provides an example of lying that enhances group identity.[83] On the negative side, Dostoevsky's liars generally follow Gogol's Khlestakov in their narcissism, disregard for truth, quest for social recognition at any price, mindless speech, and violation of social norms. In pointing out these harmful potentials in his article, the *Diary* writer advocates their positive opposites: self-control, mindfulness, and altruism.

Dostoevsky's rhetoric differs most from that of his liars, however, in its goals. Dostoevsky's liars amplify givens for self-enhancement—to win their audience's admiration or recognition, or both. Though the *Diary* writer parades his rhetorical talent, he wants to educate his audience. He elevates his readers' self-awareness by listing a series of propositions with which they identify. First he declares that all Russians are liars, citing numerous examples that are transparently universal. Then he asserts that he does not believe anyone who claims that he has never hyperbolized, bullshitted, or plagiarized, thus compelling our complicity. The *Diary* writer sweetens this identification by lauding the generosity as well as the aesthetic sense inspiring this kind of lying. In the second half of the article, however, he distances himself and his audience from the bullshitters.

When they preserve decorum, liars uphold the social order. When they indulge in excess, as they do in Dostoevsky's fiction, they demonstrate bad manners, disrupting decorum and causing scandal. Excess thus precipitates disgrace and failure. Three of Dostoevsky's lower-born liars—Lebedev, Lebiadkin, and Fedor Karamazov—lack good manners or flaunt bad manners and thus behave shamefully.[84] Though General Ivolgin and Stepan Verkhovensky preserve the good manners of their class, they both indulge in excess and fail to reckon with their audiences. As Dostoevsky repeatedly shows, rhetorical success requires self-awareness and audience awareness. In outperforming his liars, Dostoevsky demonstrates that the potential shortcomings of lying (a tendency to excess, a disregard for truth, and a stress on performance) can be balanced only by the virtues necessary for truly effective rhetoric (a sense of limits, a respect for truth, and a moral purpose). Dostoevsky thus proves the moral of his article: self-awareness enhances performance.

While four of the fictional liars I discuss in this book—General Ivolgin, Stepan Verkhovensky, Lukian Lebedev, and Captain Lebiadkin—entertain readers in Dostoevsky's authorial audience, they are often unsuccessful vis-à-vis their own audiences because of their narcissism. On the other hand, Ivan Karamazov's devil and Fedor Karamazov prove to be extremely self-conscious and audience-conscious storytellers. They tailor their stories to suit their specific audiences and thereby achieve anticipated responses. They also furnish Dostoevsky's authorial audience with evidence of his work's increasingly metaliterary character.

Dostoevsky the Reformer

Before turning to a chapter-by-chapter examination of Dostoevsky's fictional liars, I must state the obvious: their lying reveals a great deal about these speakers. Whether unconsciously (Ivolgin) or consciously (Fedor Karamazov), Dostoevsky's liars employ hyperbolic rhetoric that simultaneously conceals and reveals truths about themselves and their desires. In expressing their desires or ideals, these characters' lies reveal the gap between their desired and actual self-images. If, as Dostoevsky claims, lying intimately relates to identity and liars' shame at their own identities motivates their lying, then they inscribe their shame into their rhetorical self-presentations. Dostoevsky thus shows his authorial audience how lying manifests shame content.

Furthermore, while this book focuses on the narrative dynamics of shame to portray Dostoevsky as a social or spiritual reformer, shame issues play a larger role in Dostoevsky's fictional *oeuvre*. Dostoevsky relishes his role as Gogol's postmaster—exposing others[85] and thus gratifying readers' voyeuristic impulses. Nonetheless, by placing us in the uncomfortable position of witnessing others' shame, he reveals the price of knowledge. Once we taste the fruit of the Tree of Knowledge (albeit vicariously), we are no longer innocent—we are shamed. Knowledge of others' shame leads to an uncomfortable awareness of our own. Our discomfort as readers derives not only from the sense of vulnerability we feel as witnesses but also from the very shameful, contagious nature of shame itself. As H. B. Lewis notes,

> Before we leave our review of the phenomenologies of shame and guilt, let us note that guilt is the more respectable affective state (for both sexes), as well

as the more articulate. Shame for the failure of the self to live up to its ideals is respectable enough when it is spoken of in the abstract. When it is experienced in its concrete, living form—when the ideal is represented in consciousness as an actual other before whom one is ashamed—the experience itself evokes more shame. Shame is not only a neglected experience, it is a devalued experience because it is so feelingful and so "other"-connected. In our society, people are ashamed of themselves for being ashamed.[86]

This returns us to shame's paradox: shame isolates yet connects us. We all feel somehow defective and needy; we all want to be qualified self-presenting agents; we all need ideals to live up to and fall short of. Dostoevsky not only portrays a post-lapsarian shame-filled world but plunges his narrative audience into it affectively. We may flee—as some readers of Dostoevsky do—never to return. Those who remain may be temporarily paralyzed by affect. But Dostoevsky also provides his authorial audience with the affective and cognitive means to alleviate the pain. Dostoevsky gives us models for empathic listening—characters like Myshkin, Mme. Epanchina, Zosima, and Alesha Karamazov. These characters use their moral imaginations to hear the shame/pain inscribed in others' discourses and proffer them an empathic bridge. After making us experience the often painful ties that bind us to others, Dostoevsky shows us a way to join fully in the human community.

An examination of Dostoevsky's liars demonstrates that even when metaliterarily engaging the Russian literary tradition, Dostoevsky's work is deeply ethical and political. In verbally overstepping unspoken social boundaries, his liars reveal the social conventions governing the life of nineteenth-century educated Russians. In comically decrying their own fate, liars identify actual problems facing most educated Russians. In exposing the shame that spawns lying, Dostoevsky implicates his readers in the ethical and sociopolitical action of his work. Witnesses to others' exposed selves, we stand exposed to self-scrutiny. Thus exposed, we recognize the ties that bind us to others and refrain from passing quick judgment. Thus exposed, we may live more consciously, embracing the positive in our selves and others. Thus self-conscious, we may consciously fashion ourselves as ethical and sociopolitical beings who strive to live more harmoniously with others. Dostoevsky's fiction demonstrates that the effort at social reform begins at home.

chapter three

Shame's Legacy: Fathers and Children

"You pity me," he [Napoleon] cried, "you child, and perhaps yet another child, my son, le roi de Rome, pities me; the rest all, all hate me, and my brothers will be the first to sell me into misfortune!" I sobbed and threw myself at him; at that he couldn't restrain himself; we embraced, and our tears mingled." (8:416–7)

—GENERAL IVOLGIN, *The Idiot*

And I've been lying, decidedly my whole life, every day and every hour. In truth, I am a lie and a father of lies. Or rather, it seems, not a father of lies, I keep getting lost in texts, but a son of lies, and that will be enough. (14:41;44)

—FEDOR KARAMAZOV, *The Brothers Karamazov*

Ваш отец диавол; и вы хотите исполнять похоти отца вашего. Он был человекоубийца от начала и не устоял в истине; ибо он лжец и отец лжи.*

—John 8:44

As I have shown in chapters 1 and 2, Fedor Karamazov and General Ivolgin tell others' stories as their own and are exposed for doing so. Fedor Karamazov responds aggressively, shamelessly passing along his shame. General Ivolgin responds in a more socially expected and acceptable manner, first by denying his plagiarism and then by fleeing. They thus exemplify the two basic types of Dostoevskian liars: the shameless and the shamed. Viewed singly, each has his own story. Viewed together, they expose Dostoevsky's narrative strategies. This chapter juxtaposes two of their stories not only for what they reveal about their character narrators, General Ivolgin and Fedor Karamazov, but also for what they reveal about their creator, Fedor Dostoevsky.

---

* You are of your father the devil, and your will is to do your father's desires. He was a murderer from the beginning, and has nothing to do with the truth, because there is no truth in him. When he lies, he speaks according to his own nature, for he is a liar and the father of lies.

Shame's Legacy: Fathers and Children

General Ivolgin and Fedor Karamazov are both fathers of three legitimate children, yet during inspired exhibitionistic performances both identify themselves as sons. Naturally, their stories function as self-presentations, but they also function as Fedor Dostoevsky's vehicles for engaging and problematizing the father-children thematics of the Russian literary tradition. While his narrators portray General Ivolgin and Fedor Karamazov as irresponsible fathers who drink too much, chase after women, and neglect their children, Dostoevsky reminds readers that these opprobrious fathers are also orphaned sons. Their self-chosen surrogate fathers—Napoleon and the devil—are quintessentially Dostoevskian and thus reveal Dostoevsky's poetic hand. By introducing these legendary figures into his texts, Dostoevsky addresses sociopolitical, metaphysical, and metaliterary questions in a serious yet deeply funny manner. He also plays with shame's paradox, employing these anecdotal identifications to articulate thematics of isolation and communion. Equally importantly, however, Dostoevsky deters facile judgments by showing both sides of shame's legacy, thereby challenging readers to find sociopolitical solutions. These irresponsible fathers may pass along a legacy of shame, but they also receive one.

Both Napoleon and the devil are arch-enemies of Russia and of God, would-be usurpers, defeated enemies. Legendary figures of pride, they overstep the limits of their God-given powers. Defeated by the forces of brotherhood, they are banished from the communities over which they would rule. Linked in the popular imagination, Napoleon and the devil provide rich ground for an author concerned with conflicts between individual and community, mind and heart, atheism and belief. The Russian literary tradition had already associated Napoleon with the devil/Lucifer/Satan, demonizing Napoleon and linking historical and eschatological events.[1] Dostoevsky taps into this ready-made association and links the moral/metaphysical with the sociopolitical. In viewing General Ivolgin and Fedor Karamazov in the context of Russian history as the sons of demonic fathers, Dostoevsky exposes their heritage as well as their legacy. In Dostoevsky's novels, the demonic is associated with individualism, falsehood, deliberate dissociation from community, and discord. Fathers who choose a demonic identification pass on a legacy of selfishness and discord, helping to destroy their actual and metaphorical families. General Ivolgin's and Fedor Karamazov's exhibitionistic identifications thus have serious sociopolitical and metaphysical implications.

Father-son thematics dominate Ivolgin's page boy story. In Ivolgin's telling, he is ten years old and fatherless when he allegedly meets Napoleon—the most famous military leader of the century—who becomes his surrogate father. In Ivolgin's narrative, the immediate mutual admiration between legendary hero and young general-to-be increases, culminating in near-adoption. Napoleon first singles out the well-dressed young Ivolgin with his "eagle eye." Upon learning that Ivolgin's father was "a general, who died on the fields of the fatherland," and thus in the Napoleonic campaign, Napoleon expresses his admiration for the Russian nobility in terms that reveal his ignorance of Russian reality—"*J'aime les boyards.*" As Russian readers would know, "boyar" was a class designation abolished by Peter the Great over a century earlier.[2] With this detail, Dostoevsky reminds readers of Napoleon's self-absorption and exposes Ivolgin's narrative naïveté. As becomes increasingly evident, Ivolgin fabricates his Napoleon out of period clichés and narcissistic projection.

Dostoevsky emphasizes the projected nature of Ivolgin's Napoleon when the great general unexpectedly asks Ivolgin, "*M'aimes-tu, petit?*" This question betrays Ivolgin's need for love and acceptance. The question also tackles the issue of national identity, an issue likewise raised early in Tolstoy's *War and Peace*.[3] How can a Russian patriot admire the world conqueror invading his country? Young Ivolgin's response parodies the adult responses of Tolstoy's characters prior to the invasion of Moscow: "'The Russian heart is able to discern a great man even in the very enemy of the fatherland!' That is, strictly, I don't remember whether I expressed myself that way literally . . . I was a child . . . but that was surely the meaning!" (8:413). Ivolgin's response keys readers to the synthetic dimension of storytelling. Even though he is a naive narrator, Ivolgin senses the discrepancy between what he said and what he meant. He thus acknowledges that he rephrases in the retelling. This acknowledgment bolsters Ivolgin's claim to truth-telling, thereby beefing up his credibility early in his incredible tale. It also signals Dostoevsky's authorial interest in narrative construction.

Dostoevsky emphasizes the humor of Ivolgin's account by highlighting his narcissistic grandiosity. According to Ivolgin, his personal patriotic feelings represent national sentiment: "Napoleon was struck, he thought a moment and said to his retinue: 'I love the pride of this child! But if all Russians think like this child, then . . . ' he didn't finish speaking" [8:413].[4] Ivolgin thus fashions himself a Russian patriot whose love of country spells Napoleon's downfall. Two days later, Napoleon's page boy dies. Ivolgin is invited to replace him and quickly becomes an intimate, an eyewitness to the nocturnal "moans of that 'giant in misfortune,'" Napoleon's sounding board at critical moments, and, finally, a second son. On the eve of the French retreat, Napoleon notices the tears in young Ivolgin's eyes and recites the speech of my epigraph, a passage that ends with their mingled tears. Ivolgin's story thus follows a progression: he is singled out and becomes a political consultant, then a son.

While the Russian scholar Inna Al'mi observes that the polarity—great man/small child—is a fixed motif of boulevard novels,[5] Ivolgin's story emphasizes the father-son nature of this relationship. Napoleon equates young Ivolgin with his own young son and calls him "my child" (8:414). Ivolgin gains another general as his surrogate father. Yet this adoption story ends in separation and loss. As Napoleon leaves Moscow, he tells Ivolgin, "'I don't want to take you away from your mother and am not taking you with me!'" (8:417). The separation ends disastrously for both: Napoleon's retreat is the first step on his path to the "sultry isle" of exile; Ivolgin likewise goes into exile as he "was sent to officer training school, where I found only drilling, the coarseness of my companions, and . . . Alas! All has gone to ruin!" (8:417).

This double exile further draws readers' attention to the constructed nature of Ivolgin's Napoleon. Dostoevsky's Russian readers would recognize the "sultry isle" of exile as a quote from one of Pushkin's poems about Napoleon. The General unconsciously constructs his Napoleon from all the clichés of the period. Dostoevsky also permits a personal note to enter Ivolgin's picture. Like Ivolgin, Dostoevsky attended and disliked officer training school, an unpleasant trial replete with shame-filled experiences. For both, officer training school represents exile from the comfort of home and, for Ivolgin, a fall from the childhood glory of being Napoleon's page boy. Dostoevsky thus builds a pattern of rise and fall into Ivolgin's two stories of exile. Ivolgin and his Napoleon successfully penetrate a foreign space, achieve recognition and respect, then, under circumstances beyond their control, return home and are sent into shame-filled exile. Dostoevsky displays his own authorial savvy while reflecting Ivolgin's narrative naïveté. Ivolgin consciously chooses Napoleon as a father figure, but unconsciously chooses a figure whose story, and whose shame, recapitulate his own. More significantly, as Dostoevsky exuberantly demonstrates, Ivolgin projects his own personality traits onto the legendary hero.

In Ivolgin's story, for instance, Napoleon compares himself to Joseph and asks for reciprocal admiration, actions that reflect Ivolgin's feelings.[6] In having Napoleon liken himself to Joseph betrayed by his envious brothers at a time when he is isolated, Ivolgin comments on his own situation. Like Joseph and like the Napoleon he fashions in his own image, Ivolgin is histrionic and self-centered. He is also exiled from his brothers as a result of his own actions, yet, like his Napoleon, he blames others. Attributing his fall from the good graces of high society to a scandal about his relations with the Belokonskys' governess, Ivolgin feels betrayed by his former colleagues and friends, particularly by General Epanchin, his former brother-in-arms. In having Napoleon seek his approval, Ivolgin reveals his own desire for admiration and acceptance into the dominant community.

This scene also reveals Dostoevsky's metaliterary play. Ivolgin tells this story to Prince Myshkin, a sympathetic listener who, moreover, also lost his father at an early age. The egotistic Ivolgin regards Myshkin in the same way that Ivolgin's Napoleon regards the young Ivolgin—as a representative of the

Russian aristocracy whose acceptance he seeks. In Dostoevsky's framing, Ivolgin's story recapitulates his own situation. Ivolgin's Napoleon and Ivolgin the storyteller are both egotistic individuals seeking the approval of young sons of dead generals whom they narcissistically perceive not as individuals in their own right but as representatives of a class that can give them admiration and approval.

In having Ivolgin choose Napoleon as his surrogate father, Dostoevsky reveals the retired general's alienation from his Russian roots. Instead of identifying with his own father or with the victorious Russian tsar Alexander I, Ivolgin identifies with the defeated world conqueror who was demonized in Russian and European culture. By identifying with Napoleon but acting like a Russian patriot, Ivolgin emblemizes the Russian divided self, torn between Western culture and Russian spiritual values. In Dostoevsky's handling, his internal division also reflects a metaliterary conflict; Ivolgin is a realistic character torn between forms of romantic longing: on the one hand, admiration for the alienated, individualistic hero whose ambitions cause large-scale discord and death, and, on the other, desire for brotherhood, expressed in another cliché—his identification with Alexandre Dumas's dashingly patriotic musketeers. Ivolgin's admiration for two foreign literary models signals his alienation from Russia. His choice of Napoleon expresses a shame of origins.

The exposure scene, which I discuss in the next chapter, works out a model of shame and exile. Ivolgin becomes carried away, realizes that the Prince cannot believe him, and flees in shame. Ivolgin then takes control of his shame-filled situation by projecting blame outward and breaking off relations with the Prince, thereby exiling himself under the guise of injured honor.

A decade later, while writing *The Brothers Karamazov*, Dostoevsky ups the ante. In his portrayal of Fedor Karamazov, another father orphaned in his youth, Dostoevsky emphasizes the metaphysical dimension of alienation from Russia. As Fedor Karamazov histrionically proclaims himself first father then son of lies, thus allying himself with the devil, Dostoevsky adds new depths to his novel's father-children thematics. While commentators on this passage have focused on its poetics of misquotation,[7] they have not examined the filial import of Fedor Pavlovich's hyperbolic statement. However comic, his declaration calls attention to origins—sociopolitical, metaphysical, and literary.

On the mimetic level, the narrator of *The Brothers Karamazov* treats Fedor Pavlovich as the Karamazov *paterfamilias*. He notes without comment that Fedor Pavlovich was orphaned in his youth and then sponged off the gentry until his marriage to Dmitry's mother, Adelaida. Readers thus know that he was born into a poor gentry family. The narrator does not once mention Fedor Karamazov's father, but the text bears two traces of him. First, by Russian practice, Fedor bears his father's name, Pavel, as his patronymic Pavlovich. Second, since

Fedor Pavlovich becomes a sponger, readers assume that he was left penniless at his father's death. The ghost of Pavel Karamazov thus haunts the text in his son's name and poverty. In this way Fedor Dostoevsky indicates that Fedor Karamazov receives from his father what he gives to his sons: a legacy of shame.

On the thematic level, Pavel, the Russian form of Paul, is a first name that for Russian readers evokes the image of a murdered tsar. Son of Catherine II (the Great), Paul I was murdered in the castle he had built to protect himself. The murdered Paul was also the son of Peter III, a tsar likewise murdered by conspirators, who then placed Peter's German-born wife Catherine II on the throne. Just as important for Dostoevsky's novel, Paul I was an autocrat who established male primogeniture but distrusted his first-born son Alexander I (who was popularly believed to have known of the conspiracy to kill his father). Finally, Paul I was a strict disciplinarian who restored compulsory service and corporal punishment for nobles, thereby, like Fedor Karamazov and Dostoevsky's father, giving rise to the shame and resentment that motivated his murder. The ghosts of Paul I and Peter III, both murdered in their bedchambers, haunt Russian history as well as Dostoevsky's novel.

Paul's spectral presence also haunted Dostoevsky's youth. Dostoevsky attended the Military Engineering Academy in St. Petersburg, an institution housed in the former Mikhailovskii Castle, the site of Paul I's murder. As memoir literature reveals, a survivor from that period still lived in the building and told stories, particularly of the night when Paul was killed.[8] No student of Dostoevsky could possibly imagine that the young Dostoevsky did not number among his most avid listeners. Furthermore, while living at the site of a regicide, Dostoevsky learned of his own father's murder. Into Fedor's patronymic Dostoevsky thus thematically inscribed a whole tradition of parricide/regicide.

Dostoevsky also thematically loads Fedor Pavlovich's last name. *Kara*, the first part of the name "Karamazov," derives from the Russian word for "punishment" and the Turkish word for "black." Dostoevsky signals his readers that the Turkish root is operative in Book Four, Chapter Six, when Snegirev's feeble-minded wife addresses Alesha Karamazov as "Mr. Chernomazov" (*chernyi* being the Russian adjective for "black").[9] The Turkish *kara* would have been widely known to literate Russians as early as 1804 when the Serbs, led by "Black George" (*Karageorgii*), challenged the regnant Turkish power. An active journalist, Dostoevsky followed the situation in the region. He also would have known Pushkin's 1832 cycle of poems, *Songs of the Western Slavs*,[10] including the one that explains how Kara George got his nickname "The Black" (*Chernyi*): by killing his father, who planned to betray him to the Turks. The father-son conflict depicted in Pushkin's poem thus adds the thematic element of parricide to Dostoevsky's name choice.

But Pushkin would not have been Dostoevsky's only source linking the word *kara* with parricide. The Russian expression *karachun emu* means "death to him" and had a personal resonance for the Dostoevsky brothers. In his memoir account of their father's death, Andrei Dostoevsky notes its use. On the day of his death, their father, who was known for his arbitrary discipline, had been particularly abusive to his peasants. One peasant responded impudently and then, fearing the further consequences, called out to his companions, "*Rebiata, karachun emu!*" (Fellows, death to him!).[11] The murder of Dostoevsky's father thus recapitulates the regicide. Fearful of the arbitrary power (*proizvol*)[12] of their leader, the subordinates enact a Freudian scenario in which they unite and kill the father figure.[13] While Freud focuses on the guilt that binds the brothers-in-crime, shame provides an equally potent connecting thread for Dostoevsky. Paul I and Dostoevsky's father both imposed humiliating and painful punishments on those under their care. By association, Dostoevsky inscribes parricide into Fedor's last name as well as his patronymic.

Fedor Pavlovich's last name also bears the stamp of paradox, thereby forestalling any easy judgment of him. As the narrator tells us in the opening section of the book, some said that Fedor Pavlovich rejoiced at the death of his first wife, others said that he cried like a small child. This leads to the narrator's earlier discussed comment: "It may very well be that both were true, that is, that he both rejoiced at his liberation and sobbed for his liberator—all at the same time. In most cases, people, even wicked ones, are much more naive and simple-hearted than we generally assume. And so are we ourselves" (14:10;9). Just as Fedor Pavlovich contains opposites, so do the connotations of the second part of his last name. The many derivatives of the Russian root *maz* include the verb *mazat'* (to cover with oil, smear, anoint, soil, stain, swindle, paint) and the noun *maz'* (oil, ointment, grease, ooze).[14] From these, in turn, Russian gains words such as *mazilka* (a bad painter), *mazulia* (someone who oils or soils; a bad painter), and *mazurik* (a rogue, swindler). The combination *kara* and *maz* thus evokes a broad array of associations, many negative, and many active in Dostoevsky's portrait of the Karamazov patriarch. Yet in Dostoevsky's work, most symbols cut both ways. A bad painter may be a *mazilka*, but an icon painter is a *bogomaz'*. Bad painting suggests a source of shame, but also the covering over of shame. The image of black ooze suggests filth, but also fecundity. Blackness reminds readers of the baser parts of human nature associated with Karamazovism—vileness and lechery—but Karamazovism also suggests a thirst for life.[15] Blackness is associated with the devil, but, as Ksana Blank points out, black and white also complement one another; each gains definition by contrast.[16] Dostoevsky thus inscribes Fedor Pavlovich's paradoxical complexity into his last name.

Fedor Pavlovich Karamazov's first name points to the synthetic dimension of Dostoevsky's character as Fedor Dostoevsky names the Karamazov *paterfamilias* after himself. (For more on this, see chapter 9, where I elaborate on the kinship between the two Fedors and two black writers—Aesop and Pushkin.) Adding greatly to his mimetic and thematic richness, Fedor Pavlovich's synthetic function enhances readers' aesthetic enjoyment of Dostoevsky's text. Fedor Pavlovich, for instance, declares, "I keep getting lost in texts" (*eto ia vsë v tekstakh sbivaius'*). While this statement mimetically reflects the narrator's introduction of him as "one of the most muddleheaded madcaps of our whole district" (*odnim iz bestolkoveishikh sumasbrodov po vsemu nashemu uezdu*), thus as someone who can get mixed up while reading, Dostoevsky's unusual choice of words suggests that Fedor Karamazov's identity crisis has a metaliterary and a metaphysical dimension as well. As Vetlovskaia points out, in creating *The Brothers Karamazov*, Dostoevsky followed Dante's use of the time-honored symbol—world as book, and its reverse, book as world.[17] The verb *sbivat'sia*, used in the expressions *sbivat'sia s dorogi, sbivat'sia v chtenii*, denotes the action of misplacing or miscalculating. One can slip, lose one's footing, lose one's way, lose one's place. By slipping up "in texts," Fedor Karamazov identifies texts as paths and thus as loci of error for him. He gets lost in the written word, goes astray. Indeed, as his words testify, he *has* gone astray. He has sided with the devil and lies against Christ and truth. As a son of the devil, Fedor Pavlovich anticipates the Grand Inquisitor, the unholy father of his son Ivan's story. Both Fedor Karamazov and the Grand Inquisitor are paternal figures who go astray in the Scriptures, allying themselves with the father of lies and his followers rather than with God and his son.[18] By having Fedor Karamazov get lost in a holy text, Fedor Dostoevsky affirms the ethical importance of right reading.

Fedor Karamazov's statement about straying forms one part of his blatant blasphemy. In calling himself a father/son of lies, Fedor Pavlovich obviously distorts the biblical text. But to what end? Fedor Karamazov intends to shock his audience. Fedor Dostoevsky, on the other hand, provides a scandalous cover for the shocking notion that Fedor Karamazov is not only a father, but a son, and thus a brother. Following Meerson's rule of thumb that Dostoevsky preserves the import of biblical passages only when he taboos them, thereby working on his readers' unconscious processing, I will not dwell on the passage from John that Fedor distorts, a passage in which Christ divides his followers from the devil's.[19] Instead, I look at what Dostoevsky adds.

By having Fedor Karamazov identify himself as a son, Dostoevsky locates Fedor Karamazov as the progeny as well as the progenitor of a broken family, an increasingly frequent phenomenon in nineteenth-century Russia. On the mimetic level, Dostoevsky thus provides a partial explanation for Fedor

Karamazov's unfitness as a father: he had either no model or a poor model. By reminding readers that Fedor Karamazov is a son as well as a father, Dostoevsky also expands the meaning of the word "brothers" in his novel's title. As Meerson argues, Fedor Karamazov's three legitimate sons are ashamed of their association with Smerdiakov; they thus taboo mention of him as the fourth "brother."[20] By making Fedor Pavlovich the Karamazov family patriarch, Dostoevsky provides a place for him among fathers/rulers in readers' consciousness. But Fedor Pavlovich riotously renounces his place and declares himself a son. Dostoevsky thus scandalizes us into revisiting our views. He uses his character's scandalous words to surprise, disorient, and make us self-conscious. We regard Fedor Pavlovich as a father, not as a son: we regard Smerdiakov as illegitimate and ill-educated, thus as a servant not a brother. In shocking us, Dostoevsky forces us to realize how we collaborate in the status quo, how we exclude shame-filled and shameless characters like Pavel Fedorovich Smerdiakov and Fedor Pavlovich Karamazov from our sense of universal brotherhood. Fedor Dostoevsky challenges such facile positions. By having him call himself a "son," Dostoevsky includes Fedor Pavlovich in his theological vision of universal brotherhood.

In having General Ivolgin and Fedor Karamazov choose Napoleon and the devil as father figures, Dostoevsky adds another twist to his novels' shame dynamics. Ever the psychologist, Dostoevsky reveals the shame content of his liars' grandiose claims. In choosing a French surrogate father, Ivolgin compensates for his Russian national inferiority complex. In choosing a famous world conqueror, Ivolgin compensates for his sense of obscurity and powerlessness. He chooses a hero whose success and subsequent ignominy recapitulate his own, then he projects himself onto his hero. Though General Ivolgin intends to hide his shame with his story, its excesses expose him. He flees in shame. Yet there is no scandal. Prince Myshkin, his sole listener, fears a final break but laughs after the general departs. His aesthetic appreciation of Ivolgin's story domesticates Ivolgin's shame. He is not scandalized, nor are readers.

The shame dynamic works differently in *The Brothers Karamazov*. Fedor Karamazov openly acknowledges his shame, but he aggressively and scandalously shares it with others. He thus generates a level of audience discomfort that is not easily dispelled. Dostoevsky also broadens the metaphysical scope of his last novel and associates shame with the devil. In both the Hebrew Bible and the Gospels, the devil is associated with temptation. Dostoevsky's characters, particularly Ivan, constantly refer to the temptation of Eve and Adam in the Garden of Eden and the temptation of Christ in the wilderness. Moreover, Ivan has a devil who resembles his father and thus reminds him of his shame (see my chapter 11). Father Ferapont sees medieval-type devils who tempt him. Fedor Karamazov claims he may house a low-caliber devil. Zosima identifies shame as the source of Fedor Pavlovich's buffoonery. Fedor concurs, "That's why I'm a buffoon, a buffoon out of shame, great Elder, out of shame" (14:41;43). The epithet "buffoon" (*shut*) is associated with the devil in the Russian tradition. The devil, in Dostoevsky's portrayal, is a parasite. Fedor Pavlovich, likewise, is a parasite: he expropriates his first wife's money and becomes a moneylender, a tavern keeper, and a seller of forests. He thus lives off others, like the devil. But Dostoevsky has a sociopolitical as well as a metaphysical agenda in his novel. In making Fedor Pavlovich such a bad father, Dostoevsky raises questions about justice, social order, and responsibility. A bad father, Fedor Karamazov is selfish and destructive; he tends to his own pleasure and neglects his duties to his wives, children, and other dependents. He so relinquishes responsibility for himself that he requires the paternal care of his servant Grigory. With this portrayal of narcissistic paternity, Dostoevsky obliquely criticizes all bad fathers, including negligent landowners and tsars, parasites on the constituencies they are obligated to protect. In tackling the father-children thematics of the Russian literary tradition, Dostoevsky raises crucial questions about fatherhood as well as brotherhood. His Christological poetics leave no doubts about his position on sociopolitical organization.

In reading, we view General Ivolgin and Fedor Karamazov as fathers. By having them comically remind us that they are also sons, Dostoevsky deters automatic perception and judgment. These men may be bad fathers, but they are also deprived sons. Dostoevsky further complicates readers' response in both novels by providing alternative scenarios that demonstrate the role of free will in response to social shame. General Ivolgin's sons respond differently to their shame-filled father. Gania blames and shames him; Kolia protects him. So with Fedor Karamazov's sons. Dmitry blames and beats his father; Ivan distances himself from him; Alesha loves him; Smerdiakov kills him. Smerdiakov's act, motivated by a desire to gain Ivan's approval and thus overcome his own shame, can be seen as a desire to rid both himself and Ivan of the shame of origins. But violence, as Dostoevsky demonstrates, generates more violence.[21] Shame can be cured only by love, not by violence. Ivan's encounter with his devil represents his struggle to confront his shame positively (see my chapter 11). Alesha also works to dispel shame and create community among brothers. In addition, he finds a spiritual father, who teaches that love and acceptance heal shame.

In these two stories of fathers as sons, Dostoevsky mimetically points to our common post-lapsarian legacy: we are all children of the fall. By introducing Ivolgin's Napoleon and Fedor Karamazov's devil as father figures, he introduces metaliterary fun into the sociopolitical and metaphysical thematics of his great novels. He thus provides humorous relief from the scandalous spectacles he portrays.

chapter four

General Ivolgin: Narratives of Shame and Identity

> An innocent lie [*nevinnaia lozh'*] for a good laugh, even if it's coarse, doesn't offend the human heart. Some people even lie a bit [*lzhet-to*], if you like, simply for the sake of friendship itself, to give pleasure to their interlocutor in that way. (8:411)
>
> — GENERAL IVOLGIN, *The Idiot*

In Part Four of *The Idiot*, Dostoevsky's narrator apologizes in Gogolian fashion for devoting so much attention to the secondary character General Ivolgin (8:402). Yet Ivolgin is secondary only in the novel's plot, not in its metaliterary construction, where he joins ranks with Prince Myshkin as one of the novel's most important storytellers. In this chapter I argue that Dostoevsky uses General Ivolgin to dramatize a story of shame. Fallen from the grace of good society, the General lies to conceal his shame, yet his stories reveal as much as they conceal. Ivolgin's loss of social standing means he is excluded from the social discourse of high society. He is thus denied identity as a worthy social agent. Throughout the novel, Ivolgin attempts to return to his social position by talking his way back in. All of his stories manifest yearning for his pre-lapsarian social status; many of them also recapitulate the story of his fall. He tells most of his stories in the presence of Prince Myshkin, whom he sees as the empathic and social bridge back to his former social standing. Because his stories repackage his tale of exclusion without denying his responsibility for its occurrence, they prepare for his death-bed redemption.

Dostoevsky may also have expanded General Ivolgin's role in *The Idiot* because his drama of shame serves as an analogue to Nastasia Filippovna's. Comparing their stories thus elucidates Dostoevsky's authorial message. While General Ivolgin and Nastasia Filippovna are fallen, they do not share equal responsibility for their falls. The novel only hints at Ivolgin's wrongdoings—money missing from the regiment, an affair with Princess Belokonsky's governess. The novel lays bare Nastasia Filippovna's story, however. Seduced by her guardian, who promises marriage, she is thus betrayed by the man to whose care she has been entrusted. Ivolgin responds to his shame by denial, blaming others for his fall. Nastasia Filippovna, by contrast, turns her shame inward, into self-hatred, and outward, into vengefulness. Excluded from good society, Ivolgin unaggressively drinks and tells stories, whereas Natasha Filippovna aggressively passes on her shame. As a man, General Ivolgin has hopes of restoration; as a woman, Nastasia Filippovna has none. General Ivolgin's shame story thus functions as a variant of the novel's central action.

Dostoevsky implicates readers in Ivolgin's drama of shame and the novel's moral action of exclusion and inclusion by positioning us as witnesses to his repeated exposure as a liar. He uses the progression[1] of Ivolgin's stories to demonstrate how repeated exposure changes Ivolgin, granting him the possibility of restoration to community. Dostoevsky provides character audiences as models for the authorial audience. Finally, he exploits the parallels between lying and fiction as opportunities to reveal his own poetics and enhance the authorial audience's reading pleasure.

The Literary Tradition

In creating General Ivolgin, Dostoevsky outlines the relationship between shame and storytelling. Like Dostoevsky's other liars, who are products of the post–Petrine era and thus sufferers from a massive cultural inferiority complex, Ivolgin lies to hide his shame-filled self-image. A fictional creation who reflects Russian reality, Ivolgin follows in the footsteps of Russian literature's ur-liar, Gogol's Khlestakov. Like Khlestakov, Ivolgin is ashamed of his actual identity and represents himself as other. "Consumers" of romanticism,[2] Khlestakov and Ivolgin fashion themselves after representatives of the dominant, privileged culture. Like Khlestakov, Ivolgin wants what others around him value—social status and its companion goods. To represent himself as a man of power and privilege, Khlestakov boasts that his soup comes "direct by ship from Paris" and that he serves 700 rubles worth of watermelons; in like fashion, Ivolgin boasts of an unending dinner for 200 to 700 people. Such hyperbolic exhibitionism serves to enhance self-esteem while it aims to impress.

Narcissistically dependent on public approbation, both Khlestakov and Ivolgin believe that a speaker's importance lies in the eyes of his beholders. Both thus boast of whom they know but equally of who knows them. Khlestakov boasts that he's Pushkin's pal; Ivolgin boasts that he was Napoleon's confidant. In recounting his war stories, General Ivolgin also claims to be known by two of the era's most famous physicians and all of the Russian high command: "A man who has thirteen bullets in his chest . . . you don't believe? And yet meanwhile, for my sake alone, Pirogov telegraphed

Paris and quit besieged Sevastopol for a time, and Nelaton, the Parisian Imperial Surgeon with great difficulty obtained a leave in the name of science and showed up in besieged Sevastopol to examine me. The highest command knew about it: 'Ah, it's that Ivolgin who has thirteen bullets! . . .' That's how they talk, sir!" (8:108). This whopper demonstrates Ivolgin's predilection for Khlestakovian hyperbole. Ivolgin tells it to prove his war heroism. Dostoevsky, on the other hand, uses it to reveal Ivolgin's hyperbolic self-aggrandizement and thus to undermine his credibility with readers. Dostoevsky also introduces this patent lie to reveal Ivolgin's sense of victimhood: thirteen bullets represents a lot of internalized punishment.

Ivolgin's exhibitionist cover for internalized pain also highlights the metaliterary dimension of Dostoevsky's novel. Ivolgin proves himself an unselfconscious narrator[3] who places himself at the center of history. He introduces historical verisimilitude—the siege of Sevastopol, the Russian surgeon Pirogov, the Parisian surgeon Nelaton—to support his hyperbolic claims. By borrowing such a well-known context, Ivolgin claims international renown and thus compensates for his current obscurity.

Dostoevsky introduces one of those verisimilar details to accentuate his novel's metaliterary dimension. When Ivolgin refers to the Russian surgeon Pirogov, he speaks of a famous figure in charge of medical affairs during the siege of Sevastopol.[4] When Dostoevsky puts the name Pirogov in Ivolgin's mouth, he playfully draws readers' attention to the Russian literary tradition, as a character named Pirogov is one protagonist of Gogol's well-known story, "Nevsky Prospect."[5] For Dostoevsky, Pirogov epitomizes the split between public and private selves in the Russian national consciousness (21:124–25; 18:59). The name Pirogov thus signals a split between Ivolgin's narrative awareness and Dostoevsky's; it also signals different levels of audience awareness. Ivolgin assumes that his character audience will perceive Pirogov unambiguously as a symbol of Russian national pride. Dostoevsky counts on the dual consciousness of the authorial audience for whom the name Pirogov also emblemizes Russia's private shame. Ivolgin may be an "ingenuous" Khlestakovian narrator; Dostoevsky is not.

In fact, Ivolgin's stories constantly remind Dostoevsky's authorial audience of the Russian literary tradition, particularly the works of Gogol. Like Khlestakov, Ivolgin attempts to elevate himself through false self-representation; he also seeks the company of high society. Gogol's and Dostoevsky's ambitious characters desire, but do not attain, higher rank. They compensate for their impotence by fabricating compensatory self-images. Like Gogol's Major Kovalev ("The Nose") and his madman ("Diary of a Madman"), for example, Ivolgin believes he should be given a governor-generalship (8:81). These characters thus reveal their narrative naïveté, while their creators reveal their authorial savvy. Most strikingly, Gogol's and Dostoevsky's liars are thorough narcissists. Andrew Morrison identifies shame as a painful feeling central to narcissistic disorders. He argues that "Narcissistic vulnerability is the 'underside' of exhibitionism, grandiosity, and haughtiness—the low self-esteem, self-doubt, and fragility of self-cohesion that defines the narcissistic condition."[6] Khlestakov is a low-level bureaucrat who represents himself as Pushkin's colleague and friend; Ivolgin is a fallen general who represents himself as Napoleon's page boy and a Crimean war hero. Selfishly absorbed in their own self-presentation, they act unthinkingly. Their creators, however, document their narcissistic behavior's ethical consequences.

Stories of Identity

Ivolgin's stories are essentially stories of identity: who I was, who I knew, what I did. By having Ivolgin's stories originate in circumstances that recall his shame, Dostoevsky establishes the connection between shame and lying. Ivolgin's first meeting with the Prince, for instance, is doubly shameful: the Prince comes to the Ivolgins' as a potential boarder and thus as a reminder of the family's economic fall, at a time when they are feeling the shame of Gania's proposed marriage to Nastasia Filippovna, a "kept" woman. Ivolgin tells lies whenever he is reminded of his social exile: during Nastasia Filippovna's visit, while visiting old haunts, while sitting in debtor's prison, while attending the Prince's birthday party, following his humiliation by Lebedev, and after his ejection from the Epanchin house. In these circumstances, the General understandably experiences an overwhelming desire to reestablish his self-worth.

In what follows, I examine four of Ivolgin's stories as a progression: his Kolpakov story, his "I knew you when" story, his lapdog story, and his Napoleon's page boy story. In these stories, the General re-presents events with himself as hero in hopes of gaining audience approval and acceptance. Since audience response contributes to his sense of self, Ivolgin tells lies whenever an opportunity to impress an audience presents itself. Significantly, until his death scene, Ivolgin's audience always includes Prince Myshkin, a member of the titled nobility as well as a model listener. As Ivolgin tells his stories, Dostoevsky's narrator reveals the character audience's responses. Following their example, the narrative audience experiences either shock at Ivolgin's shamelessness or pain at his shame. The authorial audience is also positioned to see what Bakhtin calls the "surplus" of Ivolgin's stories—their analogic function—and to enjoy their hyperbolic excess. Like Prince Myshkin, we chuckle madly when we read a good whopper.

Chapter 4

The Cover-Up: General Ivolgin and Private Kolpakov

General Ivolgin tells his first extended lie in *The Idiot* about Private Kolpakov. Though ostensibly told as an episode of Prince Myshkin senior's biography, the Private Kolpakov story functions as a veiled autobiography of General Ivolgin himself. A naive character-narrator, Ivolgin presents himself as a family friend and offers Prince Myshkin information about his father's life and death. The novel's narrator uses the Kolpakov story to expose Ivolgin's narrative unreliability by showing his audience the incredulous responses of Ivolgin's character audience. Dostoevsky uses the story to highlight the novel's metaliterary dimension by employing, both in Ivolgin's Kolpakov story and in Ivolgin's own story, a plot pattern familiar in the Russian tradition: theft, humiliation, death, and resurrection.

The storytelling occurs shortly after General Ivolgin meets Prince Myshkin. Ivolgin first claims a personal connection with Myshkin by declaring that he had held him in his arms many years earlier. He presents himself as a potential father figure by telling Myshkin that he had wanted to marry Myshkin's mother. He implies narrative reliability by stating that he and Myshkin's father had been close friends. Ivolgin then rewrites the story of Myshkin's father's death. When the Prince observes that he had never ascertained the reason for his father's pre-death trial, Ivolgin rejoins:

> "Oh, that was the Private Kolpakov case. Undoubtedly the Prince would have been acquitted."
>
> "Is that so? Do you know for sure?" the Prince asked with marked curiosity.
>
> "How else!"—exclaimed the General. "The court was disbanded. Nothing was decided. The case is impossible! The case, one might say, is mysterious. Staff-Captain Larionov, the company commander, dies. The Prince is temporarily appointed to carry out duties. Good. Private Kolpakov commits a theft,—footwear from a buddy—and drinks it up. Good. The Prince—and note, in the presence of a sergeant-major and a corporal—dresses him down and threatens him with a cat-o-nine-tails. Very good. Kolpakov returns to the barracks, lies down on his bunk, and fifteen minutes later dies. Fine. But the case is unexpected, almost impossible. One way or another, Kolpakov is buried. The Prince reports it, and then Kolpakov is crossed off the rolls. What could seem better? But exactly half a year later, at the brigade inspection, Private Kolpakov appears—as if nothing had happened—in the third company of the second battalion of the Novozemliansky infantry regiment,[7] of the very same brigade and the very same division!"
>
> "What!" exclaimed the Prince, beside himself with amazement.

"That's not so! That's a mistake!" Nina Aleksandrovna suddenly turned to him, looking at him almost in anguish. "*Mon mari se trompe.*"

"But, my friend, *se trompe*, that's easy to say, but go solve a similar case yourself! Everyone was stunned. I would be the first to say '*on se trompe.*' But unfortunately, I was a witness and participated in the commission myself. All the confrontations in court showed that it was the very same, absolutely the very same Private Kolpakov, who half a year earlier had been buried with a regular parade and with a drumroll. The case is really rare, almost impossible, I agree, but . . . "

"Daddy, your dinner is served,"—announced Varvara Ardalionovna, entering the room.

"Wonderful! Superb! I've gotten hungry indeed . . . But the case, one might say, is even psychological. . . . " (8:82–3)

In this story, Ivolgin represents himself as part of the investigatory commission, and thus a judge, but he also naively identifies with both Prince Myshkin senior and Private Kolpakov, the characters being judged.

In choosing the role of judge, Ivolgin asserts his former military rank. He confirms his authority by presenting himself as an eyewitness,[8] an identity that flags shame's role in his storytelling. The shame experience characteristically includes the factors of seeing and being seen. The shamed person feels exposed and vulnerable before the gaze of others. Ivolgin constantly feels judged, that is, exposed. By representing himself as a judge, that is, an authority figure who sees and adjudicates, Ivolgin reverses roles, removing himself from the shameful position of being seen and judged. In lying, Ivolgin conceals a painful psychic reality (weak, exposed self) and creates an ideal alternative (powerful, uniformed other).

While Myshkin's father is literally on trial, Ivolgin feels as though he has already been tried and convicted, a position he immediately expresses to Myshkin: "I, you see for yourself, I have suffered, because of a tragic catastrophe; but without a trial! Without a trial! [*Bez suda!*]" (8:81).[9] By presenting himself as a victim of circumstances, Ivolgin denies responsibility for his fall. But his story reveals a more ambiguous picture: Ivolgin postulates a scenario in which an action's consequences can be undone. Myshkin's father plays the role of mortifier—he literally shames Corporal Kolpakov to death. But Kolpakov returns from the dead, a circumstance that, for Ivolgin, undoes Myshkin senior's crime. Ivolgin's judgment that Myshkin's father would be acquitted because his "victim" did not die clearly expresses his own desire to be exonerated and acquitted.

Ivolgin later identifies with Myshkin senior by claiming that they had been brothers in service. When Nastasia Filippovna arrives, Ivolgin compares himself,

Myshkin's father, and General Epanchin to the Three Musketeers. For himself, Ivolgin chooses the role of Athos, the universally admired aristocrat and natural military leader (whose sole weakness, born of woman and shame, is wine). He likens General Epanchin to Porthos, the physically imposing musketeer given to sartorial vanity[10] and luxurious living. And he assigns Myshkin's father the role of Aramis, the attractive youth torn between chivalry and church service. In identifying with the titled nobleman Athos, Ivolgin stresses his former social standing. In evoking the musketeers, Ivolgin conjures up an idealized portrait of heroic devotion to king and country. But he also invokes the famous motto "All for one and one for all," a motto that emphasizes the brotherly sharing of prosperity and poverty alike. Ivolgin thus expresses solidarity with Myshkin senior while protesting his abandonment by General Epanchin.

Ivolgin reveals a naive identification with Private Kolpakov when he says "he was crossed off the rolls," literally "excluded from the lists" (*iskliuchaiut iz spiskov*). The narrator reinforces this identification by saying the same of Ivolgin—"he was excluded" (*on byl iskliuchen*). Dostoevsky hints that Ivolgin's identification with Private Kolpakov may extend to his crime—stealing from a buddy to drink. Both Kolpakov's and Ivolgin's stories follow a pattern—the crime of theft leads to exposure, then to mortification, then to exclusion. While the text never explicitly explains Ivolgin's retirement (though theft to cover debts is a recurrent motif in Dostoevsky's *oeuvre*), the Kolpakov story prefigures Ivolgin's later theft of 400 rubles from Lebedev to repay his debt to the Captain's widow.[11] Ivolgin may have been forced into retirement and thus excluded. Yet the story he tells prefigures his own: Ivolgin's next crime is a theft, which literally leads to mortification. By having the Kolpakov story recapitulate and prefigure the story of General Ivolgin's life and death, Dostoevsky displays his narrative skill: Ivolgin naively tells the Kolpakov story to cover over his own, while Dostoevsky artfully designs an analogue story.[12]

Ivolgin's lapdog story, as a plagiarism, likewise demonstrates Ivolgin's artlessness and Dostoevsky's masterful creation of yet another analogue story. The Kolpakov story suggests a reason for Ivolgin's shameful loss of military identity. The lapdog story suggests one for Ivolgin's shameful loss of social status (another unexplained loss). If the break with the Epanchins occurred at the time of his retirement, as the lapdog story implies, then Ivolgin loses several valued roles simultaneously: his active generalship, his social position, and his traditional paternal role. As he tells his stories, Ivolgin no longer provides for his wife and children but lives as a supervised dependent. He lies to regain his place in society.

Significantly, Ivolgin presents Private Kolpakov's resurrection as a reincorporation into community. In Ivolgin's words, he is "absolutely the very same Private Kolpakov." Ivolgin's story thus reveals his own desire for restoration:

he longs to rejoin the ranks of high society and to regain his social and paternal authority. The tale told by Ivolgin reveals a naive and transparent narrator: he distances himself from the wrongdoers in his story by outranking them and naively identifies with them by portraying them as victims. The tale told by Dostoevsky, on the other hand, reveals a self-conscious storyteller, masterfully controlling structure and thematics. The numerous Gogolian references in Ivolgin's story situate it in a literary context unsuspected by the boastful general. The name Private Kolpakov, for instance, echoes those of both Captain Kopeikin (*Dead Souls*) and Major Kovalev ("The Nose"). Private Kolpakov's story even follows the pattern of theirs: public humiliation, death to the world, restoration to life and community. Dostoevsky ensures his authorial audience's pleasure at identifying the Gogolian reference by having Ivolgin quote directly from the end of "The Nose": "but the case is unexpected, almost impossible" (*sluchai neozhidannyi, pochti nevozhmozhnyi*). The Kovalev reference also suggests pretence as Kovalev obtained his rank in the Caucasus, a signal for Russian readers that he is possibly a pretender. In alluding to Kopeikin, Dostoevsky parodies Ivolgin's efforts to be recognized and rewarded for his services. Captain Kopeikin proved his war heroism in *Dead Souls* by losing limbs in service of tsar and country. Ivolgin attended a military academy and would have become a general in due course. His hyperbolic war stories, however, cast doubt on his heroism. Readers may wonder whether he was ever wounded, but we are certain he has not suffered thirteen bullets in his chest. His war stories, like his other stories, may be seen as Ivolgin's way of coping with the trauma of his fall.

Dostoevsky further exploits the Russian literary tradition by having Ivolgin's Kolpakov story steal the plot of Gogol's "Overcoat," which involves a theft, mortification by a powerful superior in the presence of a witness, and reported resurrection. Kolpakov allegedly steals footwear (*sapozhnyi tovar*), an overt authorial reference to the name of Akaky Akakievich Bashmachkin (*bashmak* = shoe). But while Bashmachkin, Kolpakov, and Ivolgin are humiliated by powerful others before witnesses, Gogol's character is also the victim of theft, whereas Kolpakov and Ivolgin are (or become) thieves. By having Ivolgin's Kolpakov story recapitulate Akaky Akakievich's but with this difference, Dostoevsky allows Ivolgin to betray his victim mentality.[13] Ivolgin's Kolpakov story not only deflects attention from Kolpakov as thief and focuses on Kolpakov as victim; it also undoes the effects of Kolpakov's humiliation: Kolpakov is no longer singled out and exposed to view but reincorporated into the ranks. Ivolgin's story thus projects his own dearest wish—to regain his rank and social status and thus his own protective covering.

Ivolgin naively recapitulates Gogol's humiliation-death-resurrection pattern with another revealing difference. Unlike Akaky Akakievich, who returns as a ghost to haunt the conscience of his unjust superior, Kolpakov returns as "the very same Kolpakov." Unlike Dostoevsky, who consciously recalls yet another story of humiliation, death, and resurrection, Ivolgin emphasizes social restoration. Kolpakov returns from the dead and undoes part, but not all, of the effects of Myshkin senior's crime: Kolpakov is restored to the ranks, but not to the same regiment. Kolpakov's theft is also overlooked, but not undone. Ivolgin's story thus contains a subtle admission of his persistent guilt.[14]

Dostoevsky, on the other hand, draws readers' attention to the story of Christ. For instance, he has his narrator note that General Ivolgin tells stories to his drinking companions in debtor's prison about the siege of Kars and about "the risen soldier" (*pro voskresshego soldata*) (8:156). The word "risen," an adjective conspicuously absent from the General's story, signals Dostoevsky's authorial hand. In having his narrator allude to the transcendent Christ, Dostoevsky reminds his readers of Ivolgin's worldly concerns as well as the novel's religious thematics, for in Dostoevsky's work lack of belief in Christ leads to narcissistic self-enclosure. Ivolgin's story lacks Christian vision because Ivolgin lacks it. Though identical to Dostoevsky's, his story lacks salvatory potential.

After Ivolgin tells his Kolpakov story, the narrator encourages his readers to view the General skeptically. His wife's embarrassed response ("*mon mari se trompe*") exposes Ivolgin's unreliability, yet he manifests no shame. He even refutes the charge of unreliability by claiming eyewitness status. While readers may feel twinges of empathic embarrassment for his wife, we feel none for him. Following the narrator's lead, we see General Ivolgin as an embarrassment.

The General with the Lapdog

Among General Ivolgin's lies, two are immediately exposed. The first is the lapdog story. The second turns out to be true: Ivolgin claims that he held Aglaia Epanchina in his arms when she was a child. Both are told in the presence of the Prince and a full company: the first at the Ivolgins', the second at the Prince's. Each is primarily intended to engage and impress the beautiful young woman present—Nastasia Filippovna and Aglaia Epanchina, respectively. These rival beauties play opposite roles in the ongoing drama of Ivolgin's exposure—Nastasia Filippovna exposes the General as a liar; Aglaia Epanchina defends him against the charge. Both exposed lies test the General and represent steps in his road to self-confrontation.

The lapdog story is framed by Nastasia Filippovna's visit to the Ivolgin apartment. Her visit is unexpected, its purpose transparent: Nastasia Filippovna intends to humiliate Gania. Gania, his mother, and his sister see this clearly; the General does not. Although moments earlier he had declared to the Prince that Gania's engagement to an "ambiguous" (*dvusmyslennaia*) woman was bringing shame on his wife and daughter, once she arrives he tries to impress her. First he boasts of his heroic military past. Next, he claims to be the "victim of slander and bullets." Then he identifies himself with the French Enlightenment, Western culture, and liberal politics[15]: "In every other way I live like a philosopher, I walk, I stroll, I play checkers in my cafe, like a bourgeois who's retired from business, and I read the '*Indépendance*.'" (8:92).

Finally, General Ivolgin tells his lapdog story: he had been smoking in a train compartment, two women with a lapdog enter, one of them throws his cigar out the window, so he throws the lapdog out the window (for the full text, see chapter 2). The company applauds, the General swaggers, but Nastasia Filippovna challenges him, asking how the woman responded. Ivolgin then supplies his version of the Epanchins' break with him:

"Her? Well, there's the whole root of the problem," the General continued, scowling, "without saying a word and without the slightest bit of warning, she up and slapped me on the cheek! A savage woman; of an absolutely savage background!"

"And you?"

The General dropped his eyes, raised his eyebrows, raised his shoulders, compressed his lips, moved his hands apart, hung fire and suddenly pronounced:

"I got carried away!"

"And badly? Badly?"

"For God's sake, not badly! A scandal ensued, but not badly. I only swatted at her, simply to swat. But Satan himself wiggled his way in: the light blue one turned out to be an Englishwoman, the governess or even some kind of friend of Princess Belokonsky's house. And the one in black was the eldest of the Belokonsky princesses, an old maid of thirty-five or so. And it's well-known what kind of relationship obtains between General Epanchin's wife and the Belokonsky house. All the princesses in a faint, tears, mourning for the beloved lapdog, six princesses' squeals, the Englishwoman's squeals—the end of the world! But, of course, I went repentantly, begged forgiveness, wrote a letter, not accepted, neither me, nor the letter, and with the Epanchins quarrels, expulsion, persecution!"

"But excuse me, how can that be?" Nastasia Filippovna asked suddenly. "Five or six days ago I read in the '*Indépendance*'—I always read the '*Indépendance*'—exactly the same story! But decidedly exactly the same! It happened on one of the Rhenish railroads, in a coach, with a Frenchman and an Englishwoman. The cigar was torn away exactly the same way, the lapdog was thrown out of the window exactly the same way, finally, it ended exactly the same way as with you. Even the dress was light blue!" (8:93–5)

The General clearly tells the lapdog story to entertain and impress others. In adapting it to explain his social ostracism, he initially presents himself as a forceful figure defending his personal dignity. His story is accepted and applauded, but his triumph is short-lived. Familiar with the story, Nastasia Filippovna asks for the outcome, thereby forcing him to reveal his humiliation. Then she unmasks him as a plagiarist. This scene thus echoes the scene in Gogol's play *The Inspector General* where Khlestakov tries to impress the mayor's wife and daughter by claiming both that he is the popular writer Baron Brambeus and that he authored the widely read novel *Iurii Miloslavskii* (written by Zagoskin). When they challenge his authorship, he tells another lie. In Gogol's play, both women accept the cover lie. In Dostoevsky's novel, the woman does not. The difference highlights Dostoevsky's goals—to portray Nastasia Filippovna's aggressive response as an example of passed-on shame.

Ivolgin's resemblance to Khlestakov underscores his victim mentality. Like Khlestakov, Ivolgin reallocates blame. Blithely ignoring the fact that he has not paid his bill for two weeks, Khlestakov accuses the innkeeper of starving him. Ivolgin portrays his travel companions as proud violators of the social contract by implying that he would have extinguished his cigar had they asked. Yet he betrays shame as he admits that he struck a woman, thereby violating a social taboo.

Ivolgin's stolen story naively reveals his moral awareness. He does not deny his wrongdoing but redresses it. His exhibitionism is the flip side of his narcissistic vulnerability and shame. His social assertiveness (smoking) and proud silence provoke the initial reaction. His excessive response reflects the extent of his narcissistic vulnerability. Like Dostoevsky's underground men, Ivolgin cannot bear nonrecognition. No longer garbed in military regalia, the external sign of his rank and place in society, he is extremely vulnerable to slights. Instead of turning the other cheek (as Myshkin does), he violates a serious social taboo, which results in his banishment.[16]

In this scene, Dostoevsky diminishes the distance readers feel between ourselves and Ivolgin after the Kolpakov scene, when Ivolgin remained unshamed. This time he is clearly shamed. Though he tries to defend himself by denial, no one believes him. Yet Ivolgin's shame at being exposed creates some sympathy where there was none. Dostoevsky here reveals shame's positive force. A character capable of shame reveals his human frailty and thus breaks down the distance between himself, other characters, and Dostoevsky's readers.

"I held you in my arms"

Dostoevsky explicitly establishes shame's positive power when Ivolgin next lies, in yet another attempt to return to high society's embrace. At the Prince's, Aglaia Epanchina, partly to pique her mother, covers for the General. After calling his friend Lebedev a fraudulent interpreter of Revelation, Ivolgin introduces himself to Aglaia:

> "I can't help but warn you, Aglaia Ivanovna, that it's all charlatanry on his part, believe me," quickly and suddenly put in General Ivolgin, who had been waiting as if on pins and needles, desiring with all his might to begin a conversation somehow. He sat himself next to Aglaia Ivanovna, "of course, a country house has its rights," he continued, "and its pleasures, and the device of such an uncommon introduction [*intrusa*] to interpret Revelation is an undertaking, like any other, and even a remarkable undertaking, mind-wise, but I . . . You, it seems, are looking at me with surprise? General Ivolgin has the honor of recommending himself. I held you in my arms, Aglaia Ivanovna."
>
> "Most pleased. I know Varvara Ardalionovna and Nina Aleksandrovna," muttered Aglaia, trying with all her might not to burst out laughing.
>
> Lizaveta Prokofievna flared up. Something that had long been boiling in her soul suddenly demanded release. She could not stand General Ivolgin, with whom she had been acquainted, only very long ago.
>
> "You're lying, my dear man, as usual with you, you never held her in your arms," she lashed out at him indignantly.
>
> "You've forgotten, Mummy, he did, for God's sake, in Tver," Aglaia suddenly affirmed. "We lived in Tver then. I was six then, I remember. He made me a bow and arrow and taught me how to shoot, and I killed a dove. Do you remember, we killed a dove together?"
>
> "And he brought me a cardboard helmet and a wooden sword then, I also remember!" Adelaida cried out.
>
> "I also remember it," affirmed Aleksandra. "You even quarreled then about the wounded dove, and you were placed in separate corners. Adelaida even stood there in her helmet with her sword."
>
> The General, in announcing to Aglaia that he had held her in his arms, had said it just so, simply to start a conversation and only because he almost always began conversations with young people in that way, if he found it necessary to get acquainted with them. But this time it happened, as if on purpose, that he had spoken the truth and, as if on purpose, even himself had forgotten that truth. So that when Aglaia suddenly now confirmed that they had shot a dove together, his memory lit up at once, and he remembered it down

Chapter 4

to the last detail, as it frequently happens that in one's declining years one remembers something from the distant past. It's difficult to convey what in this memory might have acted so strongly on the poor, and as usual, slightly inebriated general, but suddenly he was extraordinarily affected.

"I remember, I remember it all!" he exclaimed. "I was a staff-captain then. You—such a tiny thing, so cute. Nina Aleksandrovna . . . Gania . . . I was . . . received at your place. Ivan Fedorovich. . . . "

"And now you see where you've gotten to!" the general's wife rejoined. "It means that you still haven't drunk up all your noble feelings since it's affected you so strongly. But you've tortured your wife. Instead of guiding your children, you're sitting in debtor's prison. Get out of here, my dear man, go somewhere, stand behind a door in a corner and have a cry, recall your former innocence, maybe God will forgive you. Go then, go, I'm telling you seriously. There's nothing better for straightening yourself out than to remember the past with repentance."

But it was no use telling him that the speech was in earnest: the General, like all other continuously inebriated people, was very sentimental and, like all inebriated people who've fallen too far, could not easily endure memories from a happy past. He stood and quiescently turned toward the door, so that Lizaveta Prokofievna immediately felt sorry for him.

"Ardalion Aleksandrich, my dear man!" she called after him, "wait a moment. We are all sinners. When you feel that your conscience reproaches you less, come see me, we'll sit and have a chat about those old times. Maybe, after all, I am fifty times more sinful than you myself. Well, good-bye for now, go, there's nothing for you here . . . ," she suddenly feared that he would return. (8:202–4)

This lie revealed as true introduces the concept of memory. As Belknap notes, in *The Brothers Karamazov,* Dostoevsky associates memory with love, attention, and family, just as he associates forgetting with neglect and debauchery, an emotional loading that obtains in this scene of *The Idiot*.[17] Memory carries the charged affects of remembered relationships. Aglaia's act of generosity deeply touches the General. After her mother accuses him of lying, Aglaia redeems him. She not only affirms the truth of his words, she presents him positively as a warm, caring man who gave her a happy memory. Yet the memory cuts both ways for General Ivolgin. He feels shame's double edge: the poignancy of loss and the warmth of belonging. Aglaia's memory restores to him a forgotten part of himself. Her mother, Mme. Epanchina, identifies positive memories from the past as agents of change. She contrasts Ivolgin's current inebriation with his past honor, generously noting his noble feelings and counseling him to use them to remember and repent. She reminds him of divine forgiveness, advises him to forgive himself, and offers him an empathic bridge.

When Lebedev tries to avenge himself against Ivolgin's charges of charlatanry by denigrating the departing General, Mme. Epanchina forestalls him. She has set the General on the road to self-confrontation—the necessary agent for healing shame. For shame is about the self, about identity, and she has reminded him of his former self. Like her daughter, she extends a generous hand. By acknowledging the good that remains, she offers him a chance to reform himself in his own past image. Unlike Lebedev, who sees the General's drinking as the problem,[18] Mme. Epanchina sees his inebriation as a symptom of underlying shame. She hopes that remembering his nobility will help heal the General's shame. But she also realizes that he needs a helping hand. She empathically acknowledges the traces of good in him and offers him that which he seeks most—restoration to the community of good society.

Both scenes of exposure, the scenes with Nastasia Filippovna and Aglaia, differ dramatically in their nature, reception, and endings. The lapdog scene dramatizes an exposed plagiarism; the memory scene dramatizes a lie exposed as true. Nastasia Filippovna is a merciless audience; Aglaia Epanchina and her mother are merciful. Nonetheless, the two scenes portray Ivolgin as an older man trying to impress a young woman.[19] Both stories feature a weapon, a death, and discord. In both stories the phallic extensions of the General's self—the cigar, the bow and arrow—cause the death of an innocent creature (the dove emphasizes this innocence). The memory scene demonstrates Ivolgin's feckless disregard for the consequences of his actions. He teaches Aglaia to shoot and thus to kill.

The two scenes establish a progression leading to the General's self-confrontation. In the first, Nastasia Filippovna cruelly forces Ivolgin to confront his fabricated self. In the second, Mme. Epanchina urges him to compare his current and former selves, hoping memory of the latter will heal him. Moreover, in pointing Ivolgin to a moment when his actual and ideal selves coincided, Mme. Epanchina acts as the novel's social conscience.

The narrator also rouses reader sympathy for Ivolgin in this scene. His unaffected joy and pain softens Mme. Epanchina, whose ire turns to empathy. She thus serves as a guide for the narrative audience. We feel the initial distance between ourselves and Ivolgin shrink yet again. The old braggart's sincerity is touching—like Mme. Epanchina, we feel sorry for him, but we don't want him to get too close.

By the next scene portraying a lie, Ivolgin has become more self-conscious. He enacts a scene of self-awareness at being caught in a lie similiar to the one that the *Diary* writer describes in his article on lying. When General Ivolgin tells Prince Myshkin his story about being Napoleon's page boy, he gets carried away—and catches himself.

Napoleon's Page Boy

Ivolgin's extended lie about being Napoleon's page boy fills almost an entire subchapter of *The Idiot* (IV:4). In addition to being one of the funniest passages in Dostoevsky's *oeuvre* (Prince Myshkin laughs for a full ten minutes after the General leaves), the page boy story highlights the novel's father-children and isolation-community thematics, emphasizes the novel's metaliterary dimension, and lays bare the dynamics of audience response.

Dostoevsky carefully frames the scene. As the narrator makes clear, Ivolgin's story represents the General's response to an eyewitness account of the Napoleonic occupation of Moscow published in the journal *Russian Archive*. Since Myshkin had recommended the article to Ivolgin, he is the General's natural audience, but not his first. When Ivolgin schedules a private interview with Myshkin, a listener with "a heart," he obviously wants to avoid interruption by the unnamed but clearly indicated Lebedev, who "understands nothing" and is "completely, completely incapable of understanding! One must have a heart to understand!" (4:404). Whatever the original purpose of Ivolgin's meeting with Myshkin, it becomes the occasion to retell (and embellish) his story and thus counteract Lebedev's insulting response to it.

Ivolgin's interview with Myshkin begins with a discussion about memoirs and eyewitness accounts that flags the novel's metaliterary dimension. Ivolgin dismisses the journal account of the Napoleonic occupation as "crude and, of course, nonsensical. Perhaps even a lie [*lozh'*] at every step" (8:410). After the Prince defends its simple-heartedness, praising any eyewitness account as a "treasure," Ivolgin asserts, "In the editor's place, I wouldn't have published. As far as memoirs of eyewitnesses generally go, a crude, but amusing, liar [*lgunu*] is more quickly believed than a worthy person who's been in service" (8:410). The General thus raises issues of narrative reliability and audience response, issues of ongoing narrative interest in Dostoevsky's novel. A naive narrator, Ivolgin unwittingly offers a spectacular irony which distances Ivolgin from the narrative audience, which is familiar with his unreliability. Moreover, it compounds the unaccustomed distance between Ivolgin and his own audience, the Prince. The formality of the interview, as well as Myshkin's awareness that for several days Lebedev has been tormenting Ivolgin about the stolen money, discomfits the Prince. Myshkin feels "somehow strangely shy, as though his guest were porcelain, and he feared to break him at any minute." The narrator stresses the singularity of this situation: "earlier he'd never been shy with the General, it had never even occurred to him to be shy" (8:409). Dostoevsky has created a situation that demonstrates the importance of audience response to a speaker's sense of self: Myshkin understands that Ivolgin's honor is at stake.

Ivolgin's derogation of the *Russian Archive* memoir contributes to the metaliterary layering of Dostoevsky's novel. As Robin Feuer Miller points out in her groundbreaking study of narration in *The Idiot*, the novel's narrator becomes increasingly unreliable as his text unfolds. As the narrator moves away from his initially sympathetic portrayal of Prince Myshkin, the gap between narrative and authorial audiences widens.[20] In the end, while the narrative audience distances itself from the Prince, the authorial audience remains loyal to him. As Miller argues, "Dostoevsky . . . had designed a narrative style and a plot that would allow the reader, often through the very act of disagreeing with the narrator's assessment of events, to participate in the moral action of the novel."[21] One of the narrator's strategies to establish his own credibility is to discredit others' stories. Yet this is the very strategy General Ivolgin uses! Ivolgin dismisses Pavlishchev's version of Prince Myshkin's father's death. Likewise, he dismisses Lebedev's 1812 story as well as his credentials as an interpreter of Revelation. By adopting the strategy of a character whose credibility he undermines, Dostoevsky's narrator undermines his own. In a dazzling narrative parallel, Dostoevsky establishes the authority of his sympathetic authorial vision of Prince Myshkin by discrediting his narrator's story in the same way that the narrator discredits Ivolgin's. Author exposes narrator as narrator exposes character.

The opening frame of the page boy story not only signals this narrative parallel but also highlights the issue of authorial intentionality. To allay the General's suspicions about his readiness to believe him, the Prince mentions a contemporary autobiographer who begins his memoir with the story of being an infant fed by French soldiers during the occupation. The book, easily recognized by Russian readers, is Herzen's *My Past and Thoughts*. Dostoevsky thus frames Ivolgin's page boy story with a discussion of artistically constructed historical accounts, which emphasizes issues of narrative reliability, audience response, and narrative construction. Ivolgin's conscious choice of audience for his story, coupled with the narrator's observations about the Prince's sensitivity, highlights questions of audience response. Ivolgin's choice of subject permits Dostoevsky to weave together mimetic, thematic, and metaliterary issues—for Napoleon was more than a historical figure, he was a legendary hero self-consciously created by himself. Unlike Herzen, who considered his book "the reflection of history in someone who *accidentally* got in its way," Ivolgin places himself at the center of history. If the commentators are correct, Ivolgin criticizes the account of a civilian servant at the Novodevichy

Convent, the story of a marginal person at the periphery.²² Not content to have Napoleon pointed out to him, Ivolgin has Napoleon single him out. He thus represents himself as a physically small but historically central figure. Ivolgin tries to conceal the shame of his fall by fabricating a glorious past. Furthermore, in contrast to Herzen, who portrays himself as a representative of his age, Ivolgin adopts both the romantic view of himself as a unique individual and the realist view of himself as a representative of Russian national sentiment. Ivolgin thus outdoes rival accounts, portraying himself as Napoleon's sounding board. While Napoleon and Davout are considering their next move, "Suddenly Napoleon's glance falls on me by chance, a strange thought glimmers in his eyes. 'Child!' he says to me suddenly, 'what do you think: if I adopt Orthodoxy and free your slaves, will the Russians follow me or not?' 'Never!' I cried out indignantly. Napoleon was startled. 'In the eyes of this child shining with patriotism,' he said, 'I have read the opinion of the entire Russian people. Enough, Davout! It's all fantasies! Lay out your other plan'" (8:415). The other plan is the French army's entrenchment in Moscow, waiting for spring to break the Russian encirclement. In Ivolgin's account, Davout supports this. Once again, Napoleon turns to the young Ivolgin: "'My child! . . . what do you think of our intention?' It goes without saying that he asked me the way that sometimes a person of the greatest intelligence, at the last moment, flips a coin. Instead of to Napoleon, I turn to Davout and say as though inspired: 'Take yourself off, General, for home!' The project was destroyed. Davout shrugged his shoulders and, leaving, said in a whisper: *'Bah, il devient superstitieux!'* And on the next day the departure was announced" (8:416).

Ivolgin claims truth value for his story on grounds of historical accuracy: the French retreated from Moscow. In claiming responsibility for that retreat, Ivolgin leaves the path of historical verisimilitude but follows another generic convention. He portrays himself as a main character in a romantic historical novel, like those of Dumas père. He thus shows his Khlestakovian origins as a consumer of romanticism.

Ivolgin also attempts to establish his credibility by disregarding yet another story. Clearly alluding to a story Lebedev has told him, he rejects it according to strictly historical grounds of verisimilitude. He objects to Lebedev's claim that a French cannon blew his leg off by declaring that Lebedev would have been too young in 1812. When the Prince agrees, noting that Lebedev clearly has two intact legs, the General comically dismisses this fact as less relevant than his own claim that Chernosvitov had not yet invented his wooden leg: "'As far as the leg in sight—that's still, let's suppose, not completely unbelievable. He asserts that it's a Chernosvitov leg . . .' 'Ah yes, with a Chernosvitov leg, they say, one can dance.' 'I know for sure, sir. Chernosvitov, after inventing the leg, at that time ran to show me first thing. But the Chernosvitov leg was invented incomparably later. . . . And besides he claims that even his deceased wife in the course of their entire marriage didn't know that he, her husband, had a wooden leg'" (8:411). Ivolgin rejects Lebedev's story because it proposes an alternative hero. He ignores the Prince's support because mentioning Chernosvitov allows him to refocus attention on himself.

In fabricating Lebedev's rival story, Dostoevsky draws on the tale of Captain Kopeikin from Gogol's *Dead Souls*. The man who tells the tale wants to claim that the main character of Gogol's novel, Chichikov, is Captain Kopeikin, but someone observes that Chichikov isn't missing any limbs. The teller rebukes himself for losing track of this detail but tries to hedge by alluding to the current state of perfection attained by artificial limbs.

In concocting Ivolgin's Chernosvitov story, Dostoevsky also parodies history. He knew the actual Chernosvitov, a radical thinker who belonged to both Petrashevsky's and Speshnev's circles. In fact, Dostoevsky probably used him as one prototype for Peter Verkhovensky in *Demons*. In having Ivolgin claim that the notoriously secretive Chernosvitov (12:219–20) rushed to share his invention, Dostoevsky playfully shows his friends in the know how Ivolgin lacks sensitivity to others' personalities. Moreover, though Dostoevsky had other real-life models for General Ivolgin,[23] he transferred Chernosvitov's love of eloquence and Gogolian hyperbole (12:220) to Ivolgin, thus emphasizing Ivolgin's Gogolian roots.

Gogol also figures in Ivolgin's Napoleon story. After he published his "Overcoat," dress coats gained a metaliterary reference in the Russian tradition that Dostoevsky playfully inscribes into his mimetics and thematics. Ivolgin's sartorial awareness, for example, signals his realism as well as Dostoevsky's thematics of identity. Ivolgin claims that Napoleon notices him because of his nice clothes (8:413); he also remarks that he decided to become Napoleon's page boy not only because he felt personal sympathy for Napoleon, but because he was offered "a sparkling uniform, which means a lot for a child" (8:414). Keenly aware of clothing's importance as an indicator of social identity,[24] Dostoevsky frequently jots the words "uniform" and "gloves" in his notebooks to signify the assumption of roles in the public sphere; one dons the clothing and thereby assumes the role. Characters in *The Idiot* are acutely clothing conscious. Lebedev, for instance, has two dress coats. When Prince Myshkin reappears in Petersburg after his six-month absence, Lebedev leaves the room to put on his shabby dress coat, thus adopting a role of poverty. When Ivolgin lovingly describes the page boy uniform, he thereby demonstrates that he has succumbed to the era's enthusiasm for institutionalized military parades.[25]

Dostoevsky creates much of the humor in Ivolgin's page boy story by having him so thoroughly and subjectively rewrite history. Ivolgin's Napoleon becomes Ivolgin's alter ego. In Ivolgin's story, Napoleon's greatest suffering resulted not from the military nightmare of occupying Russia as winter approached, but from Emperor Alexander's silence. When the Prince notes that Napoleon wrote letters to Alexander, Ivolgin elaborates: "Strictly, we don't know precisely what kind of proposals he wrote, but he wrote every day, every hour, and letter after letter! He was horribly agitated" (8:414). In Ivolgin's account, Napoleon directs most of his energy to the single goal of gaining recognition from the Russian Emperor. Ivolgin is historically accurate: Alexander removed himself from Moscow,[26] thus making any personal communication impossible. Consequently, Napoleon, the most celebrated general of the century, could not obtain an audience with his foe. Alexander's hereditary rank undoubtedly exacerbated Napoleon's sense of being snubbed. Ivolgin's account stresses the extreme humiliation Napoleon suffers at Alexander's hands.

Dostoevsky thus has Ivolgin reflect his own story in the story he tells. As a result of his rejection by high society, particularly the hereditary nobility, Ivolgin finds himself in a position similar to that of his Napoleon. In response, he first sets out on his Napoleon's path: he writes letters. He also calls on those who reject him (which Napoleon cannot do). Like his Napoleon, he is very agitated. When his epistolary efforts fail, however, he resorts to another means of verbal compensation—lying. He constantly exaggerates his importance and fabricates a host of supporting stories. Like his Napoleon's letter writing, Ivolgin's lying can be seen as a frantic attempt to obtain recognition from a silent, rejecting, significant other.

Young Ivolgin proposes a way out of his father figure's shameful and isolating dilemma: "One night, when we were alone, I threw myself at him in tears (oh, I loved him!): 'Beg, beg forgiveness from Emperor Alexander!' I cried out. That is I should have expressed myself: 'Make peace with Emperor Alexander,' but as a child I naively expressed my whole thought" (8:414). Ivolgin's two formulas reveal two approaches to reconciliation. The child's "naive" expression, "beg forgiveness," calls for a private, personal interaction that requires humility. The adult Ivolgin's rewrite, "make peace," allows for more impersonal interaction, potentially mediated, that would reduce the humiliation inherent in Napoleon's position. The second approach might also cushion potential rejection by providing a third party to blame. Nonetheless, both are routes to the same end: reconciliation. If we regard the Napoleon in Ivolgin's story as an alter ego, a great general isolated from his natural companions by his own prideful actions, then the two formulas read as alternative scripts for reconciliation. Following the lapdog incident, Ivolgin impulsively begged forgiveness both by letter and in person. He thus followed the naive, unmediated path that his child persona urges on Napoleon. Telling the story gives him a chance to rewrite his script, however, so he does. His second suggestion, "make peace," indicates that, following adult reflection, he would try a path that requires considerably more diplomacy and potential mediation. He thus describes a script that reflects his current efforts to court Prince Myshkin.

What deters Ivolgin's Napoleon is the domino effect. While he might accept suppliant status vis-à-vis Alexander, he refuses to be humbled before his European counterparts: "'oh my child, I am prepared to kiss Emperor Alexander's feet, but on the other hand the Prussian king, and again the Austrian emperor, oh, to these an eternal hatred, and . . . finally . . . you don't understand anything about politics!'" (8:414). In historical terms, Alexander is at least Napoleon's equal, if not in some ways his superior. (One need only think of the picturesque meeting of Alexander and Napoleon at Tilsit in 1807, when the two were simultaneously rowed to the tented raft in the middle of the Nieman to negotiate.[27]) Napoleon can humble himself before the emperor of the vast kingdom that had subdued his troops but cannot grovel before those whom he has conquered. Ivolgin's story thus reveals his own social snobbery. Ivolgin fabricates this extended version of the Napoleon story following his break with Lebedev, who insists on equality between storytellers. Ivolgin perceives the blatant falsity of Lebedev's 1812 story as an act of disrespect. Like his Napoleon, Ivolgin can grovel before the Belokonskys and Epanchins, his former social equals, but he cannot make peace with Lebedev, his social inferior.

Ivolgin's story also highlights Napoleon's isolation. Surrounded by his retinue, he is nonetheless far from his family and his native France. After their mutual embrace, the general-to-be inserts himself into history by suggesting that Napoleon write to the former empress: "'Write, do write a letter to Empress Josephine!' I sobbed out to him." Napoleon's response touches on some of Dostoevsky's favorite themes—memory and love: "Napoleon shuddered, thought a bit and said to me: 'You've reminded me of the third heart who loves me; thank you, my friend'" (8:417). The Prince applauds this advice: "You acted wonderfully . . . among evil thoughts you directed him to a good feeling" (8:417).[28] The Prince's response reaffirms the positive roles of memory and love in the novel. Significantly, in this account, the European adult suffers from evil thoughts while the Russian child connects him to positive memories and emotions. Dostoevsky thus boldly inscribes his authorial message along with some of his favorite oppositions—Europe vs. Russia, adult vs. child—into Ivolgin's clichéd, sentimental story. The Russian child proposes love as consolation: Europe's greatest contemporary general may have lost his Russian campaign, but he still has his wife and son. This part of the story also reflects Ivolgin's sense of his own position. Following his break with Lebedev, Ivolgin returns home from voluntary exile at Lebedev's. The suffering General's own unconscious (the child in him) thus offers him consolation. He may have lost his friend Lebedev, but he still has his wife and children.

Ivolgin's Napoleon story culminates in a farewell scene between the defeated world-conqueror and the ten-year-old Russian patriot. As Ivolgin tells it, Napoleon turns to him and says: "'I don't want to take you away from your mother and am not taking you with me! . . . but I would like to do something for you.' He was already sitting on his horse. 'Write me something in my sister's album as a memory,' I uttered, getting timid because he was very upset and gloomy. He turned, asked for a pen, took the album. 'How old is your sister?' he asked me, pen in hand already. 'Three years old,' I answered. '*Petite fille alors.*' And he jotted into the album: '*Ne mentez jamais!* Napoléon, votre ami sincère'" (8:417). This invented interchange between a political visionary and a small-time fantasizer, like Ivolgin's Kolpakov and lapdog stories, indicates Ivolgin's growing recognition of his own weakness for lying.

This scene's comic self-consciousness also reveals Dostoevsky's authorial hand. In Dostoevsky's *Crime and Punishment*, Napoleon represents the political visionary for whom the ends justify even the most violent means. He is thus a master of *lozh'*—deliberate, self-interested lies. By having Ivolgin attribute the advice "Never lie!" to Napoleon, Dostoevsky emphasizes how Ivolgin's narcissistic projection distorts the legendary givens. He also has Napoleon, that self-creator of public image, assume the role of yet another self-created figure—Cervantes' Knight of the Mirrors. Just as Samson Carrasco takes on the role of lovesick knight errant to reflect Don Quixote back to himself, so Dostoevsky has Ivolgin attribute words to his Napoleon that reflect his growing self-awareness. This story thus reflects the beginning of Ivolgin's self-cure. Even though he is lying, the process of storytelling leads to a glimmer of truth. Ivolgin creates Napoleon in his own image. In recapitulating scenes of Napoleon's shame, Ivolgin confronts his own.

The story of Ivolgin's parting from Napoleon also echoes the scene in Gogol's *Inspector General* where Khlestakov writes in the mayor's daughter's album. Just as Khlestakov proposes verses that are inappropriate to his audience,[29] so Napoleon's command seems particularly inappropriate for a three-year-old girl. He thus proves as inflexible as Ivolgin himself, for Ivolgin is unable to abandon his public persona even in the private sphere. What gifts did he bring the Epanchin girls, after all, but weapons? Dostoevsky also entertains readers with Ivolgin's incongruous juxtaposition of public and private. Albums are repositories of public words in private places. Napoleon is not in a drawing room, however, but on a horse. Ivolgin's claim that his three-year-old sister has an album, which he happens to have with him, heightens the scene's humor and strains audience credulity. Ivolgin's claims for the document's authenticity reinforce the comic hyperbole, "That page, in a gold frame, under glass, hung all her life at my sister's in the drawing room, in the most conspicuous place, until her very death—she died in childbirth; where it is now—I do not know . . . " (8:417).[30]

Finally, by having his child persona ask for a written token of remembrance, Ivolgin shows an awareness of how words connect people. Napoleon's/Ivolgin's shame may not be undone, but the wounds can be healed by communication. Dostoevsky's authorial hand is never more present than when he emphasizes the ties that bind.

Shame and Sympathy: Audience Response

General Ivolgin's lying illustrates the two extremes of narcissism: shame and grandiosity. In stating that Napoleon asks for his advice in "the way that sometimes a person of the greatest intelligence, at the last moment, flips a coin" (8:416), Ivolgin unwittingly characterizes his own narcissistic sense of self. The Russian words for flipping a coin—*orel* (heads) and *reshka* (tails)—literally mean "eagle" and "grating." Napoleon thus turns to Ivolgin as either an eagle (the king of birds, associated in folktales and legends with royalty, historically associated with the Russian imperial emblem and with Napoleon) or as a grating (an inanimate object, usually of a baser metal, which functions as a barrier). Eagle and grating, glory and ignominy, flight and imprisonment, are two sides of the same coin. They are also two sides of Ivolgin's shame experiences: he flees shame by drinking; borrowing money to drink leads to his imprisonment. Ivolgin (the oriole) thus acknowledges his dual self-image.

Ivolgin's lying allows him to rewrite history featuring his ideal. He becomes transported by his self-fashioning, however. Before a sympathetic audience, his grandiosity and exaltation know no bounds: "'Oh Prince!' exclaimed the General, intoxicated with his story to the point that, perhaps, he already could not stop himself even before the most extreme imprudence,—you say: 'That all happened!' But there was more, I assure you, there was a lot more! All that is only the miserable, political facts. But I will tell you again, I was witness to the nocturnal tears and moans of that great man; and that no one has seen, except me!" (8:416). Ivolgin's claim to exclusive knowledge of the era's most famous figure reflects his desire to feel important. His eyewitness claim allows him to undo his own shame by witnessing someone else's. By inscribing features of Ivolgin's Kolpakov story into his Napoleon story, Dostoevsky emphasizes Ivolgin's narrative naïveté while craftily displaying his own mastery. He also cannily deepens his psychological portrait of Ivolgin. Once again Dostoevsky magnifies his novel's mimetic and metaliterary dimensions in a single stroke.

As the Prince's response makes clear, Ivolgin's sense of self depends on audience response. Sensitive to the General's fragility, the Prince reassures him:

> "You entertained and . . . finally . . . it's so interesting; I'm so grateful to you!"
>
> "Prince!" said the General, again squeezing his hand until it hurt and looking fixedly at him with gleaming eyes, as though suddenly coming to his senses and as though stunned by some unexpected thought, "Prince! You are so kind, so open-hearted, that I even feel sorry for you sometimes. I look at you with tenderness; oh, God bless you! Let your life begin and flourish . . . in love. Mine is over! Oh, forgive me, forgive me!"
>
> He exited quickly, covering his face with his hands. The Prince could not doubt the sincerity of his distress. He likewise understood that the old man had exited intoxicated by his success; but he had the presentiment nonetheless that he was one of that order of liars who, although they lie to the point of sensuality and even to the point of self-oblivion, nonetheless even at the very highest point of their intoxication still suspect to themselves that in fact they are not believed, and even that they can't be believed. In his current situation, the old man might come to himself, be ashamed beyond measure, suspect the Prince of immense compassion for him, take offense. . . .
>
> His presentiments came to pass. (8:417–18)

As this passage demonstrates, Ivolgin lacks a sense of measure, a deficiency that Dostoevsky elsewhere identifies as quintessentially Russian. Ivolgin gets so carried away by his story's success that he oversteps a limit that awakens his self-consciousness. "[A]shamed beyond measure," Ivolgin ruptures ties with the Prince, thereby isolating himself. Less than a day later, the General flees his house with his son Kolia, confesses that he has caused his wife misery, and suffers a stroke in the streets. While confessing, Ivolgin repeatedly calls his son "*le roi de Rome*," a return to his identification with Napoleon and the novel's father-children thematics. Like his Napoleon, Ivolgin consoles himself in a moment of humiliation, defeat, and exile with thoughts of his young son's loyalty.

As General Ivolgin tells his stories to different groups of people, three patterns of audience response emerge: sympathetic belief, sympathetic disbelief, antipathetic disbelief. Ivolgin tells his Kolpakov story to a fairly sympathetic audience, yet as he finishes, his embarrassed wife protests "*mon mari se trompe*." When he tells his lapdog story, Nastasia Filippovna exposes him brutally. When he declares that he had held Aglaia in his arms, Mme. Epanchina proclaims him a liar, but Aglaia and her sisters defend him. Seeing the General's emotional reaction to his reawakened memories, Mme. Epanchina relents and extends a hand of reconciliation, leaving the General to his own conscience. The Prince acts as a sympathetic audience for the General's Napoleon story, but the General gets so transported that he is ashamed and breaks with the Prince. Finally, on the day of his stroke, the General tells a story whose truth is hostilely challenged by two sons—his own son Gania and his mistress's son Ippolit. These patterns of response increase the novel's verisimilitude while modeling a range of responses for Dostoevsky's readers. By having his least sympathetic characters respond most hostilely, Dostoevsky promotes sympathy and discourages shaming.

The shame Gania inflicts upon his father drives Ivolgin out of the house. After Gania seconds Ippolit's suggestion that Captain Eropegov, the subject of Ivolgin's story, never existed, Ivolgin curses his house and flees. Gania compounds his father's shame by shouting after him, "And don't steal!" Tormented by Lebedev, expelled from her house by Mme. Epanchina, taunted by Ippolit and Gania, the General runs into the street, followed by his faithful son Kolia. In his last lengthy speech, General Ivolgin recapitulates the charges against him, denies them, pities himself, but then, for the first time in the novel, thinks of someone other than himself. He expresses pity and love for his wife and repents the grief he has caused her:

"There was no Eropegov! No Eroshka Eropegov!"—he exclaimed in a frenzy, coming to a halt in the street. "And that's my son, my very own son! Eropegov, the person who substituted as a brother for me for eleven months, for whom I at a duel . . . Prince Vygoretsky, our captain, said to him over a bottle: 'You, Grisha, where did you get your Anna [a medal], what do you say to that?'—'On the battlefields of my fatherland, that's where I received it!' I cry out: 'Bravo, Grisha!' Well, a duel resulted then and there, and then he got married . . . to Maria Petrovna Su . . . Sutugina and was killed on the battlefields. . . . A bullet ricocheted off the cross on my chest and straight into his forehead. 'I'll never forget this as long as I live!'" he cried and fell on the spot. I . . . I served honestly, Kolia; I served nobly, but disgrace—disgrace pursues me! You and Nina will come to my grave . . . 'Poor Nina!' I used to call her that, Kolia, long ago, at the beginning still, and she so loved . . . Nina, Nina! What have I done to your fate! For what can you love me, patient soul! Your mother has an angel's soul, Kolia, do you hear, an angel's!" (8:419)

In expressing his outrage and shock at Gania's betrayal, General Ivolgin illustrates the narrative dynamics of audience belief. Ivolgin's story demonstrates that belief in others is necessary for social interactions; Dostoevsky's story adds that belief in God is necessary for life itself. Significantly, the scene starts with an altercation between the General and Ippolit, whom Ivolgin calls "an atheist," who is "dying from malice and lack of faith" (8:395). Though put into the mouth of a frenzied old man, the charge that Ippolit's insolence results from his atheism expresses a Dostoevskian hobbyhorse—that religious belief is a positive moral force on earth. These charges also express the concomitant idea that lack of belief in God dissolves the bonds of community.

Ivolgin's story specifically addresses the issue of disbelief and its consequences. First of all, he confirms Eropegov's existence by providing his biography. In his telling, their superior officer, Captain Vygoretsky, a prince by birth, doubts Eropegov's bravery. Eropegov defends his honor and Ivolgin seconds him, in both word and deed, thus recalling Ivolgin's earlier self-identification as a musketeer. Ivolgin compares Eropegov to a substitute brother; he also acts as his second in a duel, thereby living up to the musketeer motto. Furthermore, Ivolgin represents his friend as a patriot and war hero, like Ivolgin himself, a detail that echoes Ivolgin's contention that his own father died fighting for his country. Thus a thematic appears, however comically, in Ivolgin's stories—belief mandates action. Belief in friends, family, and country dictates the active defense of those ideals, even at the risk of one's life. And, as Dostoevsky shows, belief works both ways. Others' belief in one contributes to one's honor and identity.

In his telling of Ivolgin's story, Dostoevsky develops this thematic: he further implies that belief in God mandates active love for one's fellow human beings. As both Lebedev and Mme. Epanchina claim (see chapter 8), belief in God creates the possibility of human community. Ivolgin's story describes the results of doubting and mockery: Prince Vygoretsky's doubts lead to a duel. Ivolgin defends his friend, an act of brotherly love. Ivolgin's speech may seem digressive and foolish, but its inner logic correlates with one of Dostoevsky's most cherished themes. In his telling, Ivolgin portrays himself as indirectly responsible for Eropegov's death—a bullet ricochets off Ivolgin's service medal and kills his friend. Ivolgin thus re-presents the experience of war—events outside of his control that lead to death and loss. The detail of Ivolgin's service medal works two ways, however. First, it evidences Ivolgin's tendency to boast—even in this narrative, he cannot resist making himself at least the equal of his fallen comrade by having an equal decoration and taking equal risks. Second, with this tragicomic detail, Ivolgin takes indirect responsibility for his friend's death. His narrative thus embellishes his self-image but does not deny his responsibility. Ivolgin (a man who claims to have thirteen bullets in his chest) should have died, but as a result of his war heroism, he wears a medal that protects him. His friend dies instead. Ivolgin further emphasizes the situation's ambiguity by claiming that he served honestly and nobly but that "disgrace pursues" him. He blames events outside his control for his disgrace and loss. In similar fashion, Ivolgin's medal represents his noble service but causes his friend's death. His admission of indirect responsibility for the loss of his friend then prepares the way for his admission of full responsibility for his wife's losses. This detail thus touches another Dostoevskian hobby-horse—the responsibility of each for all.

Eropegov's tragicomic death cry, "I'll never forget this as long as I live!" evokes yet another Dostoevskian trademark—memory. This cry could almost be Ivolgin's. He tells a story to his sympathetic son Kolia to undo the trauma of his son Gania's hostile disbelief. He dies defending himself against Gania's charges. Ivolgin's last word is the name of Eropegov's wife—a name that (along with Eropegov's) he had difficulty remembering earlier. The attempt to remember a name from the past leads him to thoughts of his own honorable past, to his current disgrace, and to his wife, Nina Aleksandrovna, his faithful companion through good times and bad. This memory, and his repentance before her, redeem him in Dostoevsky's authorial eyes.

As the culmination of a progression, this story harks back to Ivolgin's other stories and their audience reception. Ivolgin's memory of his wife recalls Ivolgin's Napoleon story and the incident that earns Prince Myshkin's praise—reminding Napoleon of his wife. At a moment when Ivolgin feels cast out and rejected by his brother figure Lebedev and his own son Gania, he remembers someone who loves him. He has thus internalized the story he told the Prince. No young Ivolgin (even though one is present) reminds him; he remembers himself. He does exactly what Mme. Epanchina prescribed for him—he remembers the past with repentance. He remembers the past merits that earned his wife's early love and compares them with his current shame; he repents in her name.

Though Ivolgin dies from shame, it is not all externally imposed. The dynamic is thus complex. The immediate cause of his stroke is the shame visited on him by Gania and Ippolit following so closely as it does the shame visited on him by Lebedev.[31] But he has also internalized a dose of shame, which is signaled by his break with the Prince. Ivolgin feels exposed after his Napoleon story, not because the Prince has been a hostile audience, but because he overindulges and then examines himself. His pre-stroke story and confession of guilt to his faithful son Kolia further evidence his self-confrontation. Ivolgin takes two steps necessary for overcoming shame and rejoining community: he focuses attention outside of himself, and he acknowledges both his guilt (responsibility for others) and his shame (the fact of his fall). This deathbed acknowledgment, in turn, increases authorial audience sympathy for the General.

Chapter 4

The Homeopathic Dose

In *The Idiot*, Dostoevsky demonstrates that shame can give rise to lying, but also to healing. As Miller points out in her paper "Dostoevsky and the Homeopathic Dose," Dostoevsky prescribes like to cure like.[32] Ivolgin lies because he is ashamed of himself. He has lost his identity as a military authority, a socially respected figure, and a head of household. His lying recalls his past status but also contains recognition of his fall. Both Mme. Epanchina and Lebedev prescribe doses of shame to cure Ivolgin, whose blameworthy actions are themselves rooted in shame. Mme. Epanchina prescribes a minute dose of shame applied internally as preparation for social reintegration. Lebedev, on the other hand, treats the General with a liberal dose of externally applied shame.[33] He shames Ivolgin before and after the General returns his money (thus undoing his crime), first by swearing he believes his friend, then by pretending the money was not returned. This ruse drives the General crazy. The Prince tries to appease his pain, but Ivolgin's sense of shame forces him to flee. Further shamed by Gania, the General collapses. Confronted externally and internally by his own shame, the General dies—literally and figuratively mortified.

Lebedev suggests to the Prince that if he shames Ivolgin sufficiently, the General will return to his wife and family. The General's death proves him wrong. Mme. Epanchina, on the other hand, holds that primary responsibility for a person's actions lies with that person. She diagnoses compassionately. She understands that shame needs no external witnesses; conscience suffices. She recommends a minute dose of self-applied shame, an acknowledgment and acceptance of shortcomings, as a corrective to shame-based behavior. And, like her relative the Prince, she proffers an empathic bridge.

All of the General's lies carry the seeds of his redemption, because they reveal that he recognizes, howeverly latently, that he bears responsibility for his actions. The Kolpakov story shifts attention away from Kolpakov's initial guilt but does not deny his crime. The lapdog story shifts blame but does not deny social transgression. The Napoleon story idealizes Ivolgin's pre-military school childhood but ends with Napoleon's admonition "*Ne mentez jamais*." The Eropegov story portrays Ivolgin as a true friend, yet one indirectly responsible for Eropegov's death. The General flees his actions and his defective, shame-ridden self by verbal self-fashioning, yet his stories reveal awareness of the cover-up and thus his conscience. Sitting in Dostoevsky's authorial audience, we see that while Ivolgin's conscience mortifies him, it also redeems him. One must be capable of feeling shame to be saved.

Authorial Strategy

A secondary character in the novel, General Ivolgin figures prominently in its metaliterary construction. Ivolgin is a storyteller, like Dostoevsky himself. In representing Ivolgin's stories, Dostoevsky raises issues about the construction of narratives. The page boy story represents a new stage in Ivolgin's storytelling. For the first time, Ivolgin is sensitive beforehand to audience response. He divides the world into listeners "with a heart," such as Myshkin, and those who are without heart and thus "completely incapable of understanding," such as Lebedev. In Dostoevsky's last novel, Fedor Karamazov likewise polarizes audience response as he anticipates Elder Zosima's sympathetic response and his relative Miusov's hostile response.

Although the General is occasionally more sensitive to his audiences, his narcissism curbs his narrative efficacy. Dostoevsky emphasizes Ivolgin's limits by having his ideal audience, Prince Myshkin, also be an ideal storyteller. As Miller writes: The Prince "constantly consolidates the events of his life into an object (or form) which he can then give as a gift, a gift of insight; he changes his own life into art. All the stories he has told have derived from his own experiences, yet he has transmuted them into symbolic myths."[34] Ivolgin's enterprise differs significantly from Myshkin's, mostly because he lacks insight. Ivolgin's Kolpakov story most blatantly exemplifies this deficiency: Ivolgin tells a story of restoration, not resurrection. By underscoring the lack of transcendence in Ivolgin's account, the narrator not only marks the novel's thematics of death and resurrection but also reveals Ivolgin's shortcomings as a narrator. Obsessed with his own identity problems, Ivolgin cannot see the mythic pattern behind his story. His narcissism degrades his narrative skill. Because he insists on mimetic truth he overlooks mythic truth.

Ivolgin's stories are stories about identity—his identity. Dostoevsky's stories are not only stories about human identity; they are also stories that express, create, and transform human identity. While Dostoevsky the author may disagree with his narrator's final stance on Prince Myshkin, thus forcing the authorial audience to judge for themselves, he and his narrator see eye to eye about General Ivolgin and can thus guide reader response. Ivolgin increases in importance as he moves from being shameless to being shamed. Ivolgin also increases in importance because his story serves as a variant of the novel's main plot. Ivolgin is not only a storyteller but also a social type—a fallen general. His lying allows him to fashion a praiseworthy self-image, but it also exposes him to critical scrutiny. The activity of lying dynamically illustrates one of the novel's themes—community vs. isolation. While Ivolgin's lying shows that he wishes to be included in a community, it also shows that he has been excluded. Furthermore, it threatens him with yet greater isolation: Ivolgin's self-absorption blinds him to audience as other and thus increases the distance between him and them.

Nonetheless, in the course of the novel, Ivolgin's lying functions therapeutically. As Dostoevsky's *Diary* writer says, "there's nothing more pleasant than to talk about one's illness, if only one finds a listener; and once one begins to talk, it's already impossible not to lie; it even cures the patient" (21:118). Ivolgin's lying exemplifies repetition compulsion. All of his stories are about honor and loss of honor. Ivolgin covers the same ground over and over; his lying reframes and repeats the trauma of his lost status. The process of storytelling, however, helps cure him of the disease he suffers most from—"narcissism" in today's parlance, "self-enclosure" in Dostoevsky's. Seen as a progression, Ivolgin's stories illustrate his developing self-awareness and concomitant awareness of others. For most of the novel, Ivolgin denies responsibility for his actions; he represents himself as a positive hero who has become a victim of contingency. Nonetheless, his stories contain seeds of recognition that he has done wrong.

Once Ivolgin can admit his guilt and face his shame, he rejoins his family and dies in its midst. Dostoevsky the author devotes so much space to Ivolgin's story because it dynamically illustrates the authorial thematics of isolation and community and the responsibility of each for all. Although a secondary character, Ivolgin contributes centrally to the authorial exploration of metaliterary issues such as the nature and purposes of fiction, the relationship of truth to fiction, the function of inserted narratives, and the dynamics of audience response. Ippolit's and Gania's hostility to Ivolgin's Eropegov story, like Nastasia Filippovna's hostility to the lapdog story, shifts readers' sympathies. Entertained by the General's outlandish stories, we are grateful, as the Prince is, for a good laugh. We are angered by Ippolit's and Gania's hostility, even though we recognize that it arises from their own shame. After all, Ivolgin has humiliated Ippolit by becoming his mother's irresponsible lover, and he has humiliated Gania by his current dissolution and loss of social position. These sons, like Nastasia Filippovna, pass on their shame, exposing the father who betrayed them. Yet, in Dostoevsky's novel, a father's judgment does not excuse that of his children. Dostoevsky takes a plot line from another literary text to arouse readers' compassion for this shame-filled father. Like Lear, Ivolgin curses his family as he flees from them. Like Lear, he goes partly mad. And like Lear, Ivolgin admits responsibility for his own fall and thus for his family's suffering.

Though readers know Ivolgin is a liar and an alcoholic, a man who has ruined himself and his family, two of the novel's most positive characters—his wife and younger son—love him and stand by him. As Dostoevsky's narrator notes in discussing Ivolgin, "Let's not forget that the reasons for human action are usually countlessly more complex and diverse than we always explain them afterwards, and they are rarely definitively outlined" (8:402). In deepening Ivolgin's character, Dostoevsky implicates his readers in the general's drama of lying and exposure in five acts. He reels us in affectively, as witnesses to another's shame, cognitively, as appreciators of the novel's metaliterary art, and ethically. In such a mimetically complex world, we cannot pass simple judgments.

Viewing Ivolgin's story as a shame drama that ends fairly well casts light on Nastasia Filippovna's tragic end. Like the General, Nastasia Filippovna is fallen. Like him, she experiences social shame and exclusion. Unlike the General, Nastasia Filippovna is a woman. Her fall occurs in late adolescence; therefore, she never has the social experiences that formed the General: being part of a social class, a military unit, a family. In short, gender politics affect her fate. She does not have an equal repository of memories of community to draw upon as she struggles with her social shame. She cannot return to her family because she does not have one. Throughout the novel, Nastasia Filippovna is greatly moved by the Prince's repeated attempts to undo her shame through his generous acts of love and acceptance. Yet Nastasia Filippovna remains focused on public opinion. She cannot envision a social world that accepts her. Like the General, she repeats her self-lacerating trauma. Unlike the General, she ultimately chooses self-destruction.

Yet, just as Dostoevsky complicates reader response to Ivolgin, so he complicates our response to Nastasia Filippovna. She does not immediately succumb to self-destruction. She vacillates before running away with Rogozhin. She attempts to gain a positive sense of self by reciprocating the Prince's compassion. She tries to give him happiness by promoting his marriage to Aglaia, the woman he loves. Like Myshkin, she comes to idealize Aglaia, whose initial openness to correspondence with her encourages Nastasia Filippovna's hope of acceptance. But Aglaia cannot and does not live up to the expectations of those who idealize her. She is a flesh-and-blood woman whose jealousy Nastasia Filippovna interprets as condescension, which reignites her sense of shame. Once shame reenters the picture, all is lost.

Shame, as Dostoevsky shows, arises unexpectedly, disorients all in its wake, and kindles a painful self-consciousness that can, in the long run, lead to change, but that, in the short run, usually leads to greater pain and shame. While confronting shame has the potential to heal, it can also ravage and destroy. Tied as it is to identity, shame can be a matter of life and death.

chapter five

Confessional Moments

> My friend, I've been lying [*lgal*] all my life. Even when I spoke the truth [*pravdu*]. I never spoke for truth's sake [*dlia istiny*], but only for my own, I knew that before, but only now do I see.... Oh where are those friends whom I have insulted with my friendship all my life? And everyone, everyone! *Savez-vous*, I, perhaps, am lying [*lgu*] even now; certainly I am lying [*lgu*] even now. The main thing is that I believe myself when I lie [*lgu*]. The hardest thing in life is to live and not lie [*ne lgat'*] . . . and . . . and not to believe one's own lies [*lzhi*], yes, yes, that's precisely it! (10:497;652)
>
> — STEPAN TROFIMOVICH VERKHOVENSKY, *Demons*

> "Blessed man! Let me kiss your hand," Fedor Pavlovich rushed up and quickly smacked the elder on his thin hand. "Just so, just so, it feels pleasurable to be offended. You put it so well, I've never heard it before. Just so, just so, I've been getting offended all my life to the point of pleasure; I've been getting offended for the aesthetics, because it's not only pleasurable, it's sometimes even beautiful to be offended;—that's what you've forgotten, great elder: it's beautiful! I'm going to jot that down! And I've been lying [*lgal*], lying [*lgal*], decidedly my whole life, every day and every hour. In truth, I'm a lie [*lozh'*] and a father of lies [*otets lzhi*]!" (14:41;44)
>
> — FEDOR PAVLOVICH KARAMAZOV, *The Brothers Karamazov*

D ostoevsky's experiments in confession not only manifest his lifelong polemic with Rousseau, they also express his lifelong interest in narrative form.[1] Both lying and confession are rhetorics of identity; they are vehicles for self-presentation. For those who lie and those who confess, audience response matters greatly. If their audiences listen generously, liars experience a bolstering of self-esteem and confessees experience a healing of shame. On the other hand, if their audiences listen skeptically, liars and confessees experience heightened shame—provided, however, that they are not shameless. This chapter, like chapter 3, pairs the shameless Fedor Karamazov with a shamed character, here Stepan Verkhovensky.

The chapter epigraphs represent two histrionic confessions that admit to the same sin, occur during a moment of insight, use biblical language, and hyperbolize. But one is an Augustinian, repentant confession; the other is unrepentant.[2] The liars who pronounce them differ radically. Stepan Verkhovensky defends aesthetics and Raphael's Sistine Madonna. Fedor Karamazov revels in scandal and desecrates icons. Stepan Verkhovensky observes social etiquette and defends it ethically. Fedor Karamazov violates social etiquette and exposes it as hypocrisy. This incongruous pair of hyperbolic liars also receives very different coverage from Dostoevsky's narrators. The narrator of *Demons* casts doubt on Stepan Verkhovensky's sincerity by presenting his confession as yet one more example of his self-deceiving friend's self-devised humiliations. By contrast, the narrator of *Brothers Karamazov* highlights Fedor Karamazov's continuous posturing but also suggests that sincerity coexists with falsity in Fedor's soul. The interchange in the monastery that leads to Fedor Karamazov's histrionic confession, however, reveals a surprising similarity between the two: both Karamazov and Verkhovensky senior derive pleasure from self-fabricated humiliations. In what follows I discuss this deep and unexpected similarity, the generic differences between the two confessions, and the narrative dynamics of shame in both novels.

Shameful Pleasures

After identifying shame as the source of Fedor's shameless buffoonery, Zosima explicates the shameful pleasure Fedor receives from exaggerating offenses:

> A man who lies to himself [*lgushii sebe samomu*] is often the first to take offense. It sometimes feels very good to take offense, doesn't it? And surely he knows that no one has offended him, and that he himself has invented the offense and told lies [*nalgal*] just for the beauty of it, that he has exaggerated to create a picture, that he has grabbed onto a word and made a mountain out of a molehill—he knows all of that, and still he is the first to take offense, takes offense to the point of pleasure, to the feeling of great satisfaction, and thus he gets to the point of true hostility. . . . Do get up from your knees and sit down, I beg you, these posturings are also false. . . . (14:41;44)

The rhetoric of this passage mimics its content. Zosima links lying and taking offense, a point he elaborates with a question— "It sometimes feels very good to take offense, doesn't it?" The subsequent sentence describes the process of self-laceration, repeating forms of the word "offense" four times just as the person who is exaggerating the offense repeats to himself with heightening emotion the self-fabricated offense, until Zosima as narrator describes the climactic emotion felt by his hypothetical person—hostility.

The passage mimics the hyperbolized, repetitious build-up of offense that then seeks release. In concluding that Fedor Pavlovich's exhibitionist gestures "are also false," Zosima compares them to the buffoon's hyperbolically self-amplified shame, and thus describes how Fedor enacts his abasement.

While elders as a group are considered particularly canny, one is nonetheless struck by the felt experience in Zosima's rhetoric. Hundreds of pages later, in Zosima's autobiographical teachings, readers find the source of Zosima's wisdom. As a young officer, Zosima is offended that the young woman with whom he had been flirting marries while he is away. When he learns that she had been engaged, he is even more offended: "'[H]ow was it possible that almost everyone knew, and I alone knew nothing?'" His shame finds release in anger. He recalls, "'I remember with astonishment that this revenge and wrath were extremely burdensome and loathsome for me, because, having an easy character, I could not stay angry with anyone for long, and therefore had to incite myself artificially, as it were, and in the end became ugly [*bezobrazen*] and absurd'" (14:269;297). With the analytical skill of a behavioral therapist, Zosima details the process of artificially inciting himself to hatred. He observes that his vanity blinded him to everything but his own merits. His rage, however, originates in shame. He may have been oblivious to her fiancé, but others were not: "'And that was what offended me most of all.'" Shame leads to anger and desire for revenge, but he cannot sustain either without fabricating a supporting fiction—that she had been laughing at him. "'Later, of course, I realized and remembered that she had not been laughing in the least, but, on the contrary, had jokingly broken off such conversations with a jest and turned to other topics instead—but at the time I could not realize that and began to burn with vengeance.'" Here Zosima describes the reactive process of turning passive to active; his shame leads him to strike out and harm someone. By pretending his love was scorned, he fans the flames of his hate and precipitates his fateful duel.

Like Zosima, Stepan Verkhovensky goads himself artificially, exaggerating imagined offenses. Like Fedor Karamazov, Stepan has made a habit of this. As the narrator of *Demons* observes, Stepan Verkhovensky's first deathbed confession (he makes three) follows a pattern that he has repeated for twenty years with Varvara Stavrogina (10:496;650): after encounters with Varvara, Stepan would rage (a typical response to shame) and slander her, then he would feel ashamed and confess—either orally to the narrator or in writing to Varvara. For example, he would send for the narrator or run to him solely to announce "that Varvara Petrovna was 'an angel of delicacy,'" while he was just the opposite" (10:13;14). Likewise, Stepan also "described more than once to her in the most eloquent letters, and confessed, over his full signature, that no more than a day ago, for instance, he had been telling some outsider that she kept him out of vanity, that she envied his learning and talents, that she hated him and was only afraid to show her hatred openly for fear he would leave her and thereby damage her literary reputation; that he despised himself on account of that and had resolved to die a violent death, and was only waiting for a last word from her that would decide it all, and so on, and so on, in the same vein" (10: 13;14). After the narrator reads one of these letters once, he begs his friend not to send it, but Stepan histrionically replies, "Impossible ... honor ... duty ... I shall die if I do not confess everything to her, everything" (10:13;14–15). Unlike Zosima, who breaks out of this cycle, and unlike Fedor Karamazov, who responds aggressively, Stepan Verkhovensky internalizes the shame and wallows in it. He creates a scenario of self-vilification with Varvara cast as his savior, another shame script.

The process that Zosima describes and that all three enact involves social transgression. By insulting his rival, Zosima transgresses social decorum; he shames his rival in public, albeit in a ritual and therefore socially acceptable manner.[3] By following the rules of ritual insult, Zosima gives his rival the opportunity to challenge him to a duel, the social ritual for restoring honor. He thus ensures the comfort of his audience and of Dostoevsky's readers, who are also positioned as witnesses.

Stepan Verkhovensky slanders Varvara Stavrogina behind her back, causing discomfort to himself, to *Demons'* narrator, Mr. G-v, and to Dostoevsky's readers. By acting dishonorably, Stepan intensifies his shame and turns to writing letters of self-condemnation for release. Given Varvara's unforgiving nature, that release never comes and the cycle repeats itself for years. Shamed by Stepan Verkhovensky's self-abasement, the narrator begs his friend not to send his effusively self-condemnatory letter to Varvara. Stepan persists. The narrator expresses his discomfort at witnessing such shame by exposing his friend's weakness.

Like Stepan Verkhovensky, Fedor Karamazov violates social decorum. Unlike Stepan Trofimovich, who does so in a cowardly fashion and who consequently suffers intense shame, Fedor Pavlovich shamelessly violates social decorum and religious space; even his ritual gestures are sacrilegious. He responds hyperbolically to Zosima's gentle rebuke by confessing his pleasure in self-abasement and kissing the elder's hand after the ritual moment for hand-kissing has passed. Thus, in contrast to Zosima, who respected decorum even when ritually violating it, Fedor Pavlovich shames his character audience by forcing them to witness sacrilege. The unexpectedness of Fedor Pavlovich's response heightens the shame. Shame is highly contagious. The more witnesses, the more shame. As witnesses to scandal, individuals unexpectedly grapple with both the shame of witnessing and the shame of being in company where others may witness their response. Our armchair privacy protects us as readers from the gaze of others but not from the shame of witnessing.

Stepan Verkhovensky and Fedor Karamazov both derive a pleasure from self-abasement that can be partially explained by shame dynamics. Their grandiosity and exhibitionism mask their narcissism and sense of injury. Stepan Verkhovensky has been living for twenty years as Varvara Stavrogina's dependent. Fedor Pavlovich was "a former sponger and therefore touchy and easily offended" (14:18;19). Both experience ongoing social humiliation—Stepan Trofimovich at Varvara's hands, Fedor Pavlovich at his cousin-in-law Miusov's hands. Their social aggression can thus be seen as a defense. In my reading, their pleasure in humiliation derives from multiple sources: exhibitionism; confirmation of negative self-image; aggressive sharing of shame; and engagement in a creative process. The process that Zosima describes as the fabrication of an offense and then its exaggeration turns the passive victim of humiliation into an active humiliator. He may be humiliated, but he is not passive. He finds pleasure in controlling the experience.

In controlling the shame experience, the shamed person eliminates shame's surprise, and thus much of its pain. Shame's pain has three essential sources: disruption, disorientation, and self-consciousness. The person who fabricates or exaggerates an offense guarantees that shame does not come upon him unawares; nor does shame disorient him, making him question the world and his place in it; finally, shame does not engender self-consciousness vis-à-vis actual others. In fabricating offense and offender alike, the shamed person defines himself, his world, and his place in it. In this scenario, the pleasure of creation offsets the pain of shame.

Pleasure may derive from another related source. In fabricating an offense against himself, the fabricator places himself at the center of attention. In his scenario, he becomes a worthy object of a significant other's contempt. The pleasure derived from the self's sense of expansion offsets the pain of the negative attention.[4] Hyperbole, the rhetorical device used to achieve this self-amplification, may also contribute to the pleasure. The self experiences the pleasure of narcissistic grandiosity as well as the exhilaration of exaggeration.

Stepan Verkhovensky and Fedor Karamazov both exemplify hyperbolic humiliation. By fabricating or exaggerating offenses, they cut themselves off from others. Having deprived themselves of meaningful social interaction, they seek an alternative source of pleasure. Their engagement in self-amplified shame provides pleasure that derives from imagined interaction. In *Demons* and *The Brothers Karamazov*, Dostoevsky demonstrates that self-amplified shame destroys the possibility of a true relationship. Zosima exposes the rhetorical strategy whereby many self-lacerating Dostoevsky characters control their shame by creating roles that define others. They thus act like

Dostoevsky's underground man: by creating the world in their own image, they deprive themselves of the means of self-understanding.[5] Shamed persons who fabricate offenses isolate themselves. As Zosima observes, fictional scenarios gain a life of their own; fabricated offenses lead to actual enmity; creating scenes of discord divides. Lies thereby replace life.

Shame and Hostility

Shame need not be self-created or self-amplified to spawn hostility, however, as the narrator of *The Brothers Karamazov* illustrates in the following show-and-tell passage. As Fedor Pavlovich prepares to leave the monastery, he remembers a moment of self-exposure, when he had admitted that his clownish behavior correlates with others' expectations. Instead of responding to shame in a standard, acceptably way by flight or denial, Fedor Pavlovich chooses retaliatory aggression:

> He wanted to revenge himself on them all for his own dirty tricks. He suddenly remembered then that some time once before he had been asked: "Why do you hate so-and-so so much?" And he had replied then in a fit of buffoonish shamelessness [*besstydstva*]: "Here's why: he never did anything to me, it's true, but I once played a most unconscionable [*bessovestneishuiu*] dirty trick on him, and the moment I did it, I immediately hated him for it." Remembering it now, he sniggered softly and maliciously in a moment's hesitation. His eyes gleamed, and his lips even trembled. "Since I've started, I may as well finish," he decided suddenly. His innermost feeling at that moment might well be expressed in the following words: "There is no way to rehabilitate myself now, so I'll go ahead and spit all over them to the point of shamelessness [*do besstydstva*]; I'll tell them, 'I won't be ashamed, and that's that!'" (14:80;86)

Dostoevsky's narrator here explains how shame leads to hostility and shamelessness.[6] Fedor Karamazov first remembers a moment of self-exposure and then decides to revenge himself on the witnesses. His hostility, in turn, reminds him of an earlier event of the same ilk: he had exposed himself by playing a dirty trick and then revenged himself upon his victim by openly hating him. The dynamic is clear: shame leads to hostility which leads to aggression. The memory of shame causes more shame, hostility, and aggression. Shame spirals: the greater the shame, the more aggressive the response. The level of aggression corresponds to the level of pain.

By exposing Fedor Karamazov's thoughts, the narrator collapses the distance between his readers and Fedor Pavlovich. By depicting Fedor Karamazov's shameless behavior, he shocks us. By explaining that Fedor Pavlovich's shamelessness originates in shame, he reinforces Zosima's diagnosis and identifies the old buffoon as our post-lapsarian brother. Dostoevsky uses the dueling incident in Zosima's biography later in the novel to remind readers that aggression is a common response to shame. By locating shame and desire for revenge in the preconversion Zosima, Dostoevsky not only demonstrates their universality but also models an alternative response. Although Zosima channels hatred for his social equal into a socially acceptable form by challenging him to a duel, he hits his social inferior, his servant Afanasy, in the face, a morally unacceptable action that shames him and changes his life. Once he confronts his own shame, Zosima sees the deep connections among all human beings. Dostoevsky structures his novel so that he reveals the source of Zosima's wisdom four books after Zosima first counsels Fedor Karamazov to stop exacerbating his sense of shame. The story of Zosima's duel illustrates the potentially fatal consequences of self-amplified shame: he was in danger of killing a man to relieve his injured pride. Fedor Karamazov aggressively shames others; Zosima shamed and physically harmed one man, shamed and almost killed another. Once the two behaviors are juxtaposed, which is more shocking?

Shame and Confession

Zosima's conversion tale illustrates shame's paradox. Initially Zosima experiences shame as a prison that exacerbates his narcissism and alienates him from those around him. But the shame he feels before his servant Afanasy proves a powerful instrument of change. Shame experienced as conscience, as a moral connection to others, has the power to liberate. Once Zosima acknowledges his shame, he can beg Afanasy's forgiveness and resolve not to hurt his dueling opponent. After allowing his opponent to fire, he throws his pistol into the air and begs his forgiveness as well.[7] Zosima thus uses confession to banish shame. As Michael Lewis observes, confession permits the shamed person to distance himself from the emotional experience of shame by providing him with the opportunity to join others in viewing himself. While laughter can also provide such distance, confession requires a confessor who possesses the ability to forgive and love.[8] Zosima endows others with the power to forgive him and thus restore his sense of connection with others. He thereby renounces self-affirmation and violence and embraces humility and love.

In *Demons*, Stepan Verkhovensky uses confession as a means of reducing his shame. He becomes addicted to confession, however, because as long as he confesses to Varvara Stavrogina, who refuses to forgive him, he can never heal. Yet, at novel's end, Stepan Trofimovich breaks the cycle. After experiencing extreme shame at the fête, Stepan Trofimovich responds in typical fashion: he flees. But this time he flees his habitual milieu as well as the scene of shame. Thus liberated, he takes his first steps outside himself: he meets Liza Tushina and worries about her. Stepan Trofimovich then confesses on his deathbed to Sophia Ulitina, a woman who can freely love and forgive him. Liberated from a cycle of confession without forgiveness, Stepan Trofimovich sees how he fits into the larger social and metaphysical picture. He does what Zosima does and what Kaufman has called "refocusing attention" back outside self, a critical step for escaping cycles of shame.[9] He repents his past actions and asks for others' forgiveness. As he lies dying, he engages in an Augustinian confession, which, in Belknap's words, takes the form: "I did (or do, or am) this, and it is wrong."[10] By repenting his actions and reaching out to others, Stepan Verkhovensky escapes the prison-house of shame.

At the very moment that Stepan Trofimovich confronts and transcends his shame, however, Mr. G-v, the narrator, finds himself mired in shame. After the fête, Stepan Verkhovensky literally and figuratively locks the narrator out. Once he sets out on his final journey, he leaves his down-to-earth narrator-confidant behind. As I discuss in the next chapter, the narrator attempts to conceal his shame at being abandoned by adopting an ironic distance from Stepan Trofimovich and exposing his friend's weaknesses. Dostoevsky, however, undercuts his narrator's strategy by imitating it. He creates a similar distance between his readers and the narrator by revealing the realist narrator's spiritual limitations as well as his physical abandonment. Dostoevsky thus exposes the narrator's shame and explains the source of his narrative irony. Although the narrator distances himself from Stepan Verkhovensky and encourages his readers to do likewise, Stepan collapses that distance as he acknowledges and then transcends his shame. He moves beyond his narcissistic injury and sees himself as an integral part of a community bound by love. In exposing the narrator's shame as well as his inability to comprehend Stepan Trofimovich's metaphysical dimension, Dostoevsky splits the narrative and authorial audiences. Readers must choose whether to believe the narrator and view Stepan Trofimovich's confession as insincere or to believe in his repentance and take a metaphysical leap. Dostoevsky thus offers readers a choice of vision: shame bound (remaining with the narrator) or shame free (joining Stepan Verkhovensky).

Shamelessness and Nonrepentance

In his last novel, Fedor Dostoevsky uses Fedor Karamazov as a focal point for shame issues and shame strategies. Zosima diagnoses shame as the source of Fedor Pavlovich's shameless behavior and identifies the consequences of self-amplified shame as loss of love and thus loss of connection to others. By elucidating shame dynamics and Fedor Karamazov's behavior, Zosima forestalls condemnation and offers acceptance. In like manner, the narrator of *The Brothers Karamazov* works against any facile understanding of Fedor Karamazov. He creates a distance between Fedor Pavlovich and readers by reporting the old buffoon's shameless behavior, but he also collapses that distance by explaining its source.

In the monastery scene, Fedor Karamazov flaunts his shame, forcing his character witnesses and Dostoevsky's readers to face scandal. Old Fedor repeatedly violates social, moral, and religious conventions. But Fedor Dostoevsky also uses his namesake to shock readers' literary sensibilities. Fedor Karamazov violates every convention in the book—including the generic conventions regulating literary confessions. Fedor buffoonishly confesses to being "a lie and a father of lies, or rather . . . a son of lies." As Belknap notes, Fedor Karamazov's is an "unrepentant confession" which "is inherently far more aggressive and defiant than a love lyric or any of the other self-expressing genres. The genre of confession presupposes that the person confessed to has some sort of authority over the one confessing. In literary confession, the reader assumes this authority, and these unrepentant confessions unmitigated by any 'but' withdraw this authority from the reader in a dramatically provocative way. The power of these passages comes from the breaking of moral and social taboos, but most powerfully from breaking these literary rules which govern our reading of more normal confessions."[11] By indulging in an unrepentant confession, which takes the form: "I did it, and it's wrong, but I don't give a damn," Fedor Karamazov deprives his audience of its privileged, superior position as dispenser of acceptance and forgiveness.[12] He provides a more difficult challenge—to accept him in all his shamelessness. Fedor Dostoevsky thus uses his namesake to surprise, disorient, and make readers painfully self-conscious. He challenges us to respond to shamelessness, something that defies all standard response.

What then to do with Fedor Karamazov's recalcitrant nonrepentance? It confounds all witnesses, except Zosima. Fedor Pavlovich's buffoonery does not surprise, disorient, or render Zosima self-conscious because he sees the shame behind the shamelessness. Zosima is the ideal confessor, a man capable of forgiving and loving. He responds to Fedor Pavlovich's shame, not to his shamelessness. He offers him acceptance as a fallen creature, but he also asks Fedor to take responsibility for himself, to give up lying, sensuality, usury. Dostoevsky thus uses Zosima hagiographically to model an ideal response—a response that places all persons in right relationship to one another. Zosima proposes a world without disgrace-shame.

Alesha models another response. Although he experiences shame in the monastery, Alesha never ceases to love his father. His nonjudgmental acceptance touches his father, awakening his dormant capacity to love. This is not to say that Dostoevsky creates an expectation that Fedor Karamazov will reform. Nonetheless, he demonstrates that Zosima's understanding and Alesha's love affect the old buffoon. After all, Fedor Karamazov initially prepares to leave the monastery, sensing that it would be improper (*neprilichno*) to remain. Although shame propels him to return with vengeance in his heart, he does not return to Zosima's cell. Nor is Alesha present as he creates the scandal in the Father Superior's rooms.

Finally, Dostoevsky provides another response to Fedor Karamazov's shame: humor. Fedor Karamazov may be shameless, but he is also funny. The unrepentant confession discussed here, for instance, may violate literary rules and deprive us of a standard response, but it also makes us laugh. By evoking a familiar biblical passage, Dostoevsky plays parodically but writes seriously. He thus engages our cognitive faculties while flooding us with shame affect. He asks us to recall the passage in John's gospel (8:44), in which Christ divides those who are with him and truth from those who choose the devil and falsity. Given the passage's metaphysical seriousness, Fedor Pavlovich's choice is most unexpected. It surprises and disorients witnesses. While those in Zosima's cell are offended by his choice, Dostoevsky's readers laugh. Who would consciously choose to side with the devil? We understand that he is clowning. Fedor Pavlovich's addition, that he is a son of lies, is even funnier. Yet it also enlarges the literary context of his buffoonery, for it evokes not only the biblical passage but also the fathers and children thematics of the Russian literary tradition. Fedor Dostoevsky uses Fedor Pavlovich's shameless avowals to provoke readers' laughter, which provides us with the aesthetic distance necessary to alleviate, but not eradicate, the shame affect unleashed by his shameless buffoonery.

Fedor Dostoevsky scandalizes his readers by creating a character who creates scandals. We cannot regard Fedor Karamazov impassively. He surprises us with shame, disorienting and making us almost as self-conscious as his character audience. Dostoevsky attenuates the shame affect roused by Fedor Pavlovich by making us laugh. But in the end, he leaves Fedor Pavlovich a paradox: a man who unrepentantly revels in post-lapsarian vice but who craves salvation: "How is it with us generally? With us, once a thing falls, it lies there. With us, if a thing once falls, it can lie there forever. I won't have it, sirs! I want to rise!" (14:82;88). Fedor Karamazov here affirms that he desires salvation, but Fedor Dostoevsky cannily shows how ambivalent that desire is. Dostoevsky also describes the scene itself. Fedor Pavlovich has just staged a humiliating scandal. He is a fallen man. Yet the old buffoon counters one inertial pattern with another: defiantly refusing to be paralyzed by humiliation, he triumphantly rises, glorying in his humiliation, and humiliates others. By staging Fedor Karamazov's fall and rise in a monastery, Fedor Dostoevsky emphasizes the contrast between secular humiliation and monastic humility. Fedor Karamazov may crave salvation, but he embraces his fallen state.

chapter six

Stepan Trofimovich Verkhovensky: Leaving the Narrator Behind

The fire is in people's minds, not on the rooftops. (10:395;516)
—GOVERNOR VON LEMBKE, *Demons*

At the end of *Demons*, Stepan Trofimovich Verkhovensky, like many 1870s youth, forsakes the comforts of home and habit and travels to Russia's heartland. There, on his deathbed, he renounces his self-image as victim and assumes responsibility for his life. Relinquishing his self-image as civic figure, he avows himself to be one of those possessed by the demons wracking Russia's body and soul; he finally declares his love for Varvara Stavrogina; and he professes belief in God. This series of deathbed pronouncements represents the culmination of a progression: following shame-filled moments that expose the gap between his actual and ideal self-images, Stepan Verkhovensky attains moments of self-awareness. In facing his personal shame, acknowledging his self-deception as well as its sociopolitical effects, and reaching out to God, Stepan escapes his narcissistic isolation and joins the larger sociopolitical and metaphysical community. In portraying Stepan Verkhovensky, Dostoevsky refashions General Ivolgin's drama of shame confronted, developing it to reveal more overtly the political and metaphysical dimensions of the personal.

Stepan Verkhovensky flees not only his past life, but also Dostoevsky's narrator, thus repeating another narrative pattern Dostoevsky developed in *The Idiot*. As Robin Feuer Miller demonstrates, Dostoevsky's disembodied but intrusive narrator in *The Idiot* creates reader sympathy for Prince Myshkin throughout the first three books of the novel. In Book Four, however, the narrator distances himself from Myshkin. This radical shift forces readers to take an ethical stand: our sympathies remain with Myshkin, not the narrator. By repeating this pattern with Stepan Verkhovensky in *Demons*, Dostoevsky involves the narrative audience in the novel's emotional drama and trains his authorial audience to evaluate the novel's action for ourselves. As I show in this chapter, Dostoevsky establishes his narrator's blatant subjectivity to create a critical distance between him and Dostoevsky's authorial audience. In doing so, Dostoevsky emphasizes his novel's metaliterary dimension: in a narrative *tour de force*, Dostoevsky the author mimics his narrator's technique. The narrator creates a critical distance between his narrative audience and most characters by exposing their pretensions and self-deceptions. Dostoevsky, in turn, creates a critical distance between his authorial audience and the narrator by exposing the latter's obvious subjectivity.

The narrator of *Demons* has attracted a lot of critical attention from Dostoevsky scholars, who have particularly noted the discrepancies between his outsider representation of Stavrogin and his insider depiction of Stepan Verkhovensky, between his eyewitness status and his occasional omniscience, and between his styles of overreporting and underreporting.[1] While scholars agree that Mr. G-v, the narrator, ironizes at Stepan Trofimovich Verkhovensky's expense, they disagree about the extent of Mr. G-v's sympathy for his best friend. I hold that Mr. G-v's irony represents his attempt to sort out his conflicting feelings for Stepan. When the narrator begins telling his story, Stepan Verkhovensky is already dead. Although the narrator portrays himself as Stepan's confidant throughout most of the novel, after the fête, Stepan literally locks him out and leaves him behind. Forced to tell the story of Stepan's wanderings from a second-hand remove, the narrator employs irony to hide his humiliation.

By creating a subjective, ambivalent narrator, Dostoevsky forces the authorial audience to be wary. For instance, we know from the novel's first paragraphs that Mr. G-v had long believed Stepan Verkhovensky's claims about himself: "Just the other day I learned, to my great surprise, but now with complete certainty, that Stepan Verkhovensky had lived among us, in our province, not only not in exile, as we used to think, but that he had never even been under surveillance! Such, then, is the power of one's own imagination! He himself sincerely believed all his life . . . " (10:8;8). While accusing his friend of self-deception, the narrator exposes his own susceptibility. Dostoevsky creates a narrator grappling with his own gullibility. As he exposes Stepan, the narrator exposes himself.

By drawing early attention to the narrator's subjectivity, Dostoevsky comments on the overt or concealed subjectivity of any narrative. He thus reproduces our everyday experience of judgment as we listen to others' stories—we assess messenger along with message. Although Mr. G-v portrays Stepan Verkhovensky ambivalently but sympathetically, he portrays Peter Verkhovensky negatively. In having him do so, Dostoevsky provides his authorial audience with guidelines for evaluating the narrator's account. Mr. G-v's attitudes toward father and son can be explained by moral criteria as well as personal sympathy. Stepan Verkhovensky is a *vrun*, a liar and idealistic self-deceiver; his son Peter is a *lzhets*, a falsifier and a deliberate deceiver of others. Readers initially trust the narrator, despite his erratic system of underreporting or overreporting, because he mirrors our moral sympathies. Stepan Verkhovensky's weaknesses inadvertently cause others harm; Peter Verhovensky's weaknesses effect death and destruction.

In this chapter, I show how the narrator exposes Stepan Verkhovensky as a self-deceiver to bolster his own credibility; how Dostoevsky undermines the narrator's credibility by exposing his subjectivity; and how Dostoevsky fuses the personal, political, and metaphysical dimensions of his novel in Stepan Verkhovensky's drama of confronted shame.

Self-Deception

During the course of the novel, the narrator reveals six incidents in which Stepan Verkhovensky experiences the shame of recognizing the discrepancy between his actual and ideal self-images. All six times Stepan acknowledges his self-deception. In calling Stepan Verkhovensky a self-deceiver, I follow the philosopher Catherine Wilson's account: "The self-deceiver does not simply possess inconsistent beliefs. He is said, rather, to have made himself believe what he knows to be not true. The active dimension in self-deception can only be accounted for on the supposition that his wants and desires are involved in the final composition of his beliefs."[2] Stepan Verkhovensky believes something he knows not to be true, that is, he believes himself to be a civic figure; he also knows that he is not. How can he do this? In Wilson's account, self-deception involves weakness of will. If confronted with the statement "I am a civic figure," based on the usual criteria and with evidence that he cannot ignore, Stepan Verkhovensky would probably accept the truth of the claim that he is not. Yet Wilson points out that self-deceivers act according to "an imaginary set of alternatives, in which the evidence does not have to be taken into account."[3] In *Demons*, the narrator provides evidence showing (a) that Stepan Verkhovensky is not a persecuted civic figure, and (b) that most of the time he willfully ignores evidence to the contrary. Yet Stepan Verkhovensky can sustain his self-deception because he and his patron Varvara Stavrogina collude in creating an environment where such evidence can be ignored.

Stepan and Varvara thereby imitate a larger cultural pattern that Lotman identifies as the dualism of post–Petrine Russian culture—a split between the world of the ideal and that of the real, worlds that coexisted but did not intersect. As Lotman explains, "This world of ideas was a play world associated with social interchange, everyday life, and the entirety of official 'facade' life—all areas in which the intrusion of reality was felt most strongly. Here, to call attention to the true state of affairs was an unforgivable violation of the rules of the game. But alongside this world was another world of bureaucratic and state life. In this world, realism was preferred: pragmatists were needed, not dreamers."[4] Lotman's description evokes the image of Potemkin villages: facades erected to represent the ideal reality. But while Lotman might consider these a way for men like Potemkin to combine "dreaming" with pragmatism, he asserts that subsequent generations had to choose: "They could pursue activity that was practical but contradicted their ideals, or an activity that was ideal but had to be pursued outside of practical life. It was necessary either to renounce one's dreams or to nullify life by living only in the imagination, substituting words, poems, 'activity' in dreams and conversations, for actual deeds. The word began to occupy a hypertrophic place in culture. This development led to the growth of creative imagination in the gifted and to 'a great talent for lying,' as Aleksandr Izmailov expressed it, in the mediocre."[5]

In colluding to present him as a persecuted civic leader, Stepan Verkhovensky and Varvara Stavrogina act as though their ideal were true, ignoring any contradictory political or social reality. Stepan Verkhovensky thus engages in self-deception by lying to himself and to others. Varvara Stavrogina collaborates in creating and sustaining an ideal that diverges from reality. They sustain the split between a sociopolitically determined ideal and an everyday reality, a split that began in post–Petrine Russia and persisted through the Soviet period, if not to this day.

By showcasing this collusion, Dostoevsky not only exposes the duality of Russian life, he also explores the underlying psychological dynamics. Like Dostoevsky's other liars, Stepan Verkhovensky wants to be other. Like the nobly born General Ivolgin, Stepan Verkhovensky has had more opportunities to realize his desire than most of Dostoevsky's other liars. Yet like the General, Stepan Verkhovensky lacks strength of will. His nocturnal crying sessions with the young Stavrogin, his hysterical one-sided correspondence with Varvara Stavrogina, his constant demands on his confidant, and his drinking all demonstrate this weakness.[6] A dreamer rather than a doer, he fabricates a compensatory self-image that gratifies his vanity. In accepting Varvara Stavrogina's job offer, Stepan Verkhovensky can maintain his self-image, for Varvara not only believes in "his reputation as a poet, scholar" and "civic figure," but amplifies it: "She invented him, and she was the first to believe in her invention. He was something like a sort of dream of hers. . . . But for that she indeed demanded a lot of him, sometimes even slavery" (10:16;15–16).[7] The initial collusion, which satisfies both parties' need for a prestigious public image, thus ends with Stepan's subjugation. Accordingly, Stepan carries two sets of books into the garden: volumes of serious writing, such as those of de Tocqueville, into the garden, which hide the salacious novels, such as those of de Kock, that he actually reads.

Being a persecuted civic figure constitutes only half of Stepan Verkhovensky's ideal self-image, however. The life story[8] the feverish Stepan tells Sophia Ulitina at the novel's end includes a second self-defining role—that of noble lover. Coming at his life's end, this version of his life story reveals the self-image Stepan Verkhovensky has long cultivated and would like others to share. He considers Sophia the perfect audience because he has chosen her "for his future path, and he was hastening to intitiate her, so to speak" (10:494;647). By telling her his story, he hopes to heal his wounded vanity: for Stepan Verkhovensky portrays himself as a man who has been misunderstood and undervalued all his life—in both the public and private spheres. On his deathbed, however, Stepan Verkhovensky examines and renounces his self-defining roles. His courage in the face of painful truths about himself inspires reader sympathy.

By excluding him from Stepan Verkhovensky's deathbed, Dostoevsky highlights the narrator's changed status; he also shows how important women are in Stepan's life. By making the narrator Stepan's best friend and confidant, Dostoevsky exposes him to the authorial audience's critical view. By sharing Stepan's intimate accounts of five shame-filled moments with readers, the narrator reveals his insider status. His secondhand remove from the sixth, the most significant moment, thus carries Dostoevsky's message: the narrator has become an outsider.

The insiders at Stepan Verkhovensky's deathbed are women. To Sophia Ulitina he confesses a lifetime of lying; to Varvara Stavrogina he confesses his love. Stepan Verkhovensky, the narrator says, "could not be without a woman" (10:494;646). His first wife's infidelities and flight scar him with a feeling of unworthiness; when she abandons him, he abandons their son. When his second wife unexpectedly dies, he accepts Varvara Stavrogina's offer to become her son's tutor. Varvara Stavrogina sustains his civic persona. Yet Stepan Verkhovensky can remain her dependent only on condition that he believes (a) that she believes in him and (b) that she loves him, albeit secretly. When Varvara destroys those beliefs, he experiences intense shame and flees—a characteristic defense against shame. Before fleeing, however, he locks himself into his quarters and writes a four-page letter to Dasha—"a pure and naive being," "a meek one" (10:377;492)—because he needs female sympathy. On the road, he meets the Bible peddler, Sophia Ulitina, another meek and sympathetic woman, to whom he pours out his soul. Unencumbered by familiar faces and places, Stepan Verkhovensky relates his life story, embellishing his civic and amatory roles. He then suffers extreme shame: "'All I told you earlier were lies—for glory, for magnificence, out of idleness—all, all, to the last word, oh blackguard,

blackguard! [*Ia vam davecha vse nalgal*]'" (10:496;650). Throughout the novel, Stepan Verkhovensky's verbal excesses move him to shame, provoking emotional crises that lead to self-understanding. Sophia Ulitina gives him both the sympathy and the text he needs to relinquish his narcissistic self-images.

The Divided Self

Throughout most of the novel, Stepan Verkhovensky entrusts his unvarnished self-image to his friend the narrator, who initially characterizes him as a noble self-deceiver:

> I will say straight off: Stepan Trofimovich constantly played a certain special and, so to speak, civic role among us, and loved this role to the point of passion—so much so that it even seems to me that he could not live without it. Not that I equate him with a stage actor: God forbid, particularly as I happen to respect him. It could all have been a matter of habit, or, better, of a ceaseless and noble disposition, from childhood on, towards a pleasant dream of his beautiful civic stance. He was, for example, greatly enamored of his position as a "persecuted" man and, so to speak, an "exile." There is a sort of classical luster to these two little words that seduced him once and for all, and, later raising him gradually in his own estimation over the course of so many years, brought him finally to some sort of pedestal, rather lofty and gratifying to his vanity. (10:7;7)

The narrator here describes the mechanics of Stepan Verkhovensky's self-deception. An idealist by disposition, he readily adopts the prestigious role of a "persecuted" man. Over time, he elevates this self-image. In differentiating Stepan Trofimovich from a stage actor, the narrator represents his friend as an unconscious role player who gradually identifies himself so completely with his self-chosen role that it becomes life-sustaining.[9] The narrator thus prepares readers for Stepan's death. Once Stepan relinquishes his treasured self-image, he loses part of his life force.

His life story plays a similarly vital role for him. As the narrator notes, Stepan chides Sophia for fussing about the details of lodging, food, and expenses, because he is anxious to tell her his life story, which is "something truly lofty for him and, to use the newest language, almost a struggle for existence" (10:494;647). Stepan thus dismisses Sophia's practical concerns about the future to focus on his present, self-defining task. She recognizes that the energy he expends in telling the story may prove fatal: "This was a sudden straining of his mental powers, which, of course—and Sophia Matveevna foresaw it with anguish throughout his story—could not but lead immediately afterwards to a great loss of strength in his already unsettled organism" (10:494;647). Like Dostoevsky's other liars, Stepan Verkhovensky focuses almost exclusively on himself and the present moment.

Stepan Trofimovich's life story has three parts: his childhood and first marriages, his role as civic figure, and his love story. The first part explains why he chooses Sophia as his third wife; the second outlines his self-image as a misunderstood man of talent; the third justifies his bachelor status on the grounds that he was the object of two womens' love. Stepan begins with a Rousseauist vision of childhood innocence that prepares Sophia for the tale of his first two marriages (10:494;647). In Stepan's telling, he moves from a state of innocence to one of love and loss (his first wife abandons him and his second wife dies).[10] Stepan's personal story thus rouses Sophia's sympathy.

Stepan's account of his civic role, by contrast, confuses her: "The fogginess increased greatly for poor, trapped Sophia Matveevna when the story turned almost into a whole dissertation on the subject of how no one had ever been able to understand Stepan Verkhovensky and of how 'talents perish in our Russia'" (10:494;648). Sophia later tells Varvara Stavrogina that his witty comments about our "progressive and governing" bewildered her and his vehement invective against the nihilists and "new people" frightened her. While Sophia is confused, readers are not, for Dostoevsky's narrator has prepared us to understand this thumbnail sketch.

At the novel's outset, the narrator observes that Stepan Verkhovensky never developed his talent. While Stepan blamed a "'whirlwind of concurrent circumstances'" for the end of his career, the narrator comments: "And just think! It turned out later that there had been not only no 'whirlwind' but not even any 'circumstances,' at least not on that occasion" (10:8;8). In the Aesopian language of the time, "circumstances" signified government repression. Stepan thus implies that he lost his lectureship because the government deemed him subversive. Yet the narrator undercuts this suggestion by noting that Stepan managed to publish a study on knights in a progressive monthly journal. Then the narrator adds, "Afterwards it was said that the sequel of the study was promptly forbidden, and that the progressive journal even suffered for having printed the first part. That could very well have happened, because what did not happen back then? But in the present case it is more likely that nothing happened, and that the author himself was too lazy to finish the study" (10:9;9). The discrepancy between Stepan's self-image as prosecuted public figure and the narrator's suggestions that Stepan fabricated those circumstances reveals Stepan Verkhovensky's tendency to project blame outward. Like Dostoevsky's other liars, he also projects himself onto others. The narrator suggests that Stepan drops his study because he succumbs to laziness.

Stepan accordingly describes Russia as a country full of lazy people: "It's simply Russian laziness, our humiliating impotence to produce an idea, our disgusting parasitism among the nations. *Ils sont tout simplement des paresseux*" (10:172;216). Moreover, while Stepan describes Russia as a parasite on other nations, to the narrator he admits that he's nothing but a sponger (10:26;28).

While Stepan Verkhovensky misses the irony in his civic message to others, Dostoevsky ensures that readers do not. Stepan calls his countrymen to work while he lives as an idle dependent: "'With us everything comes out of idleness, even what is fine and good. . . . We are unable to live by our own labor. . . . Nothing can ever be acquired gratis. If we labor we shall have our own opinion. For twenty years now I've been ringing the alarm and calling to labor! I've given my life to this call, and—madman—I believed! Now I no longer believe, but I still ring and shall go on ringing to the end, to my grave; I shall pull on the rope until the bells ring for my funeral!'" (10:32–3;36–7). By fashioning a narrator who constantly exposes the gap between his friend's actual and ideal selves, Dostoevsky prepares readers to see the situational irony of Stepan Verkhovensky's lofty rhetoric. He thus demonstrates the dynamics of self-deception.

Dostoevsky's portrayal of Stepan Verkhovensky matches Wilson's account of self-deception in a way that dovetails with Frankfurt's account of bullshitting.[11] What Frankfurt calls a disregard for truth, Wilson sees as a disregard for evidence to the contrary. The narrator shows how this operates in his friend's case. As part of his self-image, Stepan Verkhovensky believes that he was persecuted and forced to live in exile. After debunking this myth, the narrator speculates: "Had someone then convinced the most honest Stepan Verkhovensky, on irrefutable evidence, that he had nothing at all to fear, he would no doubt have been offended. And yet he was such an intelligent man" (10:8;8). When the narrator suggests to Stepan Verkhovensky that he publish an early poem that had been confiscated, "he declined the proposal with obvious displeasure. My opinion as to its perfect innocence he did not like, and I even ascribe to it a certain coolness towards me on his part, which lasted a whole two months" (10:10;10). When the poem is published abroad, Stepan Verkhovensky is apprehensive, but, as the narrator notes, "I am convinced that in the hidden turnings of his heart he was remarkably flattered" (10:10;11).

Stepan's self-image as a persecuted exile satisfies his vanity; the poem's publication satisfies his desire for recognition. When the narrator attempts to provide evidence of the poem's innocence, Stepan avoids him. When not confronted with such evidence, Stepan sidesteps it, thus acting like all individuals and nations who have a vested interest in maintaining an idealized identity. Yet when confronted with such evidence, Stepan Verkhovensky, like General Ivolgin on his deathbed, experiences grief and self-awareness. While the narrator relates these moments to expose Stepan Verkhovensky's self-deception and thus diminish reader sympathy, the opposite occurs. As the narrator recounts two crises concerning Stepan's self-image as civic figure, three centering on his self-image as unrequited lover, and the hyperbolized life story that fuses the two, reader sympathy for Stepan Verkhovensky increases.

Shame and Self-Awareness: The Public Sphere

The narrator relates the first two incidents in tandem. The first occurs after Stepan Verkhovensky's trip to Petersburg with Varvara Stavrogina at the end of the 1850s. Initially a great success with the current literati, who invite him to public literary gatherings, Stepan Verkhovensky then experiences a moment of great pride and equal humiliation:

> When he came out on the stage for the first time as a reader at one of these public literary readings, there was a burst of wild applause that continued for about five minutes. He recalled it with tears nine years later—rather more because of his artistic nature than out of gratitude. "I'll even swear to you and will wager," he himself said to me (but only to me, and as a secret), "that no one in that whole audience knew the slightest thing about me!" A remarkable confession: indeed he must have possessed keen intelligence if he could understand his position so clearly, right there on the stage, despite all his rapture; and indeed he must not have possessed very keen intelligence if even nine years later he could not recall it without feeling offended. (10:21–2;23)

This memory can be termed "self-defining," as it "is vivid, affectively charged, repetitive, linked to other similar memories, and related to an important unresolved theme or enduring concern in an individual's life."[12] For Stepan Trofimovich, this memory clearly provides pleasure as well as pain. It recalls the gratifying, intoxicating applause. Yet it presents painful evidence that he is applauded for what he represents rather than for who he is. While he would like to savor his success, he bitterly acknowledges his failure. This memory remains affectively charged precisely because it touches Stepan's sorest spot—his desire for recognition. Stepan's participation in the fête in Book Three reprises this moment. He sees his speech as his last civic duty, a performance that can neutralize this impersonal, ignominious success by allowing him to triumph in his own name.

A second moment of shame-induced self-awareness follows the first. After the fiasco in Petersburg, Varvara Stavrogina sends Stepan to Europe to recover. Less than four months later, a homesick Stepan "races back" to Skvoreshniki. Two weeks after his "ecstatic" reunion with Varvara, he confesses to the narrator, "my friend, I've discovered something new and . . . terrible for me: *je suis un* mere sponger *et rien de plus! Mais r-r-rien de plus!*" (10:26;28). Overwhelmed by the shame of his financial and emotional dependence on Varvara Stavrogina, Stepan entrusts his self-discovery to the narrator.

Shame and Self-Awareness: The Private Sphere

The narrator also relates three moments of shame-induced self-awareness involving Stepan Verkhovensky's personal relationship with Varvara Stavrogina. Because Stepan still believes in their secret romance (10:19;19), her repudiation devastates him: "Yes indeed, until then, until that very day, he had always remained certain of just one thing—namely, that despite all Varvara Petrovna's 'new views' and 'changes of ideas,' he still had charms over her woman's heart, that is, not only as an exile or as a famous scholar, but also as a handsome man. For twenty years this flattering and comforting conviction had been rooted in him, and of all his convictions it was perhaps the hardest to part with" (10:53;63–4).

The incident that provokes this revelation reveals the vital interconnection between Varvara's and Stepan's self-images. Varvara Stavrogina has identified herself so much with Stepan Verkhovensky that she bristles when others offend him, or, equally, when he does not act his part. Varvara perceives Julia von Lembke's arrival with her relative Karmazinov, the famous writer, as a challenge to her social supremacy. She berates Stepan for having "gone to seed," and she lambastes him for not living up to her, or his, ideals:

> Now that all these Lembkes, all these Karmazinovs . . . Oh, God, how you've gone to seed! Oh, how you torment me! . . . I wished these people to feel respect for you, because they're not worth your finger, your little finger, and look how you carry yourself! What will they see? What am I going to show them? Instead of standing nobly as a witness, of continuing to be an example, you've surrounded yourself with some riffraff, you've acquired some impossible habits, you've grown decrepit, you cannot live without wine and cards, you read nothing but Paul de Kock, and you write nothing, while there they all write; you waste all your time on chatter. (10:51;61)

This unvarnished truth shames and shatters Stepan. He can endure moments of self-awareness as long as he believes that Varvara values him. But to see himself through her critical eyes demolishes him: he even assimilates her language as he cries to the narrator "*Mon cher, je suis un* man gone to seed!" (10:53;63). Mired in his narcissism, Stepan does not grasp the social or political dimensions of the incident: he cannot see that Varvara feels socially threatened and that she relies on his public image to maintain her social supremacy. Again, like Dostoevsky's other liars, Stepan Verkhovensky thinks only of himself.

Varvara Stavrogina next devastates Stepan Verkhovensky when she conceives her plan to marry Stepan off to her ward Dasha. Though she presents her decision as a practical solution to his money problems, Varvara actually arranges the marriage to terminate her son Nikolai's affair with Dasha, thereby freeing him to marry Liza Tushina. When informed of her plan, Stepan is crushed: "I . . . I could never have imagined that you would decide to give me in marriage . . . to some other . . . woman!" (10:61;74). Her refusal to meet with him compounds his shame. Yet, after Varvara changes their relationship, he starts to see it differently. He admits that he would like to marry, an admission that anticipates his proposal to Sophia Ulitina. His critical awareness leads to a desire for change. Dostoevsky thus offers his readers a program for reform—critical consciousness, however painful, can free us from unhealthy habits, thereby creating new possibilities for growth.

The last humiliating interview between Stepan Verkhovensky and Varvara Stavrogina ends not so much in a moment of self-awareness as in a *profession de foi*. Thus rejected by Varvara, Stepan can see clearly. When Varvara adopts the nihilists' materialistic language and reduces their relationship to finances, Stepan indignantly defends himself: "I may have had a myriad of weaknesses. Yes, I was sponging off you, I am speaking the language of nihilism, but sponging was never the highest principle of my actions. It happened that way, of itself, I don't know how . . . I have always thought that between us remained something higher than food, and—never, never have I been a scoundrel!" (10:266;341). Stepan Trofimovich invokes their unspoken feelings for one another by citing two lines of Pushkin's 1829 poem "Once There Lived a Poor Knight": "'Filled with love that's pure/And true to the sweet dream'" (10:266;341).[13] As he bids farewell to his belief in Varvara's secretly reciprocated love, Stepan clings to his self-image as knight. He does not deceive himself in this, however, for despite his many weaknesses, Stepan Verkhovensky remains a faithful defender of his, Dostoevsky's, and Pushkin's knight's ideal—the Sistine Madonna.

In fact, when the political enters the personal realm and Varvara Stavrogina joins the ranks of his ideal's detractors, Stepan Verkhovensky takes up arms. As Stepan walks into the room, he realizes, "The woman I saw was not the one I had known for twenty years. The fullest conviction that all was over gave me a strength that amazed even her" (10:262;336). Although fortified by his sense of finality, Stepan fights back only once Varvara speaks like a nihilist:

>"You're terribly fond of exclaiming, Stepan Trofimovich. It's not at all the fashion nowadays. They talk crudely but plainly. You and these twenty years of ours! Twenty years of reciprocal self-love, and nothing more. Your every letter to me was written not for me but for posterity. You're a stylist, not a friend, and friendship is merely a glorified word, essentially a mutual outpouring of slops. . . ."

"God, all in other people's words! Learned by rote! So they've already put their uniform on you, too! You too are in joy, you too are in the sun; *chère, chère,* for what mess of pottage have you sold them your freedom!" (10:263;337)

Stepan Verkhovensky here reacts to his son Peter's words. He recognizes those charges of "writing for posterity" (10:162;199), "reciprocal self-love," and "mutual outpouring of slops" (10:239;305) from earlier conversations with Peter (10:237–41;303–37). Stepan moves to the offensive, charging Varvara with adopting the nihilists' crude language and donning their "uniform." Employing a biblical allusion, he accuses her of having sold her freedom. He fights the language of atheism with the language of faith—a clue that this argument belongs to the novel's larger political and metaphysical polemic.

In fact, this interchange reprises an 1860s polemic that Dostoevsky participated in as a journalist. In his 1861 article, "Mr. —bov and the Question of Art," Dostoevsky challenges the utilitarian view that art must be useful to be good. He adopts not the traditional opposition view of "art for art's sake" but a centrist position which claims that all art is activist and must be well made if it is to be useful, that is, act as a moral force. Dostoevsky links the aesthetic and the ethical, arguing that the better a work of art is, the more useful it is. Varvara Stavrogina voices the views and language of the utilitarian "Mr. —bov" (the radical critic Nikolai Dobroliubov), which she has acquired from Peter Verkhovensky. She declares the Sistine Madonna outdated—"No one, no one nowadays admires the Madonna anymore or wastes time over it" because "She serves absolutely no purpose" (10:264;338–9). In defending her position, she parrots the proposition of Nikolai Chernyshevsky, another utilitarian: "This mug is useful, because water can be poured into it; this pencil is useful, because everything can be written with it, but here you have a woman's face that's worse than all the faces in nature. Try painting an apple and put a real apple next to it—which would you take? I'll bet you wouldn't make any mistake" (10:264;339). Varvara Stavrogina's receptivity to the utilitarian anti-aesthetic proves equal to her earlier receptivity to Stepan Verkhovensky's aesthetic views. Offended by Stepan's acquiescence to her demand that he marry Dasha, Varvara Stavrogina rejects beauty in favor of boots.

Stepan Verkhovensky, on the other hand, defends the views of Dostoevsky himself. In this confrontation, Stepan remains uncharacteristically laconic. By saving his full rebuttal of Varvara's position for the fête, he demonstrates his understanding that his real quarrel lies with those whose materialist, utilitarian views she has adopted. At the fête, Stepan then argues that contemporary youth are pure-hearted but misguided:

> The whole perplexity lies in just what is more beautiful: Shakespeare or boots, Raphael or petroleum? . . . and I proclaim that Shakespeare and Raphael are higher than the emancipation of serfs, higher than nationality, higher than socialism, higher than the younger generation, higher than chemistry, higher than almost all mankind, for they are already the fruit, the real fruit of all mankind, and maybe the highest fruit there ever may be! A form of beauty already achieved, without the achievement of which I might not even consent to live. . . . Do you know that mankind can live without . . . science, without bread, and it only cannot live without beauty, for then there would be nothing at all to do in the world! (10:372–3;485)

Stepan Verkhovensky articulates Dostoevsky's aesthetic views in Dostoevskian language, making repeated use of climaxing lists, contrasts, and hyperbolic claims. Nonetheless, Stepan Verkhovensky as speaker differs from Dostoevsky the journalist in his narcissistic self-enclosure. Obsessed by the desire to proclaim his beliefs publicly, Stepan completely ignores his audience. His speech fails.

Shame and Self-Awareness:
The Private Moves into the Public Sphere

By portraying the personal conflict between Stepan Verkhovensky and Varvara Stavrogina as one over aesthetics vs. utility, Dostoevsky signals readers that father and son are engaged in a battle over minds and souls. Varvara voices Peter's ideas without considering their implications. Stepan, however, understands the underlying nontranscendent view of humankind. Concluding that he must defend his ideals, he decides that "defeated or victorious," he will leave Varvara's house to "go off on foot to end my life as a merchant's tutor, or die of hunger somewhere in a ditch" (10:266;341)—a characteristically hyperbolic threat, but one upon which he unexpectedly acts. By siding against him, Varvara Stavrogina shames Stepan Verkhovensky. As in the past, Stepan responds to shame with rhetorical extremes. Because Stepan has repeatedly issued similar ultimatums in the past, Varvara, like the narrator, underestimates the strength of his aesthetic convictions. Thus, like the narrator, she is completely stunned by his final departure and death. She does not realize that their private argument reflects a public polemic.[14]

In *Demons,* more powerfully than anywhere else in his *oeuvre,* Dostoevsky exposes the recursive relationship between private and public. He prepares readers for Stepan Verkhovensky's final journey to Russia's heartland, which is both a private as well as a political act, by describing the semiprivate, semipublic scandal scene in Varvara Stavrogina's drawing room at the end of Part One. As in the scene just described, Stepan responds nobly to his humiliator, in this case his son. After Peter scandalizes Varvara by telling her the contents of the letter his father had sent him about marrying "'someone else's sins,'" she banishes Stepan from her house. The narrator marvels at his dignity:

> Where did he get so much spirit? One thing I discovered was that he had been undoubtedly and deeply insulted by his first meeting with Petrusha earlier, namely, by that embrace. This was deep, *real* grief, at least in his eyes, for his heart. He had yet another grief at that moment, namely, his own morbid awareness that he had acted basely; this he confessed to me later in all frankness. And *real,* undoubted grief is sometimes capable of making a solid and steadfast man even out of a phenomenally light-minded one, if only for a short time; moreover, real and true grief has sometimes even made fools more intelligent, also only for a time, of course; grief has this property. And, if so, then what might transpire with a man like Stepan Trofimovich? A whole revolution—also, of course, only for a time. (10:163;200)

While the narrator focuses here on grief, shame initiates the reaction he describes. When confronted by the truth, Stepan Verkhovensky experiences shame. His shame causes the deep grief that gives him the courage, albeit temporary, to voice the truth. This scene, in which his shame-induced grief provides Stepan with the courage to act nobly, prefigures his last interview with Varvara as well as his final wanderings.

Fathers and Sons: The Battle over Language

The drawing-room scene ends with a father-son exchange in which Peter fights, using blunt language and role-playing (10:162;199), while Stepan politely and sincerely defends himself (10:163;201). Their conflict involves a willful deception of others versus an akratic self-deception. In this fight, each generation's rhetoric serves not only as a weapon but as the battlefield.

In *Demons,* father and son fight over rhetoric because rhetoric reflects worldviews, and the Verkhovenskys hold opposite views in the aesthetic conflict of the 1860s. Stepan Verkhovensky voices the aesthetic position, telling Varvara Stavrogina that he will speak "precisely about that queen of queens, that ideal of humanity, the Sistine Madonna, who in your opinion is not worth a glass or a pencil" (10:265;340), while his son Peter advocates a utilitarian approach—"Send your article ahead of time, don't forget, and try to do it without any humbug, if you can: facts, facts, facts, and, above all, make it short" (10:241;307). Yet Dostoevsky's narrator also reveals intergenerational similarities. For example, he repeatedly comments on both Verkhovenskys' narcissism and ignorance of reality. He exposes their preoccupation with their public and private images: both father and son are clothing- and image-conscious. Both idealize a significant other (Stavrogins) before whom they verbally abase themselves: Stepan calls Varvara "'an angel of honor and delicacy, while he was just the opposite'" (10:13;14); Peter says to Stavrogin, "You are a leader, you are a sun, and I am your wormlet" (10:324;418). Both enjoy card-playing. Praskovia Drozdova calls them both "professor" (10:102;126). Governor von Lembke's assistant Blium confuses them (10:283;364). And both are shame-ridden and quick to take offense. They differ radically on theological and metaphysical grounds, however.[15]

In general terms, Stepan Verkhovensky is an idealist who cherishes Christ, the Sistine Madonna, beauty. Unlike General Ivolgin, who is acutely aware of his fallen state and habitually intoxicates himself with lies, Stepan Verkhovensky thoroughly believes in his self-image. He has moments of vanity and conscious role-playing, as when he practices in front of a mirror before the fête, but for the most part he is a product of his manners and beliefs. The narrator emphasizes Stepan Verkhovensky's idealism by stressing his emotional and aesthetic sensibilities. As he grows in self-awareness, Stepan Verkhovensky sheds his narcissism and adopts the elder Zosima's theological position that all are responsible for all and thus that all must forgive others and hope for forgiveness in return. His son Peter, on the other hand, is a materialist driven by a will to power.[16] He is capable of appealing to others' ideals, as when he persuades Liza Tushina to join Stavrogin, but he generally debunks polite language and uses his own verbal skills to confuse, shame, and intimidate. He is a falsifier and a role-player. Finally, Peter never forgets or forgives a slight. His narcissism drives his will to power and acts as a force of discord and destruction.

Significantly, in recounting his life story, Stepan Verkhovensky omits mention of his paternal role. On this score, Stepan harbors no illusions. The narrator reveals that Stepan sent Peter away and only visited him once in sixteen years. When they meet again, Peter revenges his father's neglect: he rejects his father's overtures, shames him publicly, and destroys his relationship with Varvara Stavrogina. Dostoevsky, whose *Diary* writer proclaims that parent-child bonding results from "the ceaseless labor of love" (22:70), holds Verkhovensky senior responsible not only for abandoning his son, but also, and perhaps more importantly, for his failure to foster Peter's aesthetic sensibility. All of Stepan Verkhovensky's substitute children—Stavrogin, Dasha, and Liza—receive an aesthetic legacy from their teacher.[17] Yet when Stepan Verkhovensky visits Peter in Petersburg, he is disgusted by his son's aesthetic inadequacy: "*Enfin,* no sense of elegance whatsoever, that is, of anything higher, essential, of any germ of a future idea . . . *c'était comme un petit idiot*" (10:75–6;92). In criticizing his son, Stepan convicts himself: what he has given to others, he has not shared with his own son.

As a utilitarian, Peter employs language expediently. He speaks rudely when he wants to strip away the social veneer provided by good manners. Calling his father's and Varvara's friendship "a mutual outpouring of slops," he tells Stepan: "I proved to her like two times two that you'd been living for your mutual profit: she as a capitalist, and you as her sentimental clown" (10:239;305). He speaks rudely to shame others into doing his bidding. Thus, he intimidates the group of five into murdering Shatov by threatening their safety. As the narrator notes, "Peter Stepanovich was unquestionably guilty before them: it all could have been handled with much greater accord and *ease,* if he had only cared to brighten the reality at least a little. Instead of presenting the fact in a decent light, as something Roman and civic or the like, he had held up only crude fear and the threat to their own sins, which was simply impolite" (10:421;550–1). The narrator's extraordinary comment, that Peter's failure to provide an ideological justification for Shatov's murder is "impolite" (*chto bylo uzhe prosto nevezhlivo*), emphasizes the novel's aesthetic polemic. Stepan Verkhovensky's politeness, good manners, and elevated language express his idealism. Peter's verbal and physical crudeness underline his materialism and will to power.[18] His bad manners, here revealed as brutal truth-telling, betray him.

Varnished vs. Unvarnished Truths

Stepan's politeness and Peter's rudeness also exemplify disputes concerning truth-telling. In his article, "Something about Lying," Dostoevsky's *Diary* writer declares that most social interactions contain some hyperbole and that hyperbole is not necessarily a bad thing, but rather a sign of tact (21:119). He argues that this is because Russians do not consider the unvarnished truth sufficiently interesting. Moreover, as David Nyberg points out, telling the truth about everything all the time is not only impossible but probably also undesirable.[19] We would not want to appear in public without our public persona any more than we would want to appear without our clothes.

Peter Verkhovensky repeatedly uses truth-telling to strip others of their protective covering and thus humiliate them. When it suits his purposes, Peter supplies protective fictions. He romanticizes Stavrogin's behavior for his mother; he suggests an opera plot to Liza, thereby inspiring her self-sacrifice. Yet he brutally humiliates the group of five: "Stavrogin's flight stunned and crushed him. . . . That was why he was unable to be very tender with our people" (10:421;550–1). The narrator sardonically notes the correlation between private and public: when shamed, Peter shames others. He can encourage others' fictions to serve his own ends; but when shamed by the truth, he tells the truth to pass on the shame.

Peter enjoys shaming others. He shames the Lembkes, Lebiadkin, Karmazinov, the group of five. He particularly delights in shaming his father, who finally responds by raising doubts about Peter's legitimacy. In doing so, Stepan begins a dispute over the preservation and breaking of social taboos. When Peter reciprocates by vilifying both parents, Stepan orders his son to be silent. But Peter rejoins that Stepan was the first to violate the taboo—this time and previously. Peter informs the narrator that when Stepan visited him, he used to wake his son twice nightly: "and what do you think he told me those nights? These same indecent anecdotes about my mother" (10:240:307). Peter uses the adjective "*skoromnye*," a word denoting food proscribed during fast periods, such as Lent. Stepan responds: "Oh, that was in the loftiest sense! Oh, you didn't understand me! Nothing, you understood nothing" (10:240;307). Given Stepan's romantic imagination, readers can picture him fabricating tales of a tragic love triangle in which he ceded to the other man. But given his readiness to project blame, readers can imagine him slandering his wife. Given his own materialism, Peter would naturally seize on the more accusatory parts. Their argument pertains to varnished versus unvarnished truths.

Peter accuses his father of hypocrisy: "But, still, it comes out meaner your way than mine, meaner, admit it" (10:240;307). Stepan certainly erred in confiding his doubts about his wife to his child. The narrator notes that this is a repeated mistake. Stepan acted similarly with Stavrogin: "More than once he awakened his ten- or eleven-year-old friend at night only to pour out his injured feelings in tears before him, or to reveal some domestic secret to him, not noticing that this was altogether inadmissible" (10:35;40). Stepan Verkhovensky is weak-willed. He disregards the social conventions that protect children from inappropriate disclosures. He slanders Peter's mother, then condemns his son for doing the same.

Peter has more grievances against his father, however. Stepan Verkhovensky's inappropriate confidences raise questions about Peter's legitimacy and thus his identity. Peter denies his hurt, but it is palpable: "From my viewpoint, don't worry: I don't blame mother; if it's you, it's you, if it's the Polack, it's the Polack, it makes no difference to me. . . . And does it make any difference to you whether I'm your son or not?" (10:240;307). Peter thus identifies the real issue. He turns to the narrator: "'[H]e didn't spend a ruble on me all his life, he didn't know me at all until I was sixteen, then he robbed me here, and now he shouts that his heart has ached for me all his life, and poses in front of me like an actor. Really, I'm not Varvara Petrovna, for pity's sake!'" (10:240;307). Peter's statement reveals that he still feels abandoned and dispossessed. Peter's wounded vanity thus motivates his rage for revenge. He tells the hurtful truth to pass on a true hurt.

While Peter uses rude language to wield power, he uses obfuscating rhetoric to reveal and conceal his political purposes: "'In fact I have a tactic: I blab and blab [*ia vru i vru*], then suddenly I say some intelligent word, precisely when they are all searching for it. They surround me, and I start blabbing again [*ia opiat' nachnu vrat'*]'" (10:179;225–6). In this speech to Stavrogin, Peter uses the verb *vrat'* in its sense of "blab, blather, bullshit," that is, he speaks without reference to truth. As he explains earlier to Stavrogin, "'For pity's sake, who's going to start suspecting you of mysterious designs after that?'" (10:176;221). Peter deploys blather as a deceptive cover for his political activities.

Peter also uses obfuscating rhetoric to manipulate others. He explains to Kirillov: "'In order to be believed, you must be as obscure as possible, exactly that, with hints alone. You must show only a little corner of the truth, just enough to tease them. They will always lie to themselves more than we can and, of course, believe themselves more than us'" (10:473;621).[20] Peter's words expose him as a falsifier. He blathers to obfuscate the truth, but he also deliberately refers to the truth, only to lead his interlocutors astray. This latter rhetorical strategy of Peter's works on a fill-in-the-blank principle—hint at something and let your interlocutor elaborate. Peter deploys this strategy with Julia von Lembke, overtly manipulating her propensity for self-deception.

Varieties of Self-Deception

Like Stepan Verkhovensky, Julia von Lembke is a self-deceiver[21] who is seduced by a social role. Upon becoming the governor's wife, Julia Mikhailovna felt that she had been "called, almost anointed, one 'o'er whom this tongue of flame blazed up.'" Quoting from Pushkin's 1830 poem "The Hero," the narrator ironically conveys Julia's grandiose sense of social role.[22] Moreover, the narrator reveals her rather confused and contradictory self-image: she wants to uncover a conspiracy in the provinces, thereby earning recognition and thanks from Petersburg, yet she wants to save the youthful conspirators. She plans to both report on them and save them, "and even history and all of Russian liberalism would perhaps bless her name" (10:268;345). By encouraging her self-deception, Peter gains a hold over her.

Julia von Lembke easily succumbs to manipulation because, unlike Stepan Verkhovensky, she lacks conviction. Furthermore, she completely underrates the power of language. For instance, she believes that "phrase-mongers are not dangerous" (10:248;316). Unlike Stepan Verkhovensky, who gradually relinquishes his self-deception, Julia von Lembke obstinately clings to hers. When Peter lies outright to her at the fête, the narrator comments, "Alas, the poor woman still wanted so much to be deceived!" (10:378;493). But when Peter blames her for the morning's disaster, she must face the truth: "In fact you are lying to my face" (10:380;495). Nonetheless, Julia agrees to attend the ball, thereby becoming the scapegoat for Peter's radical activities. Then Julia von Lembke must face the price of her willful self-deception: her husband's mental health. By clinging to her fantasy self-image, she completely destroys her chances of fulfilling her own political ambitions and almost kills her husband.

Stepan Verkhovensky, on the other hand, fully appreciates rhetoric's power. He may be a self-deceiver, but he also has unshakable aesthetic and ethical beliefs. In contrast to his son, who believes that all human beings act out of self-interest, Stepan Verkhovensky vacillates between idealizing and denouncing others. Stepan strains to find a positive message in his son's blather: "My friend, the real truth [*pravda*] is always implausible, did you know that? To make the truth [*pravda*] more plausible, it's absolutely necessary to mix it with lies [*lzhi*]. People have always done so. Perhaps there's something here that we don't understand. What do you think, is there something in this victorious squealing that we don't understand? I wish there was. I do wish it" (10:172;216). Yet, by the time he reaches the fête, Stepan Verkhovensky promptly announces: "Ladies and gentlemen, I have solved the whole mystery. The whole mystery of their effect lies—in their stupidity!" (10:371;484).

To attain this understanding, Stepan Verkhovensky turns to the radicals' catechism, Chernyshevsky's novel, *What Is To Be Done?*: "I guessed that he had obtained and was *studying* the novel with a single purpose, so that in the event of an unquestionable confrontation with the 'squealers,' he would know their methods and arguments beforehand from their own 'catechism,' and, being thus prepared, would solemnly refute them all *in her eyes*" (10:238;303–4). Stepan unexpectedly discovers that "'It's our same idea, precisely ours; we, we were the first to plant it, to nurture it, to prepare it'" (10:238;304). Yet the rhetoric appalls him: "'But, God, how it's all expressed, distorted, mangled! . . . Are these the conclusions we strove for? Who can recognize in this the initial thought?'" (10:238;304). The utilitarian materialism of Peter's generation distorts Stepan's social ideals: "The enthusiasm of modern youth is as pure and bright as in our time. Only one thing has happened: the displacing of purposes, the replacing of one beauty by another! The whole perplexity lies in just what is more beautiful: Shakespeare or boots, Raphael or petroleum?" (10:372;485). Stepan fights the younger generation's materialism by defending beauty.

Peter's self-image reflects his materialism. He repeatedly calls himself a "fraud, not a socialist." When proposing his pretendership plan to Stavrogin, he argues that the most effective means of subordinating others are: (1) uniforms (i.e., roles and role-playing); (2) sentimentality; (3) frauds (i.e., a useful bunch for manipulating others); and, most critically, (4) shame of one's own opinion, the cement that binds: "I can get someone to go into the fire if only I shout at him that he is not liberal enough" (10:298–9). Peter himself deliberately plays a role; advises Stavrogin to do so (10:300;386); appeals to Liza's sentimentality (10:401;523); calls himself a fraud (10:324;418); and bullies others by shaming them (10:316;407, 10:421;549).[23]

In contrasting father's and son's rhetoric, Dostoevsky shifts readers' attention from the political to the metaphysical. Where Peter uses rhetoric to shame others, Stepan uses it to inspire them: Peter reminds others of their fallen natures, Stepan of the divine spark within. Where Peter appeals to food and money, Stepan invokes love and higher ideals. Throughout the novel, Dostoevsky highlights the theological implications of the father-son conflict. In an exchange with Kirillov, for example, the materialistic Peter denies that language has figurative content, emphasizing, rather, its utilitarian aspect: "You know these are only words" (10:469;614). Kirillov, an idealist who has accepted materialism intellectually but struggles with it emotionally, protests by articulating the human need for the transcendent: "All my life I did not want it to be only words. This is why I lived, because I kept not wanting it. And now, too, every day I want it not to be words" (10:469;614). Kirillov's materialism costs him his life. In accepting it, Kirillov denies the possibility of transcendence:

> Listen to a big idea: there was one day on earth, and in the middle of the earth stood three crosses. One on a cross believed so much that he said to another: 'This day you will be with me in paradise.' The day ended, they both died, went, and did not find either paradise or resurrection. What had been said would not prove true. Listen: this man was the highest on all the earth, he constituted what it was to live for. Without this man the whole planet with everything on it is—madness only. There has not been one like *Him* before or since, not ever, even to the point of miracle. This is the miracle, that there has not been and never will be such a one. And if so, if the laws of nature did not

pity even *This One,* did not pity even their own miracle, but made *Him,* too, live amidst a lie and die for a lie, then the whole planet is a lie, and stands upon a lie and a stupid mockery. Then the very laws of the planet are a lie and a devil's vaudeville. Why live then, answer me, if you're a man. (10:471;617)

With Kirillov's suicide, Dostoevsky demonstrates the life-and-death consequences of language and belief. Without the transcendent that Stepan Verkhovensky proclaims essential for life, Kirilov chooses death. Stepan contends with his son because he believes that it is not "only words"; he believes in the figurative behind the literal, the metaphysical behind the physical.

Dostoevsky illuminates the theological implications of the father-son conflict by outlining the trajectory of their lives. During the course of the novel, Stepan Verkhovensky changes; he is portrayed as a knight who errs but moves ever closer to the truth. Stepan Trofimovich thus dies, like the world's most famous knight, Don Quixote, expressing the hope that others will learn from his mistakes. Throughout the novel, Dostoevsky connects Stepan Verkhovensky with knight imagery. Stepan publishes a treatise on knights in a progressive journal (10:9;9). When Varvara Stavrogina adopts utilitarian rhetoric, he declares himself a knight (10:266;341). To prove he loves Varvara, he quotes Pushkin's 1829 poem about the Poor Knight (10:266;341). Like Prince Myshkin, the character associated with Poor Knight imagery in *The Idiot*, Stepan Verkhovensky defends a mother's name against a son's slander.[24] Treating Varvara as his lady, Stepan regards his speech at the fête as a last chance to "solemnly refute" the "'squealers'" "*in her eyes*" (10:238;304). Finally, just like Don Quixote, for the last week of his life Stepan Verkhovensky is confined to his bed by a fever, experiences a deathbed conversion, repents of his former life, calls it a lie, confesses to his friends and to a priest, and dies three days later.

In the end, Stepan Verkhovensky emerges from his narcissistic self-enclosure, preaches universal responsibility and forgiveness, and embraces God. He confesses to Sophia Matveevna: "My friend, I have been lying [*lgal*] all my life. Even when I was speaking the truth [*pravdu*]. I never spoke for truth's sake [*dlia istiny*], but only for my own. I did know it before this, but I only see it now" (10:497;651). He acknowledges the consequences of his self-referentiality and reaches out to others: "He suddenly remembered *Lise,* their meeting the previous morning: 'It was so terrible and—there must have been some misfortune, and I didn't ask, I didn't find out! I thought only of myself!' (10:496;650). He assumes responsibility for his own actions and sees his connection to others: "*Nous sommes tous malheureux, mais il faut les pardonner tous. Pardonnons, Lise,* and be free forever. To settle accounts with the world and be fully free—*il faut pardonner, pardonner, et pardonner!*" (10:411;537); "Oh, let's forgive, forgive, let's first of all forgive all and always. . . . Let's hope that we, too, will be forgiven. Yes, because we are guilty one and all before each other. All are guilty!" (10:491;644). Like St. Paul in First Corinthians, Stepan affirms love as the highest virtue: "And what is more precious than love? Love is higher than being, love is the crown of being, and is it possible for being not to bow before it?" (10:505;662). Moreover, he renounces his atheism: "'My friends,' he said, 'God is necessary for me if only because He is the one being who can be loved eternally....'" (10:505;662).

His son Peter, on the other hand, does not change. The narrator portrays him as a rhetorical tempter with a serpent's tongue (10: 144;180) who seeks power over others. The narrator reveals that Peter tempts Stavrogin with three offers—Liza, the Lebiadkins' deaths, Shatov's life. Like the devil he resembles, Peter systematically deceives and destroys. On a more banal level, Peter never forgives a slight; he has Shatov murdered, for example, partly because Shatov spit in his face in Geneva (10:466;611). Finally, Peter proposes to substitute an earthly pretender for God.

The way father and son exit the novel thematically underscores their differences. Peter departs by train (a form of transportation associated with apocalyptic imagery in *The Idiot*) to the European capital of Russia, St. Petersburg.[25] Furthermore, he abandons the loyal Erkel on the railroad platform to play cards in first-class. He eventually flees Russia. Stepan, on the other hand, goes on a pilgrimage to Russia's heartland. He sheds his European self-image and seeks union with the Russian Bible peddler, Sophia Matveevna Ulitina. Furthermore, he turns his dying thoughts toward others:

> The whole law of human existence consists in nothing other than a man's always being able to bow before the immeasurably great. If people are deprived of the immeasurably great, they will not live and will die in despair. The immeasurable and infinite is as necessary for man as the small planet he inhabits.... My friends, all, all of you: long live the Great Thought! The eternal, immeasurable Thought! For every man, whoever he is, it is necessary to bow before that which is the Great Thought. Even the stupidest man needs at least something great. Petrusha... Oh, how I want to see them all again! They don't know, they don't know that they, too, have in them the same eternal Great Thought! (10:506;663)

Stepan Verkhovensky's last words echo Dostoevsky's declaration in his 1861 article that art and beauty are as necessary to human existence as food and water. They also address the political and metaphysical conflicts between father and son. To Peter's call for an earthly pretender, Stepan counterposes belief in the transcendent. His words explain Kirillov's mad suicide as a longing for God.

Lying and Truth

In *Demons*, the Bible ultimately serves as the vehicle for Stepan Verkhovensky's self-understanding. Stepan's dying words refer back to the political and metaphysical revelation he experiences upon hearing the Gospel passage about Christ's exorcism of demons. As Nina Perlina observes, biblical quotation has the highest moral authority in Dostoevsky's poetics.[26] Biblical epigraphs are meant to shape readers' interpretation of the novel's events, and characters who know, quote, or understand the Gospels correctly have a special moral status. Dostoevsky thus illustrates Stepan's spiritual progress by having him move from the self-serving declaration that he will "correct the errors of that remarkable book" (10:491;645) to astutely interpreting the novel's epigraph (Luke 8:32–6). Yet as readers we often forget that Luke 8: 33–36 is the third biblical text that Sophia Matveevna reads to Stepan Verkhovensky. The two preceding texts—the Sermon on the Mount (Matthew 5.1–7.27) and the lukewarmness passage (Revelation 3:14–17)—influence his exegesis.

By confessing, Stepan Verkhovensky acknowledges and overcomes his shame,[27] thus enacting a positive model for Dostoevsky's authorial audience. The psychologist Michael Lewis explains that confession allows the self to bridge the gap between self and other. If we violate the standards, rules, and goals of the other, which we have accepted as our own, then we feel shame. By admitting to past error a person may distance the present self from the past self, thus moving from the erring self's position—the source of shame—to the other's position. Furthermore, since confession conduces to forgiveness and love, it dissipates shame through redemption.[28]

Stepan Verkhovensky confesses to lying three times: twice to Sophia Matveevna (named for Russian Orthodoxy's intermediary between God and his creation) and once to Varvara Stavrogina. He confesses twice in one scene: once before Sophia reads the Sermon on the Mount, once after. He confesses for the third time after she has read all three Gospel texts. Stepan's new understanding of the Gospel texts marks how his final two confessions differ from his first confession to Sophia, which resembles his earlier outpourings to Varvara. While I have cited the first two earlier, I cite all three together here:

(1) To Sophia Matveevna: "I lied to you earlier, all of it—for glory, for magnificence, out of idleness—all, all, to the last word, oh, blackguard, blackguard!" (10:496;651).

(2) To Sophia Matveevna: "'My friend, I've been lying all my life. Even when I was telling the truth. I never spoke for truth's sake, but only for my own, I

knew that before, but only now do I see. . . . Oh, where are those friends whom I have insulted with my friendship all my life? And everyone, everyone! *Savez-vous,* perhaps I'm lying now; certainly I'm also lying now. The worst of it is that I believe myself when I lie. The hardest thing in life is to live and not lie . . . and . . . and not believe one's own lies, yes, yes, that's precisely it! But wait, that's all for later . . . You and I together, together!' he added with enthusiasm" (10:497;651–2).

(3) To Varvara Stavrogina: "'[M]y friend, when I understood . . . that turned cheek, I . . . right then I also understood something else . . . *J'ai menti toute ma vie* all, all my life! and I'd like . . . tomorrow, though. . . . Tomorrow we shall all set off'" (10:505–6;664).

As the narrator observes, when Stepan Verkhovensky first confesses to Sophia Matveevna, he behaves just has he has with Varvara Stavrogina for twenty years (10:496;650): after shame-filled encounters with Varvara, Stepan would rage and slander her, then confess (10:13;14). In similar fashion, the day after recounting his life story to Sophia Matveevna, Stepan Trofimovich throws himself at her feet, calls her "*une marquise*" and himself "a blackguard," and confesses his failings to her.

After Stepan Verkhovensky falls seriously ill for the next two days and they miss the ferry to Spasovo (Savior's), he asks Sophia to read from the Gospels.[29] Stepan's request shows that he is returning to his Russian roots; it thus exemplifies Dostoevsky's antidote to the *otorvannost'*—the deracination or alienation—of the Russian intelligentsia, who have lost their ties to the Russian soil. Sophia Matveevna's name recalls Wisdom (Sophia) and the Gospels (Matveevna—daughter of Matthew). As a woman whose husband died during the Crimean War, she represents Russian patriotism. As a Bible peddler, she embodies a bridge between the Russian people and the upper classes. When Stepan Trofimovich asks her to read from the Gospels, Sophia reads him the Sermon on the Mount.[30] Following her reading, Stepan confesses to her the second time (10:497;651). The Sermon sensitizes him to his narcissism: he has served not his ideals but his self-image. Accordingly, he reaches out to others: "'Oh, where are those friends. . . . And everyone, everyone!'" (10:497;651). After the Gospel reading, Stepan recognizes that he must break the cycle of self-enclosure: "'The hardest thing in life is to live and not lie . . . and . . . and not believe one's own lies, yes, yes, that's precisely it!'" (10:497;651). With these words, Stepan Verkhovensky acknowledges his self-deception as well as the lies that facilitated it.

In his confession to Varvara Stavrogina, Stepan Verkhovensky again refers to the turned cheek passage from Matthew. The Gospel has sensitized him to the narcissism of his normal responses. It teaches him that one must not pass on harm or humiliation. Christ's sermon thus prepares him to embrace the Elder Zosima's command to *actively* love one's neighbor—love as hard work, love as a placing of others before self. He closes his confession by expressing reprentance and a desire to begin anew.

Stepan Verkhovensky's confessions also problematize truth's role in the novel. In *Demons* nothing is as it seems. The narrator proceeds by indirection, providing rumors, speculation, and conflicting interpretations along with his own interpretation of events.[31] So how does the reader distinguish truth from falsity in *Demons*? A quick return to "Something about Lying" provides some guidance. First, as the novel shows, Stepan Verkhovensky is not a falsifier, like his son Peter, but a liar. Moreover, he is a master hyperbolizer, an epideictic rhetor, like Dostoevsky himself. Yet he dramatically differs from Dostoevsky. His speech fails because he doesn't consider his audience. Stepan Verkhovensky hopes to win over his audience only because he wants to triumph over his enemies and vindicate himself "*in her eyes.*" Reading his hyperbolic deathbed epiphany—"I *never* spoke for truth's sake, but for my own" (emphasis mine)—as a gloss on Stepan's defense of beauty at the fête allows readers to view it as a selfish act, truth spoken for the sake of upholding his self-image.

Yet if we accept Stepan Trofimovich's hyperbolic disclaimer as a simple fact, we oversimplify his character. His defense of beauty at the fête is, paradoxically, a case of a truth spoken for its own sake. For in speaking of his ideals, Stepan Verkhovensky runs the risk that his audience will not only disagree with him but mock him, as it does. Furthermore, his hyperbole enables him to express something not entirely accessible to language. Stepan Verkhovensky uses hyperbole in the way that Razumikhin describes it—as a means to arrive at the truth. His hyperbole thus originates in metaphysical, not physical, desire.

A further question arises: for Dostoevsky, is truth spoken for its own sake really truth? To consider this, readers must refer to another passage, one very dear to Dostoevsky's heart. While reconciling with Stavrogin, Shatov paraphrases a thought from Dostoevsky's own letter to Fonvizina (28.I:176), attributing it to Stavrogin: "'But wasn't it you who told me that if someone proved to you mathematically that the truth is outside Christ, you would better agree to stay with Christ than with the truth?'" (10:198;249). For Dostoevsky, truth is never merely statically factual. Truth is spoken or lived; it is embodied and dynamic; it always matters who says things and to what end. Shatov, who often voices authorial beliefs, associates the truth with mathematical proofs and thus with rationalist thought. Dostoevsky, not a Kantian, top-down thinker, himself favored a more intuitive mode. He rejects the proposition that truth as an abstract principle has an absolute moral force. A bottom-up thinker, Dostoevsky examines individual cases to make moral judgments. For Dostoevsky, truth is embodied and dynamic, not abstract and static. Dostoevsky thus embraces Christ as an incarnate ideal.[32]

By having a compulsive liar recognize the role of rhetoric in self-deception, Dostoevsky warns readers that self-fashioning is risky and self-examination is essential. Stepan's confessions to Sophia prove necessary to the self-examination that precedes his full conversion, political as well as religious. Before he can see himself in the broader sociopolitical context, however, Stepan needs further exposure to the Bible. Sophia next reads to him from Revelation: "'And to the angel of the church in Laodicea write: The words of the Amen, the faithful and true witness, the beginning of God's creation. I know your works: you are neither cold nor hot! Would that you were cold or hot! So, because you are lukewarm, and neither cold nor hot, I will spew you out of my mouth. For you say, I am rich, I have prospered, and I need nothing; not knowing that you are wretched, pitiable, poor, blind, and naked'" (10:497;652). Stepan Trofimovich becomes very excited about the message he sees for others: "I never knew that great passage! Do you hear: sooner cold, sooner cold than lukewarm, than *only* lukewarm. Oh, I'll prove it" (10:497–8;652). While he hails the passage as a commentary on the materialists, the last verse describes the willful blindness to one's own spiritual state that constitutes self-deception; it thus further prefigures Stepan's epiphany about what he shares with the younger generation. Stepan sees the materialists' satisfaction with material goods as ignorance of their spiritual poverty. Yet this passage, taken together with the Sermon on the Mount, reveals to Stepan his own spiritual poverty: he embraces and preaches higher ideals but does not live accordingly.

Like Stavrogin, the truly lukewarm figure in the novel,[33] Stepan Verkhovensky causes suffering by his non-action. On his deathbed, he comprehends that he, too, is possessed—by the same narcissism he sees in the younger generation. When Sophia Matveevna reads him the passage he requests from the Gospel of Luke, he identifies with his spiritual children. Drawing an analogy between the possessed man and Russia, he identifies the demons who leave him and enter into the swine as "all the sores, all the miasmas, all the uncleanness, all the big and little demons accumulated in our great and dear sick man, in our Russia for centuries, for centuries!" (10:499;654). He further identifies the demon-possessed as "us, us and them, and Petrusha . . . *et les autres avec lui*, and I, perhaps first, at the head, and we will rush, insane and raging, from the cliff down into the sea, and all be drowned, and good riddance to us" (10:499;654). Once he avows that he will be saved by the divine spark within himself, he casts off his narcissism. He dies praying that others also will be saved: "Oh, how I want to see them all again! They don't know, they don't know that they, too, have in them the same eternal Great Thought!" (10:506;665). Like Dostoevsky, Stepan Verkhovensky thus identifies the transcendent as a moral force on earth.

Narrative Vision

Stepan Verkhovensky's last words reveal the novel's narrative dynamics, for they illustrate the expansion of his vision. A larger vision is just what Dostoevsky's narrator lacks and what we, the authorial audience, have gained—for during the course of the novel Dostoevsky has trained us to see. As mentioned earlier, the narrator's treatment of Stepan recapitulates, with a difference, a narrative pattern Dostoevsky worked out in *The Idiot*. Along with the narrator, we stay close to a positive character for the greater part of the novel. Then the narrator distances himself from that character, and we in the authorial audience distance ourselves from the narrator. This dynamic can be explained in terms of narrative vision. The narrator persists in seeing Stepan Verkhovensky in light of past behavior patterns. This perspective works in Lebiadkin's case—when Lebiadkin has money, he drinks and boasts. Thus he dies. But this perspective does not accommodate Stepan Verkhovensky. Stepan experiences a conversion—figuratively, he turns around, a move that enables him to see beyond his narcissistic prison. He, in turn, expands our vision.

That Dostoevsky consciously aims to expand his readers' vision can be seen more clearly in his journalism. In an 1873 *Diary of a Writer* article about the new jury system, tellingly titled *Sreda* ("The Milieu"), Dostoevsky as *Diary* writer urges his readers (narrative and authorial audiences combined) to adopt a broad view of citizenship (such as that held by English juries, for instance) when pronouncing judgment. He gives the example of the Saiapin jury, which tried the peasant Saiapin for so cruelly and repeatedly abusing his wife that she hanged herself. The *Diary* writer argues that the jury exercises false compassion when they adjudge the criminal guilty but "worthy of leniency." This, the *Diary* writer points out, is a form of tunnel vision—which we can compare to the narrator's vision in *Demons*. The *Diary* writer urges his readers to see the crime in a larger context—to imagine the consequences of leniency, which, in his view, would spell certain death for Saiapin's daughter. He wants to deter jurors from engaging in the false compassion to which Saiapin's lawyer appeals: "Backwardness, ignorance, have some pity, it's the milieu." He counters by morally contextualizing Saiapin's actions: "Yet millions of them live and not all hang their wives by their heels!"

By sharing this larger vision of individuals in relation to others, Dostoevsky hopes to nurture true compassion in his authorial audience. Dostoevsky develops his highly subjective narrator for just this purpose—to teach us to see the person standing in front of us not as an isolated figure, but as a member of the human community. Dostoevsky hopes that we, like Stepan Verkhovensky on his deathbed, can look beyond ourselves and see the larger moral and metaphysical picture.

Lying and Self-Deception

The Dostoevskian liar whom Stepan Verkhovensky most closely resembles is General Ivolgin. Though Ivolgin is a military man and Stepan Verkhovensky is a civilian, they both come from good backgrounds and have the manners and education that make them at home with their social superiors. They are both prone to sentimentality and hyperbole. They are both consumers of romanticism; in fact, they even tell similar clichéd lies about their romantic rivalries. Ivolgin, for instance, tells Prince Myshkin that he had almost fought a duel with Myshkin's father over Myshkin's mother but that their friendship had restrained them; at the last moment, they simultaneously dropped their guns and embraced, ceding her to each other (8:81). Stepan Trofimovich tells Sophia Matveevna that Varvara Petrovna's "husband had died, 'cut down by a bullet at Sevastopol,' solely because he felt unworthy of her love, giving way to his rival—that is, to the same Stepan Trofimovich" (10:494;648). Both stories function as analogues to the action in their novels' main plots. Ivolgin's story, ending with the rivals' embrace, anticipates Myshkin's and Rogozhin's brotherly embrace over the dead body of the woman they both love. Stepan Verkhovensky's story prefigures his own story—relinquishing the beloved (Varvara Stavrogina) to a rival (in this case, an ideological rival, his son Peter) results in the lover's death (his own).

When they have sympathetic audiences, both General Ivolgin and Stepan Verkhovensky exaggerate: Sophia Matveevna's shy pleasure in his love story sends "Stepan Trofimovich into utter admiration and inspiration, so that he even added quite a lot [*prilgnul*]" (10:494;648). In Stepan's telling, Varvara Stavrogina, whom the narrator describes as "a tall, yellow, bony woman with an exceedingly long face recalling something horselike" (10:18;18), becomes "a most lovely brunette ('the admiration of Petersburg and a great many European capitals')" (10:494;648).[34] Furthermore, once successful with their audiences, both General Ivolgin and Stepan Verkhovensky start to believe themselves: Stepan Trofimovich "exclaimed to Sophia Matveevna, himself almost believing everything he was telling her" (10:494–5;648). Finally, both General Ivolgin and Stepan Verkhovensky reveal their Western educations as they acknowledge themselves as liars by using the French verb *mentir*. While confessing to the lower gentry Russian Bible peddler, Sophia Matveevna, Stepan Verkhovensky uses the Russian verb *lgat'*. When he confesses to the upper-class Varvara Stavrogina, however, he uses French: "*J'ai menti toute ma vie*, all, all my life!" (10:505–506;662). This persistent use of French resonates ideologically in the novel, illustrating the alienation of the upper classes from the Russian people.

For both General Ivolgin and Stepan Verkhovensky, a combination of externally and internally induced moments of shame provokes identity crises that lead to deathbed revelations and acceptance of responsibility for their actions. Near their lives' ends, each tells an extended lie about himself to a sympathetic audience: Ivolgin tells Myshkin that he served as Napoleon's page boy; Stepan Verkhovensky tells Sophia Ulitina that he was a civic figure and an unrequited lover. Each gets transported by his storytelling. Their hyperbole gives rise to shame. Shame leads them to confess and to express concern for their families.

Their stories differ in scope. In *The Idiot*, Dostoevsky subordinates the father-and-children plot to the romantic triangle at the novel's center. In *Demons*, however, Dostoevsky foregrounds the father-and-children plot. Stepan Verkhovensky acts as the novel's representative father—both literally and figuratively. In *The Idiot*, General Ivolgin curses his son Gania. In *Demons*, Stepan Verkhovensky curses his son Peter's whole generation and its followers. He curses his son at home (10:240;307) and his ideological children at the fête (10:374;487). Furthermore, his deathbed revelation carries a public message. Stepan Verkhovensky voices the prophecy that Dostoevsky the *Diary* writer will proclaim in "The Golden Age in Our Pockets": that we all carry the divine within us, and that we would all be happy on earth if only we could see it (22:13). In this tragic novel, Stepan Verkhovensky dies with a message of hope for all.

While Stepan Verkhovensky most resembles *The Idiot's* General Ivolgin as a liar, Dostoevsky also reveals striking similarities between him and Captain Lebiadkin, the comic liar in *Demons*. In the private sphere, both Stepan Verkhovensky and Lebiadkin desire personal recognition from women and position themselves as rivals for Stavrogin's women: Stepan Verkhovensky for Dasha, Lebiadkin for Liza. Both drink too much. Both refer to themselves as cockroaches: Lebiadkin to Varvara Stavrogina in his ludicrous cockroach poem, Stepan Verkhovensky to the narrator (10:99:122). Their financial dependence on the Stavrogins links both characters to the novel's broader thematics of political parasitism. Dostoevsky associates both Stepan Verkhovensky and

Lebiadkin with poet imagery, that ultimate fusion of personal and political in Russian literature. Lebiadkin calls himself a poet; Varvara Stavrogina calls Stepan Verkhovensky one (10:57;68). Both crave public recognition for their verbal talents. Finally, both blame Russia for their failure (Lebiadkin, 10:141;175; Stepan Verkhovensky, 10:494;648). By drawing these parallels, Dostoevsky repeatedly highlights the novel's political thematics and emphasizes the links between the private and public spheres.

By including Stepan Verkhovensky among his novel's liars, Dostoevsky underlines the connections between narcissism and lying. Stepan Verkhovensky always places himself first: a widowed father, he abandons his son Peter and becomes Stavrogin's tutor; a liberal, he loses his serf Fedka in a card game; a gentleman, he wounds Dasha by his selfishness. When upset, he locks himself away. Enamored of his roles as persecuted liberal and misunderstood lover, he ignores others and their needs. Stepan Verkhovensky also violates the Russian social contract: he hyperbolizes but does not allow Varvara Stavrogina to do the same: "When you returned from abroad, you looked down your nose at me and wouldn't let me utter a word, and when I myself came and spoke with you later about my impressions of the Madonna, you wouldn't hear me out and began smiling haughtily into your tie, as if I really could not have the same feelings as you" (10:264;338). Stepan Verkhovensky's narcissism thus returns to haunt him. Varvara Stavrogina succumbs to Peter Verkhovensky's rhetoric and ideas because his father has failed to cultivate his own garden.

Even on his deathbed, Stepan Verkhovensky reveals his narcissism. He ignores Sophia's practical difficulties as he feverishly indulges in his final romance. Stepan's deathbed epiphany recalls the narrator's words about the temporary effects of great grief and its power to change a person. In these last moments, Stepan acknowledges the difficulty of sustained effort: "The hardest thing in life is to live and not lie . . . and . . . and not believe one's own lies" (10:497;652). In his next breath, however, he proclaims that he and she will journey together. Stepan understands and repents his lifelong practice of self-deception, and he understands what the cure requires. But old habits are not easily shaken. Stepan can only envision a new life of serving others by fabricating a romance. He needs a little fiction to help him on the path to truth.

In the end, Stepan Verkhovensky's idealism triumphs. When faced with shameful truths about his actual self, Stepan Verkhovensky invokes his ideal self-image and tries to realize it. In this scenario, shame works as social conscience, inducing him to abandon his narcissistic self-enclosure, to view himself in relation to others, and to do the right thing. This scenario triumphs over his habitual vacillation between self-aggrandizement and self-abasement. Dostoevsky thus closes his Stepan Verkhovensky plot with the triumph of Stepan's ideal self, the only positive death in *Demons*.

Stepan Trofimovich Verkhovensky: Leaving the Narrator Behind

In this novel of father and children, the father dies. But so do his progeny. Stepan Verkhovensky's deathbed idealism may bear fruit in Dostoevsky's readers' hearts, but his abdication of parental responsibility in the novel yields tragedy. The man who idealizes the Sistine Madonna, an icon of mother-child love, fails to transmit that ideal to the next generation. He vacillates between idealizing and vilifying two mothers—Peter's and Stavrogin's. Worse, he vilifies the mothers to their sons, thus weakening familial bonds. Stepan Verkhovensky passes on a powerful legacy of destructive selfishness. He dies faithful to his ideal. But Dostoevsky does not end his novel with Stepan's death. The novel's flesh-and-blood madonna (Marie Shatov) and her child (Stavrogin's) die when political fratricide destroys their family unit. The atheistic sons, who have rejected religious icons (Madonna and child/Christ), perpetuate the father's job of destroying social bonds. As he recognizes on his deathbed, Stepan Verkhovensky has advocated idealism but has sown schism.

Stepan Verkhovensky's deathbed epiphany completes the progression wherein Stepan repeatedly confronts the gap between his professed idealism and his actual life. It also highlights the narrator's role as exposer of his friend's self-deception and shame. While the narrator uses irony to create a critical distance between his narrative audience and his friend, his narrative strategy exposes him to analogous treatment. In exposing his friend, the narrator exposes himself. His absence from the deathbed scene is thus marked. In joining the ranks of helpers at the fête, and thus identifying himself, however tenuously, with the enemy camp, the narrator loses his access to Stepan Verkhovensky. After his speech fails, Stepan Verkhovensky locks himself away—denying the narrator access to himself, his thoughts, and his actions. While the narrator represents this exclusion as part of a pattern, Dostoevsky clearly shows that Stepan's decision marks a significant break with the past. At this point, the narrator loses us. He has created sufficient sympathy for Stepan so that when Stepan distances himself from the narrator, the authorial audience follows suit. While we may have accepted him as our travel guide up to this point, we part company with him when Stepan does. We reject his view that in journeying to Russia's heartland, Stepan is merely acting out of habit, distancing himself from those who would expose him.

Stepan Verkhovensky's deathbed confession highlights his motives and thus the gap between character and author. Making astute use of what Bakhtin has called the "double-voiced word," Dostoevsky encourages the authorial audience to regard Stepan Verkhovensky's farewell speech at the fête through the prism of his deathbed confessions. On this reading, the authorial audience judges a speaker's message by his motives. Here Frankfurt's analysis of bullshitting elucidates Dostoevsky's narrative strategy. Frankfurt argues that the bullshitter does not necessarily get things wrong;

rather bullshitting differs from other forms of discourse in how it is made and what motivates it. Stepan Verkhovensky's message is heartfelt, yet his apparently altruistic motives are largely selfish. By double-voicing Stepan's defense of beauty, Dostoevsky has Stepan say all the right things but for the wrong reasons. Dostoevsky, by contrast, places these words in his character's mouth for all the right reasons. He appeals to the authorial audience's aesthetic and moral sensibilities to create a sense of *communitas* based on shared values. And he reveals his metaliterary hand: Stepan Verkhovensky's speech fails because Stepan, unlike Dostoevsky, ignores his audience.

Demons can be read as a novel about rhetoric gone awry. It is about lying and falsification. Yet it also supplies the rhetoric that can exorcise the narcissism of the possessed. Almost all of the novel's characters are possessed or obsessed, or both. They deceive themselves and typecast others. They regard others as reflections or reflectors of themselves. They lie to one another unconsciously or deliberately to enhance their own self-image or their political power and position, or both. They rarely listen to one another. Yet Dostoevsky creates a model audience. Sophia listens to Stepan. He lies with lofty language, fashioning an ideal self-image. He chooses Sophia because she intuitively understands and because she disseminates the powerful rhetoric and message of the Bible. He lies, he confesses, and then he asks her to read. Most importantly, he listens. At first he hears the holy words only as they pertain to others, but then they speak to him. Sophia (Wisdom), mediator between the fallen world and the transcendent truth, daughter of Matthew, God's chosen scribe, listens empathically. Then she reads the Bible, thereby inspiring Stepan Verkhovensky to escape his narcissistic self-enclosure. He thinks of others, and accepts responsibility for the legacy of his selfishness. He dies praising the divine. He speaks his last words not for his own but for truth's sake.

chapter seven

Divided Selves

> Listen, I say, General, if someone else said that about you, then on the spot I would remove my head with my own hands, place it on a large platter and bring it myself on the platter to all those who doubt: "Here you go. See this head? Thus with my own head I vouch for him, and I'd go through fire for him!" That's how, I say, I'm prepared to vouch for you. (8:373)
> — LUKIAN LEBEDEV, *The Idiot*

> This I ask you: Is it true, great father, that somewhere in the Lives of the Saints it tells the story of some holy wonderworker whom they martyred for his faith, and when they finally cut off his head, he got up, raised his head, "kissed it lovingly," and walked on for a long time carrying it in his hands and "kissed it lovingly"? Is this true or not, honorable fathers? (14:42;44–5)
> — FEDOR KARAMAZOV, *The Brothers Karamazov*

Divided selves are not new in Dostoevsky's work. Starting with *The Double*, Dostoevsky has mimetically portrayed and thematically spotlighted characters' internal divisions. In *Crime and Punishment*, he underlines his protagonist's inner conflict by giving him the name *Raskolnik*ov, which means "schismatic." In *The Idiot* and *The Brothers Karamazov*, Dostoevsky goes a step farther: he inscribes doubleness into the self-representing rhetoric of his self-conscious, shameless liars, Lukian Lebedev and Fedor Karamazov.

Lebedev can be seen as an early prototype for Dostoevsky's namesake. Like Fedor Karamazov, he is highly self- and audience-conscious. He studies his interlocutors' physiognomies, plays the buffoon for his own ends, resents his social status, revenges perceived insults, and combines contradictory impulses within himself. Like Fedor Karamazov, he pursues materialist schemes yet suffers anxiety about the afterlife. And like Fedor Karamazov, Lukian Lebedev identifies both with a martyred saint and a secular sinner, thus revealing his divided soul.

As part of dialogues about belief, these two shameless liars allude to martyrs whose decapitated bodies bear witness to their faith. In positing paradoxical images of bodiless heads talking or headless bodies walking and kissing their heads, these two comic liars reveal a fascination for literally divided selves that Dostoevsky uses to reveal their figurative self-division. Lukian Lebedev and Fedor Karamazov evoke these images to provoke diverse, even contradictory, responses of belief and disbelief from their character audiences. Fedor Dostoevsky creates these scenes not only to expose his characters' souls and provoke his authorial audience's moral responses but also to enhance our aesthetic pleasure.

Swan Prophet

In the passage cited above, Lebedev evokes the image of St. John the Baptist, an identification that reveals his prophetic pretensions. Lebedev delivers this line to General Ivolgin, who has just stolen 400 rubles from Lebedev's wallet, a criminal breach of friendship that provides Lebedev with an opportunity for revenge. Lebedev goes to Prince Myshkin. Though convinced of the General's guilt, he knows that the Prince will not permit him to accuse his friend outright. Accordingly, Lebedev adopts the stance of public prosecutor and argues his case. After eliminating Keller as a suspect, he identifies Ferdyshenko as the thief, yet he points the finger at Ivolgin. He drives the Prince crazy with his double-talk—swearing to Ivolgin's innocence while revealing his guilt. For instance, Lebedev notes that when he woke the General from his "sleep of innocence" to inform him of the theft, the General blushed, turned pale, and then became incensed (all signs of guilt). Lebedev next declares that after he and Ivolgin had searched Keller, the General had demanded to be searched as well. Lebedev responds with the speech in my epigraph.

In his telling, Lebedev successfully assures the General of his loyalty but also arouses his gratitude, his guilt, and his shame. Ivolgin weeps and embraces Lebedev, calling him "the only friend who remains to me in my misfortunes!" (a line that he later attributes to his Napoleon). By arousing the General's gratitude, Lebedev augments his own emotional importance, thereby increasing Ivolgin's shame. In the face of such apparent loyalty, the General returns Lebedev's money.

By telling this story, Lebedev intends to allay the Prince's justified suspicion that he is accusing the General of theft. He thus engages in a rhetorical doubleness that confirms his sense of personal doubleness. At the very moment that he proposes to die for his friend, Lebedev is betraying him. By having Lebedev tell this story to the Prince, Dostoevsky reveals Lebedev's calculatedness, hypocrisy, and cruelty and thus deprives him of reader sympathy. Moreover, by having Lebedev swear by his head, an action that Christ specifically forbids in his Sermon on the Mount,¹ Dostoevsky condemns Lebedev's rhetoric.

Dostoevsky also makes Lebedev the site of metaliterary play. First, Lebedev's rhetoric is double-voiced: he directs his speech simultaneously at two audiences—his homodiegetic audience, the General, and his heterodiegetic audience, the Prince. By embedding Lebedev's double-voicing in his own text, Dostoevsky discloses his awareness of narrative multivoicing.² He also roguishly reveals his narrator exposing Lebedev exposing General Ivolgin.

Second, by having Lebedev reduce figurative expressions to their literal meanings, one of Gogol's favorite devices, Dostoevsky reveals Lebedev's Gogolian roots. In this passage, Lebedev reduces the figural expression *ruchat'sia golovoi*, meaning "to stake one's life," to its literal meaning, "to vouch with one's head." Dostoevsky thus exposes Lebedev as a parodic figure—he identifies with a prophet, a speaker whose rhetoric reaches beyond the literal to the figurative. Yet he acts as an antiprophet, as his rhetoric literalizes the figurative.

Lebedev's use of the image of St. John's head also conveys an awareness of his own duality, the alienation of his head from his heart. He even styles himself a "Talleyrand," the notorious statesman of the French Revolution who repeatedly switched sides yet survived. Nonetheless, as I show in the next chapter, Lebedev's nocturnal prayers for Mme. du Barry, a victim of the guillotine, demonstrate his intuitive desire for restoration to community.

Lebedev's absurd image of a body removing its head and carrying it on a platter anticipates Fedor Karamazov's story of the decapitated saint who carries his head in his hands and kisses it. Both Lebedev's and Fedor Pavlovich's stories have mimetic resonances: St. John the Baptist shames Herod's wife, and St. Denis shames his enemies because their tortures cannot stop him from talking! Furthermore, both characters tell stories about saints martyred for their religious beliefs: men of God, they challenge the state. Dostoevsky's liars thus invoke martyrs who value their souls over their bodies, thereby parodically echoing Dostoevsky's thematic linking of belief and ethics.

Lebedev's hyperbolic extravagance—a talking decapitated head—also echoes *The Idiot*'s apocalyptic thematics. However comically, Lebedev's story raises the issue of death's finality and thus the question of belief in God. Lebedev's story likewise links him with other characters in the novel. His fascination with execution (in this story and in the Countess du Barry's story) echoes Myshkin's as well as Ippolit's fascination with uncommuted death sentences. The image of a living corpse recalls Ivolgin's Kolpakov story. Whereas the stories Myshkin and Ippolit tell reflect the Prince's compassion and the dying youth's anguish, the stories Lebedev and Ivolgin tell parody the novel's thematics. These comic characters' hyperbolic rhetoric undercuts their credibility. Dostoevsky's metaliterary play, by contrast, augments readers' aesthetic delight.

The Kissing Head

In this scene, Dostoevsky does not surprise readers with shame but shows how Lebedev consciously yet cautiously exposes the General by pretending to believe him. Fedor Karamazov, on the other hand, demonstrates no restraint. Like Lebedev's story, Fedor Karamazov's (see epigraph) parodically frames a discussion of belief. It is also addressed to two audiences: the Elder Zosima and his relative Miusov. The unnamed subject of Fedor's story is St. Denis, patron saint of France and first bishop of Paris, eponym for the Enlightenment philosopher, Denis Diderot, who mocked him. The story's most outrageous features, that he lifted his decapitated head and kissed it while walking, are part of his legendary life.[3] By having Fedor Karamazov stress the kissing by mentioning it twice, Fedor Dostoevsky identifies the story as St. Denis's.[4] By choosing the moment when St. Denis walks head in hands, Dostoevsky also evokes an episode from Christ's life. Both Christ and St. Denis were historical figures who reputedly rose from the dead and were seen shortly thereafter. Readers thus sense Dostoevsky's authorial presence in the discussion that follows. While Fedor Karamazov raises poetic issues about the story's source, its content, its effect on listeners, and its teller's motive, Fedor Dostoevsky also highlights the novel's thematics of belief.

Fedor Karamazov's verbal challenge to the monks poses an even greater visual challenge to his audience and to Dostoevsky's readers: Can a head chopped off at the neck kissing itself ever be visualized, or is it a miracle that can exist only in narrative form? The art world offers a visual solution: The Princeton Index of Christian Art contains at least half a dozen images of St. Denis decapitated at the tonsure (which would permit the head to kiss itself) in addition to those where he is decapitated at the neck. Yet Dostoevsky's probable textual source for the image of St. Denis, Voltaire's *La Pucelle d'Orléans*, suggests that Dostoevsky was not offering a solution. The footnotes to Voltaire's mock epic report that St. Denis's persecutors first hanged him, but he continued to preach, so they were forced to cut him down and chop his head off at the neck. The mimetic impossibility of a head kissing itself would not only appeal to Dostoevsky, it also suggests an equally impossible image—"The Nose." In Gogol's famous story, the disembodied Nose masquerades as a high-ranking bureaucrat, at one point praying "with a pious expression on its face." For close to two hundred years now, readers have wrestled with the mimetic impossibility of Gogol's creation.[5] By evoking "The Nose," which also serves as an intertext for *The Brothers Karamazov*, Fedor Dostoevsky signals his leap to the metaliterary dimension, where Fedor Karamazov and his son Ivan also meet (see chapter 11).

While Fedor Karamazov addresses his inquiry to Zosima, once he reveals that he had heard his story from Miusov, who had heard it from a Frenchman in Paris, readers can see that Fedor introduces it to shame his relative. After all, Miusov had ridiculed him and called him a liar by declaring that his "stupid story" about Diderot "isn't true." By challenging the veracity of Miusov's story, Fedor turns the table. Refusing to be outshamed, Fedor pays Miusov back with interest. He associates Miusov, the liberal westernizer, whom he calls a "Parisian" (14:35;38), with the Frenchman who told him the story. Earlier, Fedor Pavlovich identified himself with Diderot, another Frenchman, who, like Miusov's Frenchman, was "a very learned man," who "made a special study of statistics about Russia . . . [and] lived in Russia for a long time." By equating both Miusov and himself with educated Frenchmen, Fedor Karamazov once again throws in Miusov's face the things they share.

Fedor Dostoevsky, on the other hand, uses the Frenchman/Miusov and Diderot/Fedor Karamazov parallels thematically to emphasize Russians' alienation from their people and from the sources of their faith. Both Miusov and Fedor Karamazov reveal their religious ignorance by retelling the story of a learned but ignorant Frenchman who attributed the story of St. Denis to the Lives of the Saints and claimed it was read aloud during the Orthodox liturgy. As churchgoing Russians like Dostoevsky would know, saints' lives are not read during the liturgy.[6] And while there is a Russian saint named Merkury of Smolensk who allegedly picked up his decapitated head and carried it, the kissing detail identifies the saint as St. Denis and the source as Voltaire's mock epic, *La Pucelle d'Orléans* (15:531). Voltaire's plot fits Dostoevsky's thematics. In *La Pucelle d'Orléans*, the French king dallies with his mistress, leaving France's defense to the young Joan of Arc. Fedor Dostoevsky thus has Fedor Karamazov evoke a work in which the father figure abdicates responsibility for his people, an appropriate thematic resonance for a novel in which the father abdicates responsibility for raising his sons. Finally, Fedor Dostoevsky undermines the authority of Diderot and Voltaire, the two Enlightenment atheists[7] known for their frequent mockery of the legendary St. Denis, by associating them with the dissolute Karamazov patriarch.

Fedor Pavlovich attributes the story about St. Denis to Miusov to provoke his poor in-law. He intensifies his taunting by claiming that "you, Petr Alexandrovich, shook my faith with this funny story. You didn't know it, you had no idea, but I went home with my faith shaken, and since then I've been shaking more and more. Yes, Petr Alexandrovich, you were the cause of a great fall!" (14:42;45). By emphasizing the story's effect on him, Fedor Pavlovich highlights the narrative dynamics of audience response. According to the age-old inspiration principle, miracle stories arouse wonder; believers consequently affirm their faith while skeptics scoff. Dostoevsky underscores the perversity of Fedor's unexpected response by providing Alesha's more normal one. Alesha's faith is shaken by the lack of a miracle, not the story of one. Here as elsewhere, Fedor Karamazov violates both social and narrative norms.

Fedor Karamazov's pun on the expression "shaken faith" also resonates thematically in the text. Like Gogol (see earlier) or Aesop (see chapter 9), he reduces the figurative to the literal. Like Dostoevsky, he indulges in hyperbole. Like Diderot (with whom he identifies), Fedor plays with the religious use of figurative language. Diderot had argued that, taken literally, Christ's words "this is my body" are as absurd as the story of St. Denis kissing his own decapitated head (15:531). In Dostoevsky's novel, atheists are literalists.

Fedor Karamazov's accusation that Miusov has caused "a great fall" allies Miusov (like himself) with the devil and the thematics of temptation, which figure in scenes where tempters— the Grand Inquisitor, Ivan, Rakitin, Smerdiakov, and Kolia—ply their craft upon Christ, Alesha, Iliusha, and the unnamed peasant. By introducing the image of the fall, Fedor returns to his obsession with shame and guilt. Dostoevsky also invokes the image of falling and rising from the novel's epigraph. Stories are like the seeds of Dostoevsky's biblical epigraph; they fall on all kinds of ground and may wither or bear the most unexpected fruit. Fedor Karamazov's response to Miusov's story about St. Denis may be perverse, but Fedor Dostoevsky introduces it to establish the power of storytelling. The two stories Fedor Karamazov tells about miracles (Diderot's conversion and St. Denis's head) haunt him because they reflect his preoccupation with salvation and the afterlife.

Dostoevsky reinforces the scene's metaliterary play when he has Miusov defend himself by calling the St. Denis story "just table talk." Though Miusov would not know it, saints' lives are read aloud during meals at the monastery. Dostoevsky thus contrasts monastic meals and sacred stories with secular meals and nonreligious stories; he also includes both sacred and secular stories in his own composition. By double-voicing Miusov's reference to "table talk," Dostoevsky situates this story in a literary tradition that associates eating and storytelling, food for body and food for soul.[8]

Miusov's "table talk" defense also recalls another martyr discussed at a table, whose story links the physical body with religious belief—the story of Foma Danilov. After dinner, Grigory tells Fedor and Ivan the story of "a Russian soldier stationed somewhere far away at the border who was captured by Asians and, being forced by them on pain of agonizing and immediate death to renounce Christianity and convert to Islam, would not agree to change his faith, and endured torture, was flayed alive, and died glorifying and praising Christ" (14:117;127). Fedor Karamazov then "remarked that such a soldier ought at once to be promoted to saint, and his flayed skin dispatched to some monastery: 'You'll see how people will come pouring in, and money, too.' Grigory scowled, seeing that Fedor Pavlovich was not at all moved but, as usual, was beginning to blaspheme" (14:117;127). Significantly, these two dinnertime stories about martyrs demonstrate Fedor Karamazov's perverse response. Both stories become occasions for blame or blasphemy, thereby mingling the secular and the sacred, like Dostoevsky's own novel. Moreover, since St. Denis reputedly carried his head to the monastery outside Paris that bears his name, both stories associate monasteries with pilgrimages. Finally, both stories raise the issue of miracles which Ivan and Alesha both explore later in the novel.

Audience Response

In this scene, both Fedors carefully attend to audience response. Fedor Karamazov aims his stories at Miusov and Zosima, and Fedor Dostoevsky details both men's reactions. Fedor Karamazov watches Miusov's and Zosima's responses because audience response conditions his sense of self. He focuses on Miusov, because Miusov represents the social class that rejects him, and Fedor Pavlovich is revenging himself with Aesopian wit and one-upmanship. He focuses equally on Zosima, because he seeks a nonjudgmental response.

Fedor Dostoevsky directs his readers' attention to Miusov's and Zosima's responses, because they emblemize the social drama being enacted. Miusov and Zosima represent larger constituencies on the Russian sociopolitical and religious scene. An educated liberal who subscribes to Western secular ideas, Miusov lives largely abroad, venerates decorum, and distances himself as much as possible from Fedor Karamazov, his relative by marriage. Though once a member of the same class, Zosima rejected that life and turned to Russian Orthodoxy, devoting himself to the care of people's spiritual lives. He urges Fedor Pavlovich to return to community. Fedor Karamazov's drama of identity thus plays out in polarized social, emotional, and religious field— individualism versus universal brotherhood, mind versus heart, atheism versus faith. In his journalism, Dostoevsky advocates bridging the post–Petrine gap between the Russian educated classes (represented here by Miusov) and the Russian people. Zosima represents the ultimate synthesis that Dostoevsky advocates: he combines Western education with Russian spiritual values. As Fedor Karamazov self-consciously plays the fool in Zosima's cell, he expects particular responses from his audience. From Miusov he expects rejection and vituperation. From Zosima he expects acceptance and wisdom. Fedor Karamazov gets what he expects.

Zosima's half-hour departure from the cell ushers in a conversation between the two senior monks and Ivan Karamazov; the subject is Ivan's argument in favor of the Church subsuming the state within itself. Though a seeming digression, the argument bears on Fedor Karamazov's drama, because it foregrounds the issue of how the individual should relate to the community. In a civil order, Ivan notes, criminals are punished corporally or they are sent to prison. In an ecclesiastical order, criminals are punished by their consciences. As Zosima later points out, in Ivan's exposition the Church "never loses communion with the criminal" (14:61;65), which allows the Church "to bring the excommunicated back, to deter the plotter, to regenerate the fallen" (14:61;66). Ivan's theory thus counterposes the Church's compassion, which stresses social bonds, to the state's punitiveness, which weakens them. Though Ivan's theory concerns criminals, it resonates in the novel with Miusov's and Zosima's treatment of his father. Shamed by Fedor Karamazov's words and deeds, Miusov acts like a secular authority: he tries to exclude Fedor Pavlovich and to punish him by exposing him. Yet his tactic only inspires Fedor Pavlovich to redouble his efforts; Miusov thus exacerbates the behavior he hopes to curtail. Zosima foresees this dynamic with his own argument regarding exile and corporal punishment: "All this exile to hard labor, and formerly with floggings, does not reform anyone, and the number of crimes not only does not diminish but increases all the more" (14:59;64). Zosima rejects the state's punitive measures and treats Fedor Pavlovich with compassion, appealing to Fedor's conscience. Zosima thus demonstrates the principles he preaches: he never humiliates or abandons Fedor Karamazov. By keeping dialogue alive, Zosima maintains the link necessary "to regenerate the fallen" (even if the fallen, like Fedor Karamazov, do not accept his offer).

The scene in Zosima's cell following Fedor Karamazov's Diderot anecdote illustrates the differences between the secular and ecclesiastical approaches. Fedor Karamazov, as the narrator points out, never commits a civil crime; rather he violates social taboos: "a little push, and in no time he would reach the utmost limits of some abomination—only an abomination, by the way, never anything criminal, never an escapade punishable by law. In that respect he always managed to restrain himself, and even amazed himself in some cases" (14:80;87). By telling the Diderot anecdote in Zosima's cell, Fedor Karamazov violates the sanctity of place, thereby inspiring narrative commentary:

> Indeed, something altogether impossible was taking place in the cell. For perhaps forty or fifty years, from the time of the former elders, visitors had been

coming to this cell, but always with the deepest reverence, not otherwise. . . . Even many "higher" persons . . . even some of the freethinkers . . . considered it their foremost duty—to a man—to show the deepest respect and tactfulness through the audience, and the more so as there was no question of money involved, but only of love and mercy on the one side, and on the other of repentance and the desire to resolve some difficult question of the soul or a difficult moment in the life of the heart. So that this buffoonery displayed by Fedor Pavlovich, with no respect for the place he was in, produced in the onlookers, at least in some of them, both astonishment and bewilderment. (14:39–40;42)

In short, Fedor Pavlovich violates both social and ecclesiastical norms. Miusov responds by alienating Fedor; Zosima, by accepting him.

Alienation and Union

The figures of both Diderot and St. Denis emblemize this opposition of secular banishment and sacred union. Diderot was a political martyr, exiled by the secular state. St. Denis is a spiritual father martyred by temporal authorities, a fact that situates his story at the crossroads of church and state, an area of intense scrutiny in *The Brothers Karamazov*. In the legend, St. Denis responds to the literal alienation of his head from his body and the figurative alienation of his body from the state's body with figurative acts of union. First, he picks up his head—thus holding together that which has been sundered. Next, he kisses it.

The idea of St. Denis kissing his head may haunt Fedor Karamazov because it suggests a solution to his own problem of self-alienation. After all, Zosima diagnoses the source of Fedor Pavlovich's scandalous and semiblasphemous behavior as shame (14:41;43). But his lying is a symptom whose habitual practice exacerbates Fedor's problem. Zosima thus exhorts Fedor Karamazov to stop lying, then respect himself and join in the brotherly communion of love on earth. Fedor Karamazov then asks him about St. Denis, a figure who implies self-acceptance. St. Denis's repossession of self also signals a victory over his executioners, a refusal to accept the state-mandated alienation of head from body. Fedor Karamazov's self-proclaimed obsession with the literal absurdities of this image thus signals a subliminal awareness of its figurative implications.

As a patron saint of France and first bishop of Paris, St. Denis also evokes the novel's father-son thematics, which resonate strongly in this scene. Set in Zosima's cell, this scene brings together Alesha's spiritual and physical fathers. But Fedor Pavlovich questions his own paternal status when he declares himself "a son of lies." Dostoevsky the author thus introduces his *Diary* writer's obsession with broken familes. In *The Brothers Karamazov*, Dostoevsky posits attachment to a spiritual community as the solution to family breakups. In the St. Denis legend, the body carries its head to a place outside Paris where a monastery is founded—thus establishing a religious enclave in a secular world. In Dostoevsky's novel, the hero is sent out of the monastery into the secular world where he creates a community of brothers.

Though Fedor Karamazov does not mention the saint's name, Fedor Dostoevsky undoubtedly counted on his authorial audience's recognition of the legend. Two of the anecdotes he attributes to Fedor Karamazov in Zosima's cell are about Parisians named Denis—the atheist *philosophe* and the martyred bishop—a deliberate strategy in a novel about atheism and faith. Both anecdotes involve the question of religious belief and the imagery of resurrection. And Fedor Karamazov aims both particularly at a westernized landowner and a holy elder.

Significantly, Miusov's and Zosima's responses to Fedor Karamazov reverberate with the novel's thematics about alienation. Fedor Pavlovich responds to Zosima's invitation to "feel completely at home" by confessing that he plays the buffoon because he anticipates audience ridicule and social rejection (14:41;43–4). Dostoevsky thus reveals how Fedor Karamazov takes control of shame-filled situations: to defend himself from social rejection, he provokes it by playing the fool. This dynamic explains his teasing hostility toward Miusov throughout this scene. Miusov not only represents that rejection but demonstrates it. Nonetheless, Fedor Karamazov's invocation of Diderot and St. Denis demonstrates a subliminal self-awareness. Fedor Pavlovich's self-conscious identification with Diderot indicates a latent desire for an alternative script—a penetrating wisdom that would slay the blasphemer and give birth to a new man. His St. Denis story further emphasizes Fedor Pavlovich's awareness that he can influence audience response. As Fedor Karamazov tells his stories, Fedor Dostoevsky constantly contrasts the responses of Miusov, the westernized Russian who exacerbates Fedor Pavlovich's sense of alienation from society and self, with the responses of Zosima, the Orthodox healer who propagates love and self-acceptance. Dostoevsky thus models an empathic response that can cure shame.

The image of St. Denis gains greater thematic power through association with images of decapitation in Dostoevsky's work.[9] It particularly exemplifies many forms of alienation and thus fits into the *Diary* writer's polemics on *otorvannost'* (alienation) and *obosoblenie* (dissociation),[10] if we understand *otorvannost'* and *obosoblenie* not just as alienation from one's native soil and dissociation from self and others, but, like Dostoevsky, as social, psychological, and metaphysical dynamics. Images of decapitation signify externally imposed alienation of head from body but can also signify different kinds of alienation of head from heart, which can spring from such external sources as ideology or from sources such as shame, which operates both internally and externally. Thus, for instance, Alesha acts like his spiritual father Zosima as he tells his biological father, "I know your thoughts. Your heart is better than your head" (14:124;134). Images of decapitation can also signify the alienation of the individual from the body politic. Ivan thus argues that if the Church were to subsume the state, such alienation would cease because "the Church would excommunicate the criminal and the disobedient and not cut off their heads" (14:59;63).

Fedor Karamazov's use of the image of St. Denis's head suggests both the alienation of head from heart and reunion through love and self-acceptance. Dostoevsky prepares his authorial audience to understand this thematic message through his mimetic focus on the father-son plot. Alesha's presence seems to provoke a spiritual crisis in his father. Fedor Pavlovich receives unexpected, positive responses from his son that have begun to work some internal changes. In addressing his Diderot and St. Denis stories to Zosima, Fedor Karamazov consciously tests his son's teacher. Fedor Dostoevsky thus suggests Fedor Karamazov's subliminal awareness of his spiritual illness. As Zosima tells Fedor, "You've known for a long time what you should do; you have sense enough: do not give yourself up to drunkenness and verbal incontinence, do not give yourself up to sensuality, and especially to the adoration of money, and close your taverns; if you cannot close all of them then at least two or three. And above all, above everything else—do not lie" (14:41;44). Zosima speaks the words Fedor Karamazov needs to hear to change his life. He acts out the role Fedor Karamazov scripts for him with his story of Diderot and Metropolitan Platon. In Fedor Karamazov's story, conversion comes through the power of the word. Zosima thus proves the ideal audience: he listens and hears the covert message behind Fedor Pavlovich's provocative Aesopian tale. Zosima may guess that Fedor Pavlovich will not change his ways, yet he offers empathy, thereby modeling a response for his character audience. Fedor Dostoevsky calls attention to Zosima's empathic response, thus creating a model for his authorial audience to emulate. Alesha follows Zosima's lead and sees connections to those who differ from him. Readers must do the same and read with empathy, not pride, with our hearts as well as our heads.

By inscribing metaliterary play into moments of scandal, Dostoevsky provides some aesthetic relief from the anxiety aroused. Both Lebedev and Fedor Karamazov double-voice their stories, directing them simultaneously at two audiences. Unknowingly, they thus reveal their own contradictory longings for revenge and belonging. Dostoevsky portrays their divided selves by having both refer to decapitated saints. Their choice of saints, however, reveals Dostoevsky's psychological canniness as well as his thematic concerns. The images of St. John the Baptist and St. Denis of Paris, two saints who reputedly raised their heads with their own hands, are images of violence containing within themselves images of healing—paradoxical or miraculous images of life in death.

chapter eight

Lukian Lebedev: Narrative and Exposure

> Have you noticed, Prince, that in our century everyone is an opportunist! Especially here, in Russia, in our beloved fatherland. And how that's come to be, I don't know. It seems that everything stood so solidly, but what about now? Everyone is talking about it, and everywhere they're writing about it. They are making exposures [*Oblichaiut*]. In Russia everyone is making exposures [*u nas vse oblichaiut*].
> — KOLIA IVOLGIN, *The Idiot* (8:113)

Shame works like the contents of Pandora's box. Once released, shame affects everyone in its purview—exposed, exposer, and witnesses alike. Shame destabilizes. Shame's very presence heralds the abrogation of social norms. Having no fixed script, shame deprives all parties of set responses. Shame thus contributes to the chaos of *The Idiot*, whose characters all participate at one time or another in shame scenes. Most characters participate passively as witnesses to others' shame; many experience the pain of being exposed; some actively expose others. As I have shown, Dostoevsky implicates character-witnesses and readers alike in the text's moral action by reducing the intersubjective space between those exposed and those who witness the exposure. We have all experienced shame, so we can all place ourselves in the position of the shamed—provided, of course, that the exposed person experiences shame. As Dostoevsky illustrates, a person's shame sensitivity has a positive function. A person capable of shame is capable of change.

In chapters 4 and 6, I reveal how Dostoevsky creates reader sympathy for the two shamed liars, General Ivolgin and Stepan Verkhovensky, by showing their progression from denial or self-deception to acknowledgment of shame. While Ivolgin and Verkhovensky senior share a similar progression, Dostoevsky's narrators treat them differently. The character-narrator of *Demons* creates an ambivalent sympathy for Stepan Verkhovensky. But when Stepan leaps with his creator and the authorial audience into the metaphysical realm of aesthetics and religious belief, he leaves his friend the narrator behind in the literal realm. The narrator is thus abandoned. As discussed, the semi-embodied narrator of *The Idiot* initially creates sympathy for Prince Myshkin, but he gradually distances himself from the Prince, forcing a split between the narrative and authorial audiences. He treats General Ivolgin more reliably. As the General progresses from narcissistic grandiosity to grateful acknowledgment of others, the narrator portrays him more and more sympathetically. *The Idiot*'s narrator is equally reliable vis-à-vis Lukian Lebedev but not equally sympathetic. Lebedev begins and ends the novel as a shameless liar; the narrator thus keeps his distance, and so do readers.

This chapter focuses on Lukian Lebedev and the narrative dynamics of exposure, paying particular attention to shame's role as a destabilizer. In the chapters that follow I show how Dostoevsky uses shame as a moral measure and how he uses shameless characters to highlight exposure at his novels' mimetic, thematic, and synthetic levels.

While all literature in some ways involves exposure, that is, letting readers into characters' spaces, making public that which is private, *The Idiot* consistently exposes, thematizes, and comments on the dynamics of exposure.[1] Dostoevsky foregrounds exposure mimetically by creating numerous exposure scenes, thematically by having characters tell stories about exposure scenes, and synthetically by having character audiences comment on their interlocutors' exposure narratives. As Dostoevsky shows in all of these cases, exposure cuts both ways. Those who expose others to the public eye expose themselves as well. This reciprocity works mimetically and thematically throughout the novel. Nastasia Filippovna, for instance, cannot expose the double standards and hypocrisy of the men trying to transfer control over her body without exposing herself as a fallen woman.[2] Lebedev's nephew cannot expose his uncle as an unscrupulous lawyer without exposing himself as an ungrateful dependent. Lebedev cannot expose Aglaia's correspondence with either Gania or Nastasia Filippovna without exposing himself as a shameless spy.

In addition to numerous exposure scenes, *The Idiot* features many exposure narratives that display the novel's poetics. Thus, for example, the Prince's story about the seduced peasant girl Marie and his story of an execution contribute to the novel's thematics of the fallen woman and condemnation to death; they also serve as moral tales that reflect on events in the novel. Like the inserted narratives in *Don Quixote*, the Prince's stories serve as analogue texts, highlighting and commenting on the novel's action. The Prince's stories establish his credentials as a good narrator and Dostoevsky's credentials as a metaliterary virtuoso. Aglaia exposes Myshkin as "The Poor Knight," flagging the novel's intertext *Don Quixote* and underlining the novel's Pushkin connection.[3] Ferdyshchenko's parlor game about relating one's most reprehensible act illustrates shame and narrative dynamics: narrative savvy enhances audience response while shamelessness estranges. Ippolit's "Explanation" further demonstrates how a speaker's narcissistic neediness leads him to ignore his audience. Ippolit pours out his most intimate thoughts and feelings to a largely hostile audience that is tired and restless. Not surprisingly, the hostile mock him, thus finalizing his decision to kill himself. Dostoevsky cannily replicates this action in a later scene when Ippolit, imitating his earlier detractors, mocks General Ivolgin, thereby precipitating the humiliated general's flight to death. As these examples show, Dostoevsky inscribes his poetics into *The Idiot*'s mimetic action.

Lebedev as Exposer

Although a minor character, Lebedev contributes significantly to the novel's mimetics, thematics, and poetics. As a social climber, Lebedev exposes other social climbers. As a divided self, Lebedev articulates the thematics of doubleness. As a liar and copyist, Lebedev raises poetic questions of truth and verisimilitude. As a self-fashioned lawyer and prophet, Lebedev self-interestedly exposes self-interest. But all of these identities work two ways. Throughout the novel Lebedev exposes others, but he is also exposed—as honorless, shameless, mercenary, and false. The exposer/exposed dynamic reaches its peak in Dostoevsky's *Idiot* when Lebedev's forensic and prophetic rhetoric conjoin in his cannibal speech. Like Dostoevsky's novel, my chapter builds toward that hilarious but serious speech. First, however, I show how Dostoevsky links Lebedev with the novel's thematics and poetics of exposure.

Unlike General Ivolgin, who grew in importance as Dostoevsky wrote *The Idiot*, Lukian Lebedev appears early and remains minor but central. On page 3, the unnamed Lebedev intrudes upon a conversation between the novel's two unnamed male protagonists, Prince Lev Myshkin and Parfen Rogozhin. His first words, "The veritable truth!" (*Istinnaia pravda!*), introduce Dostoevsky's double-voicing. While Lebedev uses these clichéd words to flatter Rogozhin and thus enter the conversation, Dostoevsky uses them to introduce the novel's thematics of truth and justice, all in the context of Russia's relationship to the West, another of the novel's thematics. The narrator interrupts to describe Lebedev as a "poorly dressed man, something on the order of a bureaucrat calloused by service as a copy clerk, forty years old, strongly built, with a red nose and a pimply face." In describing his rank, Dostoevsky's narrator uses the words *zakoruzlogo v pod'iachestve chinovnika*, labeling Lebedev as a low-level civil servant, probably a copy clerk (*pod'iachestvo* is a collective term for scribes). His copy-clerk identity grounds him in nineteenth-century Russian reality, where this was a large class, and reveals his connection to the written word and thus his synthetic function.[4]

Lebedev repeats the tautological cliché containing the adjectival form for the biblical word for truth (*istina*) and the unmarked noun *pravda* that means both "truth" and "justice": "The veritable truth, sir, only they (Europeans) keep senselessly transferring all those Russian resources to themselves!" (*Istinnaia pravda-s, tol'ko vse russkie sily darom k sebe perevodiat!*). Lebedev's words represent a sycophantic response to Rogozhin's assertion that Myshkin's benefactor had wasted his money on the Prince's European doctor.[5] Thus, while the narrator marks Lebedev as someone who supports himself copying others' words, Lebedev's own words mark him as a derivative flatterer. Lebedev concludes his second intrusion into the conversation with the cliché "poverty is no vice," again marking himself as a verbal borrower. Finally, in his third intrusion, Lebedev exposes himself by projecting his own excess of imagination onto the Prince, just as earlier he had projected his own parasitism onto Europe.

Lebedev's three intrusions are all forms of *oblichitel'naia literatura*, prose that exposes (what is currently called investigatory journalism), a popular genre in 1860s Russia.[6] Lebedev exposes Europeans as parasites on Russians; he exposes the Prince's poverty; and he falsely accuses the Prince of fabricating relationships.[7] By associating Lebedev with the unscrupulous investigatory journalists of his time, Dostoevsky ties him to the novel's thematics of exposure.[8] By having his narrator interrupt Lebedev's first interruption, Dostoevsky immediately flags the novel's synthetic dimension, where Lebedev figures prominently. Dostoevsky clearly identifies *Don Quixote* as one of *The Idiot*'s major intertexts. He fashions Lebedev's rhetorical rivalry with General Ivolgin and the class tensions between them to echo the relationship between Sancho Panza and Don Quixote. He also gives Lebedev roots in the Russian literary tradition. His name derives from *lebed'*, the Russian word for "swan," and is one of many bird names in the novel. It thus evokes both Gogol, whose name means "golden-eye" (a kind of duck) and Derzhavin, who wrote many poems with birds' names as titles. Lebedev's rhetorical excesses, digressions, and self-interested plotting recall Nozdrev, the compulsive, calculating, yet ineffective liar in Gogol's *Dead Souls*.[9] His name recalls one of Derzhavin's poems, titled "Lebed'." In this 1804 poem, Derzhavin compares himself to a swan and claims that his poetic status will elevate him over his social superiors; accordingly, in Dostoevsky's 1868 novel, Lebedev is obsessed with using his verbal skill to raise himself socially. While Dostoevsky will make his next swan, Captain Lebiadkin from *Demons*, a parodic poet whose verses are modeled on Derzhavin's, he makes Lebedev a parodic prophet (the other standard role of Russia's poets) whose speeches contain the mixture of high and low styles characteristic of Derzhavin and of Dostoevsky himself.

In creating Lebedev, Dostoevsky exploits the double-edged narrative dynamic in which exposer stands exposed. Time and again Lebedev eagerly exposes others to promote himself. Yet unlike General Ivolgin, who becomes increasingly shame-sensitive during the course of the novel, Lukian Lebedev remains unabashedly shameless. Lebedev's shamelessness is not an immunity to shame, however, but a defense against it. As Bernstein has shown, Lebedev is an abject character who "suffers constantly new, and usually externally imposed, slights and degradations."[10] Lebedev protects himself from real and perceived slights by shameless self-promotion; he willingly abases himself to achieve his ends. By revealing the sociopolitical roots of Lebedev's shameless opportunism, Dostoevsky exposes the destabilizing class antagonisms in nineteenth-century Russia.

The Russian Social Contract and the Politics of Exposure

Dostoevsky wrote in a period of social change that witnessed the emancipation of the serfs and the rise of industrial capitalism, both of which affected the composition of the social classes and contributed to the breakdown of Russia's rigid hierarchies. As an ambitious government clerk, Lebedev resents his social superiors. He thus embraces the unwritten rule of social interaction that Dostoevsky identifies in his 1873 article on lying and that I call the Russian social contract—lie and let lie. Dostoevsky calls this unwritten rule "the first condition of Russian society." Significantly, in Dostoevsky's formulation, the Russian social contract involves narrative—I'll tell you a story and let you tell one; I'll embellish the truth and let you do so. You believe me, and I'll believe you.

Like Rousseau's social contract, Dostoevsky's redresses inequities of birth, social station, and wealth by creating equality—not in the political, but in the social sphere. By establishing norms of reciprocity and trust, the Russian social contract undermines social hierarchies and creates democratic expectations about social interactions. But, as Dostoevsky shows repeatedly in *The Idiot*, the social harmony resulting from the reciprocity of lie and let lie can only work among actual social equals or those who agree to behave as equals while maintaining their social hierarchy (as in the engagement party in the Epanchins' drawing room). Social inequity fuels violations of the Russian social contract.

As Dostoevsky demonstrates in *The Idiot*, the Russian social contract breaks down under the strain of rhetorical and sociopolitical rivalry, especially, but not exclusively, in the rivalry between his two comic liars, Lukian Lebedev and General Ivolgin. In portraying their interaction, Dostoevsky dramatizes how class resentment disrupts the Russian social contract. In making their rhetorical rivalry echo that of Sancho Panza and Don Quixote, Dostoevsky lodges his own polemics on truth and verisimilitude in a metaliterary context. In portraying their class rivalry, Dostoevsky thematically reflects the tension between individual desires and collective harmony. In contrasting their responses to being exposed as liars, Dostoevsky establishes the positive value of shame as a measure of moral worth and thus of reader sympathy. Unlike General Ivolgin, whose sense of shame increases as the novel progresses, Lebedev remains shameless. Thus, while Dostoevsky's narrator creates increasing sympathy for General Ivolgin, his constant revelations of Lebedev's shameless opportunism keep readers at arm's length. In examining Lebedev's roles and rhetoric, I show how Dostoevsky inscribes his own awareness of the recursive relationship obtaining among storyteller, audience, and story by showing how that relationship breaks down and what happens when it does.

Rhetorical Rivalry

Dostoevsky embeds Ivolgin's and Lebedev's class rivalry in their rhetorical rivalry. Ivolgin breaches the Russian social contract and exposes Lebedev's rhetorical pretensions both times that Lebedev claims prophet status. The second, when Lebedev makes his cannibal speech, occurs at the Prince's birthday party and thus on the terrace of Lebedev's house. The company has been discussing Lebedev's interpretation of the Revelation of St. John, particularly his view that the Star of Wormwood has become manifest as Russia's network of railroads. Lebedev claims that contemporary Russians have lost touch with the transcendent. He argues that the railroads signal humanity's move toward materialism, that is, food for the body, and away from belief in a higher idea, that is, food for the soul. He illustrates his argument with the story of an aging twelfth-century cannibal who surrenders to the Inquisition for having in his lifetime killed and eaten sixty monks and six babies.

General Ivolgin immediately responds: "That can't be! . . . I frequently discuss and argue with him, gentlemen, and all about similar ideas. But most of the time he presents such absurdities, that you can't believe your ears, not an ounce of verisimilitude!" (8:313). Ivolgin thus publicly refutes Lebedev's story and exposes him as a habitual liar (and not for the first time). But Lebedev refuses to be embarrassed. He reminds the General of the social contract: "General! Remember the siege of Kars, and you, gentlemen, will recognize that my story is the naked truth. For my part I note that almost every reality, though it has its own immutable laws, is almost always incredible and lacking in verisimilitude. And even the more real it is, then sometimes it's also more lacking in verisimilitude" (8:313). Lebedev fights exposure by insisting on mutual hospitality: if he agrees to believe the General's war stories, the General must reciprocate. Social harmony demands generosity of spirit. But reciprocity breaks down in a hierarchical society. The fathers retain control of their wealth, power, and words. Though they agree to play Ferdyshenko's truth-telling game, Generals Epanchin and Totsky do not follow the rules: they recount their reprehensible deeds only to relate their praiseworthy actions. Though General Totsky seduces his ward Nastasia Filippovna, he does not marry her. Though he demands Lebedev's belief, General Ivolgin does not believe him. Rhetorical exchanges thus become battlegrounds for class and gender confrontation. Lebedev defends himself against Ivolgin by exposing the double standard.

However comic Lebedev's counterattack, those familiar with Dostoevsky's work will recognize in the second part of his defense—the inverisimilitude of reality—Dostoevsky's response to his own critics, who accused him of complete inverisimilitude even when he took his facts from the newspapers.[11] Dostoevsky thus provides Lebedev with an unexpected defender—Prince Myshkin. Myshkin's position resembles that of the narrator of Apuleius's *Golden Ass*, who addresses a scoffer, "But for you, sir, with the dense ears and the firm prejudice, you are rejecting a story which may very well be true. By Hercules, you are ignorant that man's debased intelligence calls all those matters lies which are either seldom seen or heard, or which exist on heights beyond the narrow cast of his reason. And yet if you probe these matters closely, you will find them not only understandable and clear, but even easily beheld."[12] Myshkin's support is more qualified, however: "That there were cannibals, and perhaps, very many, in that Lebedev is undoubtedly correct; only here's what I don't know, namely why did he mix monks into this and what does he mean by that?" (8:313). By defending Lebedev's mimetic truth but questioning his poetic intent, Myshkin accentuates the novel's poetics.

Myshkin's enigmatic response reveals the gap between Lebedev and himself as storytellers. Myshkin masterfully fashions his own experiences into stories with moral import. Though Lebedev's cannibal speech illustrates a moral concept dear to Dostoevsky, the nineteenth century's loss of belief in God, Lebedev's motive for introducing it is suspect. Lebedev delivers his speech like a prophet, but he represents himself as a lawyer—a clue to Lebedev's rhetorical ambition and ethical bankruptcy. The drunken Lebedev exposes himself as a false prophet: he may speak the truth, but not for truth's sake. He speaks, rather, to kindle audience admiration for his rhetorical skill. Unlike Myshkin and Dostoevsky, who tell stories meant to involve their audiences thematically and ethically, Lebedev tells stories to gain audience approval and social acceptance.

Lebedev: Liar Lawyer and Swan Prophet

Although Lebedev's rhetoric exposes him, so does Dostoevsky's narrator. In fact, the narrator's continual exposure of Lebedev prepares for the exposures that follow his cannibal speech. The narrator first exposes Lebedev's rhetorical ambitions in Book Two, when Myshkin returns to Petersburg and pays him a surprise visit. The narrator notes that Lebedev is repeating (for the fifth time) his successful courtroom speech that allowed the moneylender Zaidler to defraud an old woman of her entire 500-ruble fortune. Lebedev's insolent nephew contributes to this exposure by revealing his uncle's rhetorical vanity ("he has set out on the path of eloquence and speaks with elevated diction all the time with his children at home" [8:161]) as well as his mercenary motives ("And who did he decide to defend: not the old woman, who begged him, . . . but that very money-lender . . . because he promised to give him fifty rubles" [8:161]). His nephew's criticism anticipates Keller's later charge that Lebedev is a mercenary. Furthermore, the Prince's discovery that Lebedev lends money (8:368) identifies, Lebedev's argument that the moneylender lives by "honest labor" as a self-defense. Though Lebedev later represents himself as a prophet and thus a social conscience, he proves to be a lawyer and thus a "hired conscience." This early scene reveals a social dynamic that Dostoevsky depicts repeatedly: socioeconomic inequity fuels rhetorical rivalry. Characters who resent Lebedev discredit his rhetoric as well as his ethics. Like Cervantes, Dostoevsky utilizes scenes of exposure as opportunities for metaliterary commentary. As characters tell one another how their rivals' rhetoric fails, Dostoevsky shows how his succeeds.

During Myshkin's surprise visit, Lebedev also boasts of his skill at interpreting Revelation, claiming fifteen years of experience: "I believe and I interpret. For poor am I and naked, and an atom in people's orbit. And who respects Lebedev? Everyone mocks him and the only thing they don't do is accompany him with a kick.[13] Yet there, in yon interpreting, I am equal to a grandee. For my mind!" (8:168). Lebedev thus reveals his craving for respect. Like Ivolgin, who tries to enhance his public image by telling stories, Lebedev tries to establish his prophetic credentials by telling one. He recounts that three years earlier, his superior at work had asked Lebedev, "Is it true, that you are the Antichrist professor?"

> And I didn't conceal: "I am, I say," and I expounded and performed, and did not mitigate the terror, but mentally, unfurling the allegorical scroll, intensified it even more and correlated the numbers. And he laughed, but at the numbers and such like he started to tremble, and he asked me to close the book and leave, and he designated a reward for me for Easter week, and he gave up his soul to God on Thomas' Sunday. (8:168)

Lebedev's story clearly serves as a wish fulfillment as well as a self-vindication. In his telling, his department chief first mocks him but then respects and rewards him. Furthermore, his immediate supervisor credits Lebedev with foretelling their mutual superior's death. Lebedev thus portrays himself as a mocked figure who, by dint of his rhetorical talent and prophetic ability, wins the respect (even fear) of his social superiors. Lebedev elevates himself with elevated diction. His story enacts his victory, thereby justifying his worthiness to cross class boundaries.

Dostoevsky's version of Lebedev's story establishes the connection between Lebedev's rhetoric and his self-image: he adopts the role and rhetoric of a prophet to overcome his social shame. Dostoevsky also exposes him as a parodic imitator of the text he interprets. For instance, Lebedev swells with pride when identified as "the Antichrist professor" and grandiosely responds with biblical language "I am" (*Az esm'*). His claim to poverty also employs biblical language—"poor and naked" (*nishch i nag*). His claim to superiority employs the high-style noun "grandee" (*vel'mozh*), a noun used frequently by Gavrila Derzhavin.[14] In addition to reflecting the ongoing vacillation between his self-abasement and self-promotion, Lebedev's imagery and language reveal Dostoevsky's parodic hand. Derzhavin's "Swan" poem, for instance, contains the line "To other grandees I am not equal." Derzhavin uses it to show that while the poet may be lower born, his poet's status elevates him. Dostoevsky, however, attributes this language to Lebedev both to reveal his obsession with social status and to emphasize his rhetoric's archaic and portentous nature. Dostoevsky also uses parody to provoke a comparison. At the beginning of this subchapter, Lebedev fashions himself as a lawyer; here at the end he fashions himself as a prophet. Once he adopts these roles, readers compare him to their prototypes. Other characters continue this comparison as they reveal the gap between Lebedev's actual and projected self-images. Dostoevsky thus unmasks Lebedev as he assumes his roles.

Shame of Origins

Dostoevsky further reveals his authorial hand when Lebedev's nephew exposes his uncle as a drunkard, citing his nightly prayers for the Countess du Barry as evidence. While the nephew's exposure backfires because Lebedev's identification with the beautiful, anguished sinner earns Myshkin's admiration, Dostoevsky's exposure succeeds. In identifying with the high-class prostitute who was elevated to the rank of countess to become Louis XV's mistress, Lebedev betrays his willingness to sell himself to transcend his class limits. In telling her story, Lebedev portrays Mme. du Barry as someone who escaped from ignominy (*iz pozoru vyidia*) and rose to the apex of the social ladder and to dazzling sociopolitical heights.

She thus embodies an ideal success: Lebedev wants to escape the shame of his origins; he aspires to social respectability and power; and he is willing to sell himself to get them. Lebedev thus defends his prayers for the Countess du Barry:

> She died so that after such honor, such great former sovereignness, the executioner Sanson dragged her to the guillotine, for no fault of her own, for the amusement of the Parisian market women [*poissards*], while she does not even understand what's happening to her, from terror. She sees that he's placing her neck under the blade and urging her with kicks,—while those there laugh—and she begins to cry out: "*Encore un moment, monsieur le bourreau, encore un moment!*" Which means: "Wait one more moment, Mr. Executioner, just one more moment!"[15] And it's for that minute there that perhaps God will forgive her, for greater misery than that it's impossible to imagine with the human soul. Do you know what the word misery means? Well, there it is, misery itself. From that cry of a countess, at the single moment that I read it, I felt exactly as though my heart were seized by pincers. And what's it to you, worm, that I, going to sleep at night, thought to remember her, a great sinner, in prayer. For perhaps I remembered because for her, since time immemorial, probably no one has ever bowed his forehead in prayer, nor even thought about it. On the contrary it will be pleasant for her in the other world to feel that there has been found such a sinner as her, who at least one time on earth has prayed for her. (8:165)

Since the Prince acts as a model audience, his sympathetic response helps create some reader sympathy for Lebedev. Lebedev's story acts as an early variant of Grushenka's onion story: the speaker (Lebedev/Grushenka) earns the admiration of his/her audience (Myshkin/Alesha) for telling the story of a great sinner saved by her own experience (a moment of great suffering/one good deed). Lebedev's blow-by-blow account of her last moment, told in the present tense, creates a dramatic immediacy that touches the Prince. Lebedev's story also echoes the Prince's obsession with executions and violent deaths, guaranteeing its efficacy. The Prince's sympathetic listening to Lebedev's story counteracts his nephew's hostility.

Nonetheless, Lebedev's obsession with rank diminishes reader sympathy. In Lebedev's account, Mme. du Barry keeps the title that she acquired to become Louis XV's lover—that of countess.[16] From the novel's first pages, the narrator exposes Lebedev's passion for knowing anything and everything about his social superiors. The narrator classifies him as a type: "these Mr. Know-it-alls" (*eti gospoda vseznaiki*) (8:7). As a commoner who went from rags to riches, Mme. du Barry makes the world of wealth and prestige seem more accessible to Lebedev, who is not a democrat, like the Prince, but a social climber. He calls her a "sinner" but does not mention her early profession, her extravagant expenses, or her passion for jewelry. As he describes her second reversal of fortune (from power to powerlessness), Lebedev reveals his identification with her by repeating his earlier self-description: she is laughed at and kicked. Lebedev may also identify with Jeanne Bécu (Mme. du Barry) because she had natural talents (good taste and an aptitude for good diction), and because she was lucky: early in her career she happened to be in the right place at the right time. Lebedev clearly views himself as a man rhetorically gifted, whose appearances on the Warsaw–Petersburg train enabled him to meet the two men who make his fortune, however small. He keeps hoping that proximity to money and nobility will elevate him financially and socially.

Lebedev's prayers for Mme. du Barry also express his bereavement. Between Books One and Two, Lebedev's wife dies in childbirth. When the Prince arrives at the beginning of Book Two, Lebedev has already been mourning for five weeks. His grief, and probably guilt, over his wife's death drive him to drink. The nocturnal activities his nephew mocks—his searches for robbers and for his daughter's hidden lovers as well as his thrice-nightly prayers—are actually symptoms of his grief and anxiety. His wife's death was unexpected—after all, she had given birth without complication three times before. Thus, like Mme. du Barry's death, which Lebedev attributes to the bloodlust of the Parisian mob, his wife's death must strike him as unjust. These unexpected deaths[17] fuel Lebedev's apocalyptic anxiety: how do you avoid the horseman of death? His prayers for Mme. du Barry seem like insurance for the future—an onion proffered by one poor sinner to another.

Finally, Lebedev's version of Mme. du Barry's story demonstrates his complexity: he can feel compassion for those less fortunate than himself, while exploiting those more fortunate—here, the Prince. Unlike General Ivolgin or Stepan Verkhovensky, Lebedev calculates as he lies. In using Prince Myshkin's compassion for Mme. du Barry to snare him as his tenant at Pavlovsk,[18] Lebedev diminishes reader sympathy.

His self-confessed opportunism further reduces reader sympathy. As he explains to the Prince, good and evil war in his soul: "Well, here it is, for you, for you alone, I will pronounce the truth [*istina*], because you fathom a man: both word and deed, and lie [*lozh'*] and truth [*pravda*], are all together in me, and completely sincere. Truth and deed in me are made up of true [*istinnom*] repentance, believe it or not, I swear, and words and lie [*lozh'*] in me are made up of a hellish (and always immanent) thought: how can I ensnare a person even at that very moment, how can I gain something through tears of repentance! I swear to God, it's so! I would not tell anyone else, they'd laugh or spit;

but you, Prince, you will judge humanely" (8:259). Lebedev's dual agenda, as well as his capacity to serve two very different masters—Myshkin and Rogozhin—makes him emblematic of the duality of human nature—one of the novel's themes. Yet even Lebedev's self-awareness does not create reader sympathy. The Prince also confesses to dual thoughts, but he feels shame at his negative thoughts. Lebedev, however, feels no shame.

Lebedev's self-awareness and his self-confessed opportunism differentiate him from the narcissistically injured General. Ivolgin is an "innocent" liar; Lebedev is a role-player. Where Ivolgin is naively sincere, Lebedev is not. Where Ivolgin feels shame, Lebedev feigns it. While Ivolgin expects audience sympathy and is always surprised by audience hostility, Lebedev mostly expects hostility. While Ivolgin's narcissism makes him insensitive to others, Lebedev's class consciousness makes him hypersensitive. Most significantly, Ivolgin cherishes his honor, whereas Lebedev willingly abases himself for money.[19] He preaches the importance of the spiritual but sells himself for a profit.

My Client, My Self

Readers can thus understand why Lebedev defends the twelfth-century cannibal. He chooses as his client a man who combines good and evil in himself. In Lebedev's account, the cannibal commits evil deeds (66 murders!) but repents. For Lebedev, the cannibal's sincere repentance and desire for absolution mitigate the evil of his past actions. Lebedev thus presents himself as the defender of a client whom he fashions in his own self-image. Furthermore, Lebedev represents his client as a man who, while persisting in his sins, nonetheless experiences pangs of conscience:

> We see that the criminal, or, as they say, my client, despite the complete impossibility of finding something else edible, a few times, in the course of his curious career, displayed the desire to repent and abstained from clergymen. We see this clearly from the facts: it's been mentioned that he nevertheless ate four or six babies, a comparatively insignificant figure, but for all that significant in another respect. It's evident, that, tormented by terrible pangs (for my client is a religious and conscientious person, as I will prove) and in order to diminish his sin as much as possible, he, as a kind of experiment, exchanged a clerical for a lay diet six times. That it was a kind of experiment is again indisputable; for if it was only for gastronomic variety, then the number six would be much too insignificant: why only six figures and not thirty? (I take half and half.) But if it was only an experiment solely from despair before the terror of blasphemy and ecclesiastic offense, then in that case the number six becomes very understandable; for six experiments to satisfy the

pangs of conscience is more than enough, because the experiments could not be successful. (8:315)

Like Ivolgin, who fashions Napoleon in his own image, Lebedev fabricates a client who resembles himself. Like his cannibal, Lebedev feels a need to confess his wrongdoings. At the opening of Book Two, Myshkin exposes him: he sees that while Lebedev wrote him a letter, he did not expect him to return to Petersburg. The Prince then accuses him of writing "to cleanse his conscience" (*dlia ochistki sovesti*) (8:166).[20] In Book Four, the narrator exposes Lebedev: "Afterwards, almost on the wedding day itself, when Lebedev came to the Prince to pour out his repentance (he had the invariable habit of always coming to pour out his repentance to those against whom he intrigued, especially when it didn't come off)" (8:487). These incidents demonstrate Lebedev's habit of confessing, thereby providing readers with textual evidence that Lebedev has created his cannibal client in his own image. Lebedev's defense of the cannibal can thus be read, like his defense of the moneylender, as a self-defense.

Unlike Lebedev's cannibal speech, Dostoevsky's cannibal speech parodies forensic rhetoric. Like the lawyers Dostoevsky's *Diary* writer exposes as "hired consciences," Lebedev disregards ethics. He uses scientific language and statistics to neutralize the horror of his client's crime, a rhetorical strategy the *Diary* writer repeatedly denounces. In a speech identifying belief in God as the basis for ethical action, Lebedev identifies his client's consumption of babies not as a case of murder but as proof of the latter's desire to repent and change his ways. Dostoevsky introduces babies to augment the horror of the crime; Lebedev introduces babies to diminish it. Lebedev quantifies and reifies the babies, claiming that the cannibal's fare substitution necessarily failed: "For, in the first place, in my opinion, a baby is too small, that is, not big in size, so that for a defined period it would take three to five times as many lay babies as clerics, so that the sin, if diminished on one side, is nonetheless augmented on the other, not in quality, but in quantity" (8:314–15). By quantification, Lebedev deflects attention away from the fact that he is talking about murder victims. He even calls the innocent babes in question "numbers" (*shest' numerov*) (8:314). Dostoevsky thus makes Lebedev the early prototype for the lawyers with whom he polemicizes in later works. He discredits Lebedev's pseudoscientific rhetoric by demonstrating its ethical inadequacy. He also shows how Lebedev's rhetoric reflects his claim to be an "Antichrist professor": Lebedev chooses sixty-six as the number of murders—a clear reference to 666, the number of the beast in Revelations. Dostoevsky thus reveals the ethical ramifications of Lebedev's identification with his cannibal. Moreover, Dostoevsky's juxtaposition of the argument's defense of a transcendent idea with its rhetorical strategies of quantification and reification reinforces the image of Lebedev as a shameless opportunist.[21] The cannibal defense speech also contains within itself the mix of truth and lies that characterize its speaker. In exposing the cannibal to his audience, Lebedev exposes himself.

It Takes One to Know One

Throughout the novel, the boxer Keller serves as a parody of Lebedev. Both are self-taught wordsmiths who delight in language; both crave recognition for their rhetorical skills; and both love learned conversations. Yet Keller also serves as a foil of Lebedev: though both can be calculating, Keller is also sincere. More importantly, Keller has a sense of honor, however flawed.

Ferdyshenko's game at Nastasia Filippovna's in Part One and the reading of Keller's article in Part Two highlights the novel's thematic and poetic interest in scenes of exposure. Keller's article clearly parodies *oblichitel'naia literatura*—prose that exposes. Written in cliché-ridden and bombastic prose, the article is meant to expose the corrupt morals of the upper classes. By leaving its targets (Myshkin, Myshkin's father, Pavlishchev, and Burdovsky's mother) unnamed, the article both reveals and conceals. Hoping to expose the Burdovsky crowd as unscrupulous slanderers, undeserving of the Prince's largesse, Lebedev hands it to Mme. Epanchina. Enraged by its contents, she forces Kolia to read it aloud. But exposure always cuts both ways, and neither Mme. Epanchina nor anyone else is prepared for the resulting shame reaction. The narrator, however, reports it in detail, describing Kolia's response as a fall from childlike innocence to shameful knowledge. He observes that Kolia runs to a corner and covers his face from shame: "He was unbearably ashamed, and his childlike impressionability, which had not yet gotten used to filth, was distressed beyond all measure. It seemed to him that something extraordinary had happened, something which had destroyed everything at once, and that he was practically the cause of it for the sole reason that he had read it aloud. But everyone else, it seemed, also felt something similar" (8:221). By having his narrator observe the general shame response, Dostoevsky dramatizes shame's contagious force.

The exposers in this scene are likewise exposed. Keller shamelessly admits authorship. Ippolit informs Mme. Epanchina that Lebedev had collaborated with Keller, and she announces it out loud. Keller reveals that he paid Lebedev six silver rubles for such "facts" as the foreign shoes the Prince was wearing when he arrived in Russia,[22] the Prince's enormous appetite at Shneider's (a fabrication), and some numerical alterations: "in a word, all that aggregation [*gruppirovka*], all of that belongs to him, for six silver rubles, he didn't correct the diction, however." Lebedev responds with a counter-exposure: "I didn't correct the second half, sir, so that all that's illiterate (and there's illiterate stuff there!), so after all don't attribute that to me, sir . . . " (8:242). In addition to parodying radical prose, Dostoevsky here underscores the sociopolitical rivalry that hinders social harmony. The article's authors and those whom it was intended to benefit (Burdovsky and company) all belong to the lower classes, while their targets belong to the nobility.

Exposure does not stop with mutual recrimination—the obverse of the Russian social contract. Dostoevsky highlights the ethics of the exchange by having Mme. Epanchina emphasize Lebedev's concern—not with the article's slanderous content, but with its diction: " 'Look at what he's worried about!' exclaimed Lizaveta Prokofievna" (8:242). She focuses attention on the authors' ethics or, rather, their lack of ethics. Both Keller and Lebedev shamelessly disregard the article's slanderous content, focusing instead on their own rhetorical contributions to it. Lebedev's treacherous collaboration (for six silver rubles, the sign of a cheap Judas) not only emphasizes his moral bankruptcy but also suggests a relationship between class status and shamelessness. Mme. Epanchina's indignation at the Prince for forgiving Lebedev derives from a sense of personal honor. She clearly believes that base action springs from base character.

Once Lebedev's co-authorship is exposed, readers easily find traces of his rhetoric, particularly the detail about Burdovsky's mother being crippled (repeated twice). Lebedev used the expression "crippled" (literally "without legs," *bez nog*) in an earlier scene to characterize his wife, who was still alive, pregnant, and presumably whole-bodied. After Nastasia Filippovna throws the 100,000 rubles into the fire at her birthday party, Lebedev wails: "Little Mother! Gracious One! Order me into the fireplace: the whole of me will crawl in, I will put my entire gray head into the fire! . . . A sick crippled wife, thirteen children—all orphans, I buried my father last week, he's sitting hungry, Nastasia Filippovna!" (8:145). The first part of Lebedev's appeal reveals his willingness to abase himself for money. While Nastasia Filippovna tests Gania's honor, Lebedev demonstrates that he has none. Here, as elsewhere, Lebedev's shamelessness rouses readers' contempt.

Lebedev's last sentence betrays his rhetorical tactics. First, Lebedev uses physical disability to elicit audience pity—in this case for his supposedly unfortunate wife, in Keller's article for Burdovsky's supposedly dying mother. But women are not the only disabled characters in Lebedev's repertory. He represents the moneylender Zaidler as a "sad old man, crippled, making a living by honest labor" (8:161). Lebedev also claims to General Ivolgin that during the Napoleonic invasion one of his own legs was shot off by a cannon (he specifies which one); that he buried it in a Moscow cemetery and visits it yearly[23]; and that he sported a Chernosvitov leg that was so convincing that his wife never knew of his physical defect. Such statements reveal his blatant disregard for verisimilitude as well as truth. Lebedev appeals to his audience's emotions, not their reason.

In retrospect, this scene also reveals Lebedev's numerical exaggerations and his preoccupation with food.[24] At the time Lebedev makes his anguished plea to Nastasia Filippovna, he has three, not thirteen children (in Book Two, he has a fourth). Later Keller reports Lebedev's claim that the Prince sent Burdovsky only fifty rubles, when in fact the Prince had sent two hundred fifty. In both cases, Lebedev manipulates numbers for rhetorical effect. These scenes thus prepare for Lebedev's use of statistics in the cannibal speech. Lebedev also characterizes his father as hungry, again a clear plea for audience sympathy. Keller's article claims that the Prince ate huge amounts at the doctor's in Switzerland, a detail Lebedev fabricates to portray the Prince as a parasite. This claim thus links the Prince with Pavlishchev, whom the article overtly labels a parasite, *lezheboka i tuneiadets* (literally, a "lie-a-bed" and a parasite),[25] and with two other social parasites—the Prince's grandfather, who is labeled a spendthrift, and the Prince's father, who is labeled a thief. Lebedev's fabrication reveals the resentment of the disenfranchised. Yet his accusation is ironically self-condemnatory, for other characters unceasingly expose Lebedev as a parasite.

Finally, in Lebedev's wail to Nastasia Filippovna, he claims that his children are all orphans because he buried his father the week before (a non sequitur). Yet in the very next clause he claims that his father is "sitting hungry" (a contradiction). This claim exemplifies Lebedev's tendency to disregard truth altogether. It also fits the novel's imagery of resurrected dead. Kolpakov rises from the dead and returns to his regiment; Lebedev's bodiless head continues to speak; Lebedev's father dies in one sentence then starves in the next. These nontranscendent images recall the novel's preoccupation with Holbein's Christ and the seeming impossibility of resurrection.[26] Lebedev's rhetoric, even as reflected in Keller's article, thus constantly circles back to the novel's thematics.

While Lebedev and Keller willingly compromise others for the sake of their own verbal display, they differ significantly in their sincerity. During his long interview with Myshkin, Keller suddenly jumps to the conclusion "that he had practically lost 'every trace of morality' ('solely from lack of belief in the Most High'), that he had almost stooped to theft" (8:256). By attributing loss of morality to loss of faith, Keller reinforces Lebedev's assertion that belief in God spawns ethical action and anticipates Ivan Karamazov's famous dictum that without belief in God, "all is permitted." Keller also associates theft with loss of belief in a transcendent idea, thus providing an ethical standard for judging Ferdyshchenko's and General Ivolgin's thefts. Ferdyshchenko's lack of shame and guilt condemn him. By contrast, General Ivolgin's shame and guilt, as well as his attempt to undo his crime, redeem him.

Though tempted, Keller does not steal. Instead, he complains comically to the Prince: "Keller with unusual readiness confessed to such things that it was not possible to imagine how it was possible to talk about such things. Approaching each story, he positively averred that he was repentant and inwardly 'full of tears,' and yet he talked as though he were proud of his act, and at the same time sometimes so comically that he and the Prince chuckled in the end like madmen" (8:257). This interaction reveals Keller's narrative talent: like Dostoevsky, Keller can transform the unspeakable into something comic. Keller's confession recalls yet again Ferdyshchenko's truth-telling game. The contest, which hinges on self-presentation, establishes each speaker's rhetorical skill. Both Generals Epanchin and Totsky recount shameful incidents skillfully. Though readers may agree that the Generals have cheated Ferdyshchenko, we have no sympathy for him because he is a bad narrator.[27] Like his social superiors, Keller skillfully tells on himself. Unlike his social superiors, he creates listener sympathy. As Keller confesses, the Prince is at the height of his psychological insight in the novel. His genuine affection for the boxer and his remarks about Keller's stories model a response for the authorial audience: "The main thing is that you have a kind of childlike trustfulness and a rare truthfulness, . . . do you know that even with that alone you compensate for a lot?" (8:257). The Prince thus identifies Keller's capacity for moral intuition as a redeeming grace.

By confessing to doubleness, Keller links himself to Myshkin and Lebedev, who also articulate their ideas about the doubleness of human thoughts.[28] Keller tells the Prince that he came to visit intially because he wanted to improve himself but then he decided to borrow money as well (8:258). Keller concludes, "Isn't that base?" (*nizko*), a question that links him rhetorically to Lebedev, who calls himself "base" (*nizok*).[29] Arriving as Keller leaves, Lebedev fumes when he sees money in Keller's hand. The Prince objects that Keller was sincerely repentant. Lebedev responds, "Why indeed what kind of repentance is that! Exactly the same as me yesterday: 'Base, base am I,' and in fact it's only words, sir!" (8:259). Lebedev then confesses his own doubleness, causing the Prince to observe: "'Well, there you are, he also said the exact same thing to me just now,' exclaimed the Prince, 'and both of you praise yourselves! You even surprise me, only he's more sincere than you, for you've turned it into a real profession'" (8:259). In identifying Lebedev as an actor, the Prince exposes his calculations.[30] At the novel's outset, Lebedev gladly plays the buffoon in order to accompany Rogozhin. He confesses his baseness to Mme. Epanchina so that she will continue speaking with him. He identifies with Talleyrand. He admits his own hypocrisy to the Prince to expose Keller. The

Prince, a model audience for moral response, immediately perceives the difference in their motives. Unlike Keller, with his "childlike trustfulness," Lebedev acts from *ressentiment*. Keller wants money and respect, but he does not plot against those who have them, nor is he quick to feel slighted. Furthermore, Keller has a sense of honor, albeit a comically flawed one. He slanders the Prince to defend Burdovsky's honor, for example, yet he willingly defends Nastasia Filippovna's honor. In this way, Keller proves himself a champion of the humiliated and injured.[31] Nonetheless, Keller violates the social contract because he perceives Lebedev as a rhetorical rival.

The Cannibal's Defense

Following Lebedev's cannibal speech, both Keller and Ivolgin expose Lebedev as a phony. Keller points to the gap between Lebedev's rhetoric and his lifestyle; Ivolgin criticizes his unexpected conclusion. Alive to his audience's mockery, Lebedev defends himself: "As far as it concerns me, a nineteenth-century man, then I, perhaps, would have judged otherwise, and that's what I'm informing you about, so there's no reason, gentlemen, to curl your lips at me, and for you, General, it's positively indecent" (8:315). Lebedev takes particular offense at the General's derision because of the Russian social contract. Yet Lebedev's self-consciousness increases his rhetorical fervor, for he concludes his speech with a series of anaphoric questions and portentous imperatives that wed his forensic and prophetic talents:

> Now for the conclusion, the finale, gentlemen, the finale which contains the solution to one of the greatest questions of that time and ours! The criminal finally goes and informs against himself to the clergy and surrenders himself to the authorities' hands. One asks, what tortures awaited him at that time, what torture wheels, what bonfires and burning? Who, after all, pushed him to inform against himself? Why not just stop at the figure sixty, preserving his secret until his last breath? Why not simply give up monastics and live in repentance as a hermit? Why, finally, not become a monk himself? And here's the solution! Therefore, there was something more powerful than bonfires and burning and even a twenty-year habit! Therefore, there was an idea more powerful than all misfortunes, bad harvests, tortures, plagues, leprosy, and all that hell which humanity would not even have borne without that binding idea directing the heart and fecundating the sources of life! Show me something similar to such a power in our age of vices [*porokov*] and railroads . . . that is, one should say: in our age of steamers [*parokhodov*] and railroads, but I say: in our age of vices and railroads, because I am drunk, but right! Show me a contemporary binding idea of even half the power of that in those cen-

turies. And dare to say, finally, that the sources of life have not weakened, not grown murky under that "star," under that net entangling people. And don't scare me with your welfare, with your riches, the infrequency of famine and the speed of your roads of communication! There is greater wealth, but less power; the binding idea is gone; everything has grown soft, everything and everybody has gotten well-stewed! We've all, all, all gotten well-stewed! . . . But enough, that's not the point now, the point is how should we manage, most worthy Prince, about the *hors d'oeuvres* that have been prepared for our guests? (8:315)

Dostoevsky's lawyer-prophet concludes his speech about a people-eater by proposing that people eat. By identifying his conclusion as a "subtle, forensic twist to the case" that staves off "genuine indignation" and pacifies his opponents, Lebedev naively associates forensic rhetoric with moral manipulation. Eight years later Dostoevsky's *Diary* writer exposes the ethical cost of ending a speech with a witticism: "You know what: it seems to me that it is very difficult to remain, and, as they say, to keep yourself as an honest person when you worry so much to save the most apt remark for last, in order to leave a burst of laughter after yourself. The task is itself so petty that in the end it must drive from a person everything serious. And what's more, if the apt remark is not stored up for last, then it's necessary to make it up, and for a pretty turn of phrase 'one doesn't spare mother or father'" (22:54). Dostoevsky's later attitude to lawyers applies to Lebedev: rhetorical talent almost always leads its possessor astray. Lebedev's forensic rhetoric undercuts his moral message. Likewise his mixture of prophetic and forensic rhetoric signals the duality of his soul.

Literary Critique as Authorial Message

Dostoevsky provides his authorial audience with guidelines for judging Lebedev's bombast by having his rhetorical rivals, Keller and Ivolgin, criticize Lebedev and his speech. By exposing Lebedev's prophetic pretensions, both thus violate the Russian social contract. Keller objects to the content, the presentation, and the ethics of Lebedev's speech: "He attacks enlightenment, preaches twelfth-century fanaticism, he's affected, and even without any innocence of the heart: yet how did he himself get the means for his house, let me ask?" (8:316). Keller's first objections parodically voice the views of 1860s radicals: he condemns the religious content of Lebedev's message. Keller's next two objections spotlight authorial concerns: Lebedev's posturing and his ethics. Keller appropriates one of the narrator's verbs to characterize Lebedev: the verb "to be affected, to posture" (*krivliat'sia*) (8:212), a word with both physical and moral connotations. In colloquial Russian, the common word *krivda* (falsehood, injustice) is used as the opposite of *pravda* (truth, justice). In addition, the verb *krivliat'sia* (to be affected, to posture) gains a further sense of physical and moral distortion by association with the verb *krivit'sia* (to become crooked, to make a wry face). The narrator employs this verb at the beginning of Book Two when Myshkin finds Lebedev reciting his successful trial speech to his family (8:161). Mme. Epanchina uses it three times to describe Lebedev (8:202;212;241). By placing this verb in Keller's mouth 100 to 150 pages after Mme. Epanchina and the narrator use it, Dostoevsky emphasizes Lebedev's insincerity and role-playing. Dostoevsky's narrator also exposes Lebedev by using the verb "wriggles" (*vertet'sia*) (8:241), which his *Diary* writer later uses to describe lawyers' unscrupulousness (21:22,23). In Dostoevsky's novel, Lebedev's identification with lawyers taints his moral image.

Finally, Keller discredits Lebedev's speech by asking what kind of prophet profits from his trade? Keller thus exposes the discrepancy between Lebedev's self-presentation as a "poor" and "naked" prophet and his financial opportunism. Moreover, Keller's exposure of Lebedev reinforces an earlier exposé by Lebedev's own daughter Vera, who scolds her father for donning his raggedy old jacket instead of his brand-new one (8:160). Lebedev feigns poverty to enrich himself.

Following Keller's exposé of Lebedev, General Ivolgin argues that Lebedev's pretensions to the status of a prophet clash with his conciliatory conclusion: "'I've seen a real interpreter of Revelation,' said the General in another corner to different listeners, among them Ptitsyn whom he seized by the button, 'the deceased Grigory Semenovich Burmistrov: he, as they say, set hearts aflame. And in the first place, he put on glasses, opened a big, ancient book with black leather binding, well, and besides he had a gray beard, two medals for tithing. He would begin sternly and severely, generals bowed before him, and women fainted, well—and that one concludes with *hors d'oeuvres!* Nothing at all alike!'" (8:316). Though the General comically points to Burmistrov's props, he also stresses his rhetorical impact. Lebedev, on the other hand, avoids audience criticism by pandering to their physical comfort. He defensively asserts his qualifications to speak: "I say in our age of vice and railroads because I am drunk, but *prav!*" (8:315).[32] By playing on the double meaning of *prav*, which can mean "right" or "just," Lebedev invokes prophetic privilege. Yet his defensiveness reveals Lebedev's resentment of the class status that condemns him to role-playing.

Although Lebedev avoids mockery by inviting his guests to eat *hors d'oeuvres*, Dostoevsky uses Lebedev's invitation to parody one of the mysteries of Christian ritual—communion. The sacrament of communion unites the congregation in an act of symbolic cannibalism: members partake of the freely given body and blood of Christ and thus unite spiritually with their God through a physical act. In proposing that his guests join in a secular communion, Lebedev unwittingly acts as Dostoevsky's comic spokesperson.

Lebedev's client engages in nonsymbolic cannibalism, killing and eating unwilling victims, yet he changes in a way dear to Dostoevsky's heart—from self-imposed isolation or dissociation (*obosoblenie*), he moves to community (*vseobshchnost*').[33] Lebedev uses his client's belief in God as an indirect argument against cannibalism—when his client turns to God, he stops eating his fellow men. While Lebedev proclaims the need for a higher idea, he does not elaborate. Dostoevsky has Mme. Epanchina, the novel's social conscience, do that. Angry at the Burdovsky crowd, she exclaims, "Madmen! Vain ones! You don't believe in God, you don't believe in Christ! And in fact vanity and pride have so eaten you up, that you will end up eating one another up, this I predict to you" (8:238). Mme. Epanchina overtly links atheism and cannibalism. She also identifies vanity and pride as causes of social strife,[34] arguing that when individuals place themselves first, they destroy community. Like Lebedev's cannibal, they act narcissistically and thus harm others.

While the Prince defends the verisimilitude of Lebedev's twelfth-century cannibal, he nonetheless questions the cannibal's choice of monks. Lebedev hints that monks' homosexual proclivities made them easy prey, and Gania suggests that monastic corruption ensured monks' corpulence. But the Prince's question implies another explanation. Monks are members of religious orders who take Christ as their model. Dostoevsky thus suggests, tongue in cheek, that a religiously oriented man like Lebedev's cannibal wants to approximate the sacrament. But he fails, because he follows the letter of the ritual, not the spirit. The cannibal thus shares another of Lebedev's weaknesses. Like Lebedev, he reduces the figurative to the literal. Lebedev's cannibal partakes not of the God-man, but of God's men.

These comic critics provide Dostoevsky's authorial audience with rhetorical and ethical criteria for judging Lebedev's speech. Yet, while Keller reveals Lebedev's moral defects, Dostoevsky shows how exposure cuts two ways. Like Lebedev, his critics reveal their own moral flaws. Keller discredits himself by spouting the rhetoric and ideas of 1860s radicals. His argument—that Lebedev's speech attacks enlightenment and praises religion—rings hollow because of its unexamined clichés. In staging these critiques that discredit Lebedev, Dostoevsky turns to the comic tradition in which authors make serious thematic statements under the mimetic guise of their fools and liars. Lebedev's critics discredit him, even as his cannibal speech voices one of Dostoevsky's most cherished ideas—that belief in God unites men on earth.

Lebedev implies a moral contract: if one believes in God, one is obliged to love one's neighbor. While this is difficult to achieve, it functions like Dostoevsky's version of the Russian social contract. Lying and allowing others to lie promote tolerance and acceptance of one's neighbor, a tolerance and acceptance based on an awareness of one's own humanness. As Versilov reminds Arkady (*The Adolescent*), who wants to expose his landlord's story as a lie: "My friend, always allow a person to lie a little—it's innocent. Even let him lie a lot. First of all, it will show your tact, and second of all, for that you also will be allowed to lie—two enormous advantages—at one time. *Que diable!* one needs to love one's neighbor" (13:168). In this view, the Russian social contract operates on the principle of reciprocity and functions to strengthen the bonds of community. Arkady's impulse—to expose the lie—would disrupt the dialogue and alienate its participants.

This is what happens in *The Idiot*. Consumed by shame at their social positions, General Ivolgin and Lebedev lie. Ivolgin tells outrageous stories and Lebedev delivers forensic and prophetic speeches to impress their audiences. Their desire to undo their shame inspires them to rhetorical excesses that surpass acceptable limits. In loving their self-images more than their neighbors, they expose and humiliate each other, thus violating the Russian social contract. By doing so, they call attention to the unwritten codes of social interaction. They also expose themselves.

In fashioning these scenes of exposure, Dostoevsky lays bare his own narrative strategy. As his characters expose one another to shame, thereby implicating the character-witnesses, so Dostoevsky exposes his characters to shame, thereby implicating his readers, who are also positioned as witnesses. By making shame public, Dostoevsky plunges readers into the affective and cognitive experience of the text's action. On the cognitive level, Dostoevsky's character audiences ask the questions that Dostoevsky wants his authorial audience to ask: What are a speaker's intentions? What moves characters to act? What are the consequences, intentional and unintentional, of a given speech act or a given action? On the affective level, Dostoevsky complicates the picture: we may not feel sympathy for a character's action, but we can feel the pain of his/her exposure.

As Dostoevsky exposes his narrative strategies, he exposes his moral vision. In *The Idiot,* Dostoevsky makes a character's shame or shamelessness a moral measure: a character who is capable of shame is capable of change. As Dostoevsky shows, shame can eradicate barriers or erect them. Shame that eradicates barriers implies conscience, a moral agency that reminds us of what we share with our fellow human beings. Yet shame can be used defensively, to erect barriers, to protect exposed individuals from further scrutiny, thereby removing them from others' compassion. Shamelessness, on the other hand, only erects barriers. Whether or not it is a defensive role adopted to protect the self from narcissistic injury, shamelessness implies lack of conscience, that is, lack of the moral agency necessary for community. Yet even Dostoevsky's most shameless characters, like Lukian Lebedev and Fedor Karamazov, worry about the afterlife, indicating that a spark of conscience still lives within them. Lebedev's cannibal speech, his family loyalty, and his prayers for Mme. du Barry reveal traces of conscience in him. Nonetheless, the inertial force of role-playing overpowers his conscience. Lebedev starts and ends as a role-player. He enacts shame without feeling it. From start to finish, Dostoevsky's narrator maintains a distance from Lebedev. Dostoevsky thus metes out poetic justice—his narrator treats Lebedev as Lebedev treats others. As long as Lebedev reifies others and views them as sources of profit, he remains separated from them. In *The Idiot*, the shamed General dies in the bosom of his family; the shameless Lebedev leaves the novel the way he entered it: still plotting to enrich himself at others' expense. He has a family, but he has left them at home.

chapter nine

Metaliterary Identity

I am a slave, I am a worm, but I am not God—that is the only way I differ from Derzhavin. (10:213;269)

— CAPTAIN LEBIADKIN, *Demons*

I am not of the same society as that Aesop, that buffoon, that Pierrot. (14:78;84)

— MIUSOV, *The Brothers Karamazov*

"What Aesop?" the judge again picked up sternly.
"That Pierrot, my father, Fedor Pavlovich." (15:99;666)

— DMITRY KARAMAZOV, *The Brothers Karamazov*

While Dostoevsky foregrounds the identity crises of his bilious underground man or his tormented intellectual Raskolnikov, he conceals his liars' identity crises with comic covers. He thereby provides readers with the aesthetic pleasure that derives from comic play, but he also affords us the cognitive pleasure of looking beneath the surface for hidden depths. In this chapter, I focus on Captain Lebiadkin and Fedor Karamazov, two shameless liars who are compared both to writers and to literary characters. Captain Lebiadkin identifies himself with the eighteenth-century poet Derzhavin, with the Russian fable-writer Krylov, and with Shakespeare's Falstaff. Miusov and Dmitry Karamazov identify Fedor Karamazov as both "Aesop" and "Pierrot." By attributing these dual identifications as actual writers and comic characters to Captain Lebiadkin and Fedor Karamazov, Dostoevsky identifies them as loci for poetic display, metaliterary play, and serious commentary on the writer's art.

Liars resemble writers in their willingness to fabricate context as well as content. Liars differ from writers, however, in their ability to do so. As I show, Dostoevsky's liars' narcissism reduces their narrative efficacy because it makes their stories self-referential; it also blinds them to the nature and needs of their homodiegetic audiences. Dostoevsky, on the other hand, masterfully manipulates his authorial audience and humorously employs his liars to inscribe his own poetics into his work's mimetic action and thematics. Lebiadkin's reference to Derzhavin, for example, comically encapsulates the thematics of *Demons*, and Fedor Pavlovich's identification as "Aesop" indicates hidden depths in Dostoevsky's last novel. The surface humor of these characters' poems and stories belongs to them; the penetrating humor and thematic depth of those same poems and stories belong to Dostoevsky. By double-voicing their hyperbolic claims and self-referential fabrications, Dostoevsky adds a metaliterary dimension to his realist novels.

Although he drinks, beats his sister, sponges off the Virginskys, and distributes subversive literature as well as counterfeit money, the lower-class Lebiadkin falls in love with the aristocratic beauty Liza Tushina and styles himself a poet. The first time the narrator meets him, Lebiadkin bursts into dedicatory verse ("To a Star-Amazon") (10:95;117). He declares his love for her in epistolary verse ("To the Perfection of the Young Miss Tushina") and calls his marriage proposal to her a poem ("The letter from the infusorian is to be understood in verse") (10:106;131–2). To an irate Stavrogin he justifies his proposal with an occasional poem ("In Case She Should Break Her Leg") (10:210;266). In Liza's presence, he answers Varvara Stavrogina's query about his sister's identity with a verse fable ("The Cockroach") (10:141;177). Expecting Liza to be at the fête, he composes another occasional poem ("To the Governess") (10:362;472–3). And, self-consciously contrasting himself with a famous Russian poet, Lebiadkin declares "I am a slave, I am a worm, but I am not God—that is the only way I differ from Derzhavin" (10:213;269). As Ksana Blank has shown, Dostoevsky highlights the comic and derivative nature, as well as the weakness, of Lebiadkin's poetry by having him imitate archaic verse forms. Thus, instead of writing like his contemporaries, Lebiadkin uses eighteenth-century genres and seventeenth-century rhymes.[1]

By making Lebiadkin a parodic poet, Dostoevsky flags his novel's metaliterary dimension. While Lebiadkin naively compares himself to the eighteenth-century Russian poet Gavrila Derzhavin, for example, Dostoevsky uses the occasion parodically to encapsulate the novel's thematics and situate its metaphysics in a tragicomic and satiric political context. Lebiadkin abbreviates Derzhavin's famous line: "I am a tsar—I am a slave, I am a worm—I am God." This line belongs to an ode in which Derzhavin invokes his own "wondrous" powers as a human being to express his unity with God's creation.[2] Lebiadkin merely cites a well-known line from a Russian literary classic. Dostoevsky, however, chooses his source poem to echo the novel's metaphysical thematics. Likewise, Dostoevsky recontextualizes the poem, transferring the metaphysical to the political realm. Lebiadkin cites this line while appealing to Stavrogin for protection from Peter Verkhovensky, who threatens to expose his illegal activities. Justifiably fearing for his life, Lebiadkin emphasizes his lowly status by citing the two humble identities ("I am a slave, I am a worm"). He consciously modifies Derzhavin's line by denying his identification with God. He also, perhaps unconsciously, skips the first segment of Derzhavin's paired contrasts: "I am a tsar."

While Lebiadkin seeks Stavrogin's protection, Dostoevsky links every word of his declaration to the novel's thematics. Lebiadkin's self-identification as a "slave" links him with the nine-tenths of the population that Shigalev's theory identifies as "slaves." His self-identification as a "worm" (*cherv*) anticipates Peter Verkhovensky's declaration to Stavrogin—"I am your wormlet" (*cherviak*) (10:324;419). His omission ("I am a tsar") proleptically avoids competition with Stavrogin, whom Peter Verkhovensky later proclaims the political pretender "Ivan-Tsarevich" (10:325;421). Finally, Lebiadkin's disavowal ("but not God") recalls Kirillov, a man likewise obsessed with identity, who finally declares himself the "God-man." As Lebiadkin comically defines himself, Dostoevsky reminds his readers of revolutionary ideologies and politics.

Lebiadkin's identification with Derzhavin also highlights the novel's thematics of pretendership. Not a captain but a retired provisions clerk, not a poet but a poetaster, Lebiadkin is a self-fashioner. However comic his self-identifications as "slave" and "worm," they nonetheless reflect actual humiliations the Russian sociopolitical system inflicts even on those it most honors, such as poets.

While Lebiadkin identifies with a famous poet, Dostoevsky establishes him as a site of metaliterary play. First, Derzhavin's ornamental style and his unorthodox mixing of high and low diction and imagery make him a worthy literary model for Lebiadkin. Second, Derzhavin's low social origins, his elevation through civil service, and his poems in praise of Catherine the Great highlight the uneasy relationship between poet and political patronage in the Russian literary tradition. Third, as mentioned in chapter 8, Derzhavin compares the poet to a swan in his poem "The Swan" (*Lebed'*), a likely source for Lebiadkin's name. Moreover, Derzhavin's swan-poet claims that the muses will confer immortality on him, raise him socially, and bring him earthly fame—all claims that reflect Lebiadkin's longings. Finally, as Dostoevsky would know, Pushkin cites Derzhavin's famous line as the epigraph to Part Two of his "Egyptian Nights." Dostoevsky thus forges an added link to the Russian literary tradition. Lebiadkin's next line—"But my means, what are my means!" (10:213;269)—comically emphasizes the economic humiliation experienced by Russia's poets. By having Lebiadkin identify with Derzhavin, Dostoevsky thus inscribes his own thematic and metaliterary play into Lebiadkin's mimetic obsession.

Lebiadkin also identifies with the Russian fable writer Krylov, hyperbolically claiming that his doggerel masterpiece, "The Cockroach," is a "fable of Krylov" (*odnu basniu Krylova*). In calling his poem a fable, Lebiadkin indicates that it is an allegory containing a hidden message, which he nonetheless spells out for his audience. By calling it a "fable of Krylov," Lebiadkin imitates an eighteenth-century fable tradition: La Fontaine appropriated fables of Aesop; Krylov appropriated fables of La Fontaine.³ Dostoevsky thereby emphasizes Lebiadkin's connection to the fable tradition and thus to the cunning slave Aesop, to whom Fedor Karamazov is later compared.

Lebiadkin recites "The Cockroach" in Varvara Stavrogina's drawing room, almost immediately after his Prince de Monbars speech (discussed in the next chapter). Identifying himself as a poet, he recites it to explain why he cannot reveal his sister Marya's identity:

> 'Tis of a cockroach I will tell
> and a fine cockroach was he,
> But then into a glass he fell
> Full of fly-phagy . . .

"Lord, what is this?" Varvara Petrovna exclaimed.

"It's in the summertime," the captain hurried, waving his arms terribly, with the irritable impatience of an author whose recitation is being hindered, "in the summertime, when lots of flies get into a glass, then fly-phagy takes place, any fool can understand that, don't interrupt, don't interrupt, you'll see, you'll see . . . " (he kept waving his arms).

> "The cockroach took up so much room
> He made grumble⁴ the flies.
> 'A crowded glass, is this our doom?'
> To Jupiter they cried.
> But as the flies did make their moan
> Along came Nikifor,
> A kind, old, no-o-oble man . . .

I haven't quite finished here, but anyway, in plain words!" the captain rattled on. "Nikifor takes the glass and, in spite of their crying, dumps the whole comedy into the tub, both flies and cockroach, which should have been done long ago. But notice, Madam, notice, the cockroach does not grumble! This is the answer to your question, 'Why?'" he cried out triumphantly. "'The cockroach does not grum-ble!' As for Nikifor, he represents nature," he added in a quick patter and began pacing the room self-contentedly. (10:141–2;176)

Lebiadkin's comic poem, in which Dostoevsky parodies Miatlev's poem "Fantastic Tale,"[5] sums up his dilemma: Lebiadkin's apophatic claim that the cockroach "does not grumble" reveals his self-image.[6] While fable writers typically represent humans in animal form, Lebiadkin reveals his sense of insignificance, as well as his sense of physical size and awkwardness, by imitating Miatlev's choice of poet-cockroach.[7] By representing the rest of humanity as flies, Lebiadkin further reveals his own sense of social immobility (though they have wings, cockroaches usually crawl). Finally, in his fable, he represents himself as an outcast—persecuted for his superficial differences. Like the flies, the cockroach is caught in a trap; unlike the complaining majority, he remains silent, thereby demonstrating his moral superiority.[8] While he repudiates the vociferous majority's political infighting, Lebiadkin shares their ignoble fate. Lebiadkin gives Nikifor, whose name means "Bearer of Victory," and who "represents nature," both a servant's name and a servant's job, thereby emphasizing his role as servitor of divine will. He thus comically represents the man-made sociopolitical order as a chaotic mess and divinely creates nature as an arbitrary force. From Miatlev's poem, Lebiadkin appropriates the image of a cockroach fatally fallen into a cup. The source poem also depicts an image of grieving love, which reflects Lebiadkin's unrequited love for Liza Tushina. Furthermore, Miatlev's image of silent loyalty inspires the pretender captain, who aspires to be seen in the same way.

Lebiadkin's creator, however, would know that Miatlev's elegaic poem of melancholy love and solitude parodies an eighteenth-century elegy by A. I. Polezhaev. This makes Lebiadkin's poem a parody of a parody.[9] But Dostoevsky goes even further: he turns Lebiadkin's verse into a political and metaphysical satire.[10] Dostoevsky's addition of Jupiter and his choice of the verb "to grumble" (*roptat'*) add a metaphysical dimension missing from Miatlev's poem. Dostoevsky's first version does not mention Jupiter (11:38). His modification thus reflects Lebiadkin's comic and the novel's serious metaphysical concerns.[11] Moreover, in contrasting his meek poetic "I" with the flies' metaphysical rebelliousness, Lebiadkin uses the verb "to grumble" (*roptat'/vozroptat'*), which flags Dostoevsky's authorial reference to his beloved book of Job. Though the verb "to grumble" does not figure in the Russian Bible account of Job, it occurs in Dostoevsky's.[12] Dostoevsky's source for the verb was probably yet another eighteenth-century poem—Lomonosov's "Ode, Extracted from Job, Chapters 38, 39, 40 and 41." Lomonosov's ode opens, "Oh you, man, who vainly in your grief / grumble [*ropshchesh'*] against God / Listen, if in jealousy / He spoke awesomely from the clouds to Job!"[13] Lebiadkin narcissistically stresses his own creative powers as well as his own human suffering, while Dostoevsky gleefully parodies Lomonosov's ode, which ignores Job's suffering to emphasize God's might.

By having Lebiadkin invoke Job, Dostoevsky highlights his narcissism. Lebiadkin is not a righteous man who first earns his good fortune by hard work and devotion to God; rather he is a liar and a parasite who daily beats the sister who supports him. Nor does Lebiadkin accept his humble place on this earth; rather he rails against heaven and earth at the perceived injustices against him. He does not quietly accept his anonymous status as Stavrogin's brother-in-law; rather he does everything he can to publicize the connection. He gladly misrepresents himself to earn others' praise and recognition. Thus, as Varvara prepares to expel him from her house, Lebiadkin declares, "Madam, your magnificent halls might belong to the noblest of persons, but the cockroach does not grumble! Notice, yes, notice finally that he does not grumble, and cognize the great spirit!" (10:142;177). Lebiadkin's apophatic grumble exposes him as a shame-ridden, materialistic, vain, and rebellious man who will do anything for personal recognition. He wants praise for remaining anonymous, but he flaunts his anonymity to reveal his identity.

Lebiadkin is Dostoevky's creation. His identity is self-fabricated. The humiliations he experiences, however, have historical counterparts in Russia. Though Dostoevsky draws attention to the constructed nature of his novel as well as the constructed nature of identity, he nonetheless demonstrates with Lebiadkin's death that personal, political, and poetic identity are life-and-death matters. Lebiadkin's exhibitionist displays warn the shame-sensitive Stavrogin of what to expect once he announces his marriage to Lebiadkin's holy fool sister. Stavrogin eventually turns his purse over to Fedka, the convict who later murders the Lebiadkins. As I will show in the next chapter, the threat of shame provokes extreme responses in people's hearts. Lebiadkin may live comically, but he dies tragically.

Aesop

While General Ivolgin and Stepan Verkhovensky die after shocks to their identity, Captain Lebiadkin and Fedor Karamazov are murdered in part because they expose, or threaten to expose, others' shame. Like Lebiadkin, Fedor Karamazov responds to social shame by verbal aggression. When humiliated, or potentially humiliated, he humiliates.[14] By doing so publicly, he not only provokes a desire for revenge within his victim but also arouses audience anxiety. By doing so with stories, Fedor Karamazov earns the epithet "Aesop," which situates him at the center of metaliterary play in *The Brothers Karamazov*. Though commentators usually focus on Ivan's and Alesha's literary activities, their provocative progenitor regales those assembled in Zosima's cell with four stories that signal the novel's metaliterary dimension. Like

Aesop's stories, Fedor Karamazov's contain hidden messages. And like Aesop's, they provoke hostile audience response.

Dostoevsky reveals authorial intent to associate Fedor Karamazov with Aesop by having three characters refer to him as "Aesop" four times within a hundred pages of the novel's beginning and once at its end. Miusov calls him "Aesop" once in Book Two, Chapter 8 (14:78;84); Dmitry Karamazov once and Ivan Karamazov twice in Book 3, Chapter 9 (14:129,132;140,143); Dmitry once again in Book Twelve, Chapter 2 (15:99;666). Dostoevsky further underscores the epithet's metaliterary function by joining Miusov's first and Dmitry's last references to Fedor as "Aesop" with references to him as "that Pierrot." Aesop and Pierrot share humble social origins and ambiguous identities as well as scatological, gastronomical, and clown-like associations. Both are identified with arbitrary violence and comic wit. Both are subverters of hierarchy as well as performers. And both link Fedor Pavlovich to the European literary tradition. Though Fedor Pavlovich is referred to as "Pierrot" only twice, he is repeatedly referred to as, and even professes himself to be, a "buffoon" (*shut*), keeping his identity as a performer alive to Dostoevsky's readers.

The references to Fedor Pavlovich as "Aesop" and "Pierrot" are not only five hundred pages apart but also occur in vastly different contexts. Their placement and travel thus bear the stamp of Fedor Karamazov's eponymous creator. Miusov uses these epithets in the privacy of his own thoughts, while Dmitry declaims them in a courtroom during one of the most publicized murder trials in Russia. The epithet "Aesop" thus moves from Miusov's mind to the Karamazov house and then to the public fora of both courtroom and press. The epithet's move from private to public reflects the path of the novel's action, a family scandal that becomes a national one.

Like the legendary Aesop, Fedor Karamazov's career moves from private to public spheres. As Annabel Patterson points out in her study *Fables of Power*, most collections of Aesop's fables from the Middle Ages through the eighteenth century begin with the legendary life of Aesop.[15] Though the *Life* itself consists of a series of anecdotes, many of them scatological, Patterson points out that together they form a complex fable that was often amply illustrated. In the legendary *Life*, Aesop (or Aethiops) was an ugly,[16] black slave who acquired the gift of eloquence after he hosted two priests of Diana.[17] He was then sold to the philosopher Xanthus, whom he entertained with his wit and one-upmanship. Weary of his role as servile prankster, he achieved manumission by successfully interpreting portents. Aesop then attained international fame as a counselor, which proved his undoing, for the good citizens of Delphi, either jealous of their own reputation as readers of oracles (Patterson) or angry because Aesop reminded them of their slave origins (Daly), had him framed for sacrilegious theft and threw him over the cliff at Delphi. Patterson points out that though there were fables before and after Aesop, he became associated with animal fables employed as ruses by the underprivileged for survival in a hostile world and was thus seen as a symbolic figure of challenge from below. Furthermore, she associates him with sexual and political violence and locates him at the crossroads of gross body and ironic wit, slavery and liberty, self-destructive ambition and an ideal of emancipation. The account of Aesop in the nineteenth-century Russian encyclopedia published by Brockhaus-Efron also characterizes the father of the animal fable as a person who, though constantly humiliated by his owners as well as his fellow slaves, was able to revenge himself successfully.[18] The name "Aesop" thus evokes the image of a man who rose from servitude to independence by using his god-given wit, a legendary figure associated with physicality, sacrilege, and theft, both generating fiction and generated by it, the site of revenged humiliation and opposites clashing. What better epithet for Fedor Pavlovich Karamazov?

Skotoprigonevsk, the name that Dostoevsky chose for Fedor Karamazov's residence, also smacks of Aesop.[19] In the notes to their translation, Richard Pevear and Larissa Volokhonsky supply "Cattle-roundup-ville" as the rough meaning of the town's name. Given Aesop's association with both animal fables and political satire, the town becomes a fit location for a Russian Aesop. The first two stories that Fedor Pavlovich tells in Zosima's cell have Aesopian parallels. In examining the first one, I show how Dostoevsky exploits the tragicomic potential of revealed shame by creating a liar who self-consciously reveals his own shame in order to pass it on. In doing so, Dostoevsky deliberately explores storytelling's potential as an aggressive challenge to its audience. Furthermore, by creating a character who self-consciously violates social norms, Dostoevsky self-consciously violates reading norms, thereby challenging his audience and actively engaging us in the ethical action of his text.

When readers first meet him, Fedor Karamazov has lived and prospered by his verbal wit, the Aesopian quality he has used to raise himself in the world. He sang for his supper, as it were, during his days as a sponger. He managed to convince his first wife, an intelligent young woman with a romantic imagination, "if only briefly," that he "was one of the boldest and most sarcastic spirits of that transitional epoch" (14:8;8). From this marriage he gained enough capital to make his future fortune. Like the Aesop in Swift's "The Battle of the Books," Fedor Karamazov breaks the silence in Zosima's cell by apologizing for his son Dmitry's tardiness.[20] He introduces himself with a well-worn cliché attributed to Louis XVIII, thereby identifying himself as an imitator of social decorum: "I myself am always very punctual, to the minute, remembering that punctuality is the courtesy of kings." An upholder of social decorum, Miusov responds to his shame at witnessing

Fedor's gaucherie by acrimoniously retorting that Fedor Pavlovich is not a king. Thus, early in the novel, Dostoevsky sets up a scenario of shame and exposure that draws readers into the action. To the intense embarrassment of the homodiegetic audience, including his son Alesha, Fedor Pavlovich parries by proclaiming himself a buffoon:

> "That's quite true, I'm not a king. And just imagine, Petr Alexandrovich, I even knew it myself, by God! You see, I'm always saying something out of place! Your reverence," he exclaimed with a sort of instant pathos, "you see before you a buffoon! Verily, a buffoon! Thus I introduce myself! It's an old habit, alas! And if I lie inappropriately sometimes [*nekstati inogda vru*], I do it even on purpose, on purpose to be pleasant and make people laugh. One ought to be pleasant, isn't that so?" (14:38;40)

Fedor Pavlovich here pays lip service to the *Diary* writer's observation that most liars sacrifice themselves to their audiences, thereby hoping to provide pleasure. In Dostoevsky's article, however, audience pleasure encourages social harmony, whereas Fedor Pavlovich voices the cliché about punctuality to criticize his son. He thereby demonstrates that he is not an altruistic, but an aggressive liar. His shameless exhibitionist display also discomfits the homodiegetic audience, whose members serve as models for the narrative audience, including Alesha, a model for Dostoevsky's authorial audience. Guided by the audience in the text, Dostoevsky's readers experience the same anxiety at witnessing a flagrant violation of social norms as the character audience.

This small scenario dramatizes an instance of inappropriate wit, thus preparing both literally and thematically for the two anecdotes that immediately follow. Fedor Pavlovich's blasphemous use of the interjection "by God" (*ei-bogu*) in a monastery underlines his conscious toying with social and religious taboos. He presents himself as a self-conscious buffoon, a playactor and entertainer, a Pierrot. But he goes even further. Fedor Pavlovich recounts two anecdotes about how wit can backfire. These anecdotes wittily explain the aforementioned exchange with Miusov by anticipating their own effect; they also link him to Aesop, whose wit frequently angered his audience.

By wittily exposing himself, Fedor Karamazov aggressively shares his shame with his audience:

> I came to a little town seven years ago, I had a little business there, and went around with some of their merchants. So we called on the police commissioner, the *ispravnik*, because we wanted to see him about something and invite him to have dinner with us. Out comes the *ispravnik*, a tall man, fat,

blond, and gloomy—the most dangerous type in such cases—it's the liver, the liver. I spoke directly with him, you know, with the familiarity of a man of the world: "Mr. Ispravnik," I said to him, "be, so to speak, our Napravnik!" "What do you mean, your Napravnik?" I can see from the first split second that it's not coming off, that he's standing there seriously, but I keep on: "I wanted," I say, "to make a joke, for our general amusement. Mr. Napravnik is our famous Russian *Kappelmeister,* as it were . . ." I explained it all and compared it quite reasonably, didn't I? "I beg your pardon," he says, "I am an *ispravnik,* and I will not allow my title to be used for the construction of puns." He turned around and was about to walk away. I started after him, call out: "Yes, yes, you are an *ispravnik,* not Napravnik." "No," he says, "have it your way. I am Napravnik." And just imagine, our deal fell through! And that's how I am, it's always like that with me. I am forever damaging myself with my own courtesy! (14:38; 40–1)

Fedor Karamazov's pun, as he himself realizes, might have worked with a different audience. The word *ispravnik,* which designates a police commissioner, literally means "corrector." By contrast, *napravnik,* which literally means "director," is a fabricated word that is also the last name of the Russian composer who first directed the Mariinsky Theater, the imperial opera and ballet theater in Petersburg. Fedor Pavlovich appeals to the police commissioner not to criticize or correct, the police commissioner's literal job, but to direct Fedor Pavlovich's business enterprise. Fedor Pavlovich thus puns on the police commissioner's identity as well as his title. He asks him to be a "director," rather than a "corrector," to harmonize people rather than to isolate them. While Fedor Karamazov puns with a very concrete commercial goal in mind, Fedor Dostoevsky situates this pun in a novel that thematizes social and spiritual harmony. Fedor Dostoevsky's pun also plays with the shared root *prav,* which denotes "justice" and "truth," other thematic issues in the novel.

Fedor Karamazov's pun demonstrates his deliberately aggressive wit. He tells this anecdote about misfired wit after Miusov rudely refuted his cliché about punctuality. By telling a story about the police commissioner's humorless response to his pun, Fedor Pavlovich exposes Miusov's. At the same time he looks to his son's spiritual director, the Elder Zosima. Like the police commissioner, the Elder Zosima upholds order, in his case, spiritual order. Unlike the police commissioner, who "corrects" his charges, Zosima "directs" his spiritual flock. Fedor Pavlovich thus tells his anecdote about literal and figurative understanding to a divided audience—which either literally or figuratively understands him. Unlike most Dostoevskian liars, Fedor Karamazov is acutely aware of his audience. Dostoevsky thus uses him to inscribe his Aesopian poetics into the scene's mimetic action. In reading this scene, Dostoevsky's readers may follow the different examples of Fedor Pavlovich's homodiegetic audience. Like the police commissioner and Miusov, we may respond to his pun with shame and punish him. Or, like Zosima, we may listen to the shame behind it and respond with compassion.

Fedor Pavlovich's diagnosis of the police commissioner as a sufferer from "the liver" displays his street smarts—he understands that the police commissioner is a difficult audience because of his disposition. Fedor Dostoevsky's diagnosis links Fedor Karamazov's police commissioner with his own underground man, who uses Galen's theory of the four humors to explain behavior. As Meerson points out, this apparently physiological explanation gains theological significance in the context of Dostoevsky's biblical references, where liver illnesses suggest Jeremiah's lamentation over the desolation of Jerusalem (Lamentations 2:11).[21] Fedor Karamazov's diagnosis of the police commissioner's humorlessness thus suggests a physical disorder based on an excess of bile, while Fedor Dostoevsky's suggests a spiritual depression based on a biblical sense of loss and longing.

Fedor Karamazov's punny story also reveals the synthetic construction of Dostoevsky's novel. Fedor Karamazov's wit backfires. His story fails both because the police commissioner is humorless and because Fedor nonetheless persists in inappropriate wordplay. His story thus replicates and anticipates Miusov's humorless reactions. His story also anticipates Smerdiakov's revenge against Fedor Pavlovich for the playful Aesopian names he has given "Smerdiakov" and "Balaam's ass." The name Smerdiakov derives both from the noun *smerd* (which literally means "a stinking peasant" and figuratively "a plebian")[22] and the verb *smerdet'* ("to stink"). As Dostoevsky would know, the legendary Aesop bestows scatological or animalistic names.[23] The first words the heretofore dumb Aesop speaks, for instance, are the names of objects and animals, including an "ass." Likewise, when his master Xanthus asks Aesop why people examine their own feces, Aesop replies, " 'Because long ago there was a king's son, who as a result of the looseness of his bowels and his loose way of living, sat there for a long time relieving himself—for so long that before he knew it, he had passed his own wits. Ever since then when men relieve themselves, they look down for fear they, too, have passed their wits.' "[24] Whether or not Fedor Dostoevsky knew this particular anecdote, he too associates witlessness and excrement in the person of Lizaveta Smerdiashchaia (literally, "Stinking Lizaveta"). By attributing his mother's nickname to her son, Fedor Karamazov deeply humiliates him. As Smerdiakov tells his neighbor Maria Kondratievna, "I'd have killed anyone in a duel with a pistol for calling me a scoundrel, because I came fatherless from the Stinking One" (14:204;224).

Fedor Karamazov's second anecdote also involves word play. In it, for the sake of a pun, he slanders a woman whose husband then beats him. Though I reserve discussion of this anecdote for chapter 11, it, like Fedor Pavlovich's first anecdote, has an internal audience and is about audience response. Both anecdotes thus self-consciously anticipate Fedor Pavlovich's homodiegetic audience's responses, for they are about business or social interchanges spoiled by Fedor's love of wordplay. The dynamic of backfired wit, in turn, links Fedor Karamazov to Aesop. First of all, like Aesop, Fedor Pavlovich constantly provokes others into beating him—including his own son Dmitry. Next, like Aesop, Fedor Pavlovich is partly responsible for his own violent death: Aesop reminds the citizens of Delphi of their origins as the progeny of slaves. Likewise, Fedor Pavlovich's names for Smerdiakov remind his illegitimate son of his shameful origins.[25] Again, like Aesop, Fedor Pavlovich is betrayed by the child he takes under his roof.[26] In an Aesopian twist, in a novel about divine and human justice, the self-proclaimed "son of lies" is killed by the son of a liar.

Finally, by establishing the Aesop/Fedor Karamazov connection, Fedor Dostoevsky draws readers' attention to the covert message of Fedor's stories—for *The Brothers Karamazov* is a novel about justice and judgment. Fedor Karamazov, who worries about the Last Judgment, tells stories about being judged and punished.

Fedor Pavlovich's Aesopian identity also links him to another literary legend—Alexander Sergeevich Pushkin. In her work on Russian fables, Laura Wilhelm makes the Aesop/Pushkin connection. She notes that the *danseur* Konstantin Dembrovsky apparently maligned Pushkin in an unpreserved epigram by referring to him as "Aesop" because of his "homely physiognomy" (*nekrasivaia fiziognomiia*). Pushkin responded by appropriating the epithet in an 1819–20 epigram: "When I look into mirrors/I see, it seems, Aesop" (*Kogda smotrius' ia v zerkala,/To vizhu, kazhetsia, Ezopa*). She then outlines the parallels between Aesop and Pushkin: both emerged as champion word wielders in cultures that encuraged rhetorical display; both upstaged their superiors with their verbal wit; both experienced countless run-ins with authority figures; both thirsted for freedom and regarded poetic prophecy as a function of free speech; both valued personal expression over official views, exalting the Muses over Apollo; both experienced extremes of humiliation and lionization; and both died violent deaths at the hands of philistines.[27] Dostoevsky, an avid reader of Pushkin as well as an occasional summer neighbor of his sister, probably knew the epigram. He certainly connected Pushkin with blackness; he also linked Fedor's prototypes Lebedev and Lebiadkin to Pushkin. By inscribing blackness into Fedor Pavlovich's surname and by attributing his own first name to him, Dostoevsky linked four writers who are further connected by their provocative style.[28] In traditional Russian fashion, Dostoevsky thus fuses the poetic and the political as his linked figures of Aesop/Pushkin/Fedor Karamazov/Fedor Dostoevsky remind readers of bodily mortality, poetic immortality, and the politics of interpretation.

Fedor Karamazov and his creator pose a further problem for their audiences. Both note that positive audience response causes pleasure. Furthermore, as Fedor Karamazov's anecdotes show, negative audience response causes pain. His second anecdote underlines the fact that a disapproving audience can even beat a storyteller—as happened so frequently in Aesop's case. So why does a storyteller who knows that storytelling can provide pleasure tell stories that deliberately provoke displeasure? While I do not believe I can explain fully, I think that the shame dynamics encoded in the Aesop/Pushkin connection provide a partial explanation.

When Fedor Karamazov responds to Miusov's initial rejection by aiming his anecdotes at him, he acts like Aesop, engaging in wit and one-upmanship with a social superior. In winning the battle of wits, Aesop frequently incurred physical punishment from his master. Thus the cycle of shame and triumph would resume and continue until Aesop wins his freedom. Once free, he not only becomes his master's social equal, but also gains universal recognition as his master's intellectual superior. Fedor Pavlovich starts from an analogous position. Though he is Miusov's class equal and a relative by marriage, he is not Miusov's social equal. Miusov is ashamed of their relation by marriage. Fedor Pavlovich resents and reacts to his shame. Miusov exposes and shames Fedor Pavlovich, reminding him of his social inferiority. Fedor Pavlovich, in turn, exposes and shames Miusov. Their rivalry thus keeps shame alive for both of them. As mentioned earlier, there are three major defenses against shame: denial, flight, and fight. The first two are more conventional and socially acceptable. The decorum-conscious Miusov engages in the first, denial. Fedor Pavlovich, on the other hand, chooses aggression, which is both unconventional and unacceptable. He shares his shame, thus equalizing the relationship. Fedor Dostoevsky uses this Aesopian struggle mimetically to illustrate sociopolitical and economic inequalities in a modernizing country, thematically to raise questions of justice, and synthetically to spotlight issues of audience response.

The epithet "Aesop" functions mimetically as well as metaliterarily in Dostoevsky's novel. Aesop is smart enough to know that he should not provoke the Delphians, yet he does. Fedor Karamazov is smart enough to know that the police commissioner would resent the pun on his name, that the important official would resent the pun on his wife's honor, that the humorless Miusov would expose and shame him. But the pleasure of wordplay, a pleasure that links Fedor Karamazov with Dostoevsky's Lebedev and Lebiadkin, impels

Dostoevsky's exhibitionist liars to display themselves whatever the cost. In this, Dostoevsky's liars differ from their creator.

In literary history there are two Aesops: the Aesop of legend and the writer of fables. The name "Aesop" thus evokes the story of a slave who lives and dies by his wit. It also suggests apparently simple stories with hidden depths, thus signaling a time-honored practice favored by writers constricted by censorship. Aesopian subterfuge became a commonplace in the Russian literary tradition, where writers and readers alike conspired to inscribe forbidden materials and messages in and extract them from texts that passed through the scrutiny of government censors.[29] In attributing the epithet "Aesop" to Fedor Karamazov, Dostoevsky deliberately evokes Aesop's legendary life story as well as his poetics. As I have shown, Fedor Karamazov's life story resembles that of the legendary Aesop. But Fedor Karamazov as an Aesopian storyteller is a cover for Fedor Dostoevsky, who uses his comic namesake to plumb dangerous thematic depths. On the surface, *The Brothers Karamazov* is the story of parricide. Beneath the surface, it is the story of regicide and deicide, topics forbidden by Russian censors. Though Dostoevsky counted on his Russian audience's Aesopian reading practices, the epithet "Aesop" clues us to look for depths in Fedor's stories that we might otherwise overlook.

chapter ten

Captain Lebiadkin: Pretender Politics and Poetics

> They advised me, "Publish it anonymously." Well, what good is a "thank you" if it is anonymous?
>
> —IVAN KARAMAZOV'S DEVIL, *The Brothers Karamazov* (15:76;641)

In *Demons*, Dostoevsky's most overtly political novel, a novel where the plot dynamics of secrecy and exposure function mimetically, thematically, and metaliterarily, the secondary character Ignat Lebiadkin figures centrally in exposing authorial poetics. As Richard Kuhns writes in his book on tragedy, the presence of secrets arouses an urgent desire to unknot them.[1] Thus, while Lebiadkin is a minor character, he propels both the political and love plots of Dostoevsky's novel. An outward sign of aristocratic shame and political conspiracy, Lebiadkin lies at the center of the novel's dual plot. As a pretender, he reveals the novel's parodic and political depths. As a poetaster, he figures importantly in its metaliterary play.[2] As an anonymous letter writer, he pushes the plot with threats to expose others' personal and political secrets. As an aspiring suitor of Liza Tushina, he exposes the character-narrator's subjectivity. Finally, as a comically shameless character who mimetically threatens to upset the status quo in every way imaginable, he provokes in Dostoevsky's homodiegetic narrator, other characters, and readers alike the desire to control or contain him, thus making us all complicit in his tragic death.

Lebiadkin is famous as the author of the five ridiculous poems mentioned in chapter 9. By inscribing the novel's social, political, and metaphysical thematics into Lebiadkin's comic verses, Dostoevsky parodies the sociopolitical role of poets in Russia. More significantly for the novel's plot, however, Lebiadkin composes a spate of anonymous letters—to Praskovia Drozdova, Varvara Stavrogina, and Governor von Lembke—as well as several letters written in his own name—to Liza Tushina. By having Lebiadkin's letters pose a threat to the social order, Dostoevsky uses Lebiadkin to propel his novel's plot. Lebiadkin's anonymous letter to Varvara Stavrogina prompts her to allow him into her drawing room (10:135;168); one of his letters to Liza Tushina provokes Stavrogin's scandalous revelation that he is married to Marya Lebiadkina (10:352;456); and Peter Verkhovensky uses Lebiadkin's anonymous letter to Lembke to cement the conspiracy to murder Shatov (10:417;544). Lebiadkin's first round of letters hints at his sister Marya's identity, thus preparing the scandal that ends Part One. His second round of letters reveals Marya's identity as Stavrogin's wife, thus provoking the scandal that ends Part Two. While they figure largely in the love plot, these letters merge with the novel's pretender thematics, raising critical questions about identity.[3] The first letters reveal the presence of an unsettling secret that threatens the social order: Stavrogin's marriage to a lame, lower-class, holy fool. The second letters expose the secret, thereby disrupting the social norm that would have Stavrogin marry a social equal like Liza and produce offspring to inherit his estate. The third, Lebiadkin's anonymous letter to Governor von Lembke (10:279–80;360), figures in the political plot. The only anonymous letter that readers see, it reveals the presence of subversive political forces in Russia. It thus explains the political unrest at the end of Part Two and Shatov's murder in Part Three. By circulating it among the group of five after the Lebiadkins are murdered, Peter Verkhovensky intimidates them with fear of exposure. This letter thus compels characters and readers alike to associate exposed secrets with death.[4]

Like Dostoevsky's liars in *The Idiot*, Lebiadkin tries to expose others and thus reveal his own identity. Furthermore, as in *The Idiot*, the project of exposing others complicates plots. Lebiadkin's threats to expose Stavrogin's secret marriage and Peter Verkhovensky's political activities reveal social and political problems. Lebiadkin uncovers the age-old issue of aristocrats abusing their social inferiors. Stavrogin's momentary whim has serious consequences: Marya is a social embarrassment as well as an impediment to a real marriage.[5] In true Russian fashion, Stavrogin sends her away to a monastery. Her brother then abducts her to blackmail Stavrogin into supporting him. Eventually, Stavrogin turns a blind eye while Peter Verkhovensky has Marya, her brother, and their old servant murdered. One aristocrat plays around, and three people die. The comic turns tragic.

Lebiadkin's threats to expose Peter Verkhovensky reveal Peter's political role, particularly as disseminator of seditious political pamphlets, to readers. Exposing Peter to the authorities, however, involves exposing himself. Peter may have produced subversive literature, but Lebiadkin has distributed it. Lebiadkin's dilemma thus dramatizes the mercenary mechanics of political subversion. It also reveals his narcissistic ethical indifference: like his social superiors, Lebiadkin acts out of self-interest. Blackmailed by Peter, he blackmails Stavrogin. Unconcerned about sacrificing others, he is sacrificed.

Dostoevsky exposes Lebiadkin as a social critic who exposes injustice only when he is its target.

Lebiadkin's plans to expose his social superiors involve shame dynamics. He threatens their sense of self and relation to the world. Stavrogin and Peter Verkhovensky both have leverage over Lebiadkin, but neither can be sure of him. He threatens to disrupt their lives in embarrassing and potentially incriminating ways. He is a wild card, an ever-present reminder of that which must remain hidden. Lebiadkin also exercises that power over readers: we too feel threatened by his presence; we too want him to be contained. By having Lebiadkin press his readers' shame buttons, Dostoevsky coopts his authorial audience into the novel's ethical action. Watching Lebiadkin expose himself as he threatens to expose others rouses an anxiety that we want to eliminate. In this novel, however, elimination entails murder. Readers must then confront our response to his death.

Lebiadkin's project of exposing others also highlights the narrator's project of exposing Lebiadkin. While the heterodiegetic narrator of *The Idiot* exposes Ivolgin exposing others in order to establish his own reliability, the homodiegetic narrator of *Demons*, Mr. G-v, exposes Lebiadkin as a pretender for similar, but more personal, reasons. Lebiadkin openly courts Liza Tushina, making him a rival for the narrator, who has a crush on her. From the novel's outset, the narrator describes Lebiadkin negatively. Dostoevsky thereby challenges his authorial audience to form its own judgments about his exhibitionistic liar and his subjectively involved narrator. Willy-nilly we are drawn into the novel's ethical action. How we respond to Lebiadkin and his death thus determines the author's success in providing what Bakhtin calls "surplus vision." We must see beyond the narrator's negativity and Lebiadkin's own unreliability. In the end, the very excess of Lebiadkin's outrageousness redeems him. For while we side with the narrator against him ethically, we delight in his verbal excesses. Like Dostoevsky, we can condemn the sins but enjoy the sinner.

Anonymity and Identity

Unlike Ivolgin and Lebedev, who violate the Russian social contract by exposing one another as liars, Lebiadkin violates his economic and political contracts with Stavrogin and Peter Verkhovensky by threatening to expose their personal and political secrets. Yet he hesitates. While exposing Stavrogin's secret would allow Lebiadkin to reveal his own identity as Stavrogin's brother-in-law and thus raise his social status, it would also cut off his revenues: Stavrogin pays him for his silence. Lebiadkin faces social obstacles as well: his appearance, life-style, and class status make it "impossible" (in

Mavriky Drozdov's words) for Lebiadkin to be received in an aristocratic drawing room. Exposure is also a risky business. Exposing Peter's secret would free Lebiadkin from blackmail. On the other hand, revealing Peter's illegal activities entails revealing his own. Thus, like Peter, he could be imprisoned. Lebiadkin attempts to liberate himself from enforced anonymity by writing letters. He writes to people who would not normally receive him. Once received, he speaks. On paper and in person, Lebiadkin threatens to expose others' secrets.

Lebiadkin's project thus lies on the border between private and public spheres. Since Lebiadkin threatens to reveal both Stavrogin's embarrassing marriage and his radical politics, he links the novel's romantic and political plots. The threat of exposure raises the specter of shame. By revealing Stavrogin's marriage, Lebiadkin would expose him to social shame and thus potential exclusion. By revealing Stavrogin's political connections, he would expose him to potential arrest and exile. Revealing secrets thus threatens Stavrogin. But revealing Stavrogin's and Peter's secrets also jeopardizes Lebiadkin's own privacy. While he wants to enhance his social status, any revelation about Stavrogin's or Peter's political activities threatens his political future. Anonymity thus works like a double-edged sword. Though it offers Lebiadkin protective covering in the political sphere, anonymity frustrates him in the private sphere. All of Lebiadkin's letters betray a tension between public and private, a desire to reveal and a desire to conceal.

The first mention of anonymous letters occurs in Varvara Stavrogina's drawing room. Both Praskovia Drozdova and Varvara Stavrogina reveal that they have received anonymous letters about "some lame woman" (10:135;168). Unlike her mystified friend, Varvara has ascertained the anonymous writer's identity. She thus violates social norms by announcing that she will receive the recently arrived Lebiadkin, but she has two powerful reasons to do so: Lebiadkin has anonymously hinted that her son is married and publicly accused her ward of being his mistress.

Pretender Politics

At this point in the novel, the narrator has mentioned Lebiadkin once and encountered him twice. Readers know that Lebiadkin and his sister live in the house of Filippov on Epiphany Street, a location associating them with the novel's thematics of pretendership and revelation.[6] Liars and pretenders thrive during transitional periods, periods when social norms and structures are laid bare and individuals and groups struggle to maintain or to change the status quo. Liars and pretenders perceive and employ their historical moments as opportunities for self-fashioning, that is, they fabricate stories to establish their place in history. Like historical pretenders, Dostoevsky's liars are not members of the ruling elites. Like Gogol's Khlestakov, they are wannabes. They resemble Boris Uspensky's second category of pretenders: unlike those who truly believe themselves tsars, Dostoevsky's liars are adventurers or rogues. They lie, as Dostoevsky claims, because they are ashamed of their identity and want to be other. Like pretenders, they want the honor and wealth associated with power. And like pretenders, they model themselves after dominant social or political figures. However, they must then live with the paradox of self-fashioning. Liars and pretenders want recognition for a false identity. To balance on the edge of this paradox, they must conceal their true identity. Captain Lebiadkin shares the fate of pretenders whose self-fashioning has a political dimension. While they fashion themselves with an eye to the present, the past catches up with them. Pretenders and liars live theatrically and die tragically.

In writing *Demons,* Dostoevsky clearly drew on the nineteenth-century commonplace comparing the era of the Great Reforms with the Time of Troubles.[7] An enthusiastic reader of Karamzin and Pushkin, Dostoevsky may well have learned from them what Uspensky has noted for us: the presence of one pretender inspires the appearance of others. Dostoevsky accordingly provides pretender pedigrees for both Stavrogin and Lebiadkin.

Peter Verkhovensky proposes that Stavrogin become Ivan-Tsarevich, and Marya Lebiadkina unmasks him as the First False Dmitry when she anathematizes him as "Grishka Otrepev." Like the First False Dmitry, Stavrogin holds heterodox views: both the atheistic Westerner Kirillov and the religious Slavophilic Shatov claim discipleship; the narrator associates him with masking (10:37;43); and he figuratively abuses icons as he literally abuses three Marias. He rapes the adolescent Matroshka, commits adultery with Marie Shatov, and marries Marya Lebiadkina (who was a commoner, like Marina Mniszech, the First False Dmitry's wife). Stavrogin also engages in a pretender phenomenon that Uspensky labels "anti-behavior"—he bites the governor's ear and pulls Gaganov by the nose.

A Stavrogin wannabe, Lebiadkin likewise engages in anti-behavior. He drinks heavily, a standard form of anti-behavior, but Lebiadkin also writes unruly poetry and anonymous letters, a literary form of anti-behavior. In keeping with his parodic status, Dostoevsky gives Lebiadkin more attributes of the Second False Dmitry, whose origins, like Lebiadkin's, are obscure. The Swedes described the Second False Dmitry as a laborer, a former servant of Grishka Otrepev, and a drummer. Lebiadkin claims to be Stavrogin's steward (10:208;263) and his Falstaff (10:208;263). But he also wants to imitate an American and leave his skin to be drummed on (10:209;264). In Mogilev, the Second False Dmitry was helped by an archpriest whose wife he then seduces.

The archpriest responded by beating him up and throwing him out. Similarly, Lebiadkin has an affair with Virginsky's wife (10:213;269) and moves in with the Virginskys, but Virginsky eventually beats him up and throws him out (10:29;33). While this *ménage à trois* clearly parodies the one in Chernyshevsky's *What Is to Be Done?* Dostoevsky frequently used multiple sources. He associates this event with pretendership by having the narrator note that after Verginsky beat him, "The captain quickly concealed himself [*skrylsia*] and revealed himself [*iavilsia*] again in our town only lately, with his sister and with new goals" (10:29;33), the same words Peter Verkhovensky uses to disclose his Ivan-Tsarevich plan to Stavrogin (10:325;422). Lebiadkin's plans for himself also recall the Second False Dmitry. While the latter made former bondsmen into landowners and offered landowners' daughters to those who denounced their masters, Lebiadkin offers to replace Stavrogin's place in Liza Tushina's affections; he also makes a veiled promise to denounce Stavrogin and take possession of his land (10:106;132).

Liza Tushina's surname likewise signals pretender politics. The Second False Dmitry, whose headquarters were in Tushino, was known as the Tushinskii rogue (*Tushinskii vor*). Moreover, the Tushino period of Russian history was associated with the cynical switching of allegiance. Fittingly, Lebiadkin once distributed subversive literature (as did Marina Mniszech, wife of the First False Dmitry, during the time of the Second False Dmitry), but swears that he has repented (10:212–13;264). Like a Tushinskii rogue, Lebiadkin has changed his allegiance and calls himself a "repentant freethinker."

In proper Gogolian spirit, Dostoevsky has his narrator expose Lebiadkin not only as a pretender, but as a self-promoting one.[8] Though the narrator refers to Lebiadkin as "Captain" throughout *Demons*, he reveals early in the novel that Lebiadkin has assumed, not earned, his title. The narrator first claims that Lebiadkin "wasn't even a retired junior captain as he titled himself. He only knew how to twirl his mustache, drink, and blather the most uncouth nonsense imaginable" (10:29;32). Fifty pages later, Liputin tells the narrator that Lebiadkin is now calling himself "a retired captain; earlier he only called himself a junior captain . . . " (10:78;96). Lebiadkin thus follows the tradition of pretenders who assume a royal name in order to assume royal functions.[9]

Lebiadkin further resembles pretenders in his similarity to a mummer— a person who dons a mask and dresses in costumes. While his master Stavrogin has a face that resembles a mask, Lebiadkin dresses up to play roles. "Do you understand, you ass," he says to Shatov, "that I am in love. I bought a dresscoat, look, a dresscoat of love, fifteen silver rubles; a captain's love demands social decorum" (10:119;149). Like historical pretenders, Lebiadkin thus attempts to procure the attributes of nobility by imitating his superiors.[10]

While Lebedev's pretendership is secular, Dostoevsky gives him an address that associates him with the religious side of pretender politics. As Uspensky points out, the word "tsar" in Russian was regarded as a divinely given title.[11] Russians thus distinguished between tsars appointed by God and those appointed by men. In claiming royal birth, all pretenders professed divine election. By having Lebiadkin live in the house of Filippov, Dostoevsky links him to the revelatory politics of pretendership. Danila Filippov was the semilegendary father figure of the most extreme religious sects—the Flagellants and the Castrates. As Richard Peace observes, the house's location on Epiphany Street (*Bogoyavlenskaya ulitsa*) bears directly on Filippov himself, as it was in a monastery of that name that Filippov was imprisoned after he declared himself by throwing holy books into the Volga. As Peace notes, "The name 'Bogoyavlenskaya' therefore combines the hint of concealment with the hope of manifestation."[12] Dostoevsky echoes this linking of concealment and revelation in Peter Verkhovensky's plans for Stavrogin: "We will say that he is in hiding [*skryvaetsia*].... But he will appear, he will appear [*iavitsia, iavitsia*]" (10:325;421). Similarly, Marya Lebiadkina's identity as Stavrogin's wife is concealed, but Lebiadkin threatens to reveal it.

Finally, Dostoevsky underscores pretender thematics by associating Lebiadkin with falsification and unoriginality. He is caught distributing bogus banknotes (10:79;96), to which he later confesses (10:213;269). His sister Marya calls him a "lackey," a word Dostoevsky uses to denote derivative thinkers.[13] Moreover, Lebiadkin is not only a pretender but a plagiarist.[14] After hearing Lebiadkin's verse "To the Perfection of the Young Miss Tushina," for example, the narrator notes: "I knew a general who wrote exactly the same verses" (10:106;132). By linking Lebiadkin with plagiarism, falsification, and pretendership, Dostoevsky shows how self-interest engenders social strife.

Dostoevsky's homodiegetic narrator, Mr. G-v, is smitten with Liza Tushina. He thus resents Lebiadkin's infatuation and constantly exposes him as a pretender. The narrator of *Demons* thus follows the example of *The Idiot*'s narrator and exposes the exposer. Just as Lebiadkin exposes Stavrogin's marriage to discredit Stavrogin in Liza's eyes, so the narrator exposes Lebiadkin to discredit him as a suitor. Like Lebiadkin's, the narrator's infatuation with Liza makes him a rival of Stavrogin, and thus an unreliable source in the public sphere. By revealing how Lebiadkin's personal feelings affect his narrative reliability, Dostoevsky shows his authorial audience how to understand and interpret the narrator's subjective unreliability. What Dostoevsky starts in *The Idiot* by having his narrator mimic his character-liar, he develops in *Demons*. Dostoevsky teaches his authorial audience to be wary of narrators with personal stakes in the novel's action. Finally, the narrator's exposition of Lebiadkin is motivated by that class rivalry which serves, in *The Idiot*, to disrupt the Russian social contract. Dostoevsky gives the authorial audience lessons in judgment: the more a narrator is a character, the less reliable he is.

Shame of Origins

Lebiadkin's self-fashioning demonstrates his shame of origins. In Varvara Stavrogina's drawing room, and thus out of his normal milieu, he reveals a bitter awareness of the gap between his actual and ideal identities. Frustrated by his enforced anonymity, constrained by his new clothing,[15] and anxious to establish his worth before two otherwise inaccessible women, Lebiadkin quickly forgets his place (both his literal place—a chair by the door—and his figurative place as social inferior) and launches into a speech that blames Russia for his social shame:

> Madam, . . . I, perhaps, might wish to be called Ernest, but instead am forced to bear the coarse name of Ignat,—why's that, what do you think? I might wish to be called Prince de Monbars, yet I'm only Lebiadkin from *lebed*, the swan—why's that? I am a poet, Madam, a poet in my soul, and I could be getting a thousand rubles from a publisher, yet I am forced to live in a washtub, why, why? Madam! In my opinion, Russia is a freak of nature, nothing more! (10:141;175)

With this speech, Lebiadkin intends to show Varvara Petrovna that he is a worthy (albeit anonymous) in-law and to show Liza Tushina, whose very presence "seemed to make him terribly giddy," that he is a worthy suitor. His peroration of comparisons reveals that even his name, this most basic fact of his identity, shames him, reminding him of his lower-class origins and life's arbitrariness. After all, why should he be Ignat Lebiadkin, instead of Ernest, Prince de Monbars? Why should he be a poor, unrecognized poet instead of a published, well-paid one? The comic dissonance of this second complaint demonstrates the peculiarly literary cast of Lebiadkin's mind as cramped living space and creative genius often conjoined in the romantic imagination. Lebiadkin blames Russia for his lack of poetic recognition by hinting that his homeland deprives its citizens of outlets to express their talents.[16]

By having Lebiadkin declare himself a poet, Dostoevsky parodically evokes the image of two poets—Derzhavin and Pushkin. As noted in chapter 9, Lebiadkin consciously compares himself to Derzhavin. While he does so to enhance his self-image, Dostoevsky uses Lebiadkin's choice of an archaic poet to mock his swan's literary pretensions and tastes. In his poem "The Swan" (*Lebed'*), Derzhavin engages in a project similar to Lebiadkin's: publicizing that which has been suppressed.¹⁷ The poem's eighth and ninth stanzas refer to the rules Derzhavin had composed for the Arbitration Tribunal, rules that Alexander I received favorably but which Derzhavin's enemies kept from publication.¹⁸ By stating the intentions behind them in a published poem, Derzhavin hints at something suppressed. Dostoevsky's Lebiadkin thus imitates Derzhavin.

Lebiadkin's mentions of the marketplace and the misfortune of Russian birth in his Monbars speech also flag an authorial association with Pushkin, Dostoevsky's favorite poet. While Lebiadkin is a poetaster who produces pekoral,¹⁹ his comic woes have serious counterparts in Pushkin's life and writing. Pushkin struggled with the advantages and limitations of political patronage, the exigencies of the marketplace, and the difficulties facing talented individuals in Russia (see his May 1836 letter to his wife: "[T]he devil got it into his head to have me be born in Russia with a soul and with talent! What a joke indeed!").²⁰ Lebiadkin's comic laments thus echo actual concerns in Russian life (as in the case of Pushkin) that Dostoevsky mimetically reproduces in his novel (in the figure of Stepan Verkhovensky).

Lebiadkin's identification with the Prince de Monbars highlights other aspects of the novel's metaliterary play. By expressing the desire to bear the name of a Frenchman who was an actual historical figure as well as the hero of several literary works, Lebiadkin reveals his desire to be a recognized and admired other—to be a member of the upper class, a European, a hero. He also demonstrates his blurring of the boundaries between life and literature, proving himself, like General Ivolgin, a consumer of romantic fictions. Lebiadkin, who prides himself on his literary education and accomplishments, would have been familiar with the Monbars name, which was a commonplace in early-nineteenth-century French literature. Featured in some historical novels as a minor character, Monbars was the protagonist of Jean-Baptiste Picquenard's historical novel, *Monbars L'Exterminateur: Anecdote du Nouveau Monde* (1807), a major source for later reworkings of his story, such as Poirié Saint-Aurèle's Romantic poem, "Le Flibustier" (1827). The historical Prince de Monbars shared command of the *flibustiers*,²¹ a group of French and English men who were a cross between pirates (free agents) and corsairs (government-commissioned operatives). In the late 1700s, the *flibustiers* enriched themselves while enabling their respective governments free the West Indies from Spanish hegemony. They appealed to the early-nineteenth-century romantic imagination as a "society of exception," living a life free of conventional social restraints. While most of these maritime adventurers were opportunists who had left their own countries in search of adventure and wealth, they were seen as liberators who had emancipated indigenous West Indians from their Spanish conquerors.²² The Prince de Monbars was an important commander of

Tortue Island—a location that symbolized French defiance of Spain's territorial domination in the New World. Assuming the name "Exterminator" to demonstrate his resolve to wipe out the Spaniards, he earned great renown for such exploits as the sacking of Maracaibo and the capture of Vera Cruz.[23]

In popularizing the *filibustiers'* exploits, historical writers, such as Picquenard, still clung to historical events. Yet they also granted legendary status to the group's leaders, who all followed a heroic code. Historical writers also incongruously appealed to the legend of an ocean paradise. Following in their footsteps, many romantic nineteenth-century writers, including Balzac, Sue, Dumas père, Flaubert, and Sand (all of whom Dostoevsky read), further liberated these legendary figures from their historical moorings and romanticized them. Thus, whether or not Dostoevsky read Picquenard's account of Monbars and his adventures, he would surely have been familiar with a romanticized version. Significantly, the semifictionalized Monbars resembles Stavrogin[24] more than Lebiadkin. He is an enigmatic loner with a mysterious past. Noble by birth, he is equally at home in drawing room and tavern; he is handsome and well dressed, the ladies love him, and his enemies fear him. Monbars' move to the Antilles and Stavrogin's early travels[25] represent flights from their historical situations, attempts to do something with their talents.[26] While still young, they both attain notoriety: military notoriety for Monbars and social notoriety for Stavrogin. Monbars thus emblemizes a romantic hero and Stavrogin a reduced romantic hero. Lebiadkin, who achieves his own notoriety as a versifier, aspires to be Monbars and emulates Stavrogin. He thus comically imitates both art and life.

Literary Parody

Lebiadkin's choice of Monbars as model illuminates his own self-image as hero and suitor. Like Khlestakov, Russia's ur-liar, Lebiadkin is a consumer of literature. He chooses a romantic hero who was a member of the titled nobility—which he would like to be, who has the reputation of a brave liberator and patriot—which he would like to have, and who has a reputed weakness for women—which is how he fashions himself.

While Lebiadkin would clearly like to be seen as a hero, Dostoevsky's narrator exposes him as a coward and a parasite. Unlike the Exterminator of history and legend, the cowardly Lebiadkin does not utter a word of protest when Virginsky drags him by the hair. Afterward, however, he "became offended with all the fervor of a noble man" (10:29;33). Lebiadkin's cowardly response reveals his actual self, while his delayed bravado reveals his ideal self. By invoking rather than following the honor code, Lebiadkin proves that he is noble in word only. Similarly, while Lebiadkin would like to be seen as an independent agent, he betrays keen awareness of his financial dependence on Stavrogin: "[Y]ou are the master here, not me, and I'm only by way of being your steward, so to speak, for all the same, all the same, Nikolai Vsevolodovich, all the same I am independent in spirit! Don't take away this last property of mine!" (10:208;263). Dostoevsky underlines Lebiadkin's dependence on Stavrogin by invoking another literary model—Falstaff. Both Peter Verkhovensky and Lebiadkin himself mention the cowardly braggart warrior and liar Falstaff to explain Lebiadkin's relationship to Stavrogin. Peter emphasizes Lebiadkin's role as buffoon (10:149;185) and Lebiadkin his role as versifier (10:208;263), but both represent the role as one of paid servitor. Lebiadkin's evocation of Falstaff also underlines his political function as someone who knows too much about Stavrogin's past. Like Falstaff, Lebiadkin fears that his older and more mature master may dismiss him: "Can it be that you'll cast me off like an old, worn-out boot?" (10:213;270).[27] Finally, just as Falstaff relies on Prince Hal, Lebiadkin depends on Stavrogin's political protection.

Given his cowardice and dependence, it is little wonder that Lebiadkin would prefer to be Prince de Monbars, the swashbuckling hero whose very name spelled freedom for the oppressed. Lebiadkin also adopts Monbars's sole weakness—love. Though Lebiadkin admits to drinking as well, he fashions himself a captive of love. In fact, when the narrator first meets him, Lebiadkin bursts into rhyme:

> A cannonball with hot love loaded
> In Ignat's noble breast exploded.
> Again with bitter torment groaned
> Sevastopol's armless one. (10:95;117)[28]

The plot twist of Lebiadkin's love for Liza comes directly from Dostoevsky's own Captain Kartuzov sketch (11:31–57). Dostoevsky's notes depict Captain Kartuzov as a quixotic landowner in love with a beautiful horsewoman, who is engaged to a handsome young count. The elderly captain reconciles himself to writing poetry dedicated to her until she falls from her horse and breaks her leg. Her fiancé withdraws and Kartuzov hazards a marriage proposal. She declines. Kartuzov then literally goes crazy thinking that his proposal insulted her. He withdraws to a mental institution, composes his poem "The Cockroach" (see discussion in chapter 9), and dies shortly thereafter. In attributing Kartuzov's verses to Lebiadkin, Dostoevsky adds a covert metaliterary dimension: Lebiadkin plagiarizes from his creator!

Dostoevsky adds a plot twist to the love triangle in *Demons*, however: in pursuing a hypothetical lame woman, Lebiadkin compounds his rivalry with Stavrogin by comically imitating him.[29] Lebiadkin's first lines introduce the imagery of broken limbs that runs throughout the novel.[30] Initially Lebiadkin regards armlessness as a technical nicety, a terrific rhyme (*mukoi/ bezrukii*) (in Russian this is both a poor and archaic rhyme) (10:95;117). He opens his letter proposing marriage to Liza by citing armlessness as a sign of courage: "Mademoiselle! Most of all I regret that I did not lose an arm in Sevastopol for glory, having not been there at all" (10:106;131). While the pretender captain invokes a military context where limblessness signifies courage and honor, Dostoevsky here engages in metaliterary play by invoking Gogol's limbless Captain Kopeikin, Tolstoy's Captain Tushin, who loses an arm fighting Napoleon in *War and Peace*, and Tolstoy's "Sevastopol Sketches." Dostoevsky also exposes Lebiadkin's psychology: elsewhere in the novel and in Lebiadkin's thought, limblessness signifies insufficiency or defect.[31] By making deficiency a trophy here, Lebiadkin comically reverses the normal shame associated with defect—an example of the grandiosity that serves as a defense mechanism for his narcissistically injured self.

Independently, Lebiadkin and Liza both speculate on her future if she were to break a leg. In Varvara Petrovna's drawing room, Liza reflects that as a horsewoman she could very well break one or both of her legs. She teases Mavriky Nikolaevich: " '[Y]ou'll be assuring me from morning till night that I've become even more interesting minus a leg! But one thing is irremediable—you are immensely tall, and minus a leg I'll become so very tiny, how then will you be able to take my arm, we won't be a matching pair!'" (10:157;196). Liza aspires to lameness to be like Stavrogin's wife—and thus more interesting. Yet she also regards a broken leg as a sign of physical and moral defect—and thus a manifestation of her self-image.

Lebiadkin's attraction to a lame Liza not only signals his imitation of Stavrogin, who has a lame wife, but also his unrealistic ambition to supplant his master in Liza's affection. Lebiadkin declares to Stavrogin that he, like Gogol in his "Last Story,"[32] has written an occasional poem—"In Case She Should Break Her Leg." He explains it to Stavrogin, hoping to reestablish himself as Stavrogin's Falstaff but also to justify himself as Stavrogin's rival:

> "In Case She Should Break Her Leg," that is, in case of horseback riding. A fantasy, Nikolai Vsevolodovich, raving, but a poet's raving; I was struck once, in passing, when I encountered a girl on horseback, and asked a material question: "What would happen then?"—that is, in such a case. The case is clear: all wooers back out, all suitors vanish, so it goes and wipe your nose, the poet alone will be left with his heart squashed in his breast. Nikolai Vsevolodovich, even a louse, even he can be in love, even he is not forbidden by any law. (10:210;265)

In Lebiadkin's reading, a woman's lameness devalues her. Consequently, the man who chooses a defective wife must be truly noble or defective. Lebiadkin thus justifies his proposal to Liza with two arguments. The first argument asserts his ideal, chivalric self-image: if Liza were to break a leg, her choices of marrying would decrease. Like Liza, Lebiadkin thus conflates literal and figurative, equating a physical fall with a social one. Lebiadkin's fantasy also betrays his ignominy: he willingly debases his beloved to elevate himself. The second argument—"even a louse, even he can be in love"—reveals the Captain's actual self-image: the louse represents both his low social status and his parasitism.[33]

While the Lebiadkin love plot follows that of Captain Kartuzov, the differences are revealing. Most importantly, the horsewoman in the Kartuzov sketch actually breaks a leg and her fiancé deserts her. Lebiadkin, however, does not wait for a hypothetical accident to announce his passion. As the narrator notes, Lebiadkin is totally incapable of containing or controlling his emotions: "A trait of such people—this total incapacity to keep their desires to themselves; this uncontrollable urge, on the contrary, to reveal them at once, even in all their untidiness, the moment they arise. When he steps into society not his own, such a gentleman usually begins timidly, but yield him just a hair, and he will at once leap to impertinence" (10:140;174). In describing Lebiadkin's shamelessness, the narrator emphasizes his unconventionality and unpredictability, thereby creating the expectation of scandal.

Lebiadkin's unpredictability springs from a class rage rooted in shame of origins. Hypersensitive to his class status, he does not approach Liza when he is sober. When drunk, however, he proposes to her. What discretion-shame he possesses restrains him, for he proposes in writing. He does not send his letter until Liputin tempts him with the argument that "every man deserves the right of correspondence."[34] Lebiadkin's letter reflects his actual self-image as a nonentity as well his desired self-image as Stavrogin's rival. Expecting to receive property from Stavrogin, Lebiadkin practically offers to replace him as fiancé:

> *To the Perfection of Young Miss Tushin.*
> Dear lady, Elizaveta Nikolaevna!
> Oh, what a lovely vision
> Is Elizaveta Tushin.
> When she flies sidesaddle with her relation
> And her locks share the wind's elation,
> Or when with her mother in church she bows
> And the blush of reverent faces shows,
> Then matrimonial and lawful pleasures[35] I do desire,

> And after her, and her mother, send my tear.
> Composed by a man in an argument.

Dear lady!

I pity myself most of all for not having lost an arm at Sevastopol in the cause of glory, not having been there at all, but served the whole campaign managing vile provisions, considering it baseness. You are a goddess in antiquity, and I am nothing but have guessed at the infinite. Consider it as verse and no more, for verse is nonsense after all and justifies what is considered boldness in prose. Can the sun be angry at an infusorian if it composes to the sun from its drop of water, where there is a multitude of them, as seen in a microscope? Even the very club of philanthropy towards large cattle in Petersburg under the auspices of high society, while rightly commiserating with the dog and the horse, scorns the terse infusorian, not mentioning it at all, because it has not grown big enough. I have not grown big enough either. The thought of marriage might seem hilarious, but soon I will possess two hundred former serfs through a mankind-hater whom you should scorn. I could impart much and volunteer it according to documents—enough for Siberia. Do not scorn the proposal. The letter from the infusorian is to be understood in verse.

> Captain Lebiadkin, a humble friend,
> with much free time to spend. (10:106;131–2)

Lebiadkin's lowly status runs as a leitmotif through the letter. He calls Liza "a goddess in antiquity" and "the sun"—a poetic cliché as well as an image that ties her to Stavrogin, whom Peter Verkhovensky calls "a sun." Liza is the center of the universe, the giver of life, a celestial body, while Lebiadkin, a lowly provisions clerk, is a "nothing," "an infusorian," one of a multitude of microscopic organisms in a drop of water on earth (another image taken from Derzhavin's famous ode "God"). How then to breach the gap between them? Lebiadkin's letter proposes two solutions: his elevation to the status of propertied landowner and his denunciation of Stavrogin. The latter would eliminate his rival entirely, since being sent to Siberia would end Stavrogin's physical proximity to Liza. It would also curtail his marital prospects, as all civil marriages were dissolved upon criminal conviction.

By the time he enters Varvara Stavrogina's drawing room, Lebiadkin urgently desires to legitimate himself before both his hostess and Liza. To counteract the shame of his actual self-image as an "infusorian," and "a louse," Lebiadkin invokes a swashbuckling hero, the attractive, rich, independent

Prince de Monbars. He attempts to bridge the great gap between his actual and ideal self-images with verbal bravado. His shameless exhibitionism expresses the other side of his narcissism. The narrator emphasizes the connection between his insecurity and his vanity: "The expression of his physiognomy betrayed extreme insecurity and, at the same time, insolence and some ceaseless irritation. He was terribly scared, one could see that, but his vanity also suffered, and one could guess that out of irritated vanity, despite his fear, he might venture any sort of insolence if the occasion arose" (10:137; 171). The narrator thus describes Lebiadkin as a narcissistic time bomb.

In this drawing-room setting, Lebiadkin clearly chafes at his anonymity. Anxious to establish his rightful identity as Stavrogin's brother-in-law, he hints at his sister's identity:

> I, of course, am a negligible link. . . . Oh, Madam, rich are your halls, but poor are those of Marya the Unknown, my sister, born Lebiadkin, but for now we will call her Marya the Unknown, for now, Madam, only *for now*, for God himself will not allow it to be forever! Madam, you gave her ten rubles, and she accepted them only because they came from *you*, Madam! . . . From no one else in the world would this Unknown Marya take, otherwise her grandfather, an officer killed in the Caucasus before the eyes of Ermolov himself, would shudder in this grave, but from you, Madam, from you she will take anything. (10:138–9;174)

In this speech, Lebiadkin employs rhetorical contrasts, appeals to divine justice, and fabricates a family pedigree to establish his social qualification. He opens by self-denigration, a conciliatory gesture. After contrasting his sister's humble poverty with Varvara's patent wealth, he hints at his sister's current identity, thereby increasing Varvara's anxiety. He then devises a laudable heritage for his sister (and for himself by association) by fabricating a patriotic and military relative—a grandfather killed in combat in the Caucasus. He elevates his grandfather to heroic status by claiming that he died in front of General Ermolov himself.[36] Lebiadkin thus counteracts the shame of his actual social status by creating a socially prestigious pedigree.

Repentant Freethinker

Lebiadkin repeatedly reveals his willingness to promote himself at any price. In his letter to Liza, Lebiadkin offers to denounce Stavrogin (whom he does not name) and thus rid himself of a rival. In his anonymous letter to Governor von Lembke, Lebiadkin offers to denounce Peter Verkhovensky (whom he does not name) and thus rid himself of a blackmailer. By not naming his antagonists, Lebiadkin unconsciously consigns them to the same anonymity to which they have consigned him. In his letter to the governor, Lebiadkin offers, in return for political amnesty and a pension, to provide information on the distribution of subversive literature. Designed to save himself, Lebiadkin's anonymous letter to Lembke declares his patriotic intention of saving his country:

> Your Excellency,
>
> For by rank you are so. I herewith announce an attempt on the life of the persons of generals and the fatherland; for it leads straight to that. I myself have constantly been spreading them for a multitude of years. And godlessness, too. A rebellion is in preparation, there being several thousand tracts, and a hundred men will run after each one with their tongues hanging out, if not taken away by the authorities beforehand, for a multitude is promised as a reward, and the simple people are stupid, and also vodka. The people considering the culprit are destroying one and another, and, fearing both sides, I repented of what I did not participate in, for such are my circumstances. If you want a denunciation to save the fatherland, and also the churches and icons, I alone can. But, with that, a pardon by telegraph from the Third Department, immediately, to me alone out of all of them, and the rest to be held responsible. As a signal, every evening at seven o'clock put a candle in the doorkeeper's window. Seeing it, I will believe and come to kiss the merciful hand from the capital, but, with that, a pension, otherwise what will I live on? And you will not regret it, because you will get a star. It has to be on the quiet, or else there will be a neck wrung.
>
> Your Excellency's desperate man.
> At your feet falls
> the repentant freethinker, Incognito. (10:279–80;360)

Lebiadkin's illogical and ungrammatical letter opens by inadvertently insulting von Lembke with an insinuation that his excellence derives only from his rank. While announcing the threat to Russia's generals and Russia herself, Lebiadkin repeatedly uses the epithet "fatherland," thereby demonstrating his identification of Russia with the men who lead it. By linking atheism and political unrest, the fate of God and country, Lebiadkin's letter ties together the novel's political and metaphysical thematics, anticipating the political and metaphysical dimensions of parricide in *The Brothers Karamazov*.

Lebiadkin signs his anonymous letter to Governor von Lembke "Incognito," from the Latin for "unknown." *Incognito* also means someone in disguise or under an assumed name. It is thus a name that aptly epitomizes the paradox of pretender identity: pretenders are unknowns who want to be known, illegitimate rulers who seek to rule legitimately. As history shows, and as Dostoevsky affirms, such a state cannot sustain itself for long. The internal contradictions are too great. Though Lebiadkin's letter claims patriotic motives, his self-interest shines through: he asks for both a pardon and a pension. Ironically, Lebiadkin's plan to liberate himself from Peter Verkhovensky seals his fate. Lembke shows Peter the letter on the eve of the fête, and Peter has Lebiadkin killed that night. Peter also uses the letter to force Shatov's murder. Lebiadkin's willingness to expose others to promote his own safety leads directly to four murders. Thus, while Lebiadkin identifies generals, fatherland, and God (father figures) as those endangered by Russia's radicals,[37] he and Shatov (former collaborators/brother figures) are equally at risk. Dostoevsky makes a political point: fathers may threaten sons, but radical sons threaten fathers and kill brothers. Brotherhoods based on violence breed more violence.

In signing his anonymous letter to Governor von Lembke "repentant freethinker," Lebiadkin plagiarizes from himself, one of Dostoevsky's own favorite practices. Lebiadkin used the same tag while describing his putative will to Stavrogin. When an incredulous Stavrogin inquires about this legacy and its recipients, Lebiadkin responds:

> To the fatherland, to mankind, and to students. Nikolai Vsevolodovich, in the newspapers I read a biography about an American. He left his whole huge fortune to factories and for the positive sciences, his skeleton to the students at the academy there, and his skin to make a drum so as to have the American national anthem drummed on it day and night. Alas, we're pygmies compared to the soaring ideas of the North American States; Russia is a freak of nature but not of mind. If I were to try and bequeath my skin for a drum, to the Akmolinsk infantry regiment, for example, where I had the honor of beginning my service, so as to have the Russian national anthem drummed on it every day in front of the regiment, it would be regarded as liberalism, my skin would be banned . . . and so I limited myself only to students. I want to bequeath my skeleton to the academy, on condition, however, that a label be pasted to its forehead for ever and ever, reading: "Repentant Freethinker." There, sir! (10:209;264)

Lebiadkin's last will and testament clearly parodies Gogol's "*Zaveshchanie,*" an actual document that Dostoevsky had parodied before in his "Village of Stepanchikovo."[38] In *Demons,* Dostoevsky returns to the language and images of Gogol's last will and testament to continue his dual parody of life and literature. As a false captain, Lebiadkin reminds readers of Gogol's literary characters, the pretenders Khlestakov and Major Kovalev. His title and his surname's suffix also evoke Gogol's lower-class military hero Captain Kopeikin. As a generator of hyperbolic prose, however, Lebiadkin echoes Gogol himself.[39] Even his name, like Gogol's, derives from a bird's name.

Like Gogol's, Lebiadkin's bequests reveal their author's obsession with identity, fear of being misunderstood, and desire for public recognition. Like Gogol, Lebiadkin wants credit for mere intentions during his lifetime: "So you intend to make your will public in your lifetime and get rewarded for it?" (10:209;264).[40] Like Gogol, Lebiadkin repudiates his earlier politics. Like Gogol, Lebiadkin designates his legacy for his countrymen's "use." Yet, whereas Gogol bequeaths his literary works, particularly his *Selected Passages*, to his fellow Russians, Lebiadkin bequeaths his skeleton.[41] By calling comic attention to his body, Lebiadkin parodically echoes Gogol's obsession with his own body and his fear of being buried alive. Like all else in this Gogolian document, Lebiadkin's choice of epithet reveals Dostoevsky's parodic authorial play along with his serious thematic concerns. The epithet "Repentant Freethinker" underscores the reactionary views of Gogol's late work. In Dostoevsky's *oeuvre*, the epithet "freethinker" (*vol'nodumets*) signifies Enlightenment beliefs, particularly atheism (14:261). Lebiadkin has worked for the revolutionary atheists. As he confesses to Stavrogin, he has distributed subversive political pamphlets calling for the closing of churches, the annihilation of God and inheritance laws, the disruption of marriage, and armed rebellion. In both his confession to Stavrogin and his letter to von Lembke, Lebiadkin repents his association with atheism and revolution and affirms his fealty to Russia. (Given the radical critics' view of Dostoevsky's post-exile political conversion, Dostoevsky is probably indulging in a little self-parody as well.)

Anonymity and Identity

While Lebiadkin writes anonymously, his hyperbolic rhetoric easily betrays his identity. Although the imperceptive Praskovia Drozdova hasn't a clue to the anonymous letter writer's identity, Varvara Petrovna quickly uncovers it. Likewise, while the bumbling von Lembke hasn't a clue, the perspicacious Peter immediately identifies Lebiadkin.

Albeit a minor character, Lebiadkin is linked to many of the novel's characters, major and minor. Like Shatov, Lebiadkin is murdered by Peter Verkhovensky. Like Karmazinov, who writes a farewell piece titled "Merci," Lebiadkin composes a "last poem." Like Stepan Verkhovensky, Lebiadkin blames Russia for his lack of public recognition. Dostoevsky makes Varvara Stavrogina link these two dissimilar liars by dismissing Lebiadkin's comic hyperbolizing as "allegories" and "nonsense," the exact words she uses to dismiss Stepan Verkhovensky's hyperbolic speeches. Lebiadkin's self-identification as a "repentant freethinker" also parallels Stepan Verkhovensky's deathbed change of heart toward Russia. Finally, as mentioned earlier, Dostoevsky links Lebiadkin to Stavrogin both personally and politically. Lebiadkin's obsession with his identity links him to his chosen master, Stavrogin. Significantly, Lebiadkin is connected with all of Stavrogin's women: he is brother to Stavrogin's wife, acts as a rival for Liza Tushina, and slanders Stavrogin's mistress Dasha. Lebiadkin persistently imitates Stavrogin. Whereas Stavrogin is married to an actually lame woman, Lebiadkin obsesses about marrying a potentially lame woman. Whereas Stavrogin, in the chapter cut by Dostoevsky's publisher Katkov, plans to publish his confession, Lebiadkin plans to publish his will. Stavrogin's observation that Lebiadkin hopes to profit from publishing his will is echoed by Tikhon, who makes the same observation to Stavrogin regarding the publication of his confession. Last, Lebiadkin's continual obsession with identity echoes the novel's preoccupation with Stavrogin's enigmatic identity.

Lebiadkin's own name, part of the identity he deplores, deserves some attention. Why did Dostoevsky change his name from Captain Kartuzov (Peaked Cap or Powder Bag) to Captain Lebiadkin (Swanlet)? While there is good evidence to show that Dostoevsky deliberately refers to Derzhavin's poem "The Swan," Lebiadkin is not Dostoevsky's first swan: *The Idiot*'s Lebedev holds that honor. The striking parallels between Dostoevsky's two swans reveal authorial intention. Both Lebedev and Lebiadkin are parasitic retired clerks—one civilian, one military. Both compensate for their social insignificance by verbal exhibitionism.[42] They both love speechifying (*slovechki*). Both draw attention to their novel's thematics by employing cannibal imagery, raising the specter of limbs lost in military campaigns (reversing the shame of defectiveness), and pointing to dualities: Lebedev to humans' internal dualities, Lebiadkin to sociopolitical dualities. Both act out of self-interest and betray their benefactors. Both drink too much. And both send anonymous letters to bridge social barriers.

Writing anonymous letters gives Dostoevsky's swans a sense of power and control. Their letters bridge the gap between their actual marginality and their desired centrality. While both swans write anonymously, they write to establish an identity, to create roles for themselves. While they write to obtain the gratitude or recognition of their addressees, their letters arouse their addressees' anxiety. They thus further marginalize themselves.

In public, both swans define themselves rhetorically—Lebedev as prophet, Lebiadkin as poet. They thereby appropriate the roles of Russia's greatest and Dostoevsky's favorite poet—Pushkin. Not surprisingly, the spirit and poetry of Pushkin pervade Dostoevsky's metaliterary novels *The Idiot* and *Demons*. In *The Idiot*, as Aglaia identifies Myshkin with Pushkin's "Poor

Knight," Dostoevsky points to the works of Pushkin and Cervantes as intertexts. When Aglaia's mother wants to read Pushkin, Lebedev volunteers to sell her his set of the poet's complete works (the same edition Dostoevsky owned). A self-proclaimed prophet, Lebedev willingly alienates himself from the Russian literary and prophetic tradition for money. Fittingly, as an aspiring lawyer, Lebedev is also willing to sell his own meager talents. Dostoevsky identifies at least one Pushkin intertext for *Demons* with his choice of epigraphs—one biblical (discussed in chapter 6), one Pushkinian. The Pushkin epigraph recalls a carriage lost in a snowstorm, led astray by petty demons (*besy*). As becomes increasingly clear in the novel, Lebiadkin is a petty demon and is lost in the confusing politics of 1860s Russia.

Like Pushkin, both Dostoevsky's swans have uneasy relationships with their patrons because of their ambitious desire to achieve fame and fortune from their verbal talents. They thus remind the reader of the problems facing men of talent in Russia. Yet Dostoevsky's swans are not truly talented. Like their literary forebear, Khlestakov, they are pretenders. Neither true prophet nor true poet, they remind readers of the gap between their actual and their ideal identities—the very gap that Dostoevsky identifies as a source of their lying and thus of their identity.

Shame and Death

Through Lebiadkin, Dostoevsky demonstrates the tragic side of the political comedy being enacted. A comic pretender in a novel about serious pretendership, Lebiadkin moves from social embarrassment to political sacrifice. Like historical pretenders, Lebiadkin acts in his own self-interest but is coopted by political forces greater than himself and dies a bloody death. Lebiadkin (and his sister Marya and their servant) become the innocent victims of Peter Verkhovensky's political machinations. Lebiadkin's death also demonstrates the potential tragedy of the noncorrespondence between the ideal and the actual. To counter his actual identity as a retired provisions clerk, Lebiadkin adopts the title and role of a captain. To counter his enforced anonymity as Stavrogin's brother-in-law, he hints in letters, in taverns, and in Varvara Petrovna's drawing room at his family connection to the Stavrogins. To counter Peter Verkhovensky's hold over him, he refashions his identity, calling himself a "repentant freethinker." Lebiadkin's naive belief in the power of money and words to change reality makes him both comic and tragic. He believes that the acquisition of property and aristocratic relations can obliterate the social differences between himself and the upper class. Like pretenders before him, Lebiadkin represents himself as other in the hope that he will actually become so. In fact, the identity Lebiadkin seeks to realize kills him. Lebiadkin, the pretender captain, must die in order for Verkhovensky, the pretender-revolutionary, to realize his plan to enthrone Stavrogin as a pretender Ivan-Tsarevich. The comic Gogolian world of the pretender Khlestakov takes a tragic turn in the political climate of 1860s Russia. Lebiadkin's death gives us pause, however, for Dostoevsky uses the imagery of sacrifice to describe it (10:396;517). Lebiadkin may be a liar, a pretender, and a rogue, but his death resembles that of the real Tsarevich Dmitry—his throat is cut. Like the young innocent, Lebiadkin is sacrificed to the cause of pretender politics.

Shame dynamics move the twin plots of *Demons*. By threatening to expose others' secrets, Lebiadkin threatens the social and political status quo. Thus he must be removed. Varvara Stavrogina throws him out of her drawing room. Stavrogin relocates him—to the town's periphery.[43] Peter has him murdered. Lebiadkin thus becomes emblematic of that which must be repressed to preserve the social and political order. Lebiadkin's power is the disruptive power of shame. From Lebiadkin's first appearance in Varvara's drawing room, the narrator makes his audience complicit in getting rid of him. Like the assembled characters, readers are uneasy around Lebiadkin and want him to be thrown out—because he violates social norms. He exposes himself, thereby exposing us to his shame. While some readers delight in this exhibition, most are uncomfortable witnesses. His ejection relieves our anxiety at having to witness another's shame.

Lebiadkin's death is a critical moment for the authorial audience. Throughout the novel, we have been exposed to the narrator's open dislike of Lebiadkin. The narrator's hearsay description of Lebiadkin's death further emphasizes the pretender captain's drunkenness and animality: "On the spot I was told that the captain was found with his throat cut, on a bench, clothed, and that he was murdered, undoubtedly, while dead drunk so that he would not have heard and the blood flowed from him 'as from a bull'" (10:396;517). The details he includes, however, particularly the reported speech "as from a bull," suggest the image of sacrifice: like an animal on an altar, Lebiadkin is lying on a bench, fully dressed, his throat cut. While the narrator means to emphasize his bulk and passivity, the author invokes sacrifice. For Lebiadkin's death, Dostoevsky employs a strategy similar to the one in *Crime and Punishment*. There, as Gary Rosenshield points out, the omniscient narrator largely adopts Raskolnikov's viewpoint, looking at events through his fevered eyes, giving life to his obsessions and fears.[44] Like Raskolnikov, the narrator focuses on one death—the pawnbroker's. But as in *Crime and Punishment*, Dostoevsky complicates the murder by tripling it. Just as the pawnbroker's sister Lizaveta and her unborn child are murdered along with her, so Lebiadkin's sister and their servant are murdered along with him. In *Demons*, the narrator likewise focuses on one death—Lebiadkin's. As in *Crime and Punishment*, the narrator mentions, but marginalizes, the deaths of the meek and the humble. Dostoevsky, however, never forgets those other deaths—and we in the authorial audience come to see how we, like Raskolnikov and the narrator in *Demons*, have been guilty of tunnel vision. Lebiadkin may have been unconscious as he died, but his housemates were not. His sister Marya and their elderly servant woman have multiple wounds, evidencing their struggles. By noting as hearsay that Lebiadkin had probably been murdered while he was stone drunk, thus anesthetized by alcohol, the narrator neutralizes our response to his death. He would have felt little or nothing. He was an embarrassment, even to readers. We may even feel a little relief at his death.

The hearsay evidence of the women's struggles, however, increases our horror and gives us pause. Though the narrator introduces evidence that Lebiadkin was murdered for the money he'd been flashing the night before, making the two women innocent victims, the authorial audience knows the murder is politically motivated. We know, and the narrator confirms our suspicion, that Marya was equally targeted. Both she and her brother had to be removed. Both were sources of shame. Marya's very existence bore witness to Stavrogin's aristocratic sin. His upper-class self-indulgence thus results in the sacrifice of his wife, her brother, and their servant. And who kills them but Fedka, another source of shame, another political secret; Fedka, a peasant turned criminal after being lost at cards by the liberal father Stepan Verkhovensky; Fedka, a taboo-breaker who steals from churches and leaves mice in icon covers, who replaces holy literature with pornography; Fedka, an escaped convict turned murderer after being bought off by the revolutionary son Peter Verkhovensky; Fedka, murdered in turn for Lebiadkin's blood money. But blood cannot remove shame.

Lebiadkin's status as sacrifice restores reader pity for him. The narrator stresses his baseness, his comicality, his shamelessness. As the parodic embodiment of his social superiors' narcissistic grandiosity and self-absorption, Lebiadkin makes us laugh. His ideals derive from clichés, which make him comic. His sacrificial death, however, makes him tragic. Lebiadkin participates in his own death, but he does not deserve to die. Dostoevsky rescues him from the narrator's characterization of him as drunkard, opportunist, pretender, poetaster, and parasite, and restores to him the status of human being. For Dostoevsky portrays him as a pawn in a political struggle where the unscrupulous (Peter Verkhovensky) escape, while the virtuous (Shatov) and the innocent (Marya, the servant) are murdered. Lebiadkin, who is neither virtuous nor innocent, shares their fate.

Finally, Lebiadkin's name links the poetic and the political in *Demons*. Another possible source of Lebiadkin's name is the myth that identifies the swan as Orpheus, the poet murdered by Thracian women while he was under the influence of Bacchus. The myth links wine, song, and bloody murder, an apt poetic precedent for Dostoevsky's swan. Poets are disruptive. Lebiadkin's function as a powerful wild card, a figure who threatens to disrupt the social and political order by threatening to expose personal and political secrets, reveals the threat of the poet's power. Lebiadkin's vacillation between uneasy acceptance of a status quo that marginalizes him, denying him wealth, power, and fame, and disquieting threats to expose his superiors' sins arouses in characters and readers alike a desire to contain him. In other words, Dostoevsky uses the comi-tragic figure of Lebiadkin, Stavrogin's Falstaff and imitator, a Second False Dmitry, to give us visceral knowledge of how censorship works. Lebiadkin is a pretender poet, but like real poets, he exposes, or rather threatens to expose, truths that we would rather repress than face.

chapter eleven

Father and Son: Legacy of Shame

> And I couldn't restrain myself. . . . (14:38;41)
> — FEDOR PAVLOVICH KARAMAZOV

In their third meeting, Smerdiakov tells Ivan: "You won't want to ruin your life forever by taking such shame upon yourself in court. You're like Fedor Pavlovich, most of all, sir; of all his children you came out resembling him most of all, having the same soul as him, sir" (15:68;632). However puzzling this statement seems at first, Ivan's response is more so: " 'You're not stupid,' Ivan said as if struck; blood rushed to his face." This enigmatic interchange begs for elucidation, but the implied solution, comparing the souls of father and son, poses further problems: while Fedor Pavlovich wears his soul on his sleeve, Ivan, in Mitya's words, "is a grave" (14:101;110). In Book Eleven, however, Ivan's creator plunges into Ivan's soul and reveals a devil, a shabby sponger who shares much with Ivan's father. Around fifty years old, punsters who specialize in dirty tricks (*pakosti*), Ivan's devil and Fedor Pavlovich Karamazov are both exhibitionist liars who wield shame's rhetoric to expose shame's content. By examining these two liars and two punning anecdotes, I will expose the family connection, reveal how contrasting responses to shame shape the novel's action, and show how Dostoevsky's metaliterary play arouses a sense of pleasure that offsets but does not erase the shame affect he uses as a narrative strategy to implicate readers in the text's ethical action.

In fashioning Ivan's devil, Dostoevsky exuberantly plays with embodied shame. His devil is, in Ivan's words, "the embodiment of myself, but only one side of me . . . of my thoughts and feelings, but only the most loathsome and stupid of them" (15:72;637). Although he represents those parts of himself that Ivan is ashamed to acknowledge, Ivan's devil paradoxically provides Ivan with the occasion for self-knowledge and self-acceptance. By reflecting Ivan's worst side to him, thus causing him to confront his shame, Ivan's devil may, in fact, bring out the best in Ivan. As Robin Feuer Miller argues, Ivan's devil may operate as a homeopathic dose.[1] Shame positively applied may cure shame.

Ivan's devil appears suddenly, thus reflecting the experience of shame. By exposing Ivan to himself, the devil expresses and embodies Ivan's self-consciousness. Ivan desires to rid himself of his devil, thereby disowning painful aspects of himself. Yet Ivan's devil also tries to plant the seeds of belief in Ivan, thereby reconnecting him with others in a way that reorients him, healing his pain. The devil as Ivan's self-consciousness thus epitomizes shame's paradox. Ivan's devil represents Ivan's physical and metaphysical alienation. Yet, while his job entails division, Ivan's devil longs to join in the general "Hosanna." Ivan's devil thus reflects Ivan's divided self: his sense of alienation as well as his desire for belief and community.[2]

Dostoevsky's narrator emphasizes Ivan's shame with his lengthy description of the devil's imaginatively embodied form, including his shabby dress. He does not have a watch, a hint of his relation to another possible world where chronometric earthly time is irrelevant.[3] He does, however, have "a tortoise-shell lorgnette on a black ribbon," a sign of his role as voyeur, a role that he shares with Ivan, who adopts "The Observer" as his journalistic *nom de plume*. The devil reflects Ivan back to himself: "Indeed, you're angry at me because I did not present myself to you in some sort of red glow, 'thundering and shining,' with scorched wings, but appeared in such modest form. You're insulted, first, in your aesthetic feelings, and, second, in your pride: how, you ask, could such a banal [*poshlyi*] devil enter such a great man?" (15:81;647). The creator of the Grand Inquisitor, Ivan feels ashamed at having such a banal devil.

Ivan experiences equal shame at having such a banal father. Though the scenes that feature Ivan's devil ("The Devil. Ivan Fedorovich's Nightmare") and his father ("The Old Buffoon") are separated by nine books and five hundred pages, Dostoevsky keeps their similarities alive to readers. Most strikingly, the two are both called "buffoon" (*shut*), an epithet that is marked as the devil's in Russian folklore[4] but as Fedor's in *The Brothers Karamazov*. When Ivan calls his devil "a buffoon," he thus evokes the memory of his father. Ivan also refers to his devil as a "lie" (*lozh'*), thus recalling the memorable scene in which Fedor Pavlovich calls himself first a father, then a son, of lies (*otets lzhi/syn lzhi*). Fedor Pavlovich and the devil are both accused of exhibitionistic lying (*vran'yo*). The devil even refers to himself as an aged Khlestakov, the archetypal liar (*vrun*) of Russian literature, thereby accentuating the novel's metaliterary play. The devil's age (pushing fifty) makes him the same generation as Fedor Pavlovich (fifty-five). Fedor Pavlovich and Ivan's devil have both lived as spongers (Ivan also spent his childhood as a dependent, a shameful memory for him). The narrator further links them by associative grouping. He notes that Ivan's devil belongs to a type that encompasses bachelors or widowers; furthermore, when widowers have children, others raise them and the widowers gradually forget them—an apt description of

Fedor Pavlovich. Both Ivan's devil and Fedor Pavlovich act as divisive spirits. Finally, both tell a number of stories that resonate thematically, further linking these figurative and literal embodiments of Ivan's shame.

Dostoevsky uses the devil's mimetic dimension to reflect Ivan's shame, his thematic dimension to express Ivan's internal divisions, and his synthetic dimension to entertain his readers and enhance their aesthetic pleasure. For instance, in elaborating the devil's difficulties with incarnation, Dostoevsky evokes Gogol's story "The Nose." The devil's mimetic attempt to thank the doctor who cured his cold by placing an appreciative announcement in the newspaper metaliterarily evokes Major Kovalev's efforts to place an inquiry regarding his missing nose in the newspaper. Both stories take covert mimetic jabs at Russian censorship. Dostoevsky also thematically caricatures Ivan's Russian liberalism: Ivan's devil is rebuffed because believing in the devil is not progressive. By foregrounding the question of the devil's objective existence, this incident mimetically reflects Ivan's metaphysical doubts. The devil comically reduces the metaphysical issue to a social one by complaining about his shame: "And would you believe that incident still weighs on my heart. My best feelings, gratitude for instance, are formally forbidden solely because of my social position" (15:76;641). As a comic rhyme, this incident also reflects Ivan's own painful experience with Katerina Ivanovna: his feelings of love are forbidden because he is her fiancé's brother. Ivan's devil reveals his soul. Dostoevsky's devil reveals his art.

Dostoevsky further exposes his own poetics by having Ivan produce a devil who discusses incarnation, an issue that evokes the image of Christ and thus reflects the battle between the devil and Christ in Ivan's heart. Early in the scene, the devil complains to Ivan that he caught cold when he took on human form and was exposed to the elements. Adapting a line from Terence, the devil notes, "I become incarnate, so I accept the consequences. *Satanum sum et nihil humanum a me alienum puto*" (I am Satan and nothing human is alien to me) (15:74;639). Even as he identifies himself as Satan, Ivan's devil plagiarizes,[5] thus signaling that he is a liar. The devil comically debases incarnation by connecting it to a cold, but he also emphasizes its relationship to exposure. Being human means having a body and thus being exposed. Even though the devil (Ivan's unconscious creation) overtly reminds Ivan of the divine *Logos* later in their conversation, Dostoevsky (the devil's conscious creator) plays with the incarnation to evoke the image of Christ. Dostoevsky thus links this scene with the *Pro and Contra* scene of Book Five by deploying, and thus highlighting, the rhetorical strategy used in each. For example, before introducing the Grand Inquisitor, Ivan raises the issues of injustice and forgiveness, thereby pushing Alesha to mention Christ. In this strategy, the character narrator draws to conscious awareness an image latent in his audience's unconscious. What Ivan consciously does to Alesha, his devil (his unconscious) does to him; the devil's talk of incarnation first evokes thoughts of the incarnate God, then the devil speaks overtly of Christ as *Logos*. Dostoevsky, who stages this scene, does the same with his readers. He thereby uses a *mise en abyme* to reveal his authorial hand.

Moreover, Dostoevsky entertains his readers with thematically charged metaliterary play. He sets up a series of implicit comparisons between Christ's incarnation and the devil's. Whereas Christ takes on human form to redeem the sins of the world, Ivan's devil takes on human form to attend a cocktail party. Whereas Christ suffers mockery and humiliation, Ivan's devil suffers the air's iciness. Whereas Christ is put to death, Ivan's devil catches cold and suffers from rheumatism. These comic contrasts emphasize Christ's transcendence and the devil's worldliness, thereby reflecting the struggle in Ivan's soul between ethical action and earthly desire.

While Ivan's devil and Ivan's father both tell a number of anecdotes, I will compare two. Dostoevsky flags both anecdotes as exhibitionist lying by their ostensible motive: hospitality. Both are salacious and confessional; both relate to honor and thus to identity. They function very differently, however, as the two anecdotes represent antithetical responses to shame. While most characters in the novel engage in the standard, generally acceptable responses to shame—concealment, denial, flight, and paralysis—Fedor Pavlovich chooses the socially unacceptable response of sharing his shame. Ivan's devil represents yet another response: the confrontation of shame. As Lynd points out, confronting one's shame may be positive and revelatory.[6] Early in the novel, Zosima advises Fedor Pavlovich not to be so ashamed of himself, "for that is the cause of everything" (14:40;43); late in the novel, Ivan unconsciously enacts this advice. Ivan's devil tells a story that posits suicide as an escape from shame. He thus implicitly presents Ivan with two alternatives: to commit suicide or to face his shame publicly. Ivan chooses the latter: he resolves to expose Smerdiakov and himself at the trial.

Both the devil's and Fedor Pavlovich's anecdotes partake of Dostoevsky's metaliterary project: both are meta-confessions, that is, stories that expose shame while thematizing shame's exposure. In keeping with their metaliterary nature, both anecdotes thematize audience response as well. Fedor Karamazov tells his Aesopian anecdote in Zosima's cell in response to Miusov's taunting. Casting himself as a social inferior (as Ivan's devil will do later), he signals his subversive intentions. To illustrate his assertion that his desire to please harms him, Fedor Pavlovich declaims:

> And that's how I am, I'm always like that. Without fail I damage myself with my own courtesy [*liubeznost'*]! Once, many years ago now, I said to one influ-

ential person, "Your wife, sir, is a ticklish woman [*shchekotlivaia zhenshchina-s*]," meaning her honor, her moral qualities, so to speak. And he suddenly replied to me, "Did you tickle her? [*A vy ee shchekotali?*]." I could not restrain myself; suddenly, go ahead, I thought, I'll be courteous [*dai, dumaiu, poliubeznichaiu*]. "Yes," I said, "I did tickle her, sir [*Da, govoriu, shchekotal-s*]." Well, right then he gave me quite a tickling . . . ! [*nu tut on menia i poshchekotal*]. But that happened long ago, so it's already not shameful to tell about it. I'm forever damaging myself like that! (14:38;41)

In this anecdote, Fedor Pavlovich consciously provokes the man he constructs as his interlocutor, who then takes his revenge by beating him. By telling this anecdote, Fedor Pavlovich gleefully parodies his relationship with Miusov and predicts what happens next: he offends Miusov (his interlocutor) who then revenges himself by publicly shaming Fedor Pavlovich (a moral beating).

Fedor Pavlovich's iterated assertion "And that's how I am, I'm always like that" (*I vse-to ia tak, vsegda-to ia tak*) emphasizes his anecdote's confessional nature, thereby signaling an authorial polemic with Rousseau. As Knapp points out, in contrast to Augustinian-style confessions that describe a person's struggle to leave past ways behind and become a new person, Rousseauist confessions display the person in all his inertial glory.[7] Belknap characterizes the Augustinian or repentant confession as a statement that can take the form "I did (or do, or am) this, and it is wrong." He notes that Rousseauist largely engages in *apologia*, which takes the form "I did (or do, or am) this, and it is right." As Belknap argues, Fedor Pavlovich indulges in another kind of confession, an unrepentant confession that takes the form "I did it, it's wrong, but that's the way I am."[8] In this anecdote, Fedor Pavlovich flaunts his willingness to besmirch a woman's honor for the pun of it. As Fedor Pavlovich knows, the most effective way to provoke those who uphold the status quo—people like Miusov at whom he directs his story—is to act or speak inappropriately or shamelessly, thereby implicating his interlocutor in a breach of decorum. In thus disrupting the status quo, Fedor Pavlovich acts like a devil, whose job is to divide.

Puns are the perfect vehicle for Fedor Pavlovich. Like jokes, puns create an intimacy between speaker and audience as they assume a shared body of knowledge or beliefs. To understand a pun or a joke means that one understands the speaker's field of reference.[9] By exploiting shared references, puns can provide the cognitive pleasure of understanding; by exploiting multiple meaning and economy of expression, they can provide aesthetic pleasure. Both kinds of pleasure depend on a sharing that creates intimacy but a distance that allows for appreciation. On the other hand, depending on their content and the relationship between speaker and audience, puns can also engender pain. The puns I will discuss, for instance, provide pleasure for Dostoevsky's readers while causing pain for their fictional audiences. Fedor Pavlovich deliberately offends reluctant interlocutors with puns that assume a shared understanding. By collapsing the intersubjective boundaries between himself and his interlocutors with his story's shameful content, he removes its humor, which requires a comfortable, not a threatening intimacy. In telling this story, Fedor Pavlovich not only forces his interlocutors to witness his shame, thereby evoking feelings of shame, he also subjects them to shame by association. They feel shame at sharing cultural and linguistic ground with such a shameless buffoon. Fedor Pavlovich thus uses puns rhetorically to assault his audience. Ivan's devil, on the other hand, does not pun to cause pain, yet he causes pain by reflecting Ivan back to himself. Ivan's devil thus uses shame much the same way as Dostoevsky does: by giving Ivan a chance to confront his shame, he aims to save him.

As Fedor Pavlovich self-consciously tells the story of his own shame, his synthetic function, to reveal the constructed nature of Dostoevsky's text, rivals his mimetic function. Dostoevsky's readers are thus positioned to witness this scene of shame and respond viscerally, but also to appreciate and thus enjoy its metaliterary play. Ivan's devil has a doubly mimetic and synthetic function: first, he is the product of Ivan's unconscious as well as of Dostoevsky's pen; and second, he self-consciously tells the story of someone else's shame, thereby reflecting Ivan back to himself. The devil's anecdote reflects Ivan's semiconscious understanding of the choices facing him:

> "My friend," the visitor observed sententiously, "it's still better to have your nose put out of joint, than sometimes to have no nose at all [*s nosom vse zhe luchshe otoiti, chem inogda sovsem bez nosa*], as one afflicted marquis . . . uttered not long ago in confession to his Jesuit spiritual father. I was present—it was a delight. 'Give me back my nose!' he said. And he beat his breast. 'My son,' the priest hedged, 'through the inscrutable decrees of Providence everything has its recompense, and a visible calamity sometimes brings with it an extraordinary, if invisible, advantage. If harsh fate has deprived you of your nose, then your advantage is that now for the rest of your life no one will dare tell you that you have had your nose put out of joint' [*chto vy ostalis' s nosom*]. 'Holy father, that's no consolation!' the desperate man exclaimed. 'On the contrary, I'd be delighted to have my nose put out of joint [*ostavat'sia s nosom*] every day of my life, if only it were in the place it belongs!' 'My son,' the priest sighed, 'one cannot demand all blessings at once. That is already a grumble against Providence, which even here has not forgotten you; for if you cry out, as you have just cried out, that you would gladly have your nose put

out of joint [*ostavat'sia s nosom*] for the rest of your life, in this your desire has already been fulfilled indirectly; for, having lost your nose, you have thereby, as it were, had your nose put out of joint all the same' [*vy tem samym vse zhe kak by ostalis' s nosom*] . . . "

"Pah, how stupid!" cried Ivan.

"My friend, I merely wanted to make you laugh, but I swear that is real Jesuit casuistry, and I swear it all happened word for word as I've told it to you. That was a recent incident, and it gave me a lot of trouble. Upon returning home, the unfortunate young man shot himself that very same night; I was with him constantly up to the last moment. . . . " (15:80–1;646)[10]

Like Fedor Pavlovich's, this anecdote involves wordplay; it also takes decorum and identity as its subject. As author of both anecdotes, Dostoevsky displays his metaliterary wit as well as his deep understanding of shame dynamics.

Both liars play with the literal/figurative meanings of words. Fedor Pavlovich, for instance, activates the potential sexual connotations of the verb *shchekotat'*, "to tickle," as well as those of the verb *poliubeznichat'*, which can mean "be courteous to" or "pay court to." He thereby hints at his sexual misconduct with the influential person's wife, as well as his indecorous behavior with the man himself. As Fedor Pavlovich notes, he could not restrain himself (*ne uderzhalsia*). While Fedor Pavlovich's anecdote is not obscene in the same patent way as his farcical blessing of "the paps" that Zosima sucked as a child, it is nonetheless obscene, that is, a deliberate violation of the sense of shame.[11] His verbal play violates social decorum, earning him the same kind of reward, that is, a beating, that the legendary Aesop regularly received from his master for his verbal one-upmanship. He thus perpetuates the cycle that he describes. In telling an indecorous anecdote in a monastery, that is, in telling a story out of place, Fedor Pavlovich succeeds in shaming his interlocutors. But his triumph over his humiliators is short-lived, for his story elicits a vengeful response that once again humiliates him, thereby metaphorically returning him to his place.[12]

The devil's anecdote plays on the literal and figurative meanings of expressions using the word "nose," which not only designates the openly visible olfactory organ but also suggests the hidden sexual organ, an eighteenth-century commonplace that Gogol exploited in his well-known story, "The Nose," an intertext for Dostoevsky's anecdote. The standard expression "to be made a fool of" is *ostat'sia s nosom*. Dostoevsky introduces the concept by having Ivan, then his devil, use the verb *otkhodit'*, which literally means "to depart, to walk away" but is used figuratively to denote the process of dying. The imperfective verb stresses process rather than result. The expression *otkhodit' s nosom* links shame with the general process of dying as well as with the marquis's specific case of syphilis.[13]

The devil's anecdote also plays with the concept of place. The nose is out of place, misplaced, displaced, no place. Its out-of-placeness identifies the nose as a source of disgrace-shame, that is, shame felt after exposure. The nose reveals that the marquis has not heeded the urgings of discretion-shame, that is, shame felt before exposure, a shame that deters a person from inappropriate action and thus preserves dignity and integrity. Having exposed himself to disgrace-shame, the marquis faces personal disintegration. Dostoevsky, here as elsewhere, links ethics and aesthetics.[14]

The marquis tries to regain a sense of self by exhibiting a sense of discretion-shame. The devil's anecdote locates the marquis's confession in a confession booth—a private, appropriate place. Fedor Pavlovich confesses his shame in a monk's cell, an ostensibly appropriate place, but one inappropriate for his behavior. First, he engages in an unrepentant, self-vaunting confession that violates the spirit of the place. Second, he confesses in front of a mixed audience that has assembled for an entirely different purpose. Fedor Pavlovich thereby engages in the very behavior he incoherently denounces later: "Is it permitted to confess out loud? The Holy Fathers instituted whispered confession, only then will your confession be a secret [*tainstvom*], and that has been so from of old. Otherwise how am I to explain to him in front of everyone that I, for instance, did this and that. . . . well, this and that, you understand? Sometimes it's even indecent to say it [*Inogda ved' i skazat' neprilichno*]. Like that it's a scandal!" (14:82;88). Though both anecdotes form part of Dostoevsky's long-standing attack on Rousseau's *Confessions*, their differences reflect the characters of their tellers. Fedor Pavlovich flaunts his shame publicly. The marquis of Ivan's devil, on the other hand, proves as shame-filled as Ivan himself; he confesses his shame privately.[15]

Fedor Dostoevsky uses Fedor Karamazov's commentary on confession to stress its sacramental nature. Old Fedor uses the word *tainstvo* to characterize whispered confession. He thus uses the word in its archaic sense as "a secret," something that is kept private. Dostoevsky, however, activates *tainstvo*'s religious meanings—"sacrament" and "mystery," thus prefiguring the Grand Inquisitor's use of "miracle, mystery and authority" (*chudo, taina i avtoritet*) as "the three powers on earth that can forever conquer and capture the conscience of these weak rebels, for their own happiness" (14:232;255). Dostoevsky also reminds readers of confession's sacramental status. As a sacrament, confession allows a person to own, acknowledge, or avow unworthy or sinful thoughts or deeds. While the focus is frequently on guilt, that is, a person's actions, confession also establishes a place where shame can be acknowledged, accepted, and thereby healed. Fedor Karamazov's declamation thus anticipates the devil's anecdote.

Like Fedor Pavlovich's anecdote, the devil's takes audience response as its subject, a metaliterary move that signals Dostoevsky's authorial hand. The Jesuit in the devil's anecdote recalls Fedor Pavlovich by creating a pun that distances him from his interlocutor and thus diminishes his effectiveness. The Jesuit approaches the marquis's problem intellectually, not compassionately, thereby proving himself an inadequate spiritual counselor; the marquis kills himself. The devil thus reminds Ivan that mind is not everything. Furthermore, in a novel of situational rhymes,[16] the Jesuit's uncompassionate response contrasts with Zosima's compassionate response to Fedor Pavlovich, a response that identifies shame as the immediate cause of Fedor Pavlovich's aggressive exhibitionism. These contrasting responses to shame express a fundamental thematic opposition between unbelievers and believers, sowers of discord and sowers of love. Dostoevsky displays his narrative virtuosity as shamed characters telling stories about shame dramatize the author's social, political, and metaphysical thematics regarding Roman Catholicism and Russian Orthodoxy, materialism and spirituality, belief and unbelief, unity and separation, God and the devil in the human heart. Dostoevsky also uses the literal/figurative play in these anecdotes to promote his message: heaven is associated with figurative understanding, acceptance, and community; hell is associated with literal understanding, rejection, and isolation. The Jesuit priest thus imitates the devil (who watches over him) while Zosima imitates Christ.

The devil's Jesuit confessor recalls the Grand Inquisitor, thereby reminding readers of Ivan's authorial status. The confessor also signals Dostoevsky's authorial hand—for Dostoevsky embeds the devil's story in a novel that thematizes fictionalizing and, under mimetic cover, reveals its storytelling devices. The devil tells a story in which the Jesuit confessor fails because he does not appreciate the pain of the marquis's shame. The Jesuit thus proves himself a poor listener and a poor imitator of Christ. He lacks Christ's compassion—Christ's experiential understanding of the shame inherent in the human condition. Furthermore, by reinforcing the marquis's shame, the Jesuit acts like Miusov, the westernized Russian who serves as a negative model of audience response, rather than like Zosima, who serves as a positive model. The Jesuit's lack of compassion works paradoxically like shame. In making shamed persons acutely aware of loss, shame can also arouse a longing for what is lost. The Jesuit's lack of compassion arouses readers' sense that his response is flawed, thus evoking the missing response—compassion. The devil's story thus illustrates Ivan's unconscious and Dostoevsky's conscious rhetorical strategy: by modeling a negative response, they educe a positive response. Dostoevsky goes even further: he models both negative and positive responses and lets readers choose.

Following Dostoevsky's lead and moving by association, I return to exhibitionist lying—the rhetoric of shame. The *Diary* writer identifies shame as the second source of lying. The first is the fear that truth (*istina*) is insufficiently poetic: "In this way, we've completely lost the axiom that truth, especially in its purest form, is more poetic than anything that exists in the world" (21:119). In the context of Dostoevsky's Christological poetics, in which Christ is the ultimate truth, an incarnate God is, in fact, literally prosaic and quintessentially poetic. As the Word made flesh, Christ literalizes the figurative. In the context of the novel, imitation of Christ translates into the concept of active love—which, as Saul Morson has noted, involves not miracles, the unusual, or the poetic, but many prosaic acts.[17] Yet, however prosaic these acts may be, they are infused with love, a higher principle, thus making them poetic in the same way that Christ is, for as flesh that embodies Word, Christ is pure poetry. This returns us to Robin Feuer Miller's observation that *The Brothers Karamazov* is a novel in which so much cuts both ways.[18]

In telling their anecdotes, Fedor Pavlovich and Ivan's devil employ the comic literary strategy of literalizing figurative expressions. Dostoevsky embeds these anecdotes in a novel whose epigraph is a parable, a literary genre that works by figuralizing the literal. By choosing a strategy that inverts Christ's rhetoric, Fedor Pavlovich and Ivan's devil parody Christ. Dostoevsky thus shows readers how it is possible to coopt antithetical narrative strategies to serve a higher truth.

In the novel's progression, shame passes from father to son. But whereas Fedor Pavlovich is mired in an inertial cycle of shame and punishment that he perpetuates with his own discourse, Ivan proves to have a soul that is a true battleground for God and the devil. Though Ivan has a liar, a spiritual sponge in his soul, he also, as his devil reminds him, authors "The Grand Inquisitor" and thus has a compassionate, forgiving Christ in his soul.

Dostoevsky thus shows readers how to heal the paternal legacy of shame and pain. While Fedor Pavlovich passes his on, Ivan confronts his. *The Brothers Karamazov* closes with Ivan still unconscious. We understand that the battle within him still rages. Yet in generating a progression from father to son, Dostoevsky gives us hope. Ivan's devil may be an exhibitionistic liar, but Ivan is not. Like Dostoevsky, Ivan creates fictions that have the power to change, even to redeem, their readers. In short, Dostoevsky gives Ivan the power to redeem himself.

conclusion

In using shame as a narrative strategy, Dostoevsky floods readers with affect. He eliminates the reading experience's armchair safety by making us witnesses to exposed shame. We experience shame's contagious, paradoxical force. We want to flee or forget these painful scenes, yet we identify uncomfortably with those who experience them. Like Dostoevsky's shamed characters, we experience the disruption of shame—the effect of surprise. Like them, we experience the disorientation of shame—the effect of defamiliarization. Just as his characters find themselves in uncharted territory, we find ourselves in a state of *aporia,* a liminal state in which we are particularly open to shame's third effect: self-consciousness. Self-consciousness, like shame itself, works paradoxically: it is a state of pain but also a state of awareness. Herein lies the power of Dostoevsky's art—he not only floods readers with affect, he also captivates our intellect. He portrays shame and scandal while he poses metaphysical questions and delights us with metaliterary play. In short, he engages our minds as much as our hearts.

As we have seen in the case studies of the shamed characters General Ivolgin and Stepan Verkhovensky, Dostoevsky outlines a pattern. The shamed person starts from a position of narcissistic self-enclosure from which he regards other persons as judges. He orients himself toward them self-referentially, trusting them to collaborate in creating and maintaining his idealized self-image. Their failure to comply causes crises of self-consciousness. When self-consciousness leads to the perception of others as equally worthy self-presenting agents, shame can be overcome. The shamed person escapes from the prison-house of self and steps toward community.

The dynamics of shamelessless are more complex and varied. Shamelessness betokens an indifference to norms of social interaction, an indifference that arises from a sense of exclusion. As Dostoevsky illustrates in *The Brothers Karamazov*, shamelessness is an aggressive defense against shame or the anticipation of shame. In the Dostoevskian case studies of the shameless characters Fedor Karamazov, Lukian Lebedev, and Captain Lebiadkin, inertia prevails, that is, while their rhetoric betrays awareness of ways to overcome their isolation, their shameless behavior not only perpetuates but also exacerbates their exclusion.

The final characters in this study, Ivan Karamazov and his devil, offer yet another look at the dynamics of shame and scandal with which this study began. Before turning to them, however, I return to shame and scandal. While shame can be private or semiprivate, scandals are public. Scandal thus proves rich material for Dostoevsky's fiction, which thrusts the private into the public realm, broadens the arena of exposure, and reveals the secrets of characters' souls. Dostoevsky's work uses scandal in its biblical sense as a stumbling block, a testing ground for the human mind and heart. In portraying scenes of exposed shame, he arouses our desire to isolate ourselves, but he also whets our longing to belong. Exposed shame mobilizes our cognitive as well as our affective faculties. in portraying scandal, Dostoevsky thus plunges us experientially into the text's action, jolts our ethical sensibilities, and implicates us in the workings of conscience.

Dostoevsky's choice of shame as subject and narrative strategy reflects his ethical commitment to universal brotherhood. At shame's heart lies a paradox: separation entails union. Dostoevsky uses this dialectical opposition to demonstrate that awareness of separation implies awareness of community. An individual is isolated *from*. In his remarkable and oft-cited meditation on the death of his first wife in 1864, Dostoevsky identifies the "I" as a source of separation and an obstacle to union. He argues that the highest realization of self comes with self-sacrifice:

> To love a person, *as oneself,* according to Christ's commandment, is impossible. The law of self is binding on earth. The *I* stands in the way. Only Christ was able to, but Christ was the eternal ideal of all ages, towards which man strives and must strive, according to the law of nature . . . for man to discover, recognize and with all the force of his nature be convinced that the highest use a person can make of his self, of his fully developed *I,* is as if to destroy that *I,* to give it wholly to one and all, undividedly and selflessly. . . . [20:172] And so, man strives on earth toward an ideal *counter* to his nature. When man has not fulfilled the law of striving toward this ideal, that is, has not through *love* sacrificed his *I* to other people (I and Masha), then he experiences suffering and has called this state sin. And so, man must constantly experience

suffering, which is counterbalanced by the heavenly delight of fulfilling the law, that is, through sacrifice. (20:175)

In this meditation, Dostoevsky contrasts human nature ("the law of self") with divine nature (self-sacrifice). In his view, suffering results from self-assertion, happiness from self-sacrifice. This formula works for Dostoevsky's liars as well as his other characters. Lying is a form of rhetorical self-assertion that is a response to shame at one's identity. Fearful of social exclusion, liars try to present their ideal rather than their actual self-image. Their rhetoric thus exacerbates their sense of social exclusion: if their ideal self-image is accepted, they do not achieve their goal of being accepted as qualified social agents on their own terms. If, as happens in Dostoevsky's novels, their ideal self-image is exposed as false, their sense of exclusion is exacerbated.

Throughout his work, Dostoevsky models a path out of the enclosed self. In the barest terms, Dostoevsky advocates freeing oneself from the prison-house of ego, where shame works as chief jailer, and joining community. The first step requires an empathic bridge, which overcomes the "I" as obstacle through the refocusing of self from self to other. General Ivolgin's final story leads him to reflect not on the wrongs he has suffered, but on the suffering he has caused his wife. On his deathbed, Stepan Verkhovensky repudiates his narcissism and assumes responsibility for others' welfare. He declares his love for others, because he sees them and himself as members of a larger, metaphysical community (10:505;663). Significantly, he recognizes his narcissism when he comprehends Christ's humility, the "turned cheek" of the Gospel (10:505–6;664). Dostoevsky thus models a conversion by the book: Stepan's deep attention to the gospel message leads to an *imitatio Christi*. Dostoevsky shows that what one reads, and how one reads it, matter deeply. Stepan Verkhovensky's epiphanies about love and humility prefigure the insights of Dostoevsky's positive characters, Alesha Karamazov and the Elder Zosima. His deathbed revelations anticipate Zosima's doctrine that "each is responsible for all."

It is tempting to say that Dostoevsky has his shamed characters move from shame scripts to guilt scripts, that is, from obsessing about self and social standing to assuming responsibility for others, thereby identifying shame with the narcissistic self and guilt with the ethical self. But, as I have shown, shame frequently has an ethical component in Dostoevsky's work. His portrait of Zosima clearly demonstrates this. Zosima's life changes radically after he slaps his servant Afanasy so hard that he draws blood. The future monk, still an aristocratic career officer, not only feels guilt at his wrong action; he also feels a deep shame that he has become the kind of person who could do such a thing. As his story shows, Zosima accepts his guilt long before he can manage his shame. While the next morning he bows down to Afanasy and begs forgiveness, years pass before he can face his servant again. Zosima remains in town but sends Afanasy away: "[O]n the same day that I returned from the duel I had sent Afanasy back to his company, being ashamed to look him in the face after the way I had behaved with him that morning–so far is an unprepared man of the world inclined to be ashamed even of the most righteous act" (14:274;301). Only after eight years of wandering as a monk and praying for Afanasy daily can Zosima finally meet his former servant with equanimity and joy.

Zosima overcomes his shame through humility and love, the two paths for overcoming "the law of self" that Dostoevsky lays out in his meditation on his first wife's death. These paths are also the paths of Christ, Dostoevsky's moral ideal. Christ is himself a paradox, a God-man, a kenotic god who voluntarily assumes bodily form to redeem humanity. Dostoevsky chooses Christ because he is not an abstract, but an embodied god, a living moral exemplar. And yet, Christ's incarnation and voluntary humility have proved a scandal, a stumbling block, for conventional wisdom. As Dostoevsky shows in his last novel, Christ's freely accepted humiliation proves to be a stumbling block for many, but particularly for Ivan and Alesha—the two Karamazov brothers who share a mother.

Ivan and Alesha emblemize shamed and unshamed individuals. Following their mother's death, both are placed with relatives. Ivan responds to his dependent status with deep shame—the underside of his pride, manifest in his aloofness and self-sufficiency. Like Dostoevsky's dreamers and underground men, Ivan becomes narcissistically self-enclosed and hypersensitive to others' opinions. Alesha, by contrast, freely accepts others' care and reciprocates with gratitude and love. In like manner, they respond differently to metaphysical issues. Ivan and Alesha, shamed and unshamed, both wrestle, directly or indirectly, with Christ's kenoticism. As part of their early trials, the two brothers wrestle with metaphysical doubts occasioned by a stinker: Ivan with doubts raised by their half-brother Smerdiakov, literally "the stinker," Alesha with doubts raised by Zosima's stinking corpse.

Alesha's struggle with incarnation thus takes an indirect form. When Father Ferapont declares the elder's odor an outward sign of inward corruption, Alesha stumbles. Having expected miracles of Zosima's body, Alesha is stunned by the rapid decomposition that links it to the cycle of the natural world emphasized by the novel's epigraph.[1] The many parallels between Zosima and Christ in the novel, however, tie Zosima's stink directly to Christ's incarnation.[2] The elder's smell manifests his mortality, which he shares with the incarnate Christ. Slattery calls Zosima's stink "iconic, for it instills in the people of the town a remembrance that brings always to consciousness the words and deeds of the holy man, which certainly call to mind the prototype of Christ's life embodied and thus remembered in the old monk."[3] In having Zosima's stink recall Christ's death, Dostoevsky has Alesha struggle with a variant of the doubt Ippolit experiences in *The Idiot* after he reviews Holbein's Christ—after witnessing such an ignominious death, how could the disciples believe in Christ's divinity? In doubting his elder's holiness, Alesha, like his brother Ivan, wrestles with God.

While the story of Zosima allows Dostoevsky to present humility and love as two models for overcoming shame, the story of Ivan offers Dostoevsky the opportunity to provide another solution, one less discussed (if at all) by shame researchers and therapists: creativity.[4] In shaping Ivan, Dostoevsky drew on the thematics discussed in this book: fathers and children, divided selves, pretenders. He tackles his polemic on confession and intensifies his engagement in metaliterary play. But he also portrays a man grappling with the modern crisis of faith. Dostoevsky portrays Ivan's soul as the figurative battleground of God and the devil by revealing the workings of Ivan's unconscious—his nightmares and his writings. Mimetically, he portrays Ivan's struggle as his attraction to Alesha and his revulsion toward Smerdiakov. Thematically, he portrays Ivan's struggle as the conflict between the Christ of Ivan's Grand Inquisitor and the devil of Ivan's nightmare. Smerdiakov and the devil are on one side; Alesha and Ivan's Christ are on the other. Pairing Smerdiakov with Ivan's devil shows Dostoevsky's readers that the question of guilt raised by Smerdiakov troubles Ivan less than the question of shame raised by his devil.

Smerdiakov and the devil both dwell in Ivan's soul. Like Ivan's devil, Smerdiakov is a figure of embodied shame. Yet there are several critical differences between them. Most obviously, Smerdiakov is a real person over whom Ivan has no control, and the devil is the product of Ivan's creative unconscious. Less obviously, Smerdiakov has none of the devil's, or Fedor Karamazov's, redeeming features; in particular, he lacks their aesthetic sensibility. While both Fedor Karamazov and Ivan's devil revel in metaliterary hijinks, Smerdiakov cannot appreciate Golgol's work because he reads it literally. The most important difference, however, is that while Smerdiakov reminds Ivan of his shame, he stresses Ivan's guilt, something Ivan's devil does not even mention.

Ivan's devil is, as Ivan admits, "the embodiment of myself," but only of his shameful parts. Yet he acts as Ivan's conscience: he reflects Ivan back to himself; he reveals his secrets and his pride. Ivan's pride, his "I," is his stumbling block. Ivan's unconscious conjures up his devil in answer to his metaphysical questions, but he also attributes to his devil the most tormenting question: Will he go and inform on himself at the trial in order to act ethically? Or will he go in order to be praised for his self-sacrifice? The shame-ridden Ivan fears the latter. Not believing in God, he cannot believe in himself. Dostoevsky thus carefully fuses Ivan's self-doubt with his metaphysical doubt. Dostoevsky answers Ivan's question about the relationship of belief in God to ethical action by revealing Ivan's internal struggle.

In case readers have any doubt about the devil's actual existence, Dostoevsky provides evidence that he is, indeed, a figment of Ivan's imagination, the product of his troubled soul. First, once Ivan decides to testify against himself in court the next day, he feels joyful and acts ethically, that is, he rescues the peasant he had earlier knocked unconscious. Once he returns home rather than going to the police station, however, "something icy suddenly touched his heart, like a memory, or, rather, a reminder, of something tormenting and repulsive that was precisely in that room, now, and had been before" (15:69;634). Like the room of Dostoevsky's earlier self-tormenting intellectual, Raskolnikov, Ivan's room functions both mimetically and thematically: it is an actual place, the scene of his self-lacerating torments, and it is a symbolic place, his refuge and prison, a place that represents his self-enclosure. Like Raskolnikov, Ivan is full of shame. And like Raskolnikov, Ivan uses reason as a defense against that shame. While their consciences prompt them to right action, their minds rebel. Their rooms are scenes of self-inflicted torments. In returning to his room, Ivan returns to isolation, the prison-house of self, the devil's playground.

Dostoevsky further reinforces the idea that the devil is the product of Ivan's troubled soul with a gap in the text. Before Ivan's devil appears, the narrator notes that Ivan is on the verge of brain fever. When the devil informs Ivan that Alesha is tapping on his window, Ivan peevishly retorts that he already knew it. Then, when Alesha informs Ivan that Smerdiakov has killed himself, Ivan replies that he already knew that, his devil had told him. The devil did not, however. Ivan *knew* it the same way he *knew* that the tapping on his window was Alesha. In his fevered state, Ivan's unconscious speaks to him. As he tells Alesha, "He [the devil], by the way, told me a lot of truth about myself. I would never have said those things. You know, Alesha, you know . . . —I very much wish that he was actually *him*, and not I" (15:87;653). Although he is ill, Ivan recognizes that his devil is part of him. Ivan may dream that he throws a glass of tea at the devil, but the glass is still sitting on his table when Alesha arrives.

Finally, Dostoevsky shows readers that Alesha knows that Ivan is tormenting himself: "The torments of a proud decision, a deep conscience!" The narrator reinforces this observation, "God, in whom he did not believe, and his truth were overcoming his heart, which still did not want to submit" (15:89;655). Alesha sees how Ivan's illness manifests his internal battle. The words he uses indicate his diagnosis: Ivan's "decision" represents a conscious, mental act. That it is a "proud" decision indicates a state of mind, a mind self-consciously concerned with how others will perceive its decision. The other protagonist in Ivan's conflict is a "deep conscience," Ivan's unconscious, ethical self. The narrator thus provides readers with a clue: Ivan's pride suffers in advance for the shame he expects at the next day's trial. Ivan, "the grave," "the mystery," the self-enclosed intellectual, fears exposure, particularly public exposure. Yet he knows that to do the right thing he must expose himself. Ivan's mind resists submitting to God's will, even though his heart tells him that he must.

Readers can thus see how Christ's incarnation proves a true stumbling block for Ivan. He is proud. He fears public exposure. But he is a writer. Alesha and Dmitry have salvific dreams, whereas Ivan has hallucinations. Alesha dreams he is at the wedding feast of Cana of Galilee; Dmitry dreams that he is in a burnt-out village where the peasant women are homeless and a suckling infant cries from hunger. Ivan's unconscious bodies forth his shame. His devil embodies the connection between father and son (see last chapter), but he also reminds Ivan of the ways to escape his shame: confession to an empathic listener who has the power to forgive (Ivan's Christ; Alesha), creativity (Ivan's earlier writings), and humility (the incarnate Christ).

These three merge in Ivan's "Grand Inquisitor," a work that demonstrates how Christ proves a stumbling block for Ivan. If one clings to self and desires control, as Ivan's Inquisitor does, one cannot accept the kenotic Christ. Like his Inquisitor, Ivan is an intellectual seeker after truth. While Ivan's Inquisitor wants a god of miracle, mystery, and authority, Ivan wants a Miltonic Satan. Yet the Grand Inquisitor gets a kenotic Christ, and Ivan gets a shabby devil. Unlike the isolated Inquisitor, however, Ivan has an empathic brother, a guardian angel who rescues him from the predatory doubts and self-doubts raised by both Smerdiakov and his devil.

Ivan's writings and his hallucinations are forms of self-healing: they can help him escape shame's isolation. They function as forms of distancing self from self, of looking at self from the outside, of joining others to view self not as an object of derision but as a fellow sufferer. Like Ivan's Christ, Alesha offers healing through unconditional love and acceptance. Like Zosima's humility, Alesha's models right relations. Alesha's influence stems directly from his altruism: he can interact with proud, shame-sensitive others like his father, his brother Ivan, his beloved Lise, his reluctant pupil Kolya, because his "I" does not interfere. He finds the appropriate tone or approach because he has developed a keen sense of discretion-shame.

Significantly, Alesha repudiates Ivan's guilt as well as his shame. He denies Smerdiakov's claim that Ivan is guilty. Likewise, his arrival signals the devil's departure: Alesha thus drives away the embodiment of Ivan's shame. As Alesha watches and prays for his brother, he sees that Ivan has experienced a painful self-confrontation which leaves him with two choices: "Either he will rise into the light of truth, or . . . perish in hatred, taking revenge on himself and everyone for having served something he does not believe in" (15:89;655). Readers who have followed the careers of Dostoevsky's shame-ridden liars and intellectuals, characters such as General Ivolgin, Stepan Verkhovensky, and Rodion Raskolnikov, have hope for Alesha's brother.

In portraying shame, Dostoevsky hopes to change readers' vision. One of the Russian words for shame is *pozor* or spectacle. Dostoevsky relies on our voyeurism but also on our conscience. He puts shame on display, thereby scandalizing readers, flooding us with affect and the desire to flee. Dostoevsky's narrative strategy is thus risky. Readers who cannot bear the affective flooding flee, some never to return. Readers who remain, however, reap the rewards of full engagement. Dostoevsky plunges us into the ethical action of his texts. He arouses anxiety by breaking down the barriers between readers and characters, but he also offers relief from shame's pain. And he offers us emotional and intellectual pleasure. Relief comes in forms of intimacy or distance. Love and empathy break down barriers between individuals; laughter, confession, and forgetting create cognitive distance between the painful emotions and the self. Both intimacy and distance thus alleviate, or even heal, shame's pain. Dostoevsky helps us feel fully human by arousing the heartfelt joy of belonging to a community. But he also shares his intellectual interest in the world and the world of texts. He creates a mimetic world that displays its metaliterary construction, a world that makes us feel intensely, but one that makes us think equally intensely, a world of tears and laughter, despair and hope, a world that saddens yet beckons.

Dostoevsky creates scenes of shame that surprise yet rivet readers. He sharpens our self-consciousness—simultaneously grabbing us by the gut and galvanizing our intellect. By forcing us to directly experience our post-lapsarian state, Dostoevsky creates a sense of community for his readers. He thus exposes the private realm to foster public good. Exposed shame arouses visceral and cerebral responses that challenge us to know ourselves. It is not easy to love one's neighbor, as Ivan Karamazov says. But he also shows us that it is not easy to love one's self. Dostoevsky compellingly demonstrates that one must love self to love others. Whether we stay or flee, Dostoevsky's scenes of exposed shame remain with us, stir our ethical imaginations, inspire us. Dostoevsky surprises us by shame but leaves us a message of love.

notes

Notes to Introduction

1. Gerhart Piers and Milton Singer co-authored *Shame and Guilt: A Psychoanalytic and a Cultural Study* (1953); Helen Merrill Lynd wrote *Shame and the Search for Identity* (1958), a fundamental text for all shame researchers; and Helen Block Lewis contributed both *Shame and Guilt in Neurosis* (1971) and *Sex and the Superego* (1987), which show how shame's affective power is brought to bear on gender issues as well as on the study of shame itself. Some of the most useful shame studies include Francis Broucek, *Shame and the Self* (1991); Merle A. Fossum and Marilyn J. Mason, *Facing Shame: Families in Recovery* (1986); Gershen Kaufman, *The Psychology of Shame: Theory and Treatment of Shame-Based Syndromes* (1993); Michael Lewis, *Shame: The Exposed Self* (1992); Susan Miller, *The Shame Experience* (1993); Andrew Morrison, *Shame: The Underside of Narcissism* (1989); Donald L. Nathanson, *Shame and Pride: Affect, Sex and the Birth of the Self* (1992), and ed., *The Many Faces of Shame* (1987), and ed., *Knowing Feeling: Affect, Script and Psychotherapy* (1996); Carl Schneider, *Shame Exposure and Privacy* (1977; 1992); and Leon Wurmser, *The Mask of Shame* (1981).

2. Eve Kosofsky Sedgwick and Adam Frank, eds., *Shame and Its Sisters: A Silvan Tomkins Reader* (1995).

3. Adamson and Clark (1999, 1–33).

4. Velleman (2002, 27–52). Velleman provides an overview of philosophical discussions of shame in his footnote 2.

5. Sartre (1956).

6. Solov'ev (1996).

7. Levinas (1969, 1985).

Notes to Chapter 1

1. My discussion of scandal agrees with that of Malcolm Jones, who writes: "[W]e may say that a scandal may occur in Dostoyevsky's world when there is a radical threat to decorum. Decorum is a social device for maintaining power relationships within a social group by means of a system of stories which people tell about themselves and about each other in order to preserve the equilibrium and coherence of the group in relation both to

its parts and the world outside" (Jones 1990, 107). Fossum and Mason note the effect of scandals when they argue that crises provide individuals with a way to face their spiritual dimension (Fossum and Mason 1986, 160).

2. Russian thus follows the pattern of Greek (*aidos/aischyne*), French (*pudeur/honte*), and German (*Scham/Schande*), which have two words for shame, one or both associated with the genitals. Dal' also defines scandal as: "*soblazn, ponoshenie, nepristoinyi sluchai, postupok.*" *Soblazn* denotes "temptation"; *ponoshenie* "abuse" or "revilement"; and *nepristoinyi sluchai, postupok* "an obscene or indecent event, incident, action."

3. Citations are from F. M. Dostoevskii (1972–90). Volume and page number are given within parentheses. Although all translations of *The Idiot, The Diary of a Writer,* and Dostoevsky's letters are my own, for the benefit of non-Russian readers, I have supplied a second page number for Richard Pevear's and Larissa Volkhonsky's excellent translations of *The Brothers Karamazov* (1991) and *Demons* (1994), which I have modified as necessary.

4. See Introduction, footnote 1, for some of the most useful shame studies.

5. For a discussion of the role of inertia in Dostoevsky's works, see Knapp (1996).

6. In the memoir literature of the nineteenth century, there are repeated references to the upper classes' reverence for decorum. Nikitenko, for instance, writes in his *Diary* for 1839: "Such, however, are all members of the court. For them, decorum constitutes the highest moral law" (*Takovy, vprochem, vse tsaredvortsy. Dlia nikh, prilichie sostavliaet vysochaishii nravstvennyi zakon,* 214).

7. Fedor's response to Miusov's question about why he lies anticipates his son Dmitry's equally inconclusive response to the same question asked by the public prosecutor: "'Devil knows. In order to boast, perhaps . . . just so . . . that I squandered so much money that way. . . . In order, perhaps, to forget about that sewn-up money . . . yes, that's exactly it . . . devil . . . how many times will you ask the question? Well, I lied, and of course, once I lied I already didn't want to correct it. What does a person lie for sometimes?'" (14:447;496).

8. Schneider (1977, 34–35).

9. Jones (1984, 19).

10. For more on Potemkin villages, see Panchenko (1983, 93–104).

11. For the distinction between the mimetic, thematic, and synthetic components of a text, I am indebted to James Phelan's seminal study of the rhetorical interpretation of narrative, *Reading People, Reading Plots* (1989). Phelan defines "synthetic" as "that component of character directed to its role as artificial construction in the larger construction of the text; more generally, the constructedness of a text of an object."

12. Unfortunately, Pevear and Volokhonsky translate *pikantno* as "quaintly."

13. For a discussion of wit and sensuality in *The Brothers Karamazov* that starts with Freud and moves beyond, see Kostalevsky (2003).

14. The fourth voice continues, "But he made that up" (literally, "lied about that," *Tol'ko on eto sovral*) (15:151;723), thus giving readers a way to dismiss or otherwise come to terms with the charge that we are all the same as Fedor Pavlovich.

15. Meerson makes a similar claim by discussing the tabooing of Smerdiakov as the fourth brother in *The Brothers Karamazov*. See Meerson (1998, chap. 6).

16. Dostoevsky's works have always generated controversy. From his contemporary Mikhailovsky, who labeled him "a cruel talent," to Henry James, who labeled his works "fluid puddings," to D. H. Lawrence, who complained that "The Grand Inquisitor" chapter of *The Brothers Karamazov* was a piece of "cynical-satanical showing-off," to Cynthia

Ozick, who wrote about "Dostoevsky the Unabomber," critics have been uncomfortable with the form and content of his works.

17. Cohen (1999).

18. As Robert Jackson observes, "The moral-aesthetic spectrum of Dostoevsky begins with *obraz*—image, the form and embodiment of beauty—and ends with *bezobrazie*—literally that which is 'without image,' shapeless, disfigured, ugly. Man finds pleasure (he also calls it beauty) in *bezobrazie*, in the disfiguration of himself and others, in cruelty, violence, and above all, sensuality—and 'sensuality is always violence.' Aesthetically, *bezobrazie* is the deformation of ideal form. The humanization of man is the creating of an image, the creating of form (the verb *obrazit'*). God created man in his own image. All violence against man is a dehumanization—a deformation, finally of the divine image" (Jackson 1966, 58).

19. In heterodiegetic narration, the narrator exists at a different level of (fictional) existence from the characters. An example of this is omniscient, third-person narration, such as that in *Crime and Punishment*. Im homodiegetic narration, the narrator exists at the same level of existence as the characters. Mr. G-v, narrator-chronicler of *Demons*, exemplifies homodiegetic narration. When characters tell stories, they too act as homodiegetic narrators. Definitions taken from Phelan (1996, 217)

20. Newton (1995, 13).

21. I take the terms "disgrace-shame" and "discretion-shame" from Schneider, who draws on the distinction between two French words for shame—*pudeur* and *honte*. Characterizing *pudeur* as a sense of shame felt before an action, warning against it, and *honte* as a shame response after an act that harms, hurts, or soils, he calls the first a sense of discretion-shame and the second a sense of being ashamed or disgrace-shame (Schneider 1977, 18).

22. I take the terms "narrative" and "authorial" audiences from Rabinowitz (1987, 93–104).

23. Phelan (1996, 27).

24. I use the distinctions that Michael Lewis, a developmental and clinical psychologist, makes between two kinds of knowledge: objective self-awareness and knowledge about standards, rules, and goals (Lewis 1992, 86).

25. While shame scholars use different terminology, the concept of measuring one's actual self/one's "I" against an ideal self is fairly standard. The classic psychoanalytic terms are "ego" and "ego ideal."

26. Bakhtin identifies this sequence as one that encompasses and interprets the aleatory sequence in what he calls "the adventure novel of everyday life" (Bakhtin 1981, 118).

27. Gershen Kaufman, for example, holds that shame about shame has made shame a cultural taboo in American society (Kaufman 1989, 4). Olga Meerson discusses taboos that are rooted both in shame and in guilt in her excellent book, *Dostoevsky's Taboos* (1998).

28. Here I combine Michael Lewis's distinction between the two kinds of knowledge with Carl Schneider's distinction between the functions of shame.

29. Various shame scholars have identified these functions as superego function (psychoanalysts), moral shame (affect theorists), and conscience (Solovev and other religious thinkers).

30. This observation I owe to Leslie A. Johnson (1991, 867–78). Adam Newton, who, like Johnson, draws on the work of Emmanuel Levinas, also notes the importance of faces for identity, as do the shame scholars Carl Schneider and Leon Wurmser.

31. The Russian translation of the Bible that Dostoevsky knew uses the phrase *vozhdeleno potomu chto daet znanie* ("desired because it gives knowledge"). The participle *vozhdeleno* derives from the verb *vozhdelet'*, which means "to long for" or "to lust after."

Notes to Chapter 2

1. In her work on *The Idiot* and *The Brothers Karamazov*, Robin Feuer Miller demonstrates how Dostoevsky implicates readers in the moral action of the text. See her books, *Dostoevsky and The Idiot: Author, Narrator, and Reader* (1981) and *The Brothers Karamazov: Worlds of the Novel* (1992).
2. For this formulation I am indebted to Caryl Emerson.
3. Frank (1986, 12–13).
4. Interestingly, Makar Devushkin blames Gogol for exposing Makar's shameful economic secrets in "The Overcoat." See Makar's letter of July 8 (1:63).
5. Matveyev (1995, 535–51).
6. Bakhtin (1989).
7. Meerson examines Dostoevsky's use of the narrative device of treating a topic as a taboo. As she demonstrates, in each novel the different characters all have their own personal "sore spots," which are revealed in their interactions. In *Crime and Punishment*, for example, Dostoevsky constantly italicizes the demonstrative pronoun *eto* ("that thing"). While other characters use the demonstrative pronoun innocently, Raskolnikov always interprets it as a signifier for his crime. His interactions with others thus reveal his sense of guilt to Dostoevsky's readers (though not necessarily to Raskolnikov's interlocutors). Through examination of various taboos in Dostoevsky's work (hell in *Notes from the House of the Dead*, cuckoldry in *The Eternal Husband*, murder in *Crime and Punishment*, love and death in *The Idiot*, devils in *Demons*, Smerdiakov's brother status in *The Brothers Karamazov*), Meerson uncovers values and ideas important for Dostoevsky's own value system. While she describes a broad panorama of authorial and characterological taboos, not all of these are shame spots. The motivation for tabooing in Dostoevsky is nonetheless strikingly dependent on the tabooer's own sore spot and/or point of shame (Meerson 1998).
8. See Martinsen (2001, 51–70).
9. "But it is possible that experiences of shame if confronted full in the face may throw an unexpected light on who one is and point the way toward who one may become. Fully faced, shame may become not primarily something to be covered, but a positive experience of revelation" (Lynd 1958, 20). In his most recent book, Andrew Morrison (1996, 194) agrees that alleviating shame requires awareness of shame followed by self-acceptance.
10. Austen (1988, 208).
11. Almond and Almond (1996, 39–40).
12. Lewis (1987, 186).
13. Fear-flight, concealment-immobility, and anger-aggression are common defenses against shame (Schneider 1992, 30).
14. Lynd (1958, 50). Shame, because it is about identity, cannot easily be undone. Guilt, on the other hand, involves a transgressive action, which can then be attenuated or expiated by a compensatory action.
15. Lynd (1958, 64).
16. Mary Douglas (1996) has written about the power of those who shame by naming, excluding, or compartmentalizing.
17. Lynd (1958, 236). Dostoevsky's story "The Dream of the Ridiculous Man" opens,

"I am a ridiculous man. They call me crazy now." Though in Russian it is possible to express this impersonally, without using a pronoun, Dostoevsky pointedly uses the third person plural pronoun (*Oni menia nazyvaiut teper' sumashedshim*), thereby emphasizing the existence of the ridiculous man's detractors and his sense of connection to them.

18. I base my discussion here on Irina Reyfman's masterful cultural study of the honor code and its representation in Russian literature (Reyfman 1999).

19. Solov'ev (1996).

20. Schneider (1987, 198–200). Schneider continues his discussion of the Indo-European root *(s)*kem*-, *(s)*kam*- by noting that it "gives us not only our English word *shame*, but the Italian word *camera* (a little room, and therefore something hidden) which becomes the English *camera* (a little room which reveals); the French *chemise*, and the German *Hemd*, all involving covering or protection. Even more fascinating, the word for shame in Lithuanian derives from a second Indo-European root *(s)*que*-, *(s)*qewa*-, also meaning 'to cover,' from which root have descended our English words *custody, hide, house, hut, shoe,* and *sky*."

21. Arutiunova (1997, 59–70). Dostoevsky's narrator in *The Idiot* comments on Prince Myshkin's "freeze" response to shame: "A new, unbearable wave of shame [*styda*], almost despair, riveted him to the spot, before the very entrance to the gates. He stopped for a minute. It sometimes happens to people that way: unbearable, sudden memories, especially compounded with shame, usually stop them, for one minute, on the spot" (8:194).

22. Schneider (1992, 18–19).

23. In *Crime and Punishment,* Dostoevsky illustrates this poignantly with the plight of Sonia Marmeladova, who literally must move out of the family space once she becomes a prostitute.

24. Solov'ev (1996, 88).

25. Wurmser (1981, 65).

26. For a fuller discussion of the dynamics of second-person narration, see Phelan (1996, chap. 7, 135–53). In Dostoevsky's work, of course, there are plenty of cases where readers are implicated in the ethical action of the text without being addressed directly.

27. Some of the best studies of Dostoevsky's *Diary* writer are: Gary Saul Morson, "Introductory Study: Dostoevsky's Great Experiment," in *A Writer's Diary,* vol. 1, 1873–1876, translated and annotated by Kenneth Lantz, (1993, 1–117) V. A. Tunimanov, "Khudozhestvennye proizvedeniia v *Dnevnike pisatelia* F. M. Dostoevskogo" (dissertation Leningrad State University, 1965), and "Publitsistika Dostoevskogo: *Dnevnik pisatelia,*" in *Dostoevskii Khudozhnik i myslitel': sbornik stat'ei*, (1972, 165–209); I. L. Volgin, *Dostoevskii—Zhurnalist (Dnevnik pisatelia i russkaia obshchestvennost')* (1982); and T. V. Zakharova, "*Dnevnik pisatelia* i ego mesto v tvorchestve F. M. Dostoevskogo 1870-kh godov" (dissertation Leningrad State University, 1974).

28. If a reader interprets Dostoevsky's text, because it exemplifies hyperbole, to misrepresent in some degree the beliefs of Dostoevsky the author, then the reader imputes to the text a type of self-referentiality known since antiquity by philosophers as that which appears in the Liar Paradox. The Liar Paradox appears in numerous forms; one of the earliest is attributed to Epimenides, a Cretan, who supposedly uttered the statement, "All Cretans are liars." Had it been the case that he spoke truly, then what he said was false, and had he spoken falsely, then what he said was true. The Liar Paradox's self-referentiality and that in Dostoevsky's text differ in two ways. First, the Liar Paradox is explicitly self-referential, while Dostoevsky's is implicitly so. Second, the Liar Paradox assumes, in its self-reference, that a statement must be simply true or simply false. Dostoevsky's text, however,

contains no similar assumption: the text allows for many degrees of truth. It thus opens up questions of motive and interpretation.

29. Singer and Salovey (1993, 13).

30. For my understanding of the concept of bullshit, I am deeply indebted to Harry Frankfurt's insightful and witty analysis in his article, "On Bullshit." Harry G. Frankfurt, "On Bullshit" (1989).

31. The nineteenth-century lexicographer Vladimir Dal' defines *lgat'* as *vrat', govorit' ili pisat' lozh', nepravdu, protivnoe istine* and *vrat'* as *lgat', obmanyvat' slovami, oblyzhnichat', govorit' nepravdu, vopreki istine; govorit' vzdor, nebylitsu, pustiaki; pustoslovit', pustobaiat', molot' iazykom; khvastat', skazyvat' nebyval'shchinu za pravdu* (Dal' 1978–80).

32. Dostoevsky also uses interchangeably the nouns that derive from the verb *lgat'* and that are closely related to the verb *vrat'—lgan'yo, lgun—*with those derived from the verb *vrat'—vran'yo, vrun*. I translate the nouns *lgan'yo/vran'yo* mostly as "lying," but also as "lie," and the nouns *vrun/lgun* as "liar."

33. The Russian word for crime, *prestuplenie*, derives from the verb *perestupit'*, which literally means stepping over or transgressing.

34. Twain (1882, 220).

35. Social inexperience can also contribute to intolerance. Dostoevsky points this out in *Raw Youth*, where he has Versilov scold Arkady for attempting to interrupt his landlord's tall tale:

> "What's the matter with you? . . . In this pitiful milieu, it's impossible to live without such stories. They have many of them. Most important—it's from their lack of self-restraint. They never learned anything, don't know anything really well, and, well, he wanted to talk about something more universal, more poetic than cards and factories. . . . Who is he anyway, this Peter Ippolitovich?"
>
> "The poorest of creatures, even unfortunate."
>
> "You see, he, perhaps, doesn't even play cards! I repeat, by telling you this nonsense, he satisfies his love for his neighbors: he even wanted to make us happy. His patriotism is also satisfied. . . ." (13:167)

36. This statement also serves as Dostoevsky's self-defense against charges that his writing suffers from the fantastic.

37. See Dostoevsky's 1876 *Diary* article, "Golden Age in a Pocket" (*Zolotoi vek v karmane*) (21:12–13).

38. Frankfurt (1989, 124). Warren Kinston also illuminates the dynamics of mindlessness:

> The state of self-protection, which Freud referred to as "the stone wall" of narcissism, has a number of interesting features. The adjective "mindless" fits well, because idiosyncratic meaning cannot be assigned to situations, and sensitivity to feelings is replaced by social convention or absent altogether. The individual may therefore act in ways that show his or her lack of consideration of others or a lack of concern for himself. Such behavior destroys relationships. In the self-protective, mindless state, a person cannot grow or develop insofar as this refers to the enrichment and increasing complexity of emotional understanding. The immediate consequences of self-protection are equally serious: continuity and persistence in efforts is weak because actions are not driven by the inner coherence of the self; commitment cannot be given or counted on; decisions concerning the person's own life or future are avoided; and all significant activity is driven by expedience, wishes

to fit the expectations of others, and social conventions. The individual inevitably denies his or her own needs, experiences confusion, and becomes confused with those about him or her. (Kinston 1987, 220)

39. Fans of Baron von Munchausen are familiar with this kind of aesthetic pleasure.

40. Frankfurt (1989, 125).

41. Frankfurt (1989, 130).

42. Though Peter Verkhovensky has much in common with *vruny*—lack of self-esteem, for instance—he uses *vran'yo* as a deliberate rhetorical strategy to serve his political ends (as well as his self-aggrandizement).

43. Frankfurt (1989, 128–29).

44. Frankfurt (1989, 130–31).

45. Frankfurt never provides a specific motive for bullshitting. That is beyond the task of his essay, which is to analyze the concept of bullshit. But he does say, "It is correct to say of bullshit . . . , that those who perpetuate it misrepresent themselves in a certain way" (121). He writes that "the participants [in a bull-shit session] try out various thoughts . . . in order to discover how others respond . . . without it being assumed that they are committed to what they say" (126). This indicates a concern for self-presentation. When speculating on the reason for the prevalence of bullshit, he notes that in modernity there is more scepticism about the objective world, but this leads to the ideal of correctness vis-à-vis subjectivity. Authenticity or sincerity is now an ideal in communication. But "Our natures are . . . less stable and less inherent than the natures of other things. Insofar as this is the case, sincerity itself is bullshit" (133). These citations suggest that Frankfurt would agree that one motive for bullshitting would very often be to present oneself in a more favorable light than the bullshitter believes is warranted.

46. See his story, "Dream of a Ridiculous Man," in which lying is the first sin.

47. This is not to say that Dostoevsky's female characters never engage in fantasy or fanciful recollection. Katerina Marmeladova remembers her past fondly, especially the shawl dance, an incident she embroiders in recollecting. Marya Lebiadkina fancies Stavrogin to be a prince and fabricates a baby. Katerina's embroidered memories are hyperbolic and idealized, but Marya's status as a holy fool takes her out of the realm of liars.

48. Earlier in this century, Merezhkovsky pointed out that Khlestakov is a literary character who imitates literature (Merezhkovsky 1974, 64).

49. Lotman (1985, 150–87).

50. Morrison (1989, 66).

51. Ekman (1988, 89).

52. Lotman (1985, 153).

53. Dostoevsky was keenly aware of adolescent conflicts, as seen in his 1875 novel *Podrostok* (variously translated *The Adolescent* or *Raw Youth*).

54. Rousseau (1979, 80).

55. See Miller (1979, 89–101).

56. Rousseau (1979, 65).

57. Ibid., p. 70.

58. Ibid., p. 69.

59. Ibid., p. 71.

60. See Fermon (1997). Rousseau makes this argument in his "Second préface de *La Nouvelle Héloïse*," *Oeuvres complètes*, tom 8, 18 (1823).

61. Rousseau (1979, 73) also uses the adjective "criminal" to describe a lie that adversely affects another person.

62. What Dostoevsky identified as the "innocent" quality of liars also comes from their interest in the present (the moment upon which epideictic speeches bear) and their disregard for both past and future. Dostoevsky's liars, like Khlestakov, the archetypal Russian *vrun*, lie unpremeditatively to represent themselves as individuals who merit honor and respect.

63. Frankfurt (1989, 125).

64. Rousseau's *Confessions* clearly shocked and shock their readers because he is so open not about guilty matters, which readers expect, but about shameful matters, which embarrass his readers. Interesting essays on Dostoevsky's polemics with Rousseau's *Confessions* include R. L. Belknap, "The Unrepentant Confession," in his edited collection *Russianness* (1990), 113–23; J. M. Coetzee, "Confession and Double Thoughts: Tolstoy, Rousseau, Dostoevsky" (1985); Leonid Grossman, "Stilistika Stavrogina," in *Dostoevskii: Stat'i i materialy* (1924); Barbara Howard, "The Rhetoric of Confession: Dostoevskij's *Notes from Underground*" (1986); Iurii Lotman, "Russo: russkaia kul'tura XVIII–nachala XIX veka," in his *Russkaia literatura: kul'tura Prosveshcheniia*, vol. 1 (1998); and Robin Feuer Miller, "Dostoevsky and Rousseau: The Morality of Confession Reconsidered" (see note 56).

65. Dostoevsky's position on women's altruism strongly resembles Rousseau's. While in Paris, Rousseau's experiences led him to view women as the only humans who help others.

66. Rousseau (1979, 73).

67. Ibid., 80.

68. He coopts his opponent's rhetorical strategy particularly effectively in his February 1876 coverage of the Kroneberg trial (22:50–73). *A Writer's Diary*, vol. 1, 356–86.

69. Occasionally, exhibitionist liars can do unintentional harm. In discussing the Kroneberg affair in 1876, the *Diary* writer uses a popular Russian proverb to express the ethical consequences of trying to impress one's audience: "[F]or a pretty turn of phrase/ 'one spares neither mother nor father'" (*dlia krasnogo slovtsa/ 'ne pozhaleesh' materi i otsa*" (22:54). The *Diary* writer deems hyperbole and plagiarism natural forms of human expression but condemns eloquence achieved at another's expense.

70. Webb (1993).

71. In Levinasian terms, the idea of Infinity. See Levinas (1969, 210).

72. Interestingly, Dostoevsky associates this kind of mindless speaking with being a bird, and the names of three of the five liars I discuss derive from birds' names: Ivolgin (oriole) and Lebedev and Lebiadkin (swan).

73. Helen Block Lewis (1987, 192) notes that shame is experienced relatively nonverbally. It is undergone primarily as imagery, particularly in the mode of looking at or being looked at. The reaction described by the *Diary* writer also resembles Myshkin's discomfiture and wordless gaze when he listens to the stories of Ivolgin, or even Lebedev.

74. Dostoevsky's ability to turn a short newspaper announcement into a fictional masterpiece is also evidenced in what he does with the newspaper paragraph about the young woman who leapt out of a fourth floor window holding an icon. See "The Meek One" (sometimes translated as "The Gentle Creature"), *Diary of a Writer*, November 1876.

75. The *Diary* writer articulates this in his article: "The task of travelling pleasantly and merrily on our rail system consists in the ability to allow others to lie and to believe as much as possible; then you will also be given the chance to concoct lies effectively, if you are so tempted; therefore, a mutual advantage" (21:122).

76. See Finke (1995) for a discussion of *The Idiot* as a "meditation on the practice and pitfalls of authoring."

77. I believe that Dostoevsky's polemic with Rousseau's *Confessions* arose, in part, from

Dostoevsky's negative valuation of Rousseau's motives. What Dostoevsky perceives as Rousseau's narcissism impedes his effectiveness with Dostoevsky the reader.

78. Martin Amis dismisses the charge that Nabokov "got carried away" while writing *Lolita*: "Great writers, however, never get carried away. Even pretty average writers never get carried away" (Amis 1992, 110–11).

79. Wurmser (1981, 65).

80. The term "focalization," originating with Gerard Genette, is used to distinguish between the one who speaks (the narrator) and the one who sees (the narrator or a character). In this scene, the narrator speaks, while Prince Myshkin serves as the focalizer (Genette 1980).

81. For the discussion of epideictic rhetoric that follows, I have used the following sources: Aristotle, *The "Art" of Rhetoric*, translated by J. H. Freese (1947); George Kennedy, *The Art of Persuasion in Greece* (1963); Ch. Perelman and L. Olbrechts-Tyteca, *The New Rhetoric: A Treatise on Argumentation* (1969); Walter H. Beale, "Rhetorical Performative Discourse: A New Theory of Epideictic" (1978):221–46; Michael F. Carter, "The Ritual Functions of Epideictic Rhetoric: The Case of Socrates' Funeral Oration" (1991); Bernard K. Duffy, "The Platonic Functions of Epideictic Rhetoric" (1983); and Christine Oravec, "'Observation' in Aristotle's Theory of Epideictic" (1976).

82. Oravec (1976, 171); Carter (1991, 219–20); Duffy (1983, 87).

83. *Podrostok* (13:165–68). Versilov's landlord tells a story about a boulder in the road that Russian peasants inexpensively leveled overnight after English engineers estimated a long and costly procedure. Arkady objects that the boulder is still there. Versilov admonishes him to be more charitable, to allow the landlord the pleasure of both telling his story and indulging his patriotism. Such anecdotes are similar to tall tales, which often have many variants and serve to promote or reinforce group identity. See Brown (1987, 22, 33).

84. In Lynd's terms, lack of good manners is a cause for shame: "Nothing comparable covers lack of beauty or grace, errors of taste and congruence, weakness and certain kinds of failure, feelings of meanness or envy, rejection of the gift of oneself—situations that are experienced as exposure of deeply personal inadequacy" (1958, 64).

85. Dostoevsky has also been read as the postmaster, someone who exposes others' secrets while attempting to suppress his own. See Breger (1989, 1–12).

86. Helen Block Lewis (1987, 197).

Notes to Chapter 3

1. Gasparov (1992, 83–117).

2. Ivolgin's narcissistically projected depiction of Napoleon bears strong similarities to Leo Tolstoy's famous depiction of a self-centered Napoleon who expects Russia, and her "boyars," to conform to his preconceived, narcissistic image (*War and Peace*, Book 11, Chapter 10). While it is interesting to speculate that Dostoevsky might have been responding to Tolstoy's novel, the relevant section of *War and Peace* was probably at the publisher's, but not in print, at the time Dostoevsky wrote Ivolgin's fabricated story. Tolstoy and Dostoevsky most likely had the same sources as well as a similar agenda in portraying Napoleon as a self-absorbed foreign invader. See Orwin (1999, 87–102).

3. Dostoevsky read the early parts of Tolstoy's novel, which appeared with the title "The Year 1805" in *The Russian Messenger* (*Russkii vestnik*) in 1865/66. He considered it a "most important thing" (Orwin 1999, 97).

4. Dostoevsky further double-voices Ivolgin's account of Napoleon. In his story, Ivol-

gin has Napoleon pay homage to Catherine the Great: "I only remember that, entering the first hall, the Emperor suddenly stopped in front of a portrait of Empress Catherine, looked at it for a long time pensively, and finally uttered: 'That was a great woman!' and walked past" (8:413). Though it was obligatory in Napoleon stories to have the Emperor pay homage to something Russian, I wondered why Catherine. My thanks to Christina Shperrle and Gina Kovarsky for pointing out that Catherine was not only a ruler of foreign birth who became a symbol of national pride, but also an avid memoir writer.

5. Al'mi (1992, 167).

6. Dostoevsky will later use Zosima's evocation of Joseph and his brothers to emphasize the issue of brotherly betrayal. See *The Brothers Karamazov*, 14:266.

7. Nina Perlina (1985, 50) notes that Dostoevsky has Fedor Pavlovich use open and reaccented quotations to introduce the theme of demonic obsession. Diane Thompson (1991, 15) argues that Fedor travesties the Bible. Meerson insightfully argues that "when Dostoevsky cites or stylizes the Scriptures directly, without transforming either the style or the context, he aims much less at conveying a pious message, or correlating his message with that of the Bible, than when he actually 'distorts' the style of the Biblical intertext. . . . Like many sacred realities, Biblical quotes in Dostoevsky often are preserved as sacred only if their direct, uncorrupted version is tabooed. Interestingly, even travesty violates this taboo to a lesser extent than the direct quotation" (Meerson 1998, 188). Following Meerson's lead, I look at this passage as one where Dostoevsky throws up a smokescreen of scandal to characterize Fedor Pavlovich, yet he invites readers to examine the content of Fedor's speech.

8. See "Vospominaniia peterburgskogo starozhila," *Birzhivye vedomosti* no. 83 (30 March 1873). "Petersburgskii starozhi" was the pseudonym of the journalist Vladimir Petrovich Burnashev.

9. The lexicographer V. Dal' lists *karamazyi*, giving as its definition *chernomazyi*. See text and note 14 for discussion of *maz*.

10. Passage (1982, 94).

11. A. M. Dostoevskii (1892, 104).

12. Bruce Lincoln (1990) identifies the tension between *proizvol* ("arbitrary power") and *zakonnost'* ("lawful order") as one that governed Russian life from the time of Catherine II on. Chapter One recounts how Catherine's attempts to impose lawful order from above by encouraging limited public discussion of civic affairs laid the basis for this tension.

13. Sigmund Freud, *Totem and Taboo* (1950).

14. I have taken the nineteenth-century meanings of these words from Dal's dictionary (Dal' 1978-80, 2:288–9). In nineteenth-century Novgorodian slang, *maz'* also denoted "a lover." Novgorod was across Lake Il'men from Dostoevsky's summer home in Staraia Russa, the place where he wrote and in which he set the action of *The Brothers Karamazov*. This meaning may thus have been known to Dostoevsky, who was an avid collector of regional speech.

15. Belknap (1989, 26–31) demonstrates how Dostoevsky creates a cluster of attributes that make up Karamazovism: vileness, lechery, half-wittedness, and a thirst for life.

16. Blank, (2000, 101–116).

17. Vetlovskaia (1976, 320–21).

18. Stepan Verkhovensky, also a father who strays, initially announces to Sophia Ulitina, "In expounding it [the Bible] orally, it is possible to correct the mistakes of this remarkable book, which I, of course, am prepared to treat with great respect" (10:491;645).

19. As Meerson notes, Fedor Karamazov uses the Church Slavonic wording *lozh'l* "lie" instead of the modern Russian *lzhets* / "liar." Fedor claims to be *lozh'l* "a lie" and *otets lzhi*/ "a father of lies." In the modern Russian of the Bible that Dostoevsky knew, Christ says of the devil: *On lzhets i otets lzhi* ("He is a liar and the father of lies"). Meerson's current research details how Dostoevsky used his knowledge of the difference between Church Slavonic, which is used in Orthodox liturgies, and the modern Russian of the translated Bible to manipulate readers' unconscious responses.

20. Meerson and Morson argue that Dostoevsky intentionally troubles readers by persistently locating Smerdiakov as the fourth "brother" (Meerson 1998, Chap. 6; Morson 1986, 234–42).

21. Belknap (1967, 71–74).

Notes to Chapter 4

1. I borrow the term "progression" from James Phelan, who defines it as "the movement of a narrative from beginning to end and the principles governing that movement. Progression exists along two simultaneous axes: the internal logic of the narrative text and the set of responses that logic generates in the authorial audience as it reads from beginning to end. Though this description focuses on the movement of narrative through time from beginning to end, a concern with progression is more than a concern with narrative as linear process, precisely because it recognizes the dynamic, recursive relationships among the authorial audience's understanding of beginning, middle, and end" (Phelan 1996, 219).

2. Lotman (1985, 164).

3. General Ivolgin is a homodiegetic narrator, that is, he exists at the same level of the text as the characters to whom he tells his story. Phelan points out that homodiegetic narration is normally naive or unself-conscious: "One of the conventions of homodiegetic narration is that unselfconscious narration is the unmarked case: that is, we take the homodiegetic narrator as unselfconscious unless we are given reason to do otherwise. Thus, we assume that the homodiegetic narrator is not the source of such things as foreshadowing, patterns of imagery, parallelism of incidents, the lyricism of a particular style—unless we have some signal that calls our attention to the narrator's self-consciousness" (Phelan 1996, 81).

4. When he makes his claim that Pirogov quits Sevastopol for a while, Ivolgin is historically accurate. In June 1855, Pirogov left Sevastopol for Petersburg, returning only in September. But in citing himself as the motive for that action, Ivolgin is rewriting history. Pirogov went to Petersburg to draw the high command's attention to the neglect of their wounded.

5. Gogol's Pirogov attempts to seduce a German locksmith's wife, is soundly whipped by her husband, and reacts indignantly, but eating a pastry distracts him from his intention to report his humiliation. In his 1873 article on lying, Dostoevsky wrote,

> Lieutenant Pirogov . . . was a terribly prophetic figure, the prophecy of a genius who had foreseen the future with dreadful insight, for there are a countless number of these Pirogovs, so many that one cannot whip them all. Remember that immediately after the incident the lieutenant ate a puff-pastry and that same evening made a great impression dancing the mazurka at the birthday party of a certain eminent official. What do you think: when he was cutting capers on the dance floor and straining his so recently abused

limbs to perform the steps, was he thinking of how he had been whipped only two hours earlier? Certainly he was thinking of that. And was he ashamed? Certainly he was not! When he woke up the next morning he probably said to himself: "Ah, to hell with it! What's the point of starting anything if no one will find out?" This "What's the point of starting anything" suggests, on the one hand, a great capacity to come to terms with virtually anything and, at the same time, such a breadth of our Russian nature that before such qualities even the Unlimited grows pale and dims. Two hundred years of being unaccustomed to even the slightest independence of character and two hundred years of despising one's own Russian face have stretched the Russian conscience to such fatal dimensions, from which . . . well, what do you think you could expect from it?" (21:124–25) (Dostoevskii 1993–94, 277–28)

6. Morrison (1989, 7).

7. Dostoevsky takes the name Novozemliansky from Griboedov's *Gore ot uma* (act 3, scene 12), thus underscoring its fictional nature. The name Novozemliansky, literally "new world," further underscores the thematics of death and resurrection.

8. See Meerson (1995) for a more complete discussion of the implications of being a witness.

9. Ivolgin's preoccupation with being judged also reveals his narcissistic self-absorption. His irresponsible actions harm others—his family and the widow Terentev's family—but he acts surprised when they hold him responsible. He thus fails to understand why he is thrown into debtor's prison for issuing false promissory notes to the widow. Until his debts threaten her family's existence, the widow accepts him as the man in the family and treats him as a provider. The General's theft from Lebedev must thus be seen as an act designed to restore his badly damaged self-esteem and to restore, if only partially, his role as head of household.

10. Dostoevsky clearly intended some authorial pun here, as Epanchin's last name derives from *epancha*, the word for cloak.

11. See Harriet Murav's (1992, 130–35) discussion of prefigurement as a narrative strategy.

12. Miller (1981, 166) points out that Dostoevsky was an "inveterate user of the inserted narrative," which he used as analogues to the main action, in contrast to Western novelists like Cervantes and Fielding, who used them to create contrasts with the main action.

13. See Murav (1992, 150–69) for a discussion of recapitulation as a critical narrative strategy.

14. See Meerson (1995) for the theological implications.

15. Perhaps Dostoevsky is trying to evoke the image of Diderot here, with Lebedev cast as Rameau's nephew.

16. Dostoevsky underlines the father-son connection by having Ivolgin's son Gania raise his hand to slap his sister. Prince Myshkin's intervention, which makes him the slap's recipient, further underscores the social impropriety of this violent behavior.

17. Belknap (1990, 81). Belknap cautions that such loading is not automatic, for Dostoevsky can also load memory negatively, as in Varvara Stavrogina's lifelong grudge against Stepan Verkhovensky.

18. Significantly, those closest to him—Lebedev, Gania, and Kolia—blame the General's drinking on the widow, thus colluding with the General, who does not acknowledge the connection between his drinking and his shame. See Lewis (1971, 233–50).

19. The General has fallen so far that he differentiates little between Nastasia Filippovna and Aglaia Epanchina as audiences. Once he has an audience, he starts his work of self-presentation. Only in Book Four does he consciously choose an audience—Myshkin.

20. Miller does not use the terms "narrative" and "authorial" audiences, which I borrow from Peter Rabinowitz, but she does speak of both: "The crucial point, however, is that the actual or real reader of the novel is concurrently both readers—the narrator's reader and the implied reader. He recognizes the simultaneous responses of both within him at this moment of their clear divergence: that is, one reader condemns and the other forgives Myshkin. Through the mechanism of reading the real reader undergoes an experience parallel to that of the characters" (Miller 1981, 156).

21. Miller (1981, 89).

22. *Russkii arkhiv* no. 4 (1864):416–34.

23. Nazirov argues convincingly that Elena Shtakenshneider's uncle and nephew, Fedor Lavrent'evich Kholchinskii and Kolia Shtakenshneider, may well have been the real-life prototypes for Ivolgin and Kolia. Dostoevsky visited the Shtakenshneiders almost every Saturday after his return to Petersburg in 1860. Kholchinskii was an amusing raconteur, a civilian general who never served in combat, though he claimed to have seen action in a number of campaigns. Interestingly, his niece believed all of his stories (Nazirov 1974, 209–12). Having multiple real-life prototypes for his characters is typical for Dostoevsky.

24. Makar Devushkin suffers agonies over a popped button. The underground man exults when he obtains the proper collar for his coat, since it would allow him to bump/challenge the officer without shaming himself. Katerina Marmeladova covets Sonia's lace collars. The list of examples is endless.

25. For an insightful discussion of how Russia's rulers used ceremonies to create and enhance their self-images, see Wortman (1995). As Wortman notes, Alexander I particularly loved military reviews and great parades. "He followed the Napoleonic model of making military displays, and military men, aesthetic objects" (Wortman 1995, 205).

26. Alexander did, in fact, move to St. Petersburg, but at his generals' orders.

27. J. M. Thompson (1988, 316).

28. As Al'mi points out, the Prince's words echo Pushkin's *chto chuvstva dobrye ia liroi probuzhdal* ("that I aroused good feelings with my lyre") (Al'mi 1992, 171).

29. Instead of inscribing some sentimental or romantic verses, Khlestakov quotes the opening lines of Lomonosov's ode, "Excerpts from Job": "O, you man, who in grief murmurs in vain against God." Lomonosov (1961, 139).

30. In chapter 2, I discuss the fact that Lebedev claims Ivolgin for a brother-in-law. Lebedev's wife dies in childbirth five weeks before the action of Book Two. If his wife was actually Ivolgin's sister, then the putative document would be in Lebedev's possession.

31. "True, at another time, he, of course, would have borne something even much more humiliating than the news about the complete nonexistence of Kapiton Eropegov, would have screamed, created a scene, lost a grip on himself, but nonetheless in the end would have removed himself upstairs to his room to sleep. But now, because of the incredible strangeness of the human heart, it so happened that precisely such an offense as the doubt about Eropegov perforce ran his cup over" (8:396).

32. Miller (1998, 118–27).

33. Lebedev identifies Ivolgin as a sick man in need of treatment: "Sensitivity and tenderness alone, alone—that's all the medicine our sick man needs. You, Prince, will allow me to consider him a sick man?" (8:375).

34. Miller (1981, 187).

Notes to Chapter 5

1. Miller (1981, 11–45).

2. These terms come from Belknap (1990, 113–23).

3. For more on dueling ritual, see Reyfman (1999, 24–34). Chapter 6 also contains an insightful analysis of Zosima's duel. Reyfman shows how Zosima's partial participation in the dueling process serves both to acknowledge the duel's social function as a regulator of relations and to critique violence, even ritual violence, as a means of resolving conflicts. See especially Reyfman (1999, 253–61).

4. See Freud's discussion of aesthetic pleasure in *Beyond the Pleasure Principle*, (1961). Sir Guy Sircello discusses feelings of expansiveness, or exhilaration, as one of the pleasures to be derived from beauty. Sircello (1989, 138–45).

5. See Sutherland (1983, 179). Sutherland points out that the isolation of the underground man and Raskolnikov contributes to their lack of self-knowledge.

6. Leon Wurmser's discussion of shamelessness as a defense against shame seems particularly apt here:

> In my observations shamelessness is rather a defense against shame than an absence of it. Instead of feeling shame about violation of ethical values and moral standards, such persons feel shame when they are caught in a vulnerable position. And what would catch them so? Kindness, friendship, love, and feeling committed in any way—being trapped or intruded upon, in their vocabulary. Their ruthlessness hides how shame-sensitive they really are. This, like so much else in personality development and especially in that of morality, is not due to any defect or lack, but to counter-identification and disidentification: "I'm not like her or him, and I never want to be!" This, by the way, is one example of a kind of double jeopardy shame: to be torn between two ideal images of oneself, and inevitably to fail one or the other, which is an unending source for inner shame. (Wurmser 1987, 87)

7. As Reyfman points out, "Zosima's acceptance of the duel as a measure of human integrity allows him to make up with his opponent without losing the latter's respect" (Reyfman 1999, 255). Although Zosima's gesture initially scandalizes his opponent and fellow officers, they accept it once he announces his intention of entering a monastery. His withdrawal from a milieu where individual honor must be preserved at all costs provides him with a special status that exempts him from ritualized violence.

8. Michael Lewis identifies three groups of people who are traditionally viewed as capable of extending forgiveness: priests, the person shamed or harmed, and people of status, "people whom society has endowed with special authority by reason of their profession, wealth, power, etc. People in the healing professions, for example . . ." (Lewis 1992, 134). Lewis believes that withdrawal of love is the prototypic cause of shame. In his view, the love offered by the confessor heals the original wound: "If, as I believe, prototypic shame is caused by withdrawal of love, which is caused by violation of standards, then love through confession banishes the shame. Confession, then, is a reenactment of the original source of shame. Through it, we are able to dissipate our shame and restore our intrapsychic life to balance" (Lewis 1992, 135).

9. Kaufman (1993, 146).

10. Belknap (1990, 116).

11. Belknap (1990, 122).

12. I discuss Belknap's distinction between repentant confessions, such as St. Augustine's, and *apologia*, such as Rousseau's, in chapter 11. In between, he locates a range of

unrepentant confessions which take the form, "I did it and it's wrong, but not important, not my fault, not very wrong for me, or not so bad for others." Wilfully disreputable characters like Fedor Karamazov, he holds, "behave the way they do simply because it is their nature to do so." I have modified his characterization of Fedor's "but" which reads, "I did it, and it's wrong, but that's the way I am" to "but I don't give a damn" to emphasize Fedor's challenge to his audience. Belknap (1990, 120–21).

Notes to Chapter 6

1. For discussions of *Demons'* narrator, see Alexandrov (1984, 243–54), Fitzgerald (1982, 121–34), Jones (1999, 100–18), Kariakin (1983, 113–31), Matlaw (1984, 37–47), Moore (1985, 51–66), Tunimanov (1972, 87–162), and Vladiv (1979).

2. Wilson (1980, 58). This chapter also draws on Nyberg (1993). Nyberg's definition of self-deception agrees with Wilson's: "Self-deception is skillful maneuvering to achieve ignorance when clear, conscious understanding threatens to break through" (91).

3. Wilson (1980, 58).

4. Lotman (1985, 152).

5. Lotman (1985, 153).

6. The text stresses Stepan Trofimovich's weakness by having characters continually refer to him as a *baba* or woman (see Busch [1987, 79]). The text also draws a parallel between him and Praskovia Ivanovna Drozdova, a very weak woman, whose major complaint regarding her daughter Liza is that "her daughter is not her friend" (10:54;65). Likewise, Stepan Trofimovich always needs a friend. Furthermore, Varvara Petrovna warns Dasha to watch out for any signs that Stepan Trofimovich might commit suicide: "with such ones it even happens; not from strength, but from weakness they hang themselves" (10:57;68).

7. When Varvara Stavrogina tells Stepan Trofimovich that he is going to marry Dasha, he calls himself *un forçat* ("a convict") (10:65;79). Earlier the narrator notes Varvara Stavrogina's passion for Stepan Trofimovich's image as a civic figure. She even calls his fits of spleen "civic grief": "In the course of his twenty-year-long friendship with Varvara Petrovna he used to fall regularly, three or four times a year, into a state known among us as 'civic grief'—that is, simply a fit of spleen, but our much respected Varvara Petrovna liked the expression" (10:12;13). Or again: "Moments came over him when he would start talking about himself in a humorous vein. And there was nothing Varvara Petrovna feared more than a humorous vein" (10:12;13).

8. In using the term "life story," I am following Charlotte Linde, who holds that "Life stories express our sense of self: who we are and how we got that way. They are also one very important means by which we communicate this sense of self and negotiate it with others. Further, we use these stories to claim or negotiate group membership and to demonstrate that we are in fact worthy members of those groups, understanding and properly following their moral standards. Finally, life stories touch on the widest of social constructions, since they make presuppositions about what can be taken as expected, what the norms are, and what common or special belief systems can be used to establish coherence" (Linde 1993, 3).

9. See Liza Knapp's excellent article, "The Force of Inertia in Dostoevsky's 'Krotkaja,'" *Dostoevsky Studies* 6 (1985):143–56.

10. His personal story thus echoes his political career: he moves into the political realm, becomes successfully involved, and then suffers loss.

11. See the discussion of Harry Frankfurt's article "On Bullshit" and the similarity between Dostoevsky's liars and bullshitters in chapter 2.

12. Singer and Salovey (1993, 13).

13. What Nina Perlina has observed for *The Brothers Karamazov* holds true for *Demons* as well: "[A] hero's ability to associate his own views with and express his own ideas through the aesthetic authority of Pushkin's word indicate[s] this character's nonfinalized nature and his potential for moral transformation" (Perlina 1985, 30).

14. Unaware that their argument has moved from the private to the public sphere, Varvara Stavrogina closes on a personal note: "I know only one thing, that this is all pranks. You will never be able to carry out your threats, so filled with egoism. You will not go anywhere, not to any merchant, but will end up quite contentedly on my hands, getting a pension and holding Tuesday gatherings of your friends, who do not resemble anything. Farewell, Stepan Trofimovich" (10:266;342).

15. Stepan Trofimovich easily forgives those who slight him, provided they are sincerely repentant. The young Liza Tushina, who loved the stories he told her, "would imitate Stepan Trofimovich at home in a very funny way. He found out about it, and once caught her unawares. Embarrassed, Liza threw herself into his arms and burst out crying. So did Stepan Trofimovich, from rapture" (10:59;71).

16. Peter uses materialist language. He accuses Stepan of being "a sponger, that is a voluntary lackey. Too lazy to work, but with an appetite for a spot of cash" (10:239;305). He tries to bind Kirillov by reminding him of the money that he accepted from the Society (10:467–68;612) and to bind Stavrogin by getting him to pay for the Lebiadkins' murder. He speaks the language of intimidation and brute force. He threatens Fedka the convict: "I won't let you take a step out of here, you scoundrel, and will hand you straight over to the police" (10:429;560). And he tries to coerce Kirillov, pistol in hand: "If you get it into your head to run away tomorrow . . . I'll hang you like a fly . . . squash you" (10:429;560).

17. Stepan Verkhovensky roused Stavrogin's aesthetic sensibilities: "Stepan Trofimovich managed to touch the deepest strings in his friend's heart and to call forth in him the first, still uncertain sensation of that age-old, sacred anguish which the chosen soul, having once tasted and known it, will never exchange for any cheap satisfaction" (10:35;41). Stepan discovered and tutored Dasha Shatova. And, smitten with the eight-year-old Liza Tushina, for three years he taught her to believe in God "and told her some sort of poetic tales about the order of the world, the heart, the history of mankind" (10:59;71).

18. That their use of language is both an issue and a weapon in their conflict is clear from the following passages. Stepan Trofimovich complains to the narrator: "And note our habit of using the second person singular between father and son: it's very well when the two agree, but what if they're quarreling?" (10:172;216). Furthermore, when the narrator goes to Stepan Trofimovich's after the fête and the latter refuses to see him, the narrator responds rudely: "([O]h, I was rude and impolite; it grieves me to remember!)" (10:376;490). Stepan Trofimovich then comments on his friend's use of language: "You have not spent so long a time with them, yet you have been infected by their language and tone, *Dieu vous pardonne, mon ami, et Dieu vous garde*. But I have always noticed the germs of decency in you, and perhaps you will still think better of it—*après le temps*, of course, like all of us Russians" (10:376;491).

19. Here I am following the reasoning of the philosopher David Nyberg, whose book is the source of my chapter's subtitle.

20. As Meerson points out, using hints is one of Dostoevsky's own powerful narrative devices (Meerson 1998, chap. 3).

21. Another variety of self-deception in the novel can be identified as a form of literary idealization, that is, the idealization of a significant other in the form of a literary or

cultural type. Many characters in the novel idealize Stavrogin: his wife, Marya Lebiadkina; his would-be fiancée, Liza Tushina; his mother, Varvara Stavrogina; his brother-in-law, Ignat Lebiadkin; his disciple, Ivan Shatov; and his political associate, Peter Verkhovensky. Though the motives for it differ, this idealization often generates a role for the idealizer. If Stavrogin is a "Prince," then Marya is a Princess; if Stavrogin has a mysterious secret, then Liza is the heroine of a novel or opera; if Stavrogin is Prince Harry, then Lebiadkin is his Falstaff; if he is a great teacher, then Shatov is his disciple; if he is a new Pretender, then Peter is his henchman. This kind of idealization engenders a particular problem, one that Stavrogin encounters throughout the novel, since it is often accompanied by a form of blindness or, as Wilson would say, a tendency to ignore evidence to the contrary. Varvara, for instance, embraces the role of Hamlet for her son without seeing herself as Gertrude. Only Kirillov and Dasha see Stavrogin as a human being with weaknesses.

22. In the narrator's eyes, Stepan Verkhovensky might have lived up to the poetic stance he adopted, but Julia von Lembke could not. She assumes a Pushkinian heroic role for which the narrator finds her unsuited: " . . . and it was in this tongue [of flame] that the trouble consisted; after all, it is not a chignon that can go on any woman's head. But there is nothing more difficult than to convince a woman of this truth; on the contrary, anyone who chooses to yes her will succeed" (10:268;344).

23. In describing the guests at Virginsky's, the narrator mentions one of Virginsky's relatives, a major, who "simply could not denounce them" because "despite all his stupidity, he had been fond throughout his life of scurrying around all those places where extreme liberals are to be found; he did not sympathize himself, but liked very much to listen." In his youth, the major had been compromised: " . . . whole warehouses of *The Bell* and various tracts had passed through his hands, and though he had been afraid even to unfold them, he would still have regarded the refusal to disseminate them as perfect baseness— and there are some Russians of his sort even to this day" (10:303;391). Later in the meeting when Peter asks the assembled to vote on whether they would rather effect social and political change quickly by extreme measures such as chopping off 100,000,000 heads or to effect change slowly, through administrative reforms that might eventually cost 500,000,000 heads, the major voices a preference for the more humanitarian solution, but "since everyone [is voting for quick change], then I'm also with everyone" (10:316;407). When Peter proposes that Shatov be killed to avoid a denunciation, Virginsky protests "with all the strength of my soul against such a bloody solution." When Peter presses him further, however, he votes "for the common cause" (10:421;549).

24. Peter Verkhovensky (*Demons*) and Antip Burdovsky (*Idiot*) both associate with nihilists and slander their mothers.

25. See the first chapter of David Bethea's book, *The Shape of Apocalypse in Modern Russian Fiction* (1989).

26. Perlina (1985, 24).

27. Michael Lewis identifies four methods of dealing with shame: "owning it," which allows shame to dissipate with time; denial/forgetting; laughter, which allows individuals to distance themselves from the feeling of shame; and confession (Lewis 1992, 127–28).

28. Ibid., 132–35

29. In the hut where he meets Sophia Ulitina, Stepan Trofimovich realizes that it has been at least thirty years since he has read the Gospels and seven years since he had thought of them while reading Renan's *Vie de Jésus* (10:486;639).

30. After he first confesses and before he falls seriously ill, Stepan Verkhovensky invokes the Sermon on the Mount (Matthew 5:39: "But I say to you, Do not resist one who is evil. But if anyone strikes you on the right cheek, turn to him the other also"). Speaking to

Sophia about Varvara, he declares: "Oh, I wish her to strike my other cheek; it delights me to wish it! I'll turn my other cheek to her *comme dans votre livre!* Now, only now do I understand what it means to . . . offer the other cheek. I never understood before!" (10:496;650). He refers to the Gospels as "*votre livre*" and construes the passage very personally. In his view, Varvara Stavrogina struck him on one cheek when she adopted his son Peter's rhetoric. Stepan ran away but now he is ready to return, with Sophia, and offer Varvara his other cheek.

31. Both Meerson (1998) and Jones (1976, 1990) discuss different aspects of Dostoevsky's narrative strategies of indirection.

32. As Dostoevsky's Ridiculous Man says, "'The consciousness of life is higher than life, knowledge of the laws of happiness is higher than happiness' . . . that's what one has to fight against! And I will" [25:119]. Cervantes stands with Dostoevsky on the issue of truth. As Anthony Cascardi points out, "This is because truth, which was Descartes's concern, matters less to Cervantes than truthfulness, the means by which we render ourselves exemplars of what we know" (Cascardi 1986, 50).

33. In the excluded Tikhon chapter, the elder cites this same passage from Revelation (but in Church Slavonic rather than Russian) in reference to Stavrogin (11:11;688–89).

34. In transforming the real into an ideal, Stepan Verkhovensky acts like Don Quixote.

Notes to Chapter 7

1. "But I say to you, Do not swear at all, either by heaven, for it is the throne of God, or by the earth, for it is his footstool, or by Jerusalem, for it is the city of the great King. And do not swear by your head [*ni golovoiu tvoeiu ne klianis*], for you cannot make one hair white or black. Let what you say be simply 'Yes' or 'No'; anything more than this comes from evil [*ot lukavogo*]" (Matt. 5:34–37).

2. Dostoevsky embeds this double-voiced speech by Lebedev into his own text, thereby demonstrating his metaliterary awareness. Double-voicing "serves two speakers at the same time and expresses simultaneously two different intentions: the direct intention of the character who is speaking and the refracted intention of the author" (M. M. Bakhtin, "Discourse in the Novel" [in *The Dialogic Imagination*1981, 324]).

3. Voltaire's footnote reads as follows:

> Ce Denis, patron de la France, est un saint de la façon des moines. Il ne vint jamais dans les Gaules. "Voyez" sa légende dans le *Dictionnaire philosophique*, à l'article "Denis": vous apprendrez qu'il fut d'abord créé évêque d'Athènes par saint Paul; qu'il alla rendre une visite à la vierge Marie, et la complimenta sur la mort de son fils; qu'ensuite il quitta l'évêché d'Athènes pour celui de Paris; qu'on le pendit, qu'il prêcha fort éloquemment du haut de sa potence; qu'on lui coupa la tête pour l'empêcher de parler; qu'il prit sa tête entre ses bras, qu'il la baisait en chemin, en allant à une lieue de Paris fonder une abbaye de son nom. (Voltaire 1819, 29)

4. The Voltaire version has no adverb modifying the kissing. The Russian translation adds *nezhno* (15:531), which Dostoevsky changes to the alliterative *liubezhno*.

5. Recently, however, a Petersburg artist has fashioned a small memorial plaque featuring Gogol's "Nose." It is so popular, however, that it has been stolen several times from its location on the corner of Vosnesenskii prospekt and ulitsa Rimskogo-Korsakova.

6. Saints' lives are sometimes read prior to liturgies or during monastery vigils, but it seems that they were read during the service only in pre-Mongolian Novgorod.

7. Voltaire was actually a theist, but Dostoevsky referred to him as an atheist.

8. The tradition is as old as Homer's *Odyssey* and includes Plato's *Symposium*, Apuleius's *Golden Ass*, and Boccaccio's *Decameron*. For a scholarly romp through the Renaissance tradition, see Jeanneret (1991).

9. Not surprisingly, there is no single meaning in Dostoevsky's use of decapitation imagery. There are, however, clusters of association. The first cluster comprises images of political *tabula rasa* that can be thematically subsumed under the *Diary* writer's polemics on simplification (see Martinsen 1990). The second cluster includes images of humanity in extreme moments (Prince Myshkin's vision of the man the moment before execution or Lebedev's and the *Diary* writer's vision of Mme. du Barry on the scaffold). The third cluster comprises images of religious and political martyrdom and has a broader thematic range. The image of St. Denis fits into this third category.

10. Here I use Kenneth Lantz's translation of the word *obosoblenie*.

Notes to Chapter 8

1. Lotman claims that "The organizing thread of Russian literature was the striving for revealed truth" (Lotman 1996, 16).

2. As the novel's fallen woman, Nastasia Filippovna is an outsider uniquely positioned to reveal the seduction script: men betray, women pay.

3. As Ganna Bograd shows, Dostoevsky probably knew the unpublished verse of Pushkin's "Poor Knight" from Pushkin's sister, who lived near Dostoevsky's sister-in-law in Pavlovsk during the summer of 1865. Interestingly, it has always been clear to Dostoevsky's most careful readers that he must have known these verses. For example, see Miller (1981, 188–93). In general, this reflects the workings of Dostoevsky's metaliterary play. The extra layer is there for those who pay attention (Bograd 1994–98, 83).

4. For interesting discussions of Russian bureaucrats, see Shore (1980) and Workman (1998).

5. Lebedev also uses the verb *perevodiat*, which can mean "transfer," but also "spend," "translate," or "copy." The fixed expression *perevodit' darom* can mean "transfer for nothing" or "spend on nothing," either of which can be used here. But the gap between the verb's idiomatic denotations and its other connotations (translate, copy) raises issues of originality and authorship that Dostoevsky thus invites us to explore.

6. For a brief account of *oblichitel'naia literatura* in relation to Dostoevsky's work, see Proskurina (1997, 33–34).

7. Once again Lebedev projects his own practices onto others. Here, he accuses the Prince of fabricating his family tie to Mme. Epanchina, when it is Lebedev who fabricates a family tie to Ivolgin, who, in turn, fabricates a family tie to the Prince.

8. As Belknap writes of *oblichitel'naia literatura*, "While it lasted, this movement helped to reveal many real public abuses, and also produced some of the finest scurrility in all Russian literature" (Belknap 1997, 110).

9. Like Nozdrev's, Lebedev's inspirations of the moment impede his success. As the narrator notes in Book Four: "Lebedev really ran around for quite a while; this person's calculations always arose as though by inspiration and from excessive fervor became complicated, branched off and moved away from their starting point in all directions; that's why he managed to do so very little in his life" (8:487).

10. Bernstein clearly spells out the difference between abjection and *ressentiment* and places Lebedev in the camp of the abject:

> Abjection and "ressentiment" can be distinguished most readily by their different relations to temporality and to the urge for vengeance: abjection suffers constantly new, and usually externally imposed, slights and degradation, whereas "ressentiment" is trapped forever in the slights of the past. A lacerated vanity nourishes both abjection and "ressentiment," but repetition is less crucial to abjection than to "ressentiment," which experiences its existence as a perpetual recurrence of the same narcissistic injury. Moreover, the man of "ressentiment" is actually "proud" of his abjection, and, as in *Notes from Underground*, he sees in it both his torment and the sign of a higher consciousness. The sufferer from abjection derives no compensatory pride from his humiliation, but neither does he dwell as obsessively on fantasies of revenge on imaginary enemies. What "empowers" someone afflicted by "ressentiment" is the intensely focused, but impotent, hatred with which he feeds his sense of having been treated unfairly, and his hope of someday forcing others to suffer in his place. . . . In Dostoevsky, though, one can schematize the differences in more clear-cut ways, since he presents, along with abject and *ressentiment*-riddled souls like *The Brothers Karamazov*'s Smerdyakov, characters like *The Idiot*'s Lebedyev, who are thoroughly abject but with none of the murderous desires of *ressentiment*. (Bernstein 1992, 28)

While Bernstein's classification of Lebedev as abject but not full of *ressentiment* is largely true, Lebedev, as I show, does act on his desire for revenge. He does not, however, have the concentrated will of the true man of *ressentiment*, and his projects largely fail. Lebedev also derives some compensatory pride from his humiliation. I see him as an early prototype for Fedor Pavlovich Karamazov, whom Bernstein identifies as a character full of *ressentiment*.

11. Dostoevsky articulates this more fully in his March 1876 *Diary of a Writer*:

> *It is* always said that reality is boring, monotonous; that in order to amuse themselves people run to art, to fantasy, they read novels. For me, the opposite holds: what can be more fantastic and unexpected than reality? What can be even more improbable sometimes than reality? A novelist could never produce such impossibilities as those which reality produces for us by the thousands every day, in the form of the most ordinary things. Some could not even be thought up at all by any fantasy. And besides that, what an advantage over the novel! Try, *make up* an episode in a novel, if only with the barrister Kupernik, think him up yourself, and on the following Sunday, in a feuilleton, a critic will prove to you clearly and invincibly that you are raving and that it never happens in reality, and, most importantly, that it could never possibly happen even, because and because. It will end so that you yourself will shamefully agree. But then you're brought a copy of *The Voice*, and suddenly you read the entire episode about our marksman and—and what is it after all: at first you read in astonishment, in terrible astonishment, so that even while you are reading you don't believe anything; but as soon as you've finished reading up to the last period, you fold up the newspaper and suddenly, without knowing why, you say to yourself all at once: "Yes, it all absolutely had to happen just this way." And some person will even add: "I had a feeling this would happen." Why there is such a difference between

impressions received from novels and newspapers I don't know, but such after all is reality's privilege. (22:91–92)

Kupernik, a defense attorney in many political trials, including the Nechaev case, was returning to Moscow in February 1876. He told the stationmaster at Chernigov that if his horses weren't ready soon, he would destroy the station. As he left, he shot his revolver at the drivers several times to speed them up. A case was brought against him, but Kupernik refuted in print all charges.

12. Apuleius (1962, 34).

13. Dostoevsky later attributes this idea to Ivan Karamazov's devil, another Dostoevskian liar: "Why of all beings in the world, am I alone condemned to be cursed by all decent people, and even to be kicked with boots, for, when I become incarnate, I must occasionally take such consequences as well?" (15:82;647).

14. Dostoevsky may also have been referring to Derzhavin's "grandee" poems—the epitaph "On the Grave of the Grandee and Hero" (between 1779 and 1791), which concludes that social fame ends in dust, and "The Grandee" (1794), whose opening lines resonate with Ivolgin's criticism of Lebedev's nonresemblance to an interpreter of Scripture: "My muse today glorifies / Not the decoration of clothing / Which, in the eyes of the ignorant / Dresses up buffoons as grandees" (Derzhavin 1985, 137).

15. The *Diary* writer mentions Mme. du Barry's cry in his 1873 article, "Vlas." He compares the moment when the Russian Vlas is loading the gun to shoot at the blessed bread, the symbolic body of Christ, to the last moment on the guillotine. Loading the gun and crying out for one more moment are ways to distract one's attention from the mystical horror of one's experience. The *Diary* writer elaborates: "She would have suffered twenty times more in that gratis minute, if it were to have been given to her, yet she nonetheless cried out and prayed for it" (21:40). In general, the motif of last moments runs throughout Dostoevsky's work and can be explained autobiographically, given Dostoevsky's own experience on the scaffold.

16. The man who took her as a lover and trained her in hopes of passing her on to the king was already married. Since the king was not allowed to have lovers of base birth, M. du Barry arranged to have his brother marry her formally. The brother was compensated financially for forgoing his connubial rights. The countess left the church in a royal carriage and was in the king's bed by evening.

17. On the morning of her execution, confident that she would succeed in purchasing her freedom, Mme. du Barry disclosed the location of all her buried valuables.

18. Getting the Prince to be his tenant is clearly the inspiration of the moment. Lebedev already has a tenant, whose contract he then breaks.

19. In the scene with Lebedev's nephew at the opening of Book Two, Lebedev and his nephew argue over honor and money. The nephew confesses that he has gambled and lost money to the unnamed Keller. While Lebedev argues against payment because his nephew has been cheated, his nephew argues that as a man of honor he must take responsibility for the debt because he incurred it knowing full well that Keller might cheat him. Here, as in the scene at Nastasia Filippovna's, where Gania demonstrates his sense of honor by allowing the packet of 100,000 rubles to burn while Lebedev offers to crawl into the fire after it, Lebedev demonstrates that he prizes money over honor. Lebedev's greed and indifference to honor also explain the apparent contradiction in his sympathy for Mme. du Barry and his hostility to Natasia Filippovna, both fallen women. Lebedev can understand Mme. du Barry's shamelessness and social climbing, but he cannot comprehend either Natasia Filippovna's shame or her indifference to wealth.

20. One is reminded here of Stepan Trofimovich Verkhovensky, who feels an equal urge to confess his weaknesses and wrongdoings.

21. This fictional speech, with its justification of criminal action by invoking the theory that the milieu is responsible, anticipates Spasovich's defense of Kroneberg as portrayed in Dostoevsky's February 1876 *Diary of a Writer* (22:50–73). The *Diary* writer holds that Spasovich tries to get his client acquitted of child abuse by defending paternal authority and diminishing the child's suffering. The *Diary* writer agrees that Kroneberg should be acquitted, but he focuses his readers' attention on the child's suffering and proposes active parental love as an alternative to paternal authority.

22. The shoe motif recalls General Ivolgin's story about Corporal Kolpakov, who was accused of stealing his buddy's footwear. In this case, Lebedev is pointing to the patently foreign make of the shoes, thus emphasizing the Prince's foreignness. (He comments on the Prince's shoes at their first meeting on the train.)

23. Interestingly, Dostoevsky has Lebedev choose as epitaph for his leg's gravestone the same one the Dostoevsky brothers chose for their mother's.

24. Focus on food in Dostoevsky's *oeuvre* is frequently a sign of a character's materialism. One motif of Dostoevsky's work, which also appears in the cannibal speech scene, is the biblical "not by bread alone."

25. This language reminds readers of Lebedev's nephew, who is reclining on the couch as Lebedev delivers his successful legal speech at the beginning of Book Two.

26. See Meerson (1995).

27. Unlike the skillful narrator Rousseau, whose story Dostoevsky lends to Ferdyshchenko.

28. In an oft-cited letter of (11 April 1880; 30.1, 149), Dostoevsky wrote:
> What are you writing about your doubleness? ... It is the most ordinary trait of human beings ... who are not quite, nonetheless, ordinary. It is a trait, generally innate in human nature, but far and away not in just any human nature is it met with such force as in you. That's why you are like a family member to me, because that *duality* in you is exactly the same as that in me, and has been in me my whole life. It is a great torment, but at the same time it is also a great pleasure. It is a powerful consciousness, a mandate for self-accounting and the presence in your nature of the mandate for moral duty to yourself and to humanity. That's what that doubleness means. If your mind were not so developed, if you were more narrow, then you would be less conscientious and you would have none of that doubleness. On the contrary, great self-doubt would arise. Nonetheless this doubleness is a great torment. My dear, deeply-respected Katerina Fedorovna, do you believe in Christ and his commandments? If you believe (or you greatly want to believe) then give yourself up to him completely, and the torments from this doubleness will soften greatly and you will experience a spiritual outcome, which is the main thing.

29. This scene also echoes an earlier scene in which Lebedev's nephew confesses to losing twenty-five rubles to Keller while gambling: "Well, do you believe, Prince, I was so mean, so base [*nizok*], that I lost them!" (8:162). He continues: "But what's worst of all, is that I knew that he was a blackguard, a scoundrel and a kind of thief [Keller], and nonetheless I sat down to play with him, and that while playing for my last ruble (we were playing cribbage), I thought to myself: if I lose, I'll go to uncle Lukian, I'll bow to him—he won't refuse. That was baseness [*nizost'*], that was real baseness! That was conscious meanness!" (8:162).

30. In Book Four, the Prince asks Lebedev about the General and the theft and Lebedev feigns incomprehension. The Prince gets angry and exclaims: "Well, there it is, it's exactly as though you don't understand me at all! Oh, God, what is it Lukian Timofeich, to you everything is an act [*u vas vse za roli*]!" (8:406).

31. Significantly, Keller is identified as a "boxer." As Reyfman shows, even though Pushkin admired boxing, the Russian nobility generally despised it. Boxing was considered a plebian form of combat, but also one in which a nobleman might engage with a coachman, a crossing of class boundaries that the nobility deplored (Reyfman 1999, 137–39).

32. This defense echoes Lebedev's earlier self-defense against his nephew's attacks. Lebedev explains to the Prince that he may be "a drunkard and rake, a robber and evildoer," but that after his sister was widowed he also changed his nephew's diapers, took care of him, and even stole wood from the concierge for him.

33. The two words *obosoblenie* and *vseobshchnost'* are key words in Dostoevsky's *Diary of a Writer*. They belong to a series of oppositions that reflect two dominant underlying metaphors in the *Diary*—metaphors of separation and union. Other pairs in the series are: logic/faith, uprootedness (*otorvannost'*) / "grass-rootedness" (*pochvennichestvo*), indifference (*indifferentizm*)/living life (*zhivushaia zhizn'*), inflexibility (*priamolineinost'*)/complexity (*slozhnost'*), simplification/contextualization, and complacency (*uspokoenie*)/anxiety (*bespokoistvo*). These oppositions operate on different levels: the social and political, the psychological, and the metaphysical. Dostoevsky uses them as touchstones to explore human beings' relationships to one another as nations and individuals, as well as to explore their relationships as nations and individuals to God (Martinsen 1990, 179–80).

34. Elsewhere Lebedev discusses vanity as a stumbling block to altruism: ". . . that was already found in Malthus, friend of humanity. But a friend of humanity with a shakiness of moral principles is a cannibal of humanity, not to speak of his vanity. For offend the vanity of any friend of these innumerable friends of humanity, and on the spot he's ready to burn up the world from all four corners out of petty vengeance,—just as any of us is, however, fairly speaking, as I myself, the vilest of all, for I in fact, perhaps, would be the first to bring firewood, yet run away myself" (8:312). Thus, while Lebedev can proclaim the need for an idea to bind humanity, he is governed by his own petty vanity and desire for revenge. In his divided soul, the forces that sunder are stronger than the forces that bind. Meerson notes that this is another example of Lebedev appropriating biblical language for his own self-presentation, in this case Pauline rhetoric. Lebedev's use of the word *shatost'* here is also worth noting for the light it casts on Shatov's name (*Demons*).

Notes to Chapter 9

1. Blank (1988).

2. Derzhavin writes, "My body decays into dust, / I command my mind with thunder. I am a tsar—I am a slave; I am a worm—I am God! / But, wondrous as I am / Whence come I—It's unknown. / Yet I cannot exist by myself. / Your creation am I, Creator . . . [*Ia telom v prakhe istlevaiu, / Umom gromom povelevaiu. / Ia tsar'—ia rab; ia cherv'—ia bog! / No buduchi ia stol' chudesen, / Otkole proisshel? Bezvesten. / A sam soboi ia byt' ne mog. / Tvoe sozdan'e ia Sozdatel'. . . .*]" (Derzhavin 1985, 54).

3. Blank (1988, 4).

4. Though I consider the Pevear and Volokhonsky translations of Lebiadkin's verses quite brilliant, I have modified this line because I think the verb *ropshchet* is somewhat stronger than their rendition—"murmur"—implies.

5. Dostoevsky parodied Miatlev's poem in his notebooks for the nonrealized story of Captain Kartuzov, which he later attributes to Lebiadkin (see next chapter). The title of Miatlev's poem, "*Fantasticheskaia vyskazka*," calls attention to itself. A neologism, *vyskazka* combines the standard noun for "fairy tale" (*skazka*) and the verb *vyskazat'* (to state; to express) or, more likely, its reflexive variant *vyskazat'sia* (to state one's mind). In my translation, I have tried to preserve Miatlev's anapestic monometer: "The cockroach / As in a cup / Will land up— / Will perish; / On the glass, / It's so steep / No escape. // Such am I: / For my life / Has faded / Has fled by; / I'm captive, / I'm in love, / But with whom? // Not a thing / Will I say; / I will grieve, / While my God / Does not rob / Me of strength; // That I might / Cease to love, / And forget, / No, never; / Forever / I sadly / Won't escape / Evil grief; / I cannot / Run away, / Cannot stop / This loving— / I will live / And I'll grieve // The cockroach / As in a cup / Will land up— / Will perish; / On the glass, / It's so steep / No escape" (Miatlev 1857, 1:121–2).

6. His self-image as cockroach is only one of Lebiadkin's many explicit self-images. In his letter to Liza, he calls himself "an unlearned at a debate," "nothing," and "an infusorian." At Varvara Stavrogina's, he proclaims himself "nothing" and "an insignificant link." To Stavrogin, he refers to himself indirectly as a louse. On the positive side, he reminds Stavrogin that he has been his "Falstaff." He also asserts that he is now living "like Zosima. Sobriety, solitude, and poverty—the vow of knights of old" (10:207;261), a comic linking to Stepan Verkhovensky, who is associated with knight imagery. Lebiadkin also claims, "I am renewing myself like a snake" (10:209;264), thereby announcing that he is changing with the times, shedding his revolutionary politics along with his disordered past.

7. In his notebooks, Dostoevsky stressed the physical awkwardness (*nelovkost'*) of Captain Kartuzov, his model for Lebiadkin.

8. Lebiadkin's image of fly-phagy anticipates the claim in his letter to von Lembke that the people are destroying one another as they look for someone to blame. It also comically reprises Mme. Epanchina's prophesy in *The Idiot* that "vanity and pride have so eaten you up, that it will end up that one by one you will eat one another up" (8:238).

9. Blank (1998, 3).

10. See Martinsen (2003).

11. Ludmila Koehler's argument that the change evidences Dostoevsky's desire to further degrade Lebiadkin by adding a violation of stress misses the point (Koehler 1970, 11–23).

12. In *The Brothers Karamazov*, Zosima uses it in his sketch of Job's story, where he has the devil say to God, "Hand him [Job] over to me and you shall see that your servant will begin to grumble [*vozropshchet*] and will curse your name" (14:264). By associating the verb "to grumble" with the story of Job, Dostoevsky uses it as shorthand for metaphysical rebellion. In describing Alesha's grief and the doubts raised in him by the corruption of Zosima's body, the narrator notes: "He loved his God and believed in Him unwaveringly, even though he suddenly grumbled [*vozroptal*] against Him for a moment" (14:307;340). Pushkin also uses the verb *roptat'* to indicate metaphysical rebellion. See Gasparov (1992, 239).

13. Lomonosov (1961, 139). Lomonosov's ode was parodied by Marin. The parody, which Dostoevsky undoubtedly knew, includes the verb *ropshchesh'*.

14. As Andrew Morrison points out, "Humiliation specifically reflects the social, interpersonal manifestation of shame, or internalized representation of the 'humiliator.' . . . Humiliation is that manifestation of shame which is the product of *action* perpetrated against the self by someone else" (Morrison 1989, 15).

15. Patterson also points out that the lives were revised at various junctures, depending on the author's political agenda. Thus, for instance, La Fontaine omitted all the scatologi-

cal incidents in his version of Aesop's life (Patterson 1991).

16. Iconographically, Aesop was often contrasted to Apollo, as two antipodal images of ugliness and beauty, formlessness and form.

17. This is the pattern Patterson outlines. Depending on the translation one uses, details change. Thus, for instance, Daly's translation portrays Aesop as hospitable to a priestess of Isis (rather than to two priests of Diana) (Daly 1961).

18. *Entsiklopedicheskii slovar'* (St. Petersburg: izd. Brokgaus-Efron, 1898), vol. 27:187.

19. Dostoevsky used Staraia Russa, the town where he owned a house and where he wrote *The Brothers Karamazov*, as the model for Skotoprigonevsk. His inspiration for the town's name probably derived from the cattle market (*skotoprigonnaia ploshchad'*) at the town's edge.

20. Defender of the ancients in the battle between the ancients and the moderns, Aesop is the first to break the silence in the library of St. James, where Swift sets this satiric battle (Swift 1960, 154; "The Battle of the Books," 143–68). In Dostoevsky's novel, Fedor Karamazov would represent the moderns as he is the product of a changing social order. As a capitalist, he does battle with Miusov, a feudal landowner. As an iconoclast, he opposes the Elder Zosima.

21. Meerson (1992, 317–22). In the physiology of humors, the heart was the seat of choler, the lungs of phlegm, the stomach of black bile, and the liver of bile. Dostoevsky may also have been suggesting to readers familiar with Galen's theory that the police commissioner was a bilious man with a jaundiced view of things.

22. I take these definitions from Meerson (1998, 198).

23. The episodes relating animal and scatological are rather numerous. In one episode, Xanthus asks Aesop to allow only philosophers to his dinner party. Aesop then greets each guest with the question, "What does the dog shake?" Most guests feel Aesop is calling them a dog and leave. Only one replies, "Its tail," whereupon Aesop lets him in and announces to his master that only one philosopher has come to dine with him.

24. Daly (1961, 63–64).

25. Readers might want to remember that Dostoevsky believed that his father was murdered by his own serfs.

26. Aesop's adopted son does not kill him, however. He gets involved with the king's concubine, which angers Aesop, who threatens him, saying that anyone who touches the king's woman is asking for his own death. The boy writes a false letter in Aesop's name that he seals with Aesop's ring. He then turns the letter over to the king, who orders a captain of the guard to kill Aesop for being a traitor. The captain does not kill his friend Aesop, however, but keeps him in prison until the king, threatened by his enemies, voices his regret over having ordered Aesop's death.

27. Laura Kristan Wilhelm, "Slave Among the Slavs: An Approach to Aesopian Poetics and Its Implications for the Study of Russian Aesopianism," unpublished paper, 3–5.

28. Pushkin designed his epigrams to offend and his *Gavriliiada* to shock.

29. Laura Kristan Wilhelm, "The Aesopic Legacy in Russian Literature," unpublished article.

Notes to Chapter 10

1. "Where there are secrets we are driven to unknotting, as if the secret lies inside a tangle to be untangled; and that urgency aroused in us reinforces the urgency of the plot" (Kuhns 1991, 65).

2. While many readers have recognized the metaliterary dimension of *The Idiot*, few have noticed the metaliterary side of Dostoevsky's most overtly political novel, *Demons*. Yet Ludmila Saraskina (1990, 115) observes that two-thirds of the novel's characters either write (20 characters) or express interest in literature (another 10). Stepan Verkhovensky's and Karmazinov's literary endeavors, the literary quadrille, and Stavrogin's confession immediately spring to mind; with little effort we recall Lebiadkin's verses, von Lembke's novel, and Shigalev's political writings; but how to remember that Marya Lebiadkina read her own stories to Stavrogin or that Kirillov was writing an article, that Iuliia Mikhailovna von Lembke wrote toasts and speeches or that Liputin added a verse to Lebiadkin's poem about governesses, that Lebiadkin is writing a will and Virginsky's student sister-in-law wrote and had printed a speech about the plight of students, or that Peter Verkhovensky suspects the lame teacher of writing poetry, while Liputin suspects Peter Verkhovensky of writing the poem "Svetlaia lichnost'" about himself? Literary activity does not stop there: Varvara Stavrogina once considered publishing a journal, Liza Tushina wants to publish a yearbook about events in Russia, Peter Verkhovensky acts as literary critic for von Lembke and Karmazinov, Tikhon does the same for Stavrogin, Shatov has a buried printing press, and his wife wants to open a bookbinding shop. Needless to say, this proliferation of literary activity and interest in literature is not accidental. The action of *Demons* is set in Russia at the end of the 1860s, with an occasional peek back at literary events from the end of the 1840s and 1850s. Dostoevsky thus traces the roots of contemporary troubles back to the heyday of Russian idealism and the rise of Russian nihilism.

3. Miss Silver, Patricia Wentworth's detective, observes about the writing of anonymous letters (in this case, poison-pen letters, but the observation still holds):

> It affords an opportunity for the release of concealed resentments, suppressed desires, the envy, the grudge which has been secretly cherished. There may, or may not, have been some specific sense of injury, but I believe that in most cases it is a feeling of inferiority or frustration which provides the background of these painful cases. As in so many other circumstances, it is only the first step which is hard to take. Once that has been taken, the vice grows rapidly. In a village the effect of each letter can be observed. A sense of power and importance comes to the writer, the letters become more numerous and more poisonous, the appetite grows with what it feeds upon. (Wentworth 1992, 92–93)

4. The association between exposed secrets and death is another variant on the mortification scenario Dostoevsky plays with in *The Idiot*. Unlike General Ivolgin and the Private Kolpakov of his story, both of whom die following their exposure to humiliation (thus following the pattern of Gogol's Akaky Akakievich), Lebiadkin, though himself a shame-filled character, dies following his attempts to expose the secrets of his social superiors, Stavrogin and Peter Verkhovensky.

5. Marya is an unsuitable wife not because of her class status, but because she is a holy fool. Stavrogin marries her not because he loves her or wants to share his life with her but to violate social conventions. Since Stavrogin subsequently supports her, his marriage to Marya has been taken as an act of altruism. The secrecy surrounding the marriage and his indifference to her murder argue against that viewpoint, however.

6. For an excellent discussion of imposture in *Demons*, see Murav (1992, chap. 5). Richard Peace connects Stavrogin and the Lebiadkins with dissident religious sects (Peace 1971, 170–78). Gordon Livermore discusses the revelation politics of the Lebiadkins' address (Livermore 1984, 185). Pretendership has political connotations in Russian his-

tory, where there have been a series of pretenders to the throne. A number of these have fomented large-scale political uprisings in the provinces.

7. For more information on pretenders in Russia, see Perrie (1995) and Uspenskii (1984, 259–66). For literary and musical representations of pretenders, see Emerson (1986). For a discussion of pretendership in *Demons*, see Murav (1992, footnote 6); and for a cultural history of pretenders in the nineteenth century, see Maiorova (1999, 204–32). In what follows, I concentrate on Stavrogin and Lebiadkin as first and second False Dmitrys. In passing, however, I would like to note that Dostoevsky also provided Peter Verkhovensky with a pretender pedigree. One possible source for his first name is that of the Tsarevich Peter, a universally acclaimed impostor. Tsarevich Peter was probably the illegitimate son of a Russian mother and a Polish father who acted in the name of Dmitry and used his pretender status as a pretense to plunder. He was rumored to have escaped to Lithuania. This story resonates with Peter Verkhovensky's uncertainty about his own birth, his chosen role as political henchman, his opportunism, and his flight abroad.

8. Dostoevsky thus makes Lebiadkin an heir to Gogol's Khlestakov (*The Inspector General*) and Major Kovalev ("The Nose"). Major Kovalev obtained his rank in the Caucasus, which makes it something of a paper title, not unlike Lebiadkin's own.

9. Uspenskii (1984, 266).

10. Ibid., 272.

11. Ibid.

12. Peace (1971, 172).

13. Marya repeatedly calls Lebiadkin her "lackey." She tells Shatov, "He's my lackey. It makes no difference to me whether he's here or not. I shout at him: 'Lebiadkin, fetch water, Lebiadkin, bring my shoes,' and off he runs" (10:115;143). Shatov agrees that Marya treats her brother like a lackey, but adds, "the only difference is that he doesn't go running for water, but beats her for it, yet she's not afraid of him in the least" (10:115;143). At Varvara Stavrogina's, she advises her hostess to send Lebiadkin "to the lackey's room. Let him sit there and play his trumps with them on a bench, and we'll sit here and have coffee" (10:134;167).

14. Most of Lebiadkin's poems are taken directly from Dostoevsky's notebook sketch of Captain Kartuzov (discussed later in this chapter). But he also bowdlerizes Fet's famous verse, "*Ia prishel k tebe s privetom*" (10:119;148) and the opening line of Kukol'nik's poem "*Somnenie*" (10:140;174).

15. In Varvara Stavrogina's drawing room, Lebiadkin is out of his natural milieu and thus is extremely exposed. The narrator describes him here as "a tall, curly-haired, thickset fellow of about forty, with a purple, somewhat bloated and flabby face, with cheeks that shook at every movement of his head, with small, bloodshot, at times quite cunning eyes, with a moustache and side-whiskers, with a nascent, fleshy, rather unpleasant-looking Adam's apple. But the most striking thing about him was that he appeared now wearing a tailcoat and clean linen" (10:136;170). Lebiadkin's evident discomfort in his new clothes mirrors his social discomfort. Every detail of his dress emphasizes the fact that he does not belong in such a setting—his hat, for instance, is clearly brand-new. Furthermore, the costume that was meant to hide his origins exposes them further: his left glove, though stretched on tightly, only half-covers "his meaty left paw." The narrator further emphasizes his discomfort with a later observation: "He apparently feared for every movement of his clumsy body. For all such gentlemen, as is known, when by some odd chance they appear in society, the worst suffering comes from their own hands and the constant awareness of the impossibility of somehow decently disposing of them" (10:137;171). His stumbling

entrance, which causes his sister to laugh, further emphasizes his awkwardness. Varvara instantly puts him in his place—on a chair near the door.

16. See Lincoln (1975, 82–100). Lincoln points out that the government bureaucracy ran largely on inertia, as men of talent had few outlets for their creativity except in those rare cases where they were recognized and patronized by higher officials. Stiva Oblonskys were typical. While Lebiadkin clearly lacks talent, this comic criticism nonetheless echoes throughout the novel in the portrayal of superfluous men, both young and old. Stepan Verkhovensky never truly applies his talents—to teaching, research, or writing—but constantly retreats from the sociopolitical sphere, all the while blaming Russia's political situation for his lack of fame. In his farewell letter to Dasha, Stavrogin complains more indirectly that he has unsuccessfully tried to apply his talents. In his parodic reduction, Dostoevsky reveals a common, defining feature. However disparate these three figures—Lebiadkin, Stepan Verkhovensky, and Stavrogin—they are all "uprooted" (*otorvannye*), that is, they have lost a sense of vital connection to Russia, their country of birth, and to the Russian people.

17. *"Da, tak! Khot' rodom ia ne slaven / No, buduchi liubimets muz, / Drugim vel'mozham ia ne raven, / I samoi smert'iu predpochtus!"* (So it is! Although by birth I have no fame / Yet, as beloved of the muses / I'm not the same / As to other grandees / And death itself will favor me) (Derzhavin 1985, 251).

18. Derzhavin (1985, 360).

19. Margaret A. Rose defines *pekoral* as unintentionally comic or stylistically incompetent pieces of writing by "would-be" but untalented poets. See Rose (1993, 68).

20. Pushkin (1979, 10:454). Pushkin uses the idiomatic expression *nechego skazat'*, which is always ironic and signals the ironic intent of the word (here *Veselo*) on which it comments.

21. Dostoevsky clearly knew of Monbars' association with the *flibustiers*; he titled the chapter on the Shpigulin strike "Flibustiers. A Fatal Morning." The association is reinforced by Governor von Lembke's declaration, "Enough, the flibustiers of our time are determined. Not a word more. Measures have been taken . . . " (10:351).

22. My information on the Prince de Monbars derives from Gérard A. Jaeger's account of the *flibustiers* and their portrayal in literature. See Jaeger (1987).

23. Jaeger comments on Picquenard's heroization of Monbars, "l'exterminateur des Espagnols": "A cet égard, Picquenard nous livre son secret personnel sur Monbars en nous proposant la compagnie de l'un 'de ces hommes dont l'audace à entreprendre et la prodigieuse valeur dans l'exécution réduisaient à des jeux d'enfants même les plus fabuleux exploits des demi-dieux de la Mythologie.' Le nom 'd'exterminateur', écrit-il, devint bientôt 'le titre le plus honorable auquel un Flibustier put prétendre.' Ce sont des aventures du dernier de ces Monbars que je vais raconter" (300) (Jaeger 1987, 101).

24. In his book, Jaeger notes that in 1863, Gustave Aimard modeled the portrait of a late-seventeenth-century adventurer on that of Monbars. The description that follows, both physical and psychological, can be seen as a composite of Stavrogin and Henry V:

> [C'était] un jeune homme de vingt-sept à vingt-huit ans, écrit le romancier, aux traits mâles et accentués, au regard fixe et pénétrant; l'expression de sa physionomie était essentiellement triste, railleuse et cruelle; une pâleur mate, répandue sur son visage, ajoutait encore, s'il est possible, un cachet d'étrangeté à toute sa personne; d'une taille haute, fortement charpentée, mais souple et gracieuse, ses gestes étaient élégants et nobles, sa parole douce, les termes qu'il employait, toujours choisis; il exerçait une singulière fascination

sur ceux qui l'approchaient, ou que le hasard mettait en rapport avec lui. On se sentait à la fois repoussé et attiré vers cet homme singulier, qui semblait être seul de son espèce jeté sur cette terre, et qui, sans paraître s'en soucier, imposait à tous sa volonté, se faisait obéir d'un geste ou d'un froncement de sourcils, et ne semblait réellement vivre que lorsqu'il se trouvait au milieu de la battaille, que les feux se croisaient au-dessus de sa tête, lui formant une auréole de flamme, que les cadavres s'amoncelaient autour de lui, que le sang ruisselait à flots sous ses pieds, que les balles sifflaient à ses oreilles, se mêlant aux éclats du canon, et qu'il s'élançait ivre de poudre et de carnage sur le pont d'un navire espagnol. Voilà ce que disaient de lui ses compagnons, à ceux que sa physionomie singulière avait frappés, et qui cherchaient à le connaître; mais, à part ce portrait moral et physique de cet homme, il était impossible d'obtenir le plus léger renseignement sur sa vie passée; aucun des marins venus avec lui n'en savait le moindre épisode, ou plutôt, ce qui était probable, n'en voulait rien découvrir (459). Cette réserve romanesque tient également lieu du règle à ce genre de description où le héros doit demeurer secret le plus longtemps possible. (Jaeger 1987, 134–35)

Dostoevsky's decision to keep Stavrogin an enigma followed this novelistic tradition.

25. See Saraskina (1990, chap. 2).

26. Picquenard's Monbars describes himself as a victim of his society's corruption, a *flibustier* out of historical necessity (Jaeger 1987, 103).

27. Lebiadkin's words link him to Stepan Verkhovensky and the novel's aesthetic polemics, as the reference to boots was a cliché of materialist critics like Chernyshevsky, who argued that boots were more useful than poetry.

28. Here and following I have used Pevear and Volokhonsky's masterful translations of Lebiadkin's doggerel.

29. Saraskina also discusses the thematics of lameness (1990, 136).

30. Interestingly, the theme of decapitation in *The Idiot* is continued in *Demons*, and Lebedev's lie about his lost leg is developed into a whole theme of broken limbs. Peter Verkhovensky explains that he and Stavrogin traveled to town together because his first train had been derailed earlier outside Matveevo and "we almost broke our legs." Liza then exclaims to her mother, "Maman, maman, you and I were going to go to Matveevo last week, so we could have broken our legs too!" (10:157;195). Even in the novel's last pages, Stepan Trofimovich meets Ansim, a former servant of Gaganov's. Ansim currently lives near the Spasovo monastery at Marfa Sergeevna's, whose sister, Avdotia Sergeevna, had broken her leg when she jumped out of a carriage.

31. Having compiled a list of lame figures in Dostoevsky's works and notes, Saraskina argues compellingly that Dostoevsky uses physical lameness to denote spiritual defects. Saraskina (1984, 155).

32. Dostoevsky here pokes fun at Lebiadkin. As he and his Russian readers would know, Gogol never wrote a "Last Story."

33. Raskolnikov uses the same noun "louse" (*vosh'*) to characterize the old pawnbroker. He also applies it to himself when comparing himself to Napoleon: "[S]o am I a louse, or not?" (*Da vosh' ia, ili net?*). Lebiadkin's sentence also parodies Gogol's "Diary of a Madman," whose protagonist, the clerk Poprishchin, falls in love with his director's daughter.

34. Once again, Dostoevsky evokes Gogol's "Diary of a Madman." Poprishchin responds to the shame of his social position by imagining himself as the king of Spain.

35. In Dostoevsky's notebook sketch of Captain Kartuzov, the Captain cannot under-

stand how the word "pleasures" (*naslazhdeniia*) can give offense, since it occurs in a poem. I have modified the Pevear and Volokhonsky translation in a few places, including here, where I have replaced their "delights" with "pleasures."

36. Unwittingly or not, Lebiadkin reverses Marya's and Varvara's positions in relation to military matters with this claim: Marya may be poor and Varvara rich, but Lebiadkin claims that Marya's grandfather died in active combat, while the reader knows that Varvara's husband, a frivolous lieutenant-general, died from a stomach ailment on his way to active duty in the Crimea. Dostoevsky also takes the opportunity to invoke Tolstoy's *War and Peace*, in which Nicholas Rostov's infatuation with Alexander I inspires him to fantasize about being killed before the emperor's eyes.

37. Significantly, Peter plans to declare his father mentally unbalanced and to institutionalize him.

38. See Tynianov (1966, 153–96).

39. Lotman's article on Gogol's realism opens: "Gogol was a liar [*lgun*]. Striving to open one's soul before the reader and speak the 'truth' was considered the height of romantic art. The height of Gogol's art was to hide himself, fabricate another person instead of himself and from that persona to play a romantic vaudeville of false sincerity.... There's a peculiar curiosity in the fact that the writer who stood as the banner of the authentic portrayal of life in Russian literature, loved to lie [*vrat'*] in both his creative work and his daily life" (Lotman 1996, 11).

40. This observation can be understood as a dig at Gogol, but it also anticipates Tikhon's observation that Stavrogin wants recognition for publishing his confession during his lifetime, thus underscoring Lebiadkin's status as a parody of Stavrogin. Lebiadkin manifests his propensity to want credit for undone deeds and mere intentions earlier in his letter to Liza Tushina when he claims that he would like to have lost a limb at Sevastopol.

41. In having Lebiadkin request that his skeleton be tagged, Dostoevsky may be evoking the displays in Peter the Great's Kunstkamera, a museum that featured freaks of nature. As Anthony Anemone noted at Columbia University, the museum's collections were all meticulously labeled (Anemone 2000, 583–602). Dostoevsky may also have found inspiration for Lebiadkin's skeletal bequest from the English philosopher Jeremy Bentham, a utilitarian with whom Dostoevsky constantly polemicized. Bentham planned for his body to be turned into an "auto-icon," that is, a representation of itself. Accordingly, his body was stuffed and placed in a glass case in University College London, where it occasionally still presides over meetings of Benthamites. I have heard it said that in the society's minutes he is recorded as "present, but not voting."

42. In addition, the narrator notes that Lebiadkin performed the solo cancan at the Virginsky's picnic, thus flaunting himself physically.

43. Fittingly, Lebiadkin and his sister are moved from the Filippov House (house of a pretender) on Epiphany Street, thus a location in town, to a newly built and isolated house on the outskirts of town that its owner intended as a tavern.

44. Rosenshield (1978).

Notes to Chapter 11

1. Miller (1998, 118–27).

2. While Ivan's devil invokes Mephistopheles, he resembles Hugo's Satan, who suffered from alienation and regret. For Hugo, "Satan became a metaphor of the longing of humanity to be reintegrated into that loving spirit of life from which we have exiled our-

selves by our own foolishness and selfishness" (Russell 1988, 230). As Russell notes, at first Hugo made Satan a symbol of evil. When he turned progressive, Hugo made Satan a representative of both oppressive governments and rebellion against oppression. "Hugo felt that alienation, defeat, sadness, and regret are as inherent in evil as cruelty and selfishness, and he painted a dimension of evil that had been neglected: the poignant sadness and isolation of the sinner." In this longing for reintegration, readers of Dostoevsky recognize Ivan Karamazov's devil. Hugo's belief in the ultimate reintegration of dark and light would also appeal to Dostoevsky's sensibilities.

3. For a discussion of the physics and metaphysics of the devil's watchlessness, see Knapp (1987, 105–20).

4. My thanks to Ganna Bograd for pointing this out to me. See Dal' (1978-80) and Ivanits (1989) for corroboration.

5. Terence's line, which Freud also cites, emphasizes the human: "I am man, nothing human is alien to me." In *Crime and Punishment*, Dostoevsky gives this line to Svidrigailov, another demonic double.

6. Lynd (1958, 20).

7. Knapp (1996, 16–19).

8. Belknap (1990, 113–23).

9. I owe this insight to Ted Cohen (1999). In his *Jokes and Their Relationship to the Unconscious*, Freud also discusses the relationship between the person telling a joke and his or her audience.

10. In translating *ostavat'sia s nosom*, I have followed Pevear and Volokhonsky's translation.

11. I take this definition of the obscene from Schneider (1977, 50).

12. Like the mythic trickster figure, Fedor Pavlovich challenges and disrupts the status quo but, given his own limitations, fails in his efforts to transcend the quotidien. See Roger Anderson's discussion of the trickster figure in his chapter on *Notes from the Underground* (Anderson 1986).

13. As Dostoevsky, the creator of the dying Ippolit, well knew, the process of dying itself can be profoundly shameful. "The open display of bodily functions—defecating, great pain, the process of dying—threatens the dignity of the individual, revealing an individual vulnerable to being reduced to his bodily existence, bound by necessity. The function of shame is to preserve wholeness and integrity" (Schneider 1977, 49). The ailing marquis thus has multiple sources of shame: he is dying; he is dying from syphilis (the consequence of exposing his penis in the wrong place); and others can see the shameful cause of his death.

14. Robert L. Jackson has made the linking of ethics and aesthetics a fundamental of Dostoevsky scholarship. While the linking permeates his work, it finds early expression in his seminal work, *Dostoevsky's Quest for Form* (New Haven, CT: Yale University Press, 1966).

15. The discretion-shame and disgrace-shame that inform these anecdotes help account for audience response to father and son. To respond appropriately to Fedor Pavlovich's shameless self-flaunting requires the wisdom and tact of Zosima. Readers may enjoy Fedor's shameless antics, but, like Alesha, we also feel acutely uncomfortable witnessing the public display of normally private matters. On the other hand, characters who display discretion-shame evoke reader sympathy. While confronting his devil proves painful for Ivan, readers feel safe. Ivan confronts his shame in the privacy of his own mind. We feel his pain, but we appreciate his discretion. We are free to delight in Dostoevsky's metaliterary play without the anxiety of witnessing inappropriate behavior.

16. I borrow this term from Miller, who cites Meier (1958, 115–228) (Miller 1992, 13).

17. Morson (1993, 1–117). For Morson's discussion of prosaics in the *Diary*, see pages 97–101.

18. Miller (1992).

Notes to Conclusion

1. Anderson notes that Zosima dies and "fertilizes" the lives of those who follow, particularly Alesha's (Anderson 1986, 143–44).

2. Slattery (2000, 121–30).

3. Ibid., 124.

4. Almost all shame dynamics discussed in the current literature can be found in Dostoevsky's work. Furthermore, Dostoevsky anticipates most therapeutic treatments for overcoming shame—laughter, denial/forgetting, confessing, empathy, and love. Dostoevsky's unique contribution to shame studies, as I see it, is narrative: in the story of Ivan Karamazov and his devil, Dostoevsky demonstrates how creativity can also help cure shame.

bibliography

Adamson, Joseph, and Hilary Clark, eds. *Scenes of Shame: Psychoanalysis, Shame, and Writing*. Albany, NY: State University of New York Press, 1999.
Alexandrov, Vladimir E. "The Narrator as Author in Dostoevskij's *Besy*." *Russian Literature* 15 (1984):243–54.
Al'mi, I. L. "K interpretatsii odnogo iz epizodov romana 'Idiot' (rasskaz generala Ivolgina o Napoleone)." In *Dostoevskii: Materialy i issledovaniia*, tom 10, 163–72. St. Petersburg: Nauka, 1992.
Almond, Barbara, and Richard Almond. *The Therapeutic Narrative: Fictional Relationships and the Process of Psychological Change*, 39–40. Westport, CT: Praeger, 1996.
Amis, Martin. "Lolita Reconsidered." *The Atlantic Monthly* 270, no. 3 (September 1992):110–11.
Anderson, Roger B. *Dostoevsky: Myths of Duality*. University of Florida Humanities Monograph Series, no. 58. Gainesville, FL: University Press of Florida, 1986.
Anemone, Anthony. "The Monsters of Peter the Great: The Culture of the St. Petersburg Kunstkamera in the Eighteenth Century." *Slavic and East European Journal* 44, no. 4 (Winter 2000):583–602.
Apuleius. *The Golden Ass*, translated by Jack Lindsay. Bloomington, IN: Indiana University Press, 1962.
Aristotle. *The "Art" of Rhetoric*, translated by J. H. Freese. Cambridge, MA: Harvard University Press, 1947.
Arutiunova, N. D. "O styde i stuzhe." *Voprosy iazykoznanie* no. 2 (1997):59–70.
———. "Poniatia styda i sovesti v tekstakh Dostoevskogo." *Chelovek* no. 30 (1999):1–17.
Austen, Jane. *Pride and Prejudice*. Vol. 2 of *The Novels of Jane Austen*. London: Oxford University Press, 1988.
Bakhtin, M. M. "Forms of Time and Chronotope in the Novel" and "Discourse in the Novel." In *The Dialogic Imagination: Four Essays by M. M. Bakhtin*, translated by Caryl Emerson and Michael Holquist. Austin, TX: University of Texas Press, 1981.
———. *Problems of Dostoevsky's Poetics*, edited and translated by Caryl Emerson, with introduction by Wayne C. Booth. Vol. 8 of *Theory and History of Literature*. Minneapolis, MN: University of Minnesota Press, 1989.

Beale, Walter. "Rhetorical Performative Discourse: A New Theory of Epideictic." *Philosophy and Rhetoric* 11, no. 4 (Fall 1978):221–46.
Belknap, Robert L. *The Structure of The Brothers Karamazov.* The Hague: Mouton, 1967. Reprint, Evanston, IL: Northwestern University Press, 1989.
———. *The Genesis of The Brothers Karamazov: The Aesthetics, Ideology, and Psychology of Making a Text.* Evanston, IL: Northwestern University Press, 1990.
———. "The Unrepentant Confession." In *Russianness*, edited by R. L. Belknap, 113–23. Ann Arbor, MI: Ardis, 1990.
———. "Survey of Russian Journals, 1840–1880." In *Literary Journals in Imperial Russia*, edited by D. Martinsen, 91–116. Cambridge, UK: Cambridge University Press, 1997.
Ben-Ze'ev, Aaron. *The Subtlety of Emotions.* Cambridge, MA: MIT Press, 2000.
Bernstein, Michael Andre. *Bitter Carnival: Ressentiment and the Abject Hero.* Princeton, NJ: Princeton University Press, 1992.
Bethea, David. *The Shape of Apocalypse in Modern Russian Fiction.* Princeton, NJ: Princeton University Press, 1989.
Blackmur, R. P. *Eleven Essays in the European Novel.* New York: Harcourt, Brace and World, 1964.
Blank, Ksana. "Korni poezii kapitana Lebiadkina." Unpublished paper presented at the Third Annual Ivy League Graduate Student Conference in Slavic and Soviet Studies, Harvard University, Cambridge, MA, April 1988.
———. "The Pen-and-ink Drawing of Utopia in Dostoevsky's 'Dream of a Ridiculous Man.'" In *Utopias*, edited by N. Thomas, 101–16. *Durham Modern Language Series.* Durham, UK: University of Durham Press, 2000.
Bograd, Ganna. "Pavlovskie realiia v romane F. M. Dostoevskogo *Idiot.*" *Dostoevsky Studies* 2–6 (1994–98):73–90.
Breger, Louis. *Dostoevsky: The Author as Psychoanalyst.* New York: New York University Press, 1989.
Broucek, Francis. *Shame and the Self.* New York: Guilford Press, 1991.
Brown, Carolyn S. *The Tall Tale in American Folklore and Literature.* Knoxville, TN: University of Tennessee Press, 1987.
Busch, Robert L. *Humor in the Major Novels of Dostoevsky.* Columbus, OH: Slavica, 1987.
Carter, Michael F. "The Ritual Functions of Epideictic Rhetoric: The Case of Socrates' Funeral Oration." *Rhetorica* 9, no. 3 (Summer 1991):209–32.
Cascardi, Anthony J. *The Bounds of Reason: Cervantes, Dostoevsky, Flaubert.* New York: Columbia University Press, 1986.
Cave, Terence. *Recognitions.* London: Oxford University Press, 1988.
Coetzee, J. M. "Confession and Double Thoughts: Tolstoy, Rousseau, Dostoevsky." *Comparative Literature* 37, no. 3 (Summer 1985):193–232.
Cohen, Ted. *Jokes: Philosophical Thoughts on Joking Matters.* Chicago: University of Chicago Press, 1999.
Cohn, Dorrit. *The Distinction of Fiction.* Baltimore: Johns Hopkins University Press, 1999.
Dal', Vladimir. *Tolkovyi slovar' zhivogo velikorusskogo iazyka.* 1880–82. Reprint, 4 vols., Moscow: Russkii iazyk, 1978–80.
Daly, Lloyd W. trans. and ed. *Aesop without Morals.* New York: Thomas Yoseloff, 1961.
Derzhavin, G. R. *Sochinenii.* Moscow: Pravda, 1985.
Dostoevskii, Andrei Mikhailovich. *Vospominaniia.* St. Petersburg: Izd. Andreev i synovia, 1892.

Dostoevskii, F. M. *Polnoe sobranie sochinenii v tridtsati tomakh*. Leningrad: Nauka, 1972–90.
———. *The Brothers Karamazov*, translated by Richard Pevear and Larissa Volokhonsky. New York: Vintage Classics, 1991.
———. *A Writer's Diary*, Vol. 1: 1873–1876, Vol. 2:1877–1881, translated by Kenneth Lantz. Evanston, IL: Northwestern University Press, 1993–94.
———. *Demons*, translated by Richard Pevear and Larissa Volokhonsky. New York: Vintage Classics, 1994.
Douglas, Mary. *Purity and Danger*. Routledge, 1996.
Duffy, Bernard. "The Platonic Functions of Epideictic Rhetoric." *Philosophy and Rhetoric* 16, no. 2 (1983):79–93.
Ekman, Paul. *Why Kids Lie*. New York: Scribner's, 1988.
Emerson, Caryl. *Boris Godunov: Transpositions of a Russian Theme*. Bloomington, IN: Indiana University Press, 1986.
Entsiklopediskii slovar'. St. Petersburg: Izd. Brokgaus-Efron, 1898, vol. 27: 187.
Fermon, Nicole. *Domesticating Passions: Rousseau, Woman, and Nation*. Middletown, CT: Wesleyan University Press, 1997.
Finke, Michael. *Metapoesis: The Russian Tradition from Pushkin to Chekhov*. Durham, NC: Duke University Press, 1995.
Fish, Stanley. *Surprised by Sin*. New York: St. Martin's Press, 1967. Reprint, Berkeley, CA: University of California Press, 1971.
Fitzgerald, Gene. "Anton Lavrent'evic G-v: The Narrator as Re-creator in Dostoevskij's *The Possessed*." In *New Perspectives on Nineteenth-Century Prose*, edited by G. J. Gutsche and L. G. Leighton, 121–34. Columbus, OH: Slavica, 1982.
Fossum, Merle A., and Marilyn J. Mason. *Facing Shame: Families in Recovery*. New York: W. W. Norton, 1986.
Frank, Joseph. *Dostoevsky: The Seeds of Revolt, 1821–1849*. Princeton, NJ: Princeton University Press, 1976.
———. *Dostoevsky: The Years of Ordeal, 1850–1859*. Princeton, NJ: Princeton University Press, 1983.
———. *Dostoevsky: The Stir of Liberation, 1860–1865*. Princeton, NJ: Princeton University Press, 1986.
———. *Dostoevsky: The Miraculous Years, 1865–1871*. Princeton, NJ: Princeton University Press, 1995.
Frankfurt, Harry. "On Bullshit." In *The Importance of What We Care About*, by Harry Frankfurt, 119–33. Cambridge, UK: Cambridge University Press, 1989.
Freud, Sigmund. *Totem and Taboo*, translated by J. Strachey. New York: W. W. Norton, 1950.
———. *Beyond the Pleasure Principle*, translated by J. Strachey. New York: W. W. Norton, 1961.
———. *Jokes and Their Relationship to the Unconscious*, translated by J. Strachey. New York: W. W. Norton, 1989.
Gasparov, Boris. *Poeticheskii iazyk Pushkina kak fakt istorii russkogo literaturnogo iazyka*, Wiener Slawistischer Almanach, Sonderband 27. Vienna: Wiener Slawistischer Almanach, 1992.
Genette, Gerard. *Figures III*. Paris: Seuil, 1972. Reprinted (in English) in *Narrative Discourse*. Ithaca, NY: Cornell University Press, 1980.
Gourevitch, Victor. "Rousseau on Lying: A Provisional Reading of the *Fourth Reverie*." *Berkshire Review* 15 (1980):93–107.

Grossman, Leonid. "Stilistika Stavrogina." In *Dostoevskii: Stat'i i materialy,* tom 2, edited by A. S. Dolinin, 138–48. Leningrad: Mysl', 1924.

Howard, Barbara. "The Rhetoric of Confession: Dostoevskij's *Notes from Underground.*" In *Critical Essays on Dostoevsky*, edited by R. F. Miller, 64–72. Boston: G. K. Hall, 1986.

Ivanits, Linda. *Russian Folk Belief.* New York: M. E. Sharpe, 1989.

Jackson, R. L. *Dostoevsky's Quest for Form.* New Haven, CT: Yale University Press, 1966.

Jaeger, Gérard A. *Pirates, Flibustiers et Corsaires: Histoire et légendes d'une société d'exception.* Avignon: Aubanel, 1987.

Jeanneret, Michel. *A Feast of Words: Banquets and Table Talk in the Renaissance*, translated by Jeremy Whitely and Emma Hughes. Cambridge, UK: Polity Press in association with Basil Blackwell, 1991.

Johnson, Leslie A. "The Face of the Other in *Idiot*." *Slavic Review* 50, no. 4 (Winter 1991):867–78.

Jones, Louisa E. *Sad Clowns and Pale Pierrots: Literature and the Popular Comic Arts in 19th-Century France.* Lexington, KY: French Forum, 1984.

Jones, Malcolm V. *Dostoyevsky: The Novel of Discord.* London: Paul Elek, 1976.

———. *Dostoyevsky after Bakhtin: Readings in Dostoyevsky's Fantastic Realism.* Cambridge, UK: Cambridge University Press, 1990.

———. "The Narrator and Narrative Technique in Dostoevsky's *The Devils*." In *Dostoevsky's The Devils: A Critical Companion*, edited by W. J. Leatherbarrow, 100–18. Evanston, IL: Northwestern University Press, 1999.

Kariakin, Iu. "Zachem khroniker v *Besakh*?" In *Dostoevskii: Materialy i issledovaniia*, tom 5, 113–31. Leningrad: Nauka, 1983.

Kaufman, Gershen. *The Psychology of Shame: Theory and Treatment of Shame-Based Syndromes.* London: Routledge, 1993. First published New York: Springer, 1989.

Kennedy, George. *The Art of Persuasion in Greece.* Princeton, NJ: Princeton University Press, 1963.

Kinston, Warren. "The Shame of Narcissism." In *The Many Faces of Shame*, edited by D. L. Nathanson, 214–45. New York: Guilford, 1987.

Knapp, Liza. "The Force of Inertia in Dostoevsky's 'Krotkaja.'" *Dostoevsky Studies* 6 (1985):143–56.

———. "The Fourth Dimension of the Non-Euclidean Mind: Time in *Brothers Karamazov* or Why Ivan Karamazov's Devil Does Not Carry a Watch." *Dostoevsky Studies* 8 (1987):105–20.

———. *The Annihilation of Inertia: Dostoevsky and Metaphysics.* Evanston, IL: Northwestern University Press, 1996.

Koehler, Ludmila. "The Grotesque Poetry of Dostoevskij." *Slavic and East European Journal* 14, no. 1 (1970):11–23.

Koepke, Wulf. "Nothing but the Dark Side of Ourselves? The Devil and Aesthetic Nihilism." In *The Fantastic Other: An Interface of Perspectives*, edited by Brett Cooke, George E. Slusser, and Jaume Marti-Olivella. *Critical Studies,* vol. 11, 143–63. Amsterdam: Rodopi, 1998.

Kostalevsky, Marina. *Dostoevsky and Soloviev: The Art of Integral Vision.* New Haven, CT: Yale University Press, 1997.

———. "The Pain and Pleasure of Thinking: Sensual Minds in *The Brothers Karamazov.*" In *Focus on Brothers Karamazov*, edited by R. L. Jackson. Evanston, IL: Northwestern University Press, 2003.

Kovacs, Arpad. "Poeticheskaia motivatsiia v romane Dostoevskogo *Besy*." *Acta Litteraria Academiae Scientiarum Hungaricae* 24, nos. 1–2 (1982):27–56.

Kuhns, Richard. *Tragedy: Contradiction and Repression*. Chicago: University of Chicago Press, 1991.

Levinas, Emmanuel. *Totality and Infinity: An Essay on Exteriority*, translated by Alphonso Lingis. Pittsburgh: Duquesne University Press, 1969.

———. *Ethics and Infinity: Conversations with Philippe Nemo*, translated by Richard A. Cohen. Pittsburgh: Duquesne University Press, 1985.

Levitt, Marcus. *The Pushkin Celebration of 1880 and the Politics of Literature in Russia*. Ithaca, NY: Cornell University Press, 1989.

Lewis, Helen Block. *Shame and Guilt in Neurosis*. New York: International Universities Press, 1971.

———. *Sex and the Superego*. Hillsdale, NJ: Lawrence Erlbaum Associates, 1987.

Lewis, Michael. *Shame: The Exposed Self*. New York: Free Press, 1992.

Lincoln, Bruce. "The Daily Life of St. Petersburg Officials in Mid-Nineteenth Century." *Oxford Slavonic Papers* 8 (1975):82–100.

———. *The Great Reforms: Autocracy, Bureaucracy, and the Politics of Change in Imperial Russia*. De Kalb, IL: Northern Illinois University Press, 1990.

Linde, Charlotte. *Life Stories: The Creation of Coherence*. London: Oxford University Press, 1993.

Livermore, Gordon. "Stepan Verkhovensky and the Shaping Dialectic of Dostoevsky's *Devils*." In *Dostoevsky: New Perspectives*, edited by R. L. Jackson, 176–92. Englewood Cliffs, NJ: Prentice Hall, 1984.

Lomonosov, M. V. *Sochinenii*. Moscow-Leningrad: Izd. khudozhestvennoi literatury, 1961.

Lotman, Iurii. "Concerning Khlestakov." In *The Semiotics of Russian Cultural History*, translated by Louisa Vinton, edited by Alexander D. Nakhimovsky and Alice Stone Nakhimovsky, 150–87. Ithaca, NY: Cornell University Press, 1985.

———. "O realizme Gogolia." In *Trudy po russkoi i slavianskoi filologii. Literaturovedenie II, novaia seria*. Tartu: Tartu University Press, 1996.

———. "Russo: russkaia kul'tura XVIII-nachala XIX veka." In *Russkaia literatura i kul'tura Prosveshcheniia*, tom 2, 139–206. Moscow: OGI, 1998.

Lynd, Helen Merrill. *On Shame and the Search for Identity*. New York: Harcourt, Brace, and Company, 1958.

Maiorova, Olga. "Tsarevich-Samozvanets v sotsial'noi mifologii poreformennoi epokhi." *Rossiia* no. 3 (1999):204–32.

Martinsen, Deborah A. "Dostoevsky and the Temptation of Rhetoric." Dissertation, Columbia University, 1990.

———. "Shame and Punishment." *Dostoevsky Studies*, New Series, vol. 5 (2001):51–70.

———. "Identity via Parody: Captain Lebiadkin, Poet-Cockroach." In *Against the Grain: Parody, Satire and Intertextuality in Russian Literature*, edited by Janet Tucker. Columbus, OH: Slavica, 2003.

Matlaw, Ralph. "The Chronicler of *The Possessed*: Character and Function." *Dostoevsky Studies*, vol. 5 (1984):37–47.

Matveyev, Rebecca Epstein. "Textuality and Intertextuality in Dostoevsky's *Poor Folk*." *Slavic and East European Journal* 39, no. 4 (1995):535–51.

Meerson, Olga. "Old Testament Lamentation in the Underground Man's Monologue: A Refutation of the Existentialist Reading of *Notes from the Underground*." *Slavic and East European Journal* 36, no. 3 (1992):317–22.

Meerson, Olga. "Ivolgin and Holbein: Non-Christ Risen vs. Christ Non-Risen." *Slavic and East European Journal* 39, no. 2 (1995):200–13.

———. *Dostoevsky's Taboos*. Dresden: Dresden University Press, 1998.

Meier, J. M. "Situation Rhyme in a Novel of Dostoevsky." In *Dutch Contributions to the Fourth International Congress of Slavists, Moscow, September 1958*, Slavistic Printings and Reprintings no. 20, 115–228. The Hague: Mouton, 1958.

Merezhkovsky, Dmitry. "Gogol and the Devil." In *Gogol from the Twentieth Century*, translated and edited by Robert A. Maguire, 55–102. Princeton, NJ: Princeton University Press, 1974.

Miatlev, I. P. *Polnoe sobranie sochinenii*. St. Petersburg: Izd. D. Fedorova, 1857.

Miller, Robin Feuer. *Dostoevsky and The Idiot: Author, Narrator, and Reader*. Cambridge, MA: Harvard University Press, 1981.

———. "Dostoevsky and Rousseau: The Morality of Confession Reconsidered." In *Dostoevsky: New Perspectives*, edited by Robert L. Jackson, 82–98. Englewood Cliffs, NJ: Prentice Hall, 1984.

———. *The Brothers Karamazov: Worlds of the Novel*. New York: Twayne, 1992.

———. "Dostoevskii and the Homeopathic Dose." In *American Contributions to the 12th International Congress of Slavists*, edited by Robert A. Maguire and Alan Timberlake, 118–27. Columbus, OH: Slavica, 1998.

Miller, Susan. *The Shame Experience*. Hillsdale, NJ: Analytic Press, 1993.

Moore, G. M. "The Voices of Legion: The Narrator of *The Possessed*." *Dostoevsky Studies*, vol. 6 (1985):51–66.

Morrison, Andrew. *Shame: The Underside of Narcissism*. Hillsdale, NJ: Analytic Press, 1989.

———. *The Culture of Shame*. New York: Ballantine Books, 1996.

Morson, Gary Saul. "Verbal Pollution in *The Brothers Karamazov*." In *Critical Essays on Dostoevsky*, edited by R. F. Miller, 234–42. Boston: G. K. Hall, 1986.

———. "Introductory Study: Dostoevsky's Great Experiment." In *A Writer's Diary*, vol. 1: 1873–1876, translated and annotated by Kenneth Lantz, 1–117. Evanston, IL: Northwestern University Press, 1993.

Murav, Harriet. *Holy Foolishness: Dostoevsky's Novels: The Poetics of Cultural Critique*. Stanford, CA: Stanford University Press, 1992.

Nathanson, Donald L., ed. *The Many Faces of Shame*. New York: Guilford, 1987.

———. *Shame and Pride: Affect, Sex and the Birth of the Self*. New York: W. W. Norton, 1992.

———, ed. *Knowing Feeling: Affect, Script and Psychotherapy*. New York: W. W. Norton, 1996.

Nazirov, R. G. "O prototipakh nekotorykh personazhei Dostoevskogo." In *Dostoevskii: Materialy i issledovaniia*, tom 1, 209–12. Leningrad: Nauka, 1974.

———. "Petr Verkhovenskii kak estet." *Voprosy literatury* 10 (1979):231–49.

Newton, Adam Zachary. *Narrative Ethics*. Cambridge, MA: Harvard University Press, 1995.

Nyberg, David. *The Varnished Truth: Truth Telling and Deceiving in Ordinary Life*. Chicago: University of Chicago Press, 1993.

Oravec, Christine. "'Observation' in Aristotle's Theory of Epideictic." *Philosophy and Rhetoric* 9, no. 3 (1976):162–74.

Orwin, Donna. "The Return to Nature: Tolstoyan Echoes in *The Idiot*." *The Russian Review*, vol. 58 (January 1999):87–102.

Panchenko, A. M. "Potemkinskie derevni' kak kul'turnyi mif." *XVIII vek,* sbornik 14, 93–104. Leningrad: Nauka, 1983.
Passage, Charles E. *Character Names in Dostoevsky's Fiction.* Ann Arbor, MI: Ardis, 1982.
Patterson, Annabel. *Fables of Power: Aesopian Writing and Political History.* Durham, NC: Duke University Press, 1991.
Peace, Richard. *Dostoyevsky: An Examination of the Major Novels.* Cambridge, UK: Cambridge University Press, 1971.
Perelman, Ch., and L. Olbrechts-Tyteca. *The New Rhetoric: A Treatise on Argumentation,* translated by John Wilkinson and Purcell Weaver. Notre Dame, IN: University of Notre Dame Press, 1969.
Perlina, Nina. *Varieties of Poetic Utterance: Quotation in* The Brothers Karamazov. New York: University Presses of America, 1985.
Perrie, Maureen. *Pretenders and Popular Monarchism in Early Modern Russia: The False Tsars of the Time of Troubles.* Cambridge, UK: Cambridge University Press, 1995.
Phelan, James. *Reading People, Reading Plots.* Chicago: University of Chicago Press, 1989.
———. *Narrative as Rhetoric: Technique, Audiences, Ethics, Ideology.* Columbus, OH: Ohio State University Press, 1996.
Piers, Gerhart, and Milton Singer. *Shame and Guilt: A Psychoanalytic and a Cultural Study.* Springfield, IL: Charles C. Thomas, 1953. Reprint, New York: W. W. Norton, 1971.
Proskurina, Iu. M. "Oblichitel'naia literatura." In *Dostoevskii: Estetika i poetika, Slovar'-spravochnik,* edited by G. K. Shchennikov, 33–34. Cheliabinsk: Metall, 1997.
Pushkin, A. S. *Polnoe sobranie sochinenii v desiati tomakh.* Leningrad: Nauka, 1979.
Rabinowitz, Peter J. *Before Reading: Narrative Conventions and the Politics of Interpretation.* Ithaca, NY: Cornell University Press, 1987.
Reyfman, Irina. *Ritualized Violence Russian Style: The Duel in Russian Culture and Literature.* Stanford, CA: Stanford University Press, 1999.
Rose, Margaret A. *Parody: Ancient, Modern, and Post-modern.* Cambridge, UK: Cambridge University Press, 1993.
Rosenshield, Gary. *Crime and Punishment: The Techniques of the Omniscient Author.* Lisse: Peter de Ridder Press, 1978.
Rousseau, Jean-Jacques. *Oeuvres complètes.* Paris: P. Dupont, 1823.
———. *Reveries of the Solitary Walker,* translated and introduction by Peter France. London: Penguin Books, 1979.
Russell, Jeffrey Burton. *The Prince of Darkness: Radical Evil and the Power of Good in History.* Ithaca, NY: Cornell University Press, 1988.
Saraskina, Ludmila. " 'Protivorechiia vmeste zhivut . . .': Khromonozhka v *Besakh* Dostoevskogo." *Voprosy literatury* no. 11 (1984):151–76.
———. *Besy: Roman-preduprezhdenie.* Moscow: Sovetskii pisatel', 1990.
Sartre, Jean-Paul. *Being and Nothingness,* translated by Hazel E. Barnes. New York: Philosophical Library, 1956.
Schneider, Carl. *Shame Exposure and Privacy.* New York: W. W. Norton, 1992; first published Boston: Beacon Press, 1977.
———. "A Mature Sense of Shame." In *The Many Faces of Shame,* edited by D. L. Nathanson, 194–213. New York: Guilford, 1987.
Sedgwick, Eve Kosofsky, and Adam Frank, eds. *Shame and Its Sisters: A Silvan Tomkins Reader.* Durham, NC: Duke University Press, 1995.
Shchennikov, Gury, ed. *Dostoevskii: Estetika i poetika, Slovar'-spravochnik.* Cheliabinsk: Metall, 1997.

Shore, Rima. "Scrivener Fiction: The Copyist and His Craft in Nineteenth-Century Fiction." Dissertation, Columbia University, 1980.
Singer, Jefferson A., and Peter Salovey. *The Remembered Self: Emotion and Memory in Personality*. New York: Free Press, 1993.
Sircello, Sir Guy. *Love and Beauty*. Princeton, NJ: Princeton University Press, 1989.
Slattery, Dennis Patrick. *The Wounded Body: Remembering the Markings of the Flesh*. Albany, NY: State University of New York Press, 2000.
Solov'ev, Vladimir. *Opravdanie dobra*. Moscow: Respublika, 1996.
Sutherland, Stewart R. "The Philosophical Dimension: Self and Freedom." In *New Essays on Dostoyevsky*, ed. Malcolm V. Jones and Garth M. Terry, 169–85. Cambridge: Cambridge University Press, 1983.
Swift, Jonathan. *A Tale of the Tub and Other Satires*. New York: Dutton, 1960.
Thompson, Diane Oenning. *The Brothers Karamazov and the Poetics of Memory*. Cambridge, UK: Cambridge University Press, 1991.
Thompson, J. M. *Napoleon Bonaparte*. Oxford: Basil Blackwell, 1988.
Tunimanov, V. A. "Khudozhestvennye proizvedeniia v Dnevnike pisatelia F. M. Dostoevskogo." Dissertation Leningrad State University, 1965.
———. "Publitsistika Dostoevskogo: *Dnevnik pisatelia*." In *Dostoevskii Khudozhnik i myslitel': sbornik stat'ei*, 165–209. Moscow: Khudozhestvennaia literatura, 1972.
———. "Rasskazchik v *Besakh* Dostoevskogo." In *Issledovaniia po poetike i stilistike*, edited by V. V. Vinogradov, 87–162. Leningrad: Nauka, 1972. Excerpt (in English) in *Dostoevsky: New Perspectives*, edited by R. L. Jackson, 145–75. Englewood Cliffs, NJ: Prentice Hall, 1984.
Twain, Mark. "On the Decay of the Art of Lying." In *Stolen White Elephant*, by Mark Twain. Boston: James R. Osgood & Co., 1882.
Tynianov, Iurii. "Dostoevskii i Gogol': K teorii parodii." In *O Dostoevskom: Stat'i*, with an introduction by Donald Fanger, 153–96. Providence, RI: Brown University Press, 1966.
Uspenskii, Boris. "Tsar and Pretender: *Samozvanchestvo* or Royal Imposture as a Cultural-Historical Phenomenon." In *The Semiotics of Russian Culture*, by Iurii Lotman and Boris Uspenskii, edited by Ann Shukman, *Michigan Slavic Contributions*, no. 11, 259–66. Ann Arbor, MI: Michigan Slavic Contributions, 1984.
Valagin, A. P. "Sistema obrazov v romane F. M. Dostoevskogo *Besy*." Dissertation, Voronezh State University, 1980.
Velleman, J. David. "The Genesis of Shame." *Philosophy and Public Affairs* 30, no. 1 (Winter 2001): 27–52.
Vetlovskaia, Valentina. "Srednevekovaia i fol'klornaia simvolika u Dostoevskogo." In *Kul'turnoe nasledie drevnei Rusi*, 315–22. Moscow: Nauka, 1976.
Vladiv, Slobodanka V. *Narrative Principles in Dostoevskij's Besy: A Structural Analysis*. Berne: Peter Lang, 1979.
Volgin, I. L. *Dostoevskii—Zhurnalist (Dnevnik pisatelia i russkaia obshchestvennost')*. Moscow: Izd. Moskovskogo Universiteta, 1982.
Vol'pert, L. I. "Napoleonovskii 'mif' u Pushkina i Stendalia." In *Pushkinskie chteniia: Sbornik stat'ei*, 88–107. Tallinn: EESTI RAAMAT, 1990.
Voltaire. *Oeuvres complètes de Voltaire*, vol. 9. Paris: L'Imprimerie de Crapelet, 1819.
Webb, Stephen. *Blessed Excess: Religion and the Hyperbolic Imagination*. Albany, NY: State University of New York Press, 1993.
Wentworth, Patricia. *Poison in the Pen*. New York: Harper Perennial, 1992.

Wilhelm, Laura Kristan. "Slave among the Slavs: An Approach to Aesopian Poetics and Its Implications for the Study of Russian Aesopianism." Unpublished paper, from a chapter in her dissertation, "The Fate of the Fable in Modern Russian Literature," University of Kansas, 1994.
———. "The Aesopic Legacy in Russian Literature." Unpublished article, n.d.
Williams, Bernard. *Shame and Necessity*. Berkeley, CA: University of California Press, 1993.
Wilson, Catherine. "Self-Deception and Psychological Realism." *Philosophical Investigations* 3, no. 4 (1980):47–60.
Wollheim, Richard. *On the Emotions*. New Haven, CT: Yale University Press, 1999.
Workman, Nancy. "Unrealism: Bureaucratic Absurdity in Nineteenth-Century Russian Literature." Dissertation Columbia University, 1998.
Wortman, Richard. *From Peter the Great to the Death of Nicholas I*, vol. 1 of *Scenarios of Power: Myth and Ceremony in Russia's Monarchy*. Princeton, NJ: Princeton University Press, 1995.
Wurmser, Leon. "Shame: The Veiled Companion of Narcissism." In *The Many Faces of Shame*, edited by D. L. Nathanson, 64–92. New York: Guilford, 1987.
———. *The Mask of Shame*. Baltimore: Johns Hopkins University Press, 1981. Reprint, Northvale, NJ: Jason Aronson, 1997.
Zakharova, T. V. "*Dnevnik pisatelia* i ego mesto v tvorchestve F. M. Dostoevskogo 1870-kh godov." Dissertation Leningrad State University, 1974.
Zembaty, Jane S. "Aristotle on Lying." *Journal of the History of Philosophy* 31 (January 1993):7–29.

index

Adamson, Joseph, xv
Aesop
   Aesopian language (coded words), 109
   Fedor Pavlovich Karamazov, 59, 170–71, 173, 175–83, 210
   historical, fictional aspects of, 173, 175–83, 213
   parallels with Pushkin, 181–82
Alexander I, tsar, 57, 80–81
Al'mi, Inna, 54
atheism, 4–5, 86, 140
audience
   authorial audience, 12–13, 99
   character audience, 6, 92, 95, 99, 211–12
   narrative audience, 12–13
Austen, Jane, 21–23

Bahktin, M. M., 19, 65, 134, 186
Baron Brambeus, 72
"The Battle of the Books" (Swift), 177
Belknap, Robert L., 74, 99–100, 211
Bernstein, Michael Andre, 151, 244–45n.11
Bible
   in *The Brothers Karamazov*, 60
   confessions, biblical language used in, 92
   in *Demons*: Sophia Matveevna Ulitina as Bible peddler, 124, 126; and Stepan Trofimovich Verkhovensky, 125–26, 128–29, 134, 219
   First Corinthians, 124
   Garden of Eden, 13–18, 25, 60
   Job, 174–75
   John 12:24, 13
   Psalms 14 and 53, 5
   Revelation, 154–55, 159, 166
Blank, Ksana, 58, 171
THE BROTHERS KARAMAZOV
Afanasy, 98, 219–20
Father Ferapont, 60, 220
Grigory, 61
Karamazov, Alesha, and brothers, 210, 220–24; and father, 3, 61, 101, 178; and Zosima, 140, 145, 175
Karamazov, Dmitry, 10, 14, 226n.8; and father, 61, 176–77, 181
Karamazov, Fedor Pavlovich
   and Aesop, 59, 170–71, 175–83, 210
   and confession, 100, 211, 214
   and other literary characters: Lukian Lebedev, 135–36; Pierrot, 8, 170, 176
   and other characters in *The Brothers Karamazov*: Alesha, 3, 61, 101, 178; Dmitry, 61, 176–77, 181; Ivan, 176; and Smerdiakov, 61, 180–81, 221; Petr Aleksandrovich Miusov, 2–7, 10, 142, 176, 178, 189, 211; Zosima, 93, 95–97, 142, 177, 180, 210–11
   and puns, 178–81, 210–11, 213, 215
   and shamelessness, xv, 52, 95–98, 100–101, 169, 210
   and stories: Diderot story, 4–10, 142–43; St. Denis story, 137–41, 143–46; police commissioner story, 178–80
   as buffoon, 2–3, 6–8, 61, 100, 178
   as exhibitionist liar, 52, 170, 178, 182–83, 214
   as father/son of lies, 92, 100
   as sponger, 3, 7, 57, 96, 177, 208

Karamazov, Ivan, 61, 141–42
    and brothers: Alesha, 210, 220–21, 223–24; Pavel Smerdiakov, 207, 221
    and Christ, 223–24
    and devil of, 207–10, 212–16, 218, 221–23, 255n.1
    and father, 176
    and Grand Inquisitor, 34, 59, 215–16, 221, 223
    and Katerina Ivanovna, 209
    as writer, 175, 208, 216
Miusov, Petr Aleksandrovich, 2–10, 137–46, 176, 178–79, 187, 211
Smerdiakov, Pavel, 60–61, 107, 180–81, 207, 221–23, 226n.16
Smerdiashchaia, Lizaveta, holy fool, 9, 180
Zosima, 4–10, 40-1, 93–8, 100–102, 138–46, 177–80, 210–11, 215, 219–20, 238–39n.7, 238n.3, 239n.8

Catherine II (Catherine the Great), 3, 8–9, 57, 172
censorship
    Aesopian language (coded words), 109
    circumvention of, 46, 183
Chernosvitov, 78–79
Chernyshevsky, Nikolai, 114, 121, 189
Christ, 215–16, 218-20, 223
    in *The Brothers Karamazov*, 60, 209–10, 221, 223–24
Clark, Hilary, xiii
commedia dell'arte, 8
confession, xvii, 92, 98–100, 123, 125–27, 202, 210–15, 239n.8
Confessions (Rousseau), 39, 214
Confessions (St. Augustine), 16
conversion, 4, 8

Dal', Vladimir, 2, 226n.2
Daly, Lloyd W., 176
Dante, 16, 18
Dashkova, Princess, 3, 8–9
Dead Souls (Gogol), 69
decapitation images, 145, 177–78, 243n.9, 254n.30
decorum, xvi, 7, 93, 95, 177–78, 225–26n.1, 226n.6
Dembrovsky, Konstantin, 181
DEMONS
Drozdova, Praskovia, 117, 184, 187, 202
Karmazinov, 112, 202
Kirillov, 120, 122–23
Lebiadkin, Captain Ignat 170–75, 184–206

and writers: Derzhavin, 170–72; Krylov, 170, 172–73; Pushkin, 181, 191–92
and historical/literary figures: Prince de Monbars, 191–94
and other literary characters: Captain Kartuzov, 194, 196, 202; Falstaff, 170, 188, 194; Job, 174–75; Lebedev, 149, 202
and other characters from *Demons*: Governor von Lembke, 184–85; Liza Tushina, 171, 174, 184–85, 189, 195–200; Marya, his holy fool sister, 173, 175, 185, 187, 198, 251n.5, 252n.13; Nikolai Stavrogin, 171–72, 175, 185–87, 195, 198–206; Peter Verkhovensky, 171–72, 185–87, 199–204; Stepan Verkhovensky, 131–32, 202; Varvara Stavrogina, 173, 175, 184–85, 187, 191, 201, 203
anonymity, 184–85, 187, 199–204
as exposer, 185–87, 206;
as plagiarist, 194–200;
as poet, 171–74, 190, 194–97, 203
    "The Cockroach," 171–74, 94
    "In Case She Should Break Her Leg," 171, 195–96
    "To the Perfection of Young Miss Tushin," 171, 190, 196–97
    "To a Star-Amazon," 171
as pretender, 186, 189–90, 203; and pretendership, 172, 187–88, 203
as repentant freethinker, 199–201, 203–4
as sacrifice, 204–5
as swan, 202, 206
murder of, 175, 185, 200–5
self-images of, 171–4; 198, 248–49n.6
Lebiadkina, Marya, holy fool, 173, 175, 185, 187–88, 190, 198, 203, 205, 251n.5, 252n.13
narrator, Mr. G-v,
    as friend to Stepan Verkhovensky, 93–95, 99, 103–108, 133–38
    as narrator, relationship to Captain Lebiadkin, 186, 190–91, 198, 204–5; infatuation with Liza Tushina, 190, 252n.13; portrayal of Peter Verkhovensky, 104–105
Shatova, Dasha, 113–14, 118, 132, 239–40n.7
Shatov, Ivan, 124, 127–28, 185, 200–2
Stavrogin, Nikolai Vsevolodovich, 106, 124, 127–28, 171–72, 175, 185–88, 190, 193–94, 197–205
Stavrogina, Varvara Petrovna, 94–95, 99, 105–107, 109, 111–17, 120, 123,

Index

125–26, 130–33, 173, 175, 184–85, 187, 191, 201–3,
Tushina, Liza, 113, 117, 119, 122–24, 171, 174, 184–85, 189, 195–200
Ulitina, Sophia Matveevna, 107–109, 123–24, 126, 130–32, 134
Verkhovensky, Peter Stepanovich, xv, 34, 104–105, 114–21, 124, 132, 171, 185–8, 190, 199–200, 203–5, 251n.5
Verkhovensky, Stepan Trofimovich, 92–96, 99, 103–11, 113–16, 124, 133, 147, 217–19, 240n.8
  Bible and, 125–26, 128–29, 134, 219
  compared with Captain Lebiadkin, 131–32, 202; General Ivolgin, 130–31
  confessions of, 98–99, 123, 125–27
  conversion experience of, 129
  and other characters: Dasha, 113–14, 118–19, 132, 239–40n.7; Fedka, 205; Liza Tushina, 118; Mr. G-v, 93–95, 104, 107–108, 133–38; his son Peter, 104–105, 114–20; Sophia Ulitina, 107–109, 123, 125–26, 128–32, 134; Stavrogin, 106, 118–19; Varvara Stavrogina, 94–95, 99, 105–107, 111–17, 123, 126, 130–33
  self-deception of, 105–11, 130–34
von Lembke, Governor, 117, 184–85, 199–201
von Lembke, Julia, 112, 120–21
Derzhavin, Gavriil Romanovich
  and Captain Lebiadkin, 170–72
  "God," 197
  "Lebed'" (The Swan), 150, 155, 172, 191–92, 202
Descartes, René du Perron, 42
devil
  Fedor Karamazov and, 4, 59
  Ivan Karamazov and, 207–10, 212–16, 218, 221–23, 255n.1
  Napoleon, Russian association with, 53
Diderot, Denis, 138–39
  Diderot story and, 3–10, 40–41, 140, 142–43
  St. Denis story and, 137–41, 143–46
divided selves, xvii, 135–46, 149
Divine Comedy (Dante), 16
Dmitry
  First False Dmitry, 188–89
  Second False Dmitry, 188–89, 206
  Tsarevich Dmitry, 204
Dobroliubov, Nikolai, 114
Don Quixote *(Don Quixote)* (Cervantes), 82, 123, 148, 150, 152, 154, 203

Dostoevsky, Fedor Mikhailovich
  and Aesop, 59
  and belief in God, 4, 18, 59, 86, 103, 123–24, 162, 167–68, 215–16
  and ethics of discourse, 38–43
  Mikhail Dostoevsky
  his brother, 19
  his father, 57–58
  and Military Engineering Academy, 57
  and narrative, 2, 10–11, 13, 18, 20, 22, 46–51, 170–75, 217–24
  works of
    The Adolescent, 168
    The Brothers Karamazov, 12–13
    Crime and Punishment, 10, 12, 20
    Demons, 184
    Diary of a Writer
      "Something about Lying," 4, 23–24, 27–30
      "Sreda" (The Milieu), 129–30
    The Double, 22, 135
    "Dream of the Ridiculous Man," 20
    The Humiliated and the Injured, 20
    The Idiot, 15
    "Mr.—bov and the Question of Art," 114
    Poor Folk, 19, 22
    "Village of Stepanchikovo," 201
double-voicing
  in *The Brothers Karamazov,* 146, 171
  in *Demons,* 134, 171
  in *The Idiot,* 149
dueling, 85–86, 94–95, 98, 238–39n.7, 238n.3
Dumas, Alexandre, *père,* 56, 78

ethics, xv, 12, 15, 18, 25, 38–43, 228n. 1

fallen woman, xv, 19, 43, 46, 62, 65, 91, 148, 243–44n.2
Falstaff (Shakespeare), 170, 188, 194
Filippov, Danila, 190
Flagellants, 190
flibustiers, 192–93
Frankfurt, Harry, 33–35, 39, 110, 134, 230n.31
Freud, Sigmund, 18, 49

Galen, 180
Garden of Eden (Bible), 13–15, 17–18, 25
Gogol, Nikolai
  Dead Souls, Captain Kopeikin, 69
  "Diary of a Madman," madman, 64–65
  The Inspector General, 19–20, 50, 72. *See* Khlestakov

"Nevsky Prospect," Pirogov, 63
"The Nose," 64, 69, 209, 213,
    Major Kovalev, 64–65, 69, 209
"The Overcoat," 69, 79
    Akakii Akakievich Bashmachkin, 69–70
Selected Passages, 201
"Zaveshchanie," 201
The Golden Ass (Apuleius), 153
Great Reforms, era of, 188
guilt, 14, 20, 23

Herzen, Alexander Ivanovich, 77–78
Holbein, Hans, The Younger, 162, 221
honor code of the nobility, 24–25, 229n.18
humor, as response to shame, 101
hyperbole. *See* lying

identity, xiv–xv, 4, 14, 20, 24–25, 36–38, 46, 89–92, 149, 170
THE IDIOT
Barashkova, Nastasia Filippovna, 43–47, 62–63, 65, 70<-.72, 75, 90–91, 148, 160–62, 243–44n.2
Epanchina, Aglaia Ivanovna, 47, 70, 73–75, 91, 148
Epanchin, General, 45, 153, 163
Epanchina, Lizaveta Prokofievna, 48, 73–76, 85–86, 88, 160–61, 166–67
Ferdyshenko, 136, 148–49, 153, 160, 163
Ivolgin, Ardalion Aleksandrovich, General
    and Aglaia Epanchina story, 73–75
    and Captain Eroshka Eropegov story, 85–88, 90, 238nn.31, 33
    and Crimean War story, 63–65
    and lapdog story, 43–47, 68, 70–73, 88, 90
    and Napoleon story, 47–48, 52–56, 60–66, 76–85, 88–89, 130–31
    and Private Kolpakov story, 65–70, 88
    Gogolian roots of, 63, 79
    and Lukian Lebedev, 65, 68, 75–82, 85, 88, 149–53, 158, 165–68, 238 nn.31, 33
    and Nastasia Filippovna, 43–47, 62, 65, 70–72, 75, 90
    and Russian social contract, 152–53
    and the Three Musketeers, 56, 68, 86
    and Stepan Verkhovensky, 130–31
Ivolgin, Gania Ardalionovich, 45, 61, 65, 71, 85, 87–88, 90, 148
Ivolgin, Kolia, 61, 84–85, 87, 90, 160
Ivolgina, Nina Aleksandrovna, 67, 73, 85, 87, 90
Ivolgina, Varvara Ardalionovna, 67, 73

Ippolit, 85–87, 90, 137, 149, 160, 221
Keller, 136, 154, 160–68, 247n.32
Lebedev, Lukian, 149–58, 162, 202, 244–45n.11
    and 1812 story, 76–79, 161–62
    and Antichrist professor story, 154–55
    and St. John the Baptist story, 135–38, 146
    and cannibal speech, 149, 152, 154, 158–60, 164–68
    as divided self, 135, 149, 158, 163, 202
    as exposer, 150–51, 202–3
    as prophet, 150, 154, 165, 181, 203
    as interpreter of Revelation, 154–55, 159, 166
    as lawyer, 154, 159–60, 166. *See also* cannibal speech
    and other characters: General Ivolgin, 65, 68, 75–76, 81–82, 88, 149–52, 158, 165–68, 238nn.31, 33; Keller, 160–68; Mme. Epanchina, 160–61, 166–67; Nastasia Filippovna, 160–62; Prince Myshkin, 153, 155–59, 166–67, 246n.19; compared with: Captain Lebiadkin, 202; Fedor Karamazov, 135–36
    and exposure, 148, 151, 166
    Gogolian roots of, 137
    and Russian social contract, 151–53
Myshkin, Lev Nikolaevich, Prince, 47–48, 55–56, 62, 65–70, 76–85, 88, 91, 130–31, 147–48, 150, 153, 155–59, 160–64, 166–67, 246n.19, 256n.16
narrative strategy in, 15, 47, 147, 168–69
narrator, 62, 147–48
Rogozhin, Parfen, 45, 91, 150, 158, 164
Totsky, General, 45, 153, 163
The Iliad (Homer), 22
The Inspector General. *See* Gogol, Nikolai

Job, 174–75
John 12:24, 13
Johnson, Leslie A., 15, 227n.30
John the Baptist story, 135–38
Jones, Malcolm V., 225–26n.1(2)
juries, 129–30

Kant, Immanuel, 128
Katkov, publisher of Dostoevsky, 202
Kaufman, Gershen, xv, 99
Khlestakov *(The Inspector General)* (Gogol), 19, 36–37, 63, 65, 72, 193
kissing head (St. Denis) story *(The Brothers Karamazov)*, 137–41, 143–46
Knapp, Liza, 211

Kock, Charles Paul de, 107, 112
Kohut, Heinz, xii
Kolpakov story *(The Idiot)*, 65–70, 88
Krylov, 170, 172–73
Kuhns, Richard, 184

Lacan, Jacques, xv
La Fontaine, Jean de, 173
lapdog story *(The Idiot)*, 43–47, 68, 70–73, 88, 90
lawyers, 130, 159–60, 166
Lear (Shakespeare), 90
"Lebed" (The Swan) (Derzhavin), 150, 155, 172, 202
Levinas, Emmanuel, xv, 227n.30
Lewis, Helen Block, xiv, 22, 50–51
Lewis, Michael, 98, 125, 239n.8, 242n.28
liars, xvi–xvii, 3, 11–12, 15, 18–20, 26–27, 31–37, 50, 63, 170, 193, 217
  shamed liars, 217. *See also* General Ivolgin, Stepan Verkhovensky
  shameless liars. *See* Captain Lebiadkin; Fedor Karamazov; Lukian Lebedev
Linde, Charlotte, 240n.8
Lives of the Saints *(The Brothers Karamazov)*, 139
Lomonosov, Mikhail, 174
  "Ode, Extracted from Job, Chapters 38, 39, 40 and 41," 174
Lotman, Iurii, 36–37, 105–106
Louis XV, 155–56
Louis XVIII, 177
lying
  bullshitters, 33–35, 161–62
  bullshitting, 30–31, 35, 134, 230n. 31
  conceals, discloses shame, 4
  and ethics of discourse, 38–43
  deliberate lies, *(lozh)*, 31, 33–35, 105, 117, 120
  exhibitionist lying *(vran'yo)*, 3, 6, 27–35, 182–83, 216
  hyperbole, 6, 30, 42–43, 79, 201
  identity, xvi, 92, 219
  plagiarism, 6–7, 23–24, 27–30, 43–47, 72
  as social contract, 32–33
  and "Something about Lying" (Dostoevsky), 4, 23–24
Lynd, Helen Merrill, xiv, 24, 210

Madame du Barry, Becu, Marie Jeanne, (Comtesse du Barry), 137, 155–57, 169, 246n. 16

Major Kovalev ("The Nose"), 64–65, 69, 209
Makar Devushkin *(Poor Folk)*, 19–20, 26
Meerson, Olga, 59–60, 180, 226n.16, 228n.7
metaliterary play, xvi, 217
  in *The Brothers Karamazov*, xvi, 5, 10, 146, 170, 175
  in *Demons*, 170, 172, 184, 195, 250–51n. 2
  in *The Idiot*, 15
Miatlev, I. P., "Fantastic Tale," 174
Miller, Robin Feuer, 77, 88–89, 103, 207, 216, 228n.1
monastery, 93, 101–102, 142–44, 177–78
Monbars, Prince de, 191–94
Morrison, Andrew, xiv, 65
Morson, Gary Saul, 216
murder
  in *The Brothers Karamazov*, 8
  in *Crime and Punishment*, 21
  in *Demons*, 185, 200–6
My Past and Thoughts (Herzen), 77–78

Napoleon and Napoleon story, 20, 47–48, 52–56, 60–61, 63–66, 76–85, 88–89, 130–31
Nathanson, Donald, xv
Newton, Adam Zachary, 227n.30
Nikitenko, 226n.6
"The Nose" (Gogol), 64, 69, 138–39, 209, 213
nose story *(The Brothers Karamazov)*, 212–14
Nyberg, David, 118

Otrepev, Grishka, 188
"Overcoat" (Gogol), 69, 79

paradox
  Christ as, 220
  shame's paradox, xvi, 2, 12, 98, 217, 220
Patterson, Annabel, 176–77
Paul I, tsar, 57–58
Peace, Richard, 189
Père Goriot (Balzac), 22
Perlina, Nina, 125
Peter III, tsar, 9, 57
Peter the Great, tsar, 35, 54
Pevear, Richard, 177, 226n.3
Phelan, James, 13, 226n.11
Picquenard, Jean-Baptiste, 192–93
Pierrot, 8, 170, 176
Piers, Gerhart, xiv
plagiarism. *See* lying
Plato, 5

police commissioner story (*The Brothers Karamazov*), 178–80
Poor Folk (Dostoevsky), 19, 22
"Poor Knight." *See* Pushkin
Potemkin, Grigori Alexandrovich, 3, 8–9, 106
pozor (shame), 2, 224. *See also* shame
pretenders
    Captain Ignat Lebiadkin *(Demons)* as, 186, 189–90, 203–4
    First False Dmitry, 188–89
    Khlestakov as *(The Inspector General)* (Gogol), 19, 201
    Major Kovalev as ("The Nose"), 201
    Peter Verkhovensky as (*The Idiot*), 204
    Second False Dmitry, 188–89, 206
    Stavrogin as "Ivan-Tsarevich" (*Demons*), 172, 188, 204
pretendership, in *Demons,* 172, 187–88, 190
Pride and Prejudice (Austen), 21–23
Prince Hal (Shakespeare), 194
Psalms 14 and 53, 5
punning, 178–81, 210–15
Pushkin, Alexander Sergeevich, 18, 55, 57–59, 63, 65, 172, 188, 191–92, 203
    parallels with Aesop, "black writer," 59, 181–82
    "Egyptian Nights," 172
    "Once There Lived a Poor Knight," 43, 113, 123, 148, 203
    "The Hero," 120

Raphael, 93, 115, 122
Raskolnikov *(Crime and Punishment),* 12, 20–21, 135, 170, 204–5, 222
Razumikhin *(Crime and Punishment),* 42–43
readers, xiii–xvii, 1–2, 10–13, 16–18, 22, 26–27, 129–30, 217
reform, Dostoevsky and, 22, 50–51
repentance, 23, 85
Revelation (St. John), 152, 154–55, 159, 166
Reyfman, Irina, 238–39n.7, 238n.3
rhetoric. xvii, 3, 46–50, 92, 165–68, 216, 219
Rosenshield, Gary, 204–5
Rousseau, Jean-Jacques, 38–43, 46, 92, 109, 214
    Reveries of the Solitary Walker, 38–39
Russian culture, 27–29, 32–38, 60, 105–106, 109, 141
Russian literary tradition, 7, 53, 63–64, 150, 172, 229 n. 18
Russian social contract, 7, 32–33, 151–53, 165–68

Saiapan, peasant, 129–30
Saint-Aurèle, Poirié, 192
Salovey, Peter, 30
Sartre, Jean Paul, xvi
scandal, xvi, 1–2, 6, 10, 93, 146, 218, 220
Schneider, Carl, 8, 25, 229n.20
self-consciousness, 1, 2, 16, 23, 26–27, 91, 96, 217
Shakespeare, William, 18, 115, 122, 170
shame, xiv–xvii, 98, 224
    contagiousness of, 2, 12, 26–27, 95, 217
    discretion-shame, 12–13, 15, 25, 100, 227n.21
    disgrace-shame, 12–13, 15 25, 100, 227n.21
    disorientation, 2, 23, 96, 217
    disruption, 2, 23, 96, 217
    dynamics, xiv–xvi, 2, 4, 8, 10–15, 20–27, 38, 46, 50–51, 88, 95–96, 152, 217–24, 227 n. 30
    Indo-European root of, 25, 229n.20
    liars, xvi, 26–27, 217
        shamed liars. *See* General Ivolgin; Stepan Verkhovensky
        shameless liars. *See* Captain Lebiadkin; Fedor Karamazov; Lukian Lebedev
    lying, xvii, 3–6, 11–12, 23–24, 30–35, 42–43, 79, 134, 161–62, 201, 230n. 31
    as narrative strategy, xiii–xvii, 1–2, 9–11, 15–16, 18, 22, 91–94, 204, 216–24
    paradoxicality of, xiv, 2, 6, 12, 98, 217
    passed-on shame, 23, 90, 216
    pozor (shame), 2, 224
    self-amplified shame, 96
    and self-consciousness, 16, 91
    shamelessness, xiii, 93–94, 97, 100, 217–18
    sram, 2
    studies, xiii–xv, 225n.1(1), 226n.4
    styd, 2
    unexpectedness of, 2, 12, 16, 91, 95
Singer, Jefferson, 30
Singer, Milton, xiv
Sistine Madonna (Raphael), 93, 113–14, 117, 132–33
Skotoprigonevsk, residence of Fedor Karamazov, 177, 249n.19
Skvoreshniki, estate of the Stavrogins, 111
Slattery, Dennis Patrick, 220–21
social class, xvi, 6, 141, 149, 171–72, 190–92, 204
Solovev, Vladimir, xv, 25–26, 30, 41
"Something about Lying" (Dostoevsky), 4, 23–24

sons, xvii, 53, 59–60, 122, 144, 200
Speshnev, Nikolai, 79
sponger
   Fedor Pavlovich Karamazov as, 3, 7, 57, 96, 177, 208
   Ivan Karamazov's devil as, 208
   Captain Lebiadkin as (*Demons*), 171
   Stepan Verkhovensky as, 106–107, 110–11, 113
St. Augustine, 16
St. Denis (kissing head) story, 137–41, 143–46
St. John the Baptist story (*The Idiot*), 135–38, 146
St. John, Revelation of, in *The Idiot*, 152, 154–55, 159, 166
St. Paul, 124
suicide, xiv, 149, 222
Swift, Jonathan, 177

taboos, 14–20, 26–27, 60, 100, 119, 205, 226n. 16
Talleyrand, Charles Maurice de, 137
Three Musketeers, 56, 68, 86
Time of Troubles, 188

Tocqueville, Alexis de, 106–107
Tolstoy, Lev Nikolaevich, 18, 22–23, 40, 54
   "Sevastopol Sketches," 195
   War and Peace, 195
Tomkins, Silvan, xiv–xv
truth, 5–6, 20, 32, 35, 38, 89, 119, 127, 157–58
Twain, Mark, 32

underground man of Dostoevsky, xv, 170
unexpectedness of shame, 2, 12, 16, 91, 95
Uspenskii, Boris, 188, 190

Velleman, David, xv
Vetlovskaia, Valentina, 59
Volokhonsky, Larissa, 177, 226n.3
Voltaire, 138–39
   La Pucelle d'Orléans, 138–39
vran'yo. *See* lying

What Is to Be Done? (Chernyshevsky), 121, 189
Wilhelm, Laura Kristan, 181
Wilson, Catherine, 105, 110
writer's art, commentary on, 170–75

The Theory and Interpretation of Narrative Series
James Phelan and Peter J. Rabinowitz, Editors

Because the series editors believe that the most significant work in narrative studies today contributes both to our knowledge of specific narratives and to our understanding of narrative in general, studies in the series typically offer interpretations of individual narratives and address significant theoretical issues underlying those interpretations. The series does not privilege any one critical perspective but is open to work from any strong theoretical position.

Misreading Jane Eyre: *A Postformalist Paradigm*
JEROME BEATY

Invisible Author, Last Essays
CHRISTINE BROOKE-ROSE

Narratologies: New Perspectives on Narrative Analysis
EDITED BY DAVID HERMAN

Telling Tales: Gender and Narrative Form in Victorian Literature and Culture
ELIZABETH LANGLAND

Matters of Fact: Reading Nonfiction over the Edge
DANIEL W. LEHMAN

Breaking the Frame: Metalepsis and the Construction of the Subject
DEBRA MALINA

Framing Anna Karenina: *Tolstoy, the Woman Question, and the Victorian Novel*
AMY MANDELKER

Surprised by Shame: Dostoevsky's Liars and Narrative Exposure
DEBORAH A. MARTINSEN

Politics, Persuasion, and Pragmatism: A Rhetoric of Feminist Utopian Fiction
ELLEN PEEL

Narrative as Rhetoric: Technique, Audiences, Ethics, Ideology
JAMES PHELAN

Understanding Narrative
EDITED BY JAMES PHELAN AND PETER J. RABINOWITZ

Before Reading: Narrative Conventions and the Politics of Interpretation
PETER J. RABINOWITZ

Narrative Dynamics: Time, Plot, Closure, and Frames
EDITED BY BRIAN RICHARDSON

The Progress of Romance: Literary Historiography and the Gothic Novel
DAVID H. RICHTER

A Glance beyond Doubt: Narration, Representation, Subjectivity
SHLOMITH RIMMON-KENAN

Psychological Politics of the American Dream: The Commodification of Subjectivity in Twentieth-Century American Literature
LOIS TYSON

Ordinary Pleasures: Couples, Conversation, and Comedy
KAY YOUNG

Having a Good Cry: Effeminate Feelings and Pop-Culture Forms
ROBYN R. WARHOL

www.ingramcontent.com/pod-product-compliance
Lightning Source LLC
Chambersburg PA
CBHW030108010526
44116CB00005B/155